CW01044885

201416385

HIMMLER'S DIARY 1945

A CALENDAR OF EVENTS
LEADING TO SUICIDE

PETER WITTE AND STEPHEN TYAS

FONTHILL

Acknowledgements

The authors would like to thank the following friends and colleagues who assisted with sources of information: Andrej Angrick, Rainer Fröbe, Peter Klein, Dieter Pohl, Ian Whittaker and Michael Wildt. For providing some of the illustrations, thanks also go to Michael Miller, Marc Rikmanspoel, Ian Sayer and, especially, Max Williams. We are also indebted to the British Army's Medical Services Museum at Aldershot, for allowing us to use the photograph of Himmler's death mask.

Fonthill Media Limited
Fonthill Media LLC
www.fonthillmedia.com
office@fonthillmedia.com

First published in the United Kingdom and United States of America 2014

Copyright © Peter Witte and Stephen Tyas 2014

ISBN 978-1-78155-257-5

Typeset in 10pt on 12pt Minion Pro
Printed and bound in England

Connect with us

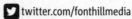

facebook.com/fonthillmedia   twitter.com/fonthillmedia

CONTENTS

Methodology and Sources

Methodology and Terminology

In presenting this research we have employed a three-fold methodological approach. First, there is a statement about the military situation over which Reichsführer-SS Himmler had no control. On some days there were no changes in the general military situation and therefore when this is the case these statements are omitted. Secondly, we made extensive use of Himmler's own desk diary in which he noted his meetings and appointments. These are handwritten entries by Himmler and can therefore be treated as entirely accurate. Unfortunately with the quickening pace of Allied armies advancing across Germany, Himmler made his last entry on 14 March 1945 before sending his diary to safety at his home in southern Germany. Lastly we have noted "Events" which are statements from various sources which involve actions and activities that included Himmler. Primarily these are from similar wartime diaries (Propaganda Minister Joseph Goebbels and Nazi Party leader Martin Bormann who also acted as Hitler's secretary), early post-war interrogations of Himmler's personal staff including his adjutants (Werner Grothmann and Heinz Macher) and the later memoirs and biographies of Nazi leaders and others who met Himmler during 1945.

In comparing and contrasting the widely different sources there is rarely any dispute between the timings and occurrences taking place. Where dates and times are obviously wrong, we have pointed this out. The timetable of events leading up to Himmler's death from the time of his capture has been re-constructed from British army sources.

Any publication involving non-English sources is fraught with language pitfalls and difficulties. To avoid making this terminology even more difficult we have maintained throughout a certain amount of German terms that are self-explanatory. For instance, *Reichsführer-SS* has no pertinent or correct English term and therefore we have maintained the original German term. To complicate matters *Reichsführer-SS* was abbreviated in different ways by individuals whose works we have quoted; thus we have RFSS, RF-SS, RfSS, Rf.SS and Rf-SS and all mean *Reichsführer-SS*. Rather than change the quotations we decided to keep to historical accuracy of the quoted work.

Similarly many works translated from German into English appear to have created their own literary terminology. Typically this occurs with the German word *führer* when used as a suffix, and seen translated as a capitalized noun *Fuhrer* (quoted with and without umlaut) when attached to someone's SS-rank. Throughout we have quoted whatever has been used.

This brings us to the German use of *the Führer* as an individual. It was common parlance among Germans alike—from the man in the street to Heinrich Himmler—that their shared use of *the Führer* always meant Adolf Hitler. The diaries of Himmler, Goebbels and Bormann all mention meetings with *the Führer* and no other information was necessary to indicate this meant Hitler. We have endeavoured to keep to correct names where possible. It is Joseph Goebbels and not *Josef* Goebbels, it is Adolf Hitler and not *Adolph* Hitler.

All SS ranks have no literal English translation, SS-Sturmbannführer may translate as SS Storm Troop Leader but its more precise equivalent is SS-Major. A list of SS ranks and their typical recognizable equivalents is included at the end. Similarly a list of abbreviations is also included.

The Sources for this Work

The primary sources we have used in writing this book are freely available in archives in Germany, Britain and the USA. Some were declassified decades ago; some more recently. For the first time, we have brought them together in a coherent chronology of events. In common with all government ministers, Heinrich Himmler found his life in government was not always his own and therefore there was a need to regulate his life through his desk diary. There are many diaries by Himmler that have proved invaluable to historians when documenting his life from the early days through to 1945, though the last entry is 14 March 1945. The diary entries quoted are little more than lines on a page with his occasional mistakes. For historians they show where Himmler was and, just as importantly, who he was with. A combination of times and people can establish why. Himmler regarded his diaries as part of his archive and for security reasons he had them sent south to Bavaria where they were lodged at his home in Gmund on the Tegernsee. Discovered when US troops searched the house after the war, they were recovered as part of the American Captured German records programme. In the 1950s, these records were returned to the West German government and placed in the Federal German Archives (*Bundesarchiv*). These original paper diaries of Heinrich Himmler are today lodged in the archives at Berlin-Lichterfelde.

The second and no less unique primary source we have used are the German police decrypts held at the National Archives at Kew (London). These decrypts are the only remaining record of German messages from the 1945 period still in existence, the originals having been either destroyed by air-raid damage or purposely burned at the time. Because British and American air raids on German cities and installations destroyed, among other things, the communications infrastructure that enabled teleprinter operations, the SS and police became reliant on radio operations capable of being intercepted in the ether. British wireless operators intercepted thousands of German messages and this particular stream of German police decrypts, deciphered at Bletchley Park, have proved extremely useful in tracking Himmler's movements and orders sent by radio. These German radio messages were originally declassified in 1997; a second series of separate German radio messages assembled by Britain's Secret Intelligence Service (MI6) were declassified several years later along with another unique set of deciphered radio messages entitled 'Decrypts of Intercepted Diplomatic Communications'. These diplomatic messages have a value in showing how Hitler and Himmler varied their responses to different foreign audiences; for example, we have quoted examples of Chinese and Japanese diplomatic messages that reveal information not provided by German sources.

In the immediate post-war period, Himmler's two adjutants, Grothmann and Macher, were extensively interrogated by British intelligence officers. From these interrogation reports we have added a good deal of extra material to show Himmler's movements in April and May 1945. It is our opinion that additional interrogation reports of Grothmann and especially Macher are still in the possession of Britain's intelligence agencies. In searching files declassified by these agencies at the UK's National Archives there are several references to the 'Himmler Book'; this, too, has not been declassified despite his death in British custody sixty-eight years ago.

It is worth noting that almost all of Himmler's personal staff maintained a loyal silence after release from US and British post-war internment. Many years ago, Peter Witte interviewed Werner Grothmann at his home but he said nothing that was not already in the public domain. Macher died in 2001, Grothmann in 2002.

Wartime documents have also been examined and quoted, especially those used by the International Military Tribunal at Nuremberg, 1945-46. Kaltenbrunner's defence attempted to mitigate his involvement in mass murder by using testimony from delegates of the International Committee of the Red Cross in the rescue of Jews in April 1945. Such testimony illustrated Kaltenbrunner's attempts at stopping Himmler's own rescue arrangements. Kaltenbrunner went to the gallows in 1946.

We have also made use of the wartime diaries of Joseph Goebbels and Martin Bormann, published in translation and the original German, as well as the post-war memoirs of Grand Admiral Karl Dönitz, Minister Albert Speer and SS General Walter Schellenberg. We have taken their words at face value, especially in the case of Schellenberg, whose memoirs are a mix of personal aggrandisement and avoidance of guilt. Schellenberg cut a poor figure under interrogation in London in 1945, his examiners declaring that he 'has not produced any evidence of outstanding genius as appears to have been attributed to him'. For Himmler's SD Chief of Foreign Intelligence, hardly a glowing report. However, Count Folke Bernadotte, representative of the Swedish Red Cross in Germany in 1945, also published a memoir which can be judged against Schellenberg's view of the Himmler–Bernadotte meetings and negotiations.

A Biographical Introduction

Of all the members of the Nazi elite who have been subject to the endless fascination of historians, Heinrich Himmler is second only to Adolf Hitler. Whereas Hitler placed himself directly at the head of German politics and government throughout the Nazi era from 1933 to 1945, Himmler was at first content to remain in the shadows. Following the outbreak of war in September 1939, his public persona began to grow, largely as a result of the increasingly sinister influence on public life of his secret police, the Gestapo, and by early 1945 he had risen to become No. 2 in the Nazi hierarchy following the political demise of Hermann Göring, the Führer's deputy, brought about by the Luftwaffe's failure to protect the skies over Germany. As Göring's influence declined, Himmler's star rose and he came to believe that he could become Hitler's successor. Göring was arrested by Himmler's SS men at Berchtesgaden following his attempt to usurp Hitler on 23 April 1945, but six days later Himmler's own bid for power resulted in Hitler stripping him of all his positions of state. Rejected by both old and new German regimes and having failed in his attempts to engage the Western Allies in peace talks, Himmler committed suicide on 23 May 1945, following capture by the British, some three weeks after the Führer had taken his own life in the Berlin bunker on 30 April. At the end, the only loyalty left to Himmler was that of his personal staff, who remained resolute in that loyalty until their own deaths many years later.

Heinrich Luitpold Himmler, born on 7 October 1900 in Munich to a schoolteacher and his wife, was the middle of three sons, all of whom were brought up with a sense of hard work, Catholic values and the good manners expected of middle-class children. The Himmler family had good relations with Bavarian Wittelsbach royalty who visited them each Christmas; Prince Heinrich of Wittelsbach was his godfather. In 1906, young Heinrich began his years of schooling in Munich, first at a catholic primary school and later at the *Gymnasium* (grammar school). The family moved in 1913 to Landshut where his father had been appointed deputy headmaster of the grammar school that Heinrich now attended. When the First World War began he was too young to serve and instead joined a local cadet unit. On 23 December 1917, Heinrich was called up as an officer-candidate by the 11th Infantry Regiment, reporting for training on 2 January 1918 at Regensburg, but at the time of the armistice he was still an officer-cadet in training and had seen no active service. His objective of becoming an army officer was now unachievable.

The end of the war meant that Heinrich had to obtain his *Abitur* (matriculation certificate) in order to enable him to enlist at university. He also joined the local Landshut Free Corps and the regional Oberland Free Corps in the hope that this might lead to an army commission, a hope that was ultimately dashed. In July 1919, he decided to study agriculture and later that summer his father accepted a post as headmaster of the Ingolstadt grammar school and the family moved there. Heinrich was fortunate to find a one-year practical placement on a nearby farming estate, but he was not cut out for practical farming work and very soon fell ill and was hospitalised. After more medical examinations, the farming placement was cancelled and in October 1919 he began studying at the Technical University in Munich. He joined a duelling fraternity and involved himself in veterans' associations. In June 1922, he finished his agricultural studies and received his diploma, and was now intent on studying politics at Munich University. Since 1919, he had dabbled in right-wing politics and participated in a variety of militant actions against the Bavarian government. His readings and writings of this time indicate an increasing interest in Jewish matters and a growing attitude of anti-Semitism. Militant political action was now in the Munich air, and Himmler joined in with his affiliation to the Oberland Free Corps and new membership of Ernst Röhm's *Reichskriegsflagge* militia, both paramilitary organisations.

On 2 August 1923, Himmler became member No. 14303 of the nascent Nazi Party and later that year, when the Bavarian government declared a state of emergency, Hitler attempted a coup – the Beer Hall Putsch – marching with armed supporters, including Himmler as flag-bearer, to the Bavarian army headquarters in Munich. There was an exchange of gunfire and the marchers fled, with some being arrested and subsequently imprisoned – including Hitler – but the putsch was over. With the Nazi Party now in disarray Himmler set about rallying the members, visiting towns and making speeches. In 1924, he began working for Gregor Strasser whose mixture of Nazi policy and Bavarian nationalism appealed to Nazi Party members. Strasser won a seat in the Bavarian parliamentary elections and later that year moved to Berlin following his election to the national parliament, the *Reichstag*, leaving Himmler behind. Following his release from Landsberg prison in December 1924, Hitler resumed his political work and Himmler joined him to organise the members, continuing to travel widely, give speeches and write columns for Nazi publications.

The fledgling SS (*Schutzstaffel*) organisation under *Reichsführer-SS* Julius Schreck was handed over to Erhard Heiden in March 1927, Himmler becoming his deputy. At this time the SS had a small elite membership and operated as a strong-arm squad, and Himmler set about recruiting new members and reorganising the SS into a Party intelligence service, placing its role at the ideological centre of Nazi policy. In January 1929, Hitler relieved Heiden and appointed Himmler as *Reichsführer-SS*. Although the SS began life subordinate to the Nazi mass movement, the SA (*Sturmabteilung*), Himmler had no desire for the status quo to remain under his leadership. The following year saw a crisis at the top of the SA caused by SA–SS friction, and the SA national commander, Franz Pfeffer von Salomon, resigned, to be eventually replaced by Ernst Röhm. Himmler had been friendly with Röhm since the early days of the Party, and the two acted in the best interests of the respective organisations. At the national elections in September 1930, Himmler was elected to the *Reichstag* as a Nazi Deputy. Thereafter he continued to reorganise the SS and expand its intelligence service, and at the beginning of August 1931, when looking for a suitable person to develop this section further, he appointed a discharged naval officer, Reinhard Heydrich, as head of the intelligence service.

Over the next eleven years Himmler and Heydrich conceived a number of plans, including increasing the membership, subsuming the police services of the independent German states into a national body, and participating in policymaking at the top level of government. These and many other plans were brought to fruition. In 1931 alone, SS membership increased from 2,272 to over 13,000 fee-paying members and the following year, regional SS organisations were established across Germany, further encouraging membership and promoting a Nazi revolution. More importantly, the Himmler–Heydrich partnership was to lead to the control by the SS of the sinister Gestapo and industrial mass murder programmes.

A Nazi government was established in Germany following national elections on 30 January 1933. Göring, the most powerful man in the regime after Hitler, after being appointed as Minister of the Interior for Prussia used his Berlin base to organise the first *Geheime Staatspolizei*, the Gestapo – a secret state police that became synonymous with state terrorisation of its political opponents. Throughout the period from 1923 to 1933, when the Nazi Party went from birth to government, independent political police departments of the regional German states under the Weimar Republic had sought to undermine and gather intelligence on this threat to the State. The Nazi government therefore desired to take over political police offices, root out anti-Nazi officials and install its own trusted people. With Göring taking over in Prussia and Berlin, Himmler and Heydrich had to be content with taking control in Bavaria and Munich.

The Bavarian political police proved to be the ideal stepping stone to taking over the other regional political police departments before finally assuming control in Berlin during April 1934. Himmler and Heydrich could now extend their dominance in the area of state terror. By June 1934, Hitler had decided that the SA needed to be brought back into line and neutralised, as its leadership had been critical of Party propaganda lines. However, this could not be achieved whilst Röhm and other senior SA figures were in charge and, on 30 June 1934, SS units across Germany began arresting SA leaders. Himmler authorised the liquidation of Röhm and Himmler's earlier friend Gregor Strasser. Described as the Röhm Putsch, SS action resulted in the liquidation of almost 200 people over a few days. The outcome, announced by Hitler on 20 July 1934, was removal of SS subordination to the SA and autonomy in its own right. There was another reward given to Himmler: the SD (*Sicherheitsdienst*) was commissioned as the Party's intelligence service. Himmler's role raised his profile within the Party and similarly Heydrich now came to the Party's attention.

After resolution of the SA problem, the plan to centralise Germany's police services under Himmler's control was pushed through, finally being implemented on 18 June 1936 when he was appointed Chief of the German Police. With his appointment came a change in operation for the police. The rule of law according to statute was no longer the law of the land; the police would now act according to the rules of the Nazi leadership. Whilst the public would continue to see the uniformed police patrolling the streets, the political police would confront opponents of the Nazi Party whatever their political colour, and detention without trial became a foundation stone of Nazi rule as carried out by the SS. On behalf of the SS, the Inspectorate of Concentration Camps established at Dachau began taking control of a number of concentration camps across Germany.

The German Communist Party had been resolute in its enmity towards the Nazi Party, and rallies by both sides in the 1920s and early 1930s had seen incidents of brawling resulting in the occasional death. The Nazi government began taking its vengeance using the SS, arresting thousands of communist members and incarcerating them in concentration camps. During 1935 alone, about 14,000 communists were arrested and held under the infamous 'Protective Custody' laws that had been brought in to provide a legal framework for detention without trial. These laws were used by the Gestapo to detain anyone – including social democrats, religious leaders and priests, prostitutes, alcoholics, homosexuals, the 'workshy', gypsies and professional criminals – believed to pose a threat to the government. News of such a wide spectrum of offenders filtered through to the public, and a knock on the door by the sinister Gestapo was anticipated with fear.

The concentration camps of the 1930s were learning centres for the SS rather than extermination centres, and the 'Dachau model' was the archetype for many such camps built in Germany before the outbreak of war. Those at Dachau, Buchenwald and Sachsenhausen trained many officers and NCOs later found in Auschwitz, Majdanek and Stutthof, and many camps, surrounded by high walls rather than a wire fence, with watch towers either brick-built into the wall or standing on wooden stilts, were constructed using prisoner labour. Before the war, SS policy was to intimidate and terrorise before allowing the release of some prisoners. Following the outbreak of war, both male and female prisoners became a slave labour force to be used wherever the SS could make a financial profit, many industries benefiting from the employment of such prisoners, from stone quarrying to aircraft and rocket component assembly. In 1943, local Gestapo offices organised over one hundred Workers' Education Camps (*Arbeitserziehungslager*) where prisoners, according to *Reichsführer–SS* Himmler's decree, could be detained for fifty-six days and then released. In practice the fifty-six-day rule could be set aside and release allowed by the Gestapo when a prisoner was deemed re-educated. These camps held German citizens opposed to the Nazi regime, as well as many hundreds of Russian, Dutch, French, Italian and Belgian nationals.

While Himmler was organising the concentration camps, Heydrich had been establishing the security police (Criminal Police and Gestapo) and the SD. Members of the security police were civil servants employed by the government, whereas the SD was a Nazi Party organisation employed as an internal intelligence service. At this juncture the SD was more involved in acquiring information from a wide series of informants in the government, the armed forces, industry and the public at large to produce a monthly digest of what the German people were thinking. These monthly reports were often at odds with the findings of Goebbels' Propaganda Ministry. Hitler himself was occasionally disparaged by the SD informants, information the Nazi elite would prefer not to read – dictators and their supporters prefer a diet of manipulated good news rather than the honest opinion of the general public. The man behind the SD monthly digests was Otto Ohlendorf, who believed in telling the Party the truth about how the public perceived them, but in return he was castigated for his honesty and when an opportunity arose, Himmler and Heydrich sent him off to command an SS Task Force (*Einsatzgruppe*) in Russia. In the twelve months between June 1941 and June 1942, Ohlendorf's unit executed over 90,000 Jews, Soviet state officials, communists, prisoners of war and many others. After the war, Ohlendorf was tried by the Americans for these crimes and executed at Landsberg Prison in 1951.

Himmler now turned his attention to reorganising the Order Police – the uniformed police service of the towns and villages. In 1938, the Order Police numbered over 100,000 men, but their numbers increased with the wartime German occupation of the eastern territories. In order to delegate his authority over the police services regionally, Himmler established the role of Higher SS and Police Leader (HSSPF – *Höhere SS- und Polizeiführer*) and nominated his SS generals to the posts. The first appointees took office in March of that year and others followed. This unification of the police and SS was not without its problems and confusions at the beginning, but gradually these were resolved and the HSSPF structure was later used throughout Nazi-occupied Europe, allowing Himmler to extend his authority and ensure SS and police control over millions of people throughout the continent.

By the outbreak of war, Himmler's empire extended beyond the control of the police services and concentration camps, and throughout the wartime years the SS continued to expand to over 500,000 members. Its interests extended from controlling ethnic German populations across Europe, with many being brought to resettlement areas in Poland, to overseeing the proposed marriages of SS men and maintaining their 'racial purity', to the SS legal office's role of maintaining standards and the *Waffen-SS*. All these organisations were accountable to *Reichsführer-SS* Himmler and he managed them dictatorially. Whether it was rebuking SS generals when they overextended their authority or insisting that sentences of death be carried out when SS men of every rank were tried and convicted by SS courts of crimes judged to merit a death sentence, Himmler had the last word in all such cases.

Naturally the war brought changes and Himmler embraced them, driving through programmes in the Nazi cause. One such was the 'Final Solution to the Jewish Question' in Nazi-occupied Europe. Before the war, Jewish migration from Germany and Austria was encouraged in an operation led by Adolf Eichmann, but the war denied further emigration mainly due to the British blockade of German shipping and embargo of Jewish refugees travelling to Palestine. Until summer 1941, Jews were systematically denied their rights and their lives were restricted. The wearing of a yellow star was compulsory. Following the invasion of Russia in June 1941, the 'Final Solution' was put into practice. In the rear areas of German-occupied Russia, *SS-Einsatzgruppen* began killing the Jewish populations wherever they were found. There were few remonstrations about the killings, which numbered almost a million Jews within twelve months in Russia.

However, this murderous event in Russia was to be overshadowed by even more killings in Poland. Himmler embarked upon a second stage to the 'Final Solution' by establishing industrial extermination centres in Poland. There were two key elements to this programme. The first was an extermination programme known as Operation Reinhard (after the recently assassinated Heydrich) and involved three purpose-built camps: Belzec, Sobibor and Treblinka. The second stage began with deportations to these camps of all Jews from the German occupied territories of eastern and western Europe. Gas chambers were built at these camps, and trains brought the victims from every corner of Europe. Adolf Eichmann's department arranged the trains and their loading, uniformed police squads forming the train escorts to ensure there were no escapes. Between 1942 and 1943, the three Operation Reinhard camps gassed to death over one and a half million Jews; on 31 December 1942, after its first seven/eight months of operation, some 1,274,166 victims were reported. At Auschwitz-Birkenau extermination centre over two million people were killed between 1942 and 1944.

The 'Final Solution to the Jewish Question' initiated by the Himmler–Heydrich partnership had resulted in the murder of at least six million Jews and many millions of non-Jews in a systematic operation of ethnic and political cleansing. Following Heydrich's assassination in Prague in June 1942, Himmler was left to direct the programme of mass murder, a programme only brought to an end by the advance of the Allied armies.

On 1 January 1945, even the most resolute Nazi must have realised that the war was lost. From east and west, the Allied armies were facing Germany's borderlands, having retaken most of the land occupied by Nazi troops in 1943. All of the Nazi-occupied regions of the Soviet Union were now back in Soviet hands, and Soviet troops had retaken most of Poland. Most of France had been liberated along with Belgium and parts of Holland. Soviet armies were moving through Hungary and Anglo-American armies were advancing through Italy. Germany was exhausted and militarily incapable of stemming the Allied advances. Himmler had now added military command to his responsibilities, first in south-west Germany and later, in mid-January 1945, transferring to the Eastern Front. His Army Group Vistula had the task of halting the Russian advance at the River Vistula, a natural division between Poland and Germany. Poorly equipped and poorly trained, the demoralised troops were asked to stem and indeed attack overwhelmingly superior Soviet forces. Any German soldier suffering battle fatigue, cowardice or mental trauma and retreating without papers or orders found himself facing a field court martial and an SS firing squad; SS Colonel Carl von Salisch, Police President of Bromberg, was shot for cowardice after fleeing his post before the Russians arrived.

Throughout January and February 1945, Himmler managed his Army Group and also occasionally commuted to Berlin for the daily military conferences in the bunker with Hitler and the army general staff, but at the beginning of March he fell ill and was confined to bed for almost two weeks with influenza – two weeks during which Soviet advances towards the Vistula could not be halted. General Guderian visited Himmler and finally persuaded him to resign his army command in favour of a trained army commander. Indeed, Goebbels had had misgivings about Himmler as an army commander: 'Unfortunately he allowed himself to be diverted by the quest for military laurels, in which, however, he failed totally.'

In January 1945, Himmler held the first negotiations with the former Swiss President Musy about the release of Jews and other prisoners and their transfer to Switzerland in return for money or goods. The first transfer of 1,200 Jews from Theresienstadt to Switzerland took place on 5 February 1945, American Jewish organisations paying 5 million Swiss francs in return. On 21 February 1945, Count Bernadotte of the Swedish Red Cross visited Berlin and met separately with the German Foreign Minister von Ribbentrop and Himmler's foreign intelligence chief SS General Walter Schellenberg before meeting with Himmler himself. As a result of these talks, Himmler agreed to issue exit visas from Germany for all Swedish-born women. Bernadotte also raised the question of Danish and Norwegian prisoners held in German prisons and camps, and Himmler agreed that they would be transferred from their place of imprisonment to Neuengamme concentration camp near Hamburg where the Swedish Red Cross would provide welfare support. During February 1945, SS General Karl Wolff, the senior SS and police commander in Italy, took steps to contact Allied intelligence agencies in Switzerland secretly and discuss a surrender in Italy. Himmler continued negotiations with Bernadotte in northern Germany and Wolff in Switzerland during March, and also began negotiating an agreement with his Finnish doctor, Felix Kersten, pledging a safe handover of concentration camps to Allied advancing troops, ordering a stop to the killing of Jews in these camps and giving a tacit agreement to release 10,000 Jews to Sweden. Following meetings between SS General Kaltenbrunner, Chief of the Security Police and SD, and the International Committee of the Red Cross in April, 300 French women prisoners from Ravensbrück camp were transferred to Switzerland.

But despite these humanitarian gestures, the business of the SS security services continued as usual. On 29 March 1945, Himmler issued an order for drastic measures to be taken against German civilians who draped white towels on their homes in a sign of surrender to Allied forces. During a short visit to Vienna at the end of March, Himmler demanded that his senior SS men bolster their defences in eastern and southern Austria against the Soviet armies. He also ordered that no more Jews be killed, a demand widely viewed as a future bargaining chip.

April 1945 was a difficult month for Himmler. German troops could not repel the advancing Allied armies, and Germany's V-weapons and new jet aircraft had simply been developed too late to protect the nation. Buchenwald camp was liberated by American troops; four days later, when Bergen-Belsen camp was handed over to British forces, the appalling conditions discovered there made newspaper headlines all over the world. On 23 April, Himmler had his last meeting in the Berlin bunker with Hitler, now a shambling wreck of a man. Berlin was in ruins and Soviet armies would soon capture the city. The first sign that Himmler had broken with Hitler was at a meeting with Bernadotte, at which Schellenberg was present, when Himmler, without the Führer's knowledge, asked Bernadotte to convey a proposal of peace to Prime Minister Churchill and President Truman whereby Germany would surrender to Great Britain and the United States but would be permitted to continue fighting the Soviet Union. The response of the British, American and Soviet governments was that only an unconditional surrender on all fronts would be acceptable. On 27 April, Bernadotte met with Schellenberg to confirm this message, to Himmler's bitter disappointment. The following day Himmler's offer to the Western Allies became public knowledge and on 29 April Hitler took his revenge. Despite no longer having the power to have Himmler killed, in his last political testament Hitler expelled both Himmler and Göring from the Nazi Party and all offices of state and appointed Grand Admiral Dönitz as his successor. But it was all too late. Martin Bormann, the General Secretary of the Party, informed Dönitz of Himmler's treachery, but Dönitz did nothing in response, and when he began forming a government of sorts after Hitler's death, Himmler pledged his support. With Berlin taken by the Soviets and Germany now split in two by the meeting of the American and Soviet armies it was clear to everyone that Germany had lost the war completely. Only the unconditional surrender remained to be negotiated.

In the first days of May, Himmler made daily visits to Dönitz, both men having set up in Flensburg, as had groups of officers from various SS organisations. At a meeting with officers from the now redundant concentration camp administration, Himmler said he was making contact with the British Army commander Field Marshal Montgomery to arrange an armistice in the west whilst continuing to fight in the east. A large number of Himmler's SS generals were also there, and on 5 May he had a last group meeting with them. Himmler was apparently optimistic about the situation, but his optimism was dashed the following day when Dönitz asked him to resign from all his offices of state. A letter prepared by Himmler and addressed to Montgomery requested a meeting to discuss an alliance between the Western Powers and Germany against the Soviet Union was later destroyed by General Alfred Jodl, unbeknownst to Himmler.

The unconditional surrender was signed between Germany and Allied forces on 8 May 1945. The same day, Himmler shaved off his moustache and reduced his staff to about sixteen men and four vehicles. For three more days he remained in Flensburg awaiting an answer to his letter, until the decision was made to head south to the Harz mountains. During the night of 15–16 May, Himmler and his group crossed the Elbe estuary on a fishing boat, all dressed in something resembling civilian clothes and carrying false papers. Now on foot, along with thousands of similarly dressed soldiers and displaced persons, the group marched forty miles south to Bremervörde. On 21 May 1945, Himmler and his two adjutants, Werner Grothmann and Heinz Macher, were arrested by two Russian soldiers attached to a British security control unit in the town. Himmler, who was using the name 'Hizinger', was not recognised. The three were taken to a nearby internment camp and remained there overnight.

On 23 May 1945, the last day of Heinrich Himmler's life, he and his two adjutants were taken to Westertimke camp and it was there that Himmler finally made his identity known. He was separated from his adjutants, searched and questioned. Senior intelligence officers from Montgomery's staff arrived at Westertimke later that day and it was decided to take Himmler immediately to the Lüneburg centre, a private house taken over for the purpose, where he could be questioned more closely. The party arrived at Lüneburg shortly after 10 p.m. and during a body search the British doctor asked Himmler to open his mouth, which he did only reluctantly. Finally recognising that any plans for the future he might have had were now over, Himmler shook his head, crunched the doctor's fingers in his mouth and bit down on a cyanide phial he had concealed in his mouth. Efforts to resuscitate him were unsuccessful; Himmler died at 11.23 p.m. The following day he was buried in an unmarked grave in the surrounding Lüneburg forest.

Reichsführer-SS Heinrich Himmler Positions in 1945

NSDAP member	2 Aug 1923–29 April 1945
SS member	Feb 1925–29 April 1945
Reichsführer-SS	6 Jan 1929–29 April 1945
Chief of the German Police	17 June 1936–29 April 1945
Reich Commissioner for the Strengthening of Germanism (RKFDV)	7 Oct 1936–29 April 1945
Minister of the Interior	25 Aug 1943–29 April 1945
Supreme Commander of Volkssturm	21 July 1944–29 April 1945
Commander of Replacement Army	20 July 1944–29 April 1945
Commander, Army Group Upper Rhine	26 Nov 1944–20 Jan 1945
Commander, Army Group Vistula (Weichsel)	20 Jan–22 March 1945

Although Hitler stripped Himmler of all his offices and appointments effective 29 April 1945, the new German Government under Grand Admiral Dönitz took no notice of Hitler's decision. Himmler therefore continued in his offices and appointments until Dönitz asked him to resign them all on 6 May 1945.

January 1945

January, date unclear

From a post-war interrogation of Oberstleutnant Ohletz (Abwehr):
"In Jan 45, Schellenberg told PW [Ohletz] that important events were imminent. Oshima [Japanese Ambassador to Germany] was in touch with the Führer HQ, in connection with a peace feeler from Russia. Himmler was very worried lest this step should succeed. Later PW saw a report on the discussion (he is not sure whether the report came to him by mistake or whether it had been purposely sent to him in error). At the end of the report it said 'The Imperial Ambassador escaped bodily injury only by a hurried exit.'"[1]

Monday, 1 January 1945

Meetings & Appointments of the Reichsführer-SS on 1.1.1945[2]

08:00 hrs	Arrival of Sz.[3] Steiermark at Pforzheim-Weissenstein[4]
14:00 hrs	·Meal with
	SS-Obergruppenführer von dem Bach
	SS-Gruppenführer Ostendorff[5]
15:30 hrs	SS-Obergruppenführer von dem Bach
	SS-Gruppenführer Ostendorff
17:00 hrs	SS-Obersturmbannführer Grothmann
20:00 hrs	Meal
22:00 hrs	Oberstleutnant Suchanek

Events:
Former Swiss President Dr Jean-Marie Musy states he had negotiations with Himmler on this day, but this is questionable due to Himmler's other known commitments.[6]

Tuesday, 2 January 1945

Meetings & Appointments of the Reichsführer-SS on 2.1.1945 (Pforzheim-Weissenstein)

14:00 hrs	Meal
17–18:00 hrs	Walk
20:00 hrs	Meal

Events:

Himmler issued three Orders of the Day, in his capacities as Reichsführer SS, C-in-C Reserve Army and Minister of Interior. All reflected on successfully managing a testing 1944 and stressed the part played by "our beloved Führer". For the future, he said, 1945 would "bring us nearer to victory and peace". Finally, Himmler urged civil servants to become "friendly and understanding helpers" of the populace suffering from increasing Allied air-raids.[7]

Martin Bormann writing from Führerhauptquartier, on 2 January 1945, to his wife Gerda, stated: "I should very much like to pay one visit to Schluchsee and combine it, if possible, with a visit to Himmler; he has his quarters – that is to say, his train – either in the vicinity of one of the Murgtal tunnels or near Triberg."[8]

Wednesday, 3 January 1945

Meetings & Appointments of the Reichsführer-SS on 3.1.1945 (Pforzheim-Weissenstein)

14:00 hrs	Meal with SS-Standartenführer [Rüdiger] Pipkorn[9]
16:00 hrs	SS-Standartenführer Pipkorn
19:00 hrs	Journey to Baden-Baden
20:30 hrs	Military headquarters, XIV. SS-A.K.
	SS-Obergruppenführer von dem Bach
	SS-Obergruppenführer von dem Bach
	and Gauleiter [Robert] Wagner to Sassbach-Walden
22:00 hrs	Evening meal with commanders of XIV. SS-A.-K.
24:00 hrs	Speech of Reichsführer-SS before the commanders of
	14th SS-Army Corps (XIV. SS-A.-K.)
01.30 hrs	Return to Pforzheim-Weissenstein on Sz. Steiermark

Events:

Himmler's speech in Sasbachwalden (Baden) given before commanders of Heeresgruppe Oberrhein (Army Group Upper Rhine) and XIV. SS-A.K.[10]

KdS Radom [Joachim Illmer] issued instructions, 3 January 1945, to his local offices (Gestapo, Criminal Police and SD): "In anticipation of the expected major Russian offensive in the General Government [Poland], the Reichsführer-SS [*Himmler*] attaches special importance and focus on partisans and the destruction of Russian scouting parties and terrorist groups, as well as communist groups."[11]

Thursday, 4 January 1945

Meetings & Appointments of the Reichsführer-SS on 4.1.1945

14:00 hrs	Meal with
	SS-Obergruppenführer Pohl
	SS-Gruppenführer Kammler

SS-Obersturmbannführer [Ekkehard] Albert[12]
Bürgermeister Volpert
16:00 hrs   SS-Obergruppenführer Pohl
18:00 hrs   SS-Obersturmbannführer Albert
18:30 hrs   Bürgermeister Volpert
20:00 hrs   Meal with
    SS-Obergruppenführer Pohl
    SS-Gruppenführer Kammler
    SS-Obersturmbannführer Albert

Friday, 5 January 1945

Meetings & Appointments of the Reichsführer-SS on 5.1.1945
04:10 hrs   Arrived Triberg
13:00 hrs   SS-Gruppenführer Ostendorff
13:20 hrs   Military briefing
14:45 hrs   Meal with
    SS-Obergruppenführer Pohl
    SS-Obergruppenführer Heissmeyer
    SS-Obergruppenführer Hofmann
    SS-Brigadeführer Görlitz (?)
    SS-Gruppenführer Klopfer
    Gebietsführer Petter (*sic* – Pette)
    SS-Sturmbannführer Rußland (?)
16:30 hrs   SS-Gruppenführer Klopfer
17:00 hrs   SS-Obergruppenführer Heissmeyer
18:30 hrs   SS-Obergruppenführer Heissmeyer
    SS-Gruppenführer Klopfer
    SS-Brigadeführer Görlitz (?)
    Gebietsführer Petter (*sic* – Pette)
    SS-Standartenführer Dr Brandt
20:30 hrs   Meal with
    SS-Obergruppenführer Heissmeyer
    SS-Gruppenführer Klopfer
    SS-Brigadeführer Görlitz (?)
    SS-Obergruppenführer Hofmann
    Gebietsführer Petter (*sic* – Pette)
22:30 hrs   SS-Obergruppenführer Hofmann
23:45 hrs   SS-Obergruppenführer Pohl
    SS-Gruppenführer Ostendorff

Events:

Himmler attended an awards investiture in which he presented Oak Leaves (*Eichenlaub*) to twelve recipients aleady holding the Ritterkreuz (see illustrations section).

German radio message intercepted by Bletchley Park on 5 January 1945, issued as part of the daily intelligence brief for Prime Minister Churchill; the message was addressed to SS-Oberst-Ogruf Josef "Sepp" Dietrich:

Dear Sepp,

I note from a [divisional] report that detachments of the 12 SS Panzer Division HITLER JUGEND, during the fighting in the first battle period of 16th and 17th December [1944], busied themselves behind the front snatching weapons from the dead of another Division – in particular assault rifles [model] 44. That such a course must have an appalling effect on the discipline of the troops is obvious. That the HITLER JUGEND Division has done such a thing is shameful. How can a Division that bears this name behave in so base a manner? This has nothing to do with the scrounging of weapons. Just calmly tell the G.O.C. [General Officer Commanding] that for the present I do not recognise this Division, since I do not associate with such people.

Heil Hitler!

(signed) H.Himmler[13]

Listing by SS-WVHA of award of the Deutschen Kreuzes in Silver to SS-Gruf. Richard Glücks with note, dated 13 January 1945, by Oswald Pohl on the tile page: "Award was agreed verbally by RFSS [*Himmler*] on 5 January 1945".[14]

On 25 January 1945, General Burgdorf noted on the basis for this award to Glücks: "Awarded by the Führer on 25.1.45."[15]

Saturday, 6 January 1945

Meetings & Appointments of the Reichsführer-SS on 6.1.1945 (Triberg)

12:30 hrs	Military briefing
13:30 hrs	Meal
14:15 hrs	Departure for Trossingen
16:00 hrs	Afternoon tea with
	Familie Kiehn
	Frau Heydrich
	SS-Obergruppenführer [Karl Hermann] Frank
	Major Hoffmann (Adjutant)
17:00 hrs	Frau Heydrich
18:45 hrs	SS-Obergruppenführer Frank
20:15 hrs	Evening meal
21:30 hrs	SS-Obergruppenführer Frank
23:15 hrs	Departure from Trossingen
00:45 hrs	Arrival Sz. Steiermark
	followed by briefing report by SS-Gruppenführer Ostendorff

Sunday, 7 January 1945

Meetings and Appointments of the Reichsführer-SS on 7.1.1945
13:30 hrs	Military briefing
14:30 hrs	Meal with 5 army sharpshooters:
	Unteroffizier Bühler
	Feldwebel Pfandke
	Obergefreiter Heinrich Franken
	Gefreiter Back
	Unteroffizier Koschorrek
20:00 hrs	Evening meal (alone)
22:00 hrs	Military briefing

Events:

OKW War Diary: "On 7.1. [1945] on order of the Führer the earlier appointment as ObdE [*Himmler*] assigned to the office of the Chef der Heeresrüstung is cancelled. The remaining office will be handed over to General Bühle, Chef des Heeresstabes, who has now been assigned to this position by the Führer"[16]

[Beginning January 1945:] Following direct intervention of Speer with Hitler, Himmler and his representative Jüttner retained management of Heeresrüstung (army armaments).[17]

Radio message dated 7 January 1945 from Reich Defence Commissioner Schlessmann (in Essen) to Himmler:

> To be forwarded via SS-Hauptamt to Rf.SS, Pg. Himmler, Feldquartier.
>
> Dear Reichsführer!
>
> For Army Group H, Generaloberst Blaskowitz, will be given older men from the Volkssturm for employment in the rear. Firstly, 1000 men. More will follow. For Army Group B, Generalfeldmarschall Model, additional Volkssturm men cannot be provided from Gau Essen. RVK Essen, signed Schlessmann, deputy Gauleiter.[18]

Monday, 8 January 1945

Meetings & Appointments of the Reichsführer-SS on 8.1.1945 (Triberg)
[Time?]	Professor Osenberg[19]
[Time?]	Deputation from I.G.a.u.E.Btl. Lissa
	SS-Obersturmführer Seidel
	SS-Hauptscharführer Oswald
	SS-Rottenführer Boppert
	brought WHW-Collection[20]
[Time?]	Generaloberst Stumpf
[Time?]	Generalmajor von Oppen
[Time?]	SS-Sturmbannführer [Götz] Persch[21]
20:00 hrs	Meal with SS-Unterscharführer [Walter] Jenschke (Ritterkreuzträger)[22]

Tuesday, 9 January 1945

Meetings & Appointments of Reichsführer-SS on 9.1.1945

13:00 hrs	Military Briefing
14:00 hrs	General von Oppen
14:15 hrs	Meal with
	SS-Gruppenführer Ostendorff
	General von Oppen
17:00 hrs	Walk
18:30 hrs	Oberstleutnant Suchanek
20:00 hrs	Ritterkreuzträger SS-Unterscharführer Jenschke
20:15 hrs	Meal with Gaupropagandaleiter Schmidt
	Oberstleutnant Harnack
	Major Roth
22:00 hrs	Military briefing
22: 45 hrs	SS-Gruppenführer Ostendorff

Events:

SS-Gruf. Otto Hellwig, appointed deputy of Prützmann, HSSPF Nordost in Königsberg.[23]

Kurt Becher promoted SS-Standartenführer.[24]

From a post-war interrogation of Kurt Becher: "I was twice with Himmler. The first time at the end of December [1944] and again on 9 January [1945], I know this exactly, as at this time Himmler promoted me to SS-Standartenführer. There was a radio message from Budapest, from General Pfeffer-Wildenbruch to Himmler, where he asked what were his instructions for the Jews in Budapest."[25]

Werner Grothmann, when interrogated after the war: "I can remember, that at the time in January 1945 at the field quarters of the Reichsführer [*Himmler*] I received permission to travel abroad. I reported this to my staff. A few days later you [Kurt Becher] telegraphed me that once again I should register my departure with the Reichsführer.[26]

Wednesday, 10 January 1945

Military situation:

Midday military briefing at Führer headquarters "Adlerhorst" near Ziegenberg, 17:06 to 19:15 hrs. "The Führer: I must mainly say: Himmler had a couple of things, which he did and did very well. He has reconnoitred everything very well."[27]

Meetings & Appointments of the Reichsführer-SS on 10.1.1945 (Triberg)

20:00 hrs	Meal with
	Obergefreiter Finger
	Obergefreiter Walter Meyer (sharpshooter)
	Gefreiter Paul Maier
22:15 hrs	Oberstleutnant Suchanek

23:00 hrs	Military briefing
00:30 hrs	Played card games (Doppelkopf) with
	SS-Standartenführer Dr Brandt
	Oberstleutnant Suchanek
	SS-Sturmbannführer Kiermaier

Thursday, 11 January 1945

Meetings & Appointments of the Reichsführer-SS on 11.1.1945 (Triberg)

13:00 hrs	SS-Standartenführer Bickler
	SS-Obersturmbannführer Rausch
13:45 hrs	Military briefing
14:30 hrs	Meal with
	Reichsleiter von Schirach
	SS-Obersturmführer Wieshofer
	Oberleutnant Döscher
	SS-Standartenführer Bickler
	Oberstleutnant Harnack
16:30 hrs	Walk with
	Reichsleiter von Schirach
	Oberleutnant Döscher
	SS-Sturmbannführer Kiermaier
	Oberstabsarzt Dr Müller
20:00 hrs	Meal with
	Unteroffizier Mülders [?], (sharpshooter)
22:00 hrs	Military briefing
23:30 hrs	Departure for Forbach Gausbach
	SS-Standartenführer Bickler

Events:

The SS journal *Das Schwarze Korps*, 11 January 1945, published Himmler's New Year message dated 31 December 1944:

> The Reichsführer-SS has issued the following command to men of the Waffen-SS and Police: Men of the Waffen-SS and Police! The year 1944 has ended. Its difficult examinations have been passed by the entire German people. The year 1945 will give us great German victories and bring peace decisively nearer. Again we promise to bring about those promises that we Leaders made at the beginning of the war in 1939.
> We will do more than our duty!
> Long live our beloved Führer Adolf Hitler![28]

Notes made by Botschaftsrat Hilger for Ribbentrop:

> In the last days SS-Oberführer Kroeger was at field headquarters of the Reichsführer-SS [*Himmler*] to give his report. On his return Kroeger informed me as follows:

1) The RFSS is very happy with current developments of the Wlassow activities and, in this connection, he is especially happy about the good comradely co-operation between the Foreign Office and the SS-Main Office [under Gottlob Berger].

…

3) The RfSS was extremely sharp and often derogatory about Reich Minister Rosenberg and the activities derived by him from his Ministry, referred to as a 'national disaster'. The RfSS seems doubtful that the time has come to completely dissolve the Reich Ministry for the Occupied Eastern Territories (*Reichsministerium für die besetzten Ostgebiete*).

…

6) In the opinion of the RFSS, given time the Wlassow-Aktion will form a basis for future formation of the Eastern areas. The RFSS believes that the German Reich could live in friendship with a strong Russia if it waived its imperialistic tendencies towards the west, and oriented itself more to the east.

…

8) In regard to the treatment of Eastern workers, the RFSS opined that discriminatory measures must go, however for the moment security police reasons the marking of Eastern workers cannot be dispensed with.

9) The RFSS intends to receive General Wlassow quite soon at his field headquarters. This visit of Wlassow will probably be at Münsingen, where the formation of the first Russian Division is coming to and end.[29]

Dr Rezsö Kasztner, Budapest, noted:

11 January: Becher returned from his visit with Himmler. On the occasion of his audience he had been promoted Standartenführer of the Waffen-SS and visibly happy… Do not be afraid. In this way I spoke with Himmler. The RFSS told me that he will refrain from taking hostages during this period. Prague was liberated six days (*sic*) later.[30]

11 January 1945, Kammler wrote to Dr Brandt with a graph attachment:

…factory constructions of bomb-proof underground plants completed [by the SS] in 1944 on orders of the Reich Minister for Armaments and War Production.[31]

Friday, 12 January 1945

Military situation:

The huge Soviet military offensive into Germany (Ukrainian Front under Marshal Konev) began at the Baranow bridgehead. The weak defensive line of the 4th Panzer Army (under Tank General Graeser) was quickly pierced.[32]

The "greatest offensive in military history": an attack by three million Soviet soldiers against 750,000 poorly armed German soldiers.[33]

Meetings & Appointments of the Reichsführer-SS on 12.1.1945
12:00 hrs   SS-Standartenführer Bender
                    SS-Sturmbannführer Giesselmann

12:15 hrs	Generalfeldmarschall v. Rundstedt
	General Westphal
	SS-Gruppenführer Ostendorff
	SS-Obergruppenführer v.d. Bach
13:30 hrs	Meal with
	Generalfeldmarschall v. Rundstedt
	General Westphal
	SS-Gruppenführer Ostendorff
	SS-Obergruppenführer v.d. Bach
	Leutnant v. Rundstedt
	SS-Sturmbannführer Studnick [Studnitz?]
	SS-Gruppenführer Simon
14:30 hrs	SS-Gruppenführer Ostendorff
15:00 hrs	SS-Obergruppenführer von dem Bach
	SS-Gruppenführer Ostendorff
	SS-Brigadeführer Harmel
16:30 hrs	SS-Gruppenführer Simon
17:00 hrs	SS-Standartenführer Bender
	SS-Sturmbannführer Giesselmann
20:00 hrs	Meal with
	Reichsbahn-Vizepräsident Kraft
00:30 hrs	Played cards (Doppelkopf) with
	SS-Standartenführer Dr Brandt
	SS-Obersturmbannführer Grothmann
	SS-Sturmbannführer Kiermaier
02:00 hrs	General Decker

Saturday, 13 January 1945

Meetings & Appointments of the Reichsführer-SS on 13.1.1945 (Forbach-Gausbach)

14:00 hrs	Meal with
	SS-Gruppenführer Ostendorff
	SS-Obergruppenführer [Friedrich-Wilhelm] Krüger
	SS-Oberführer Maack
	SS-Sturmbannführer Seyda
20:00 hrs	Meal with
	SS-Obergruppenführer Jeckeln
	SS-Obergruppenführer [Friedrich-Wilhelm] Krüger (V.K.)
	General von Mühlen
	SS-Gruppenführer Ostendorff
	Oberstleutnant Dankworth
	SS-Hauptsturmführer Beier

Events:

In mid January 1945, Rudolf Brandt reported "Feldkdo Stelle moved to Forberg-Gausberg (*sic*)".[34]

Sunday, 14 January 1945

Meetings & Appointments of the Reichsführer-SS on 14.1.1945

14:00 hrs	Meal with
	SS-Obergruppenführer Krüger
	SS-Obergruppenführer Jeckeln
	SS-Gruppenführer Ostendorff
20:00 hrs	Meal with
	SS-Obergruppenführer Krüger
	SS-Obergruppenführer Jeckeln
	SS-Gruppenführer Ostendorff
	SS-Obergruppenführer v. Herff
	SS-Obersturmbannführer Franke-Grieksch (sic)
22:00 Hrs	Military briefing
23:30 hrs	Played cards (Doppelkopf) with
	SS-Standartenführer Dr Brandt
	SS-Obersturmbannführer Grothmann
	SS-Sturmbannführer Kiermaier

Events:

Order by v. Herff from Himmler's Feldkommandostelle: promotion of Dr Fritz Arlt to SS-Standartenführer approved.[35]

Reply by Himmler to a letter dated 6 January 1945 from HSSPF Slowakei, SS-Ogruf· Hermann Höfle, on a "defence matter".[36]

Monday, 15 January 1945

Meetings & Appointments of the Reichsführer-SS on 15.1.1945 (Forbach-Gausbach)

14:00 hrs	Meal with
	SS-Obergruppenführer Jeckeln
	General Abraham
17:45 hrs	General Abraham
19:00 hrs	General Abraham
19: ? hrs	Journey to Wildbad (Hotel Post)
	Meal with
	[Dr Jean-Marie] Musy (former Swiss Bundespräsident)
22:00 hrs	Meeting with Musy
	SS-Brigadeführer Schellenberg

23:45 hrs	Depart from Wildbad with SS-Brigadeführer Schellenberg
	Return to Forbach-Gausbach
01:30 hrs	Arrive on Sz. Steiermark

Events:

In a report dated 18 January 1945, Himmler described his meeting with Musy:

> On Monday, 15.1.1945, I had a meeting with the President Dr Jean Marie Musy in Wildbad. He addressed me clearly on behalf of the Americans, whether a generous solution of the Jewish Question could not be found. He saw opportunities. From my information, on behalf of the ~~Swiss~~ [crossed out in original] Jioint (*sic* – Joint) in Switzerland, a Jew Sally Meier (*sic*), was together with representative Becher, and surprised by meeting together with the American Maclelland (*sic* – McClelland). After a long conversation a number of points remained:
>
> 1) He wants to determine, what tasks Sally Meier has and who is the American government really in touch with? Is it a Rabbi – Jew or is it the Jioint?
>
> 2) I have again told him this is my exact point of view. The Jews are working for us, understandably, in hard work such as road construction, working on canals, in mines and have a high mortality rate. Since the meetings an improvement in conditions for Jews is taking place, they are used in normal work and naturally will work like any German in the armaments industry. Our point of view for the Jewish Question is: What interests us, is the position of Jews taken by America and England. It is clear that we in Germany and German spheres of life, from decades of experience in world wars, do not want them and no discussions about getting involved with them. We would welcome America taking them. There are exclusions that must be guaranteed, any Jews released to Switzerland must not be sent to Palestine. We know that the Arabs reject the Jews as much as we Germans and it is inappropriate for these people to be tormented by a new influx of Jews.
>
> 3) Economically we are in the position of America. Just as every immigrant to the United States has to pay a fee of 1,000 dollars, we must impose a fee of 1,000 dollars for every emigrant from the German sphere of influence. Money as foreign currency does not interest us. We want delivery of goods in accordance with the laws of neutrality, undertaken in Switzerland, therefore money itself does not interest us and nor does medical supplies such as Cibasol that we manufacture ourselves. Our interest is in tractors, trucks and machine tools.... President Musy immediately went travelling and wanted to return as soon as possible. He stressed again and again that the Jewish Question was only minor, because the main objective was initiating major developments.[37]

Walter Schellenberg also made a note of this meeting in his memoirs:

> ... The following agreement was then reached through my active intervention:
>
> 1) Every fourteen days a first-class train would bring about 1,200 Jews to Switzerland.
>
> 2) The Jewish organization with which Herr Musy was working would give active support in solving the Jewish problem according to Himmler's suggestions. At the same time, the beginning of a basic change in the world-wide propaganda against Germany was to be brought forward.
>
> 3) According to my suggestion, it was agreed that the money should not be paid over directly to the International Red Cross, as had originally been decided, but should be handed to Musy as trustee.[38]

As a result of the meeting, Schellenberg appointed SS-Obersturmführer Kriminalkommissar Franz Göring (RSHA Amt VI Wi: Economic Matters, Foreign Intelligence Service of the SD) with technical supervision of the transports to Switzerland.[39]

In 1944-1945, emigration of Jews was pinned again money or goods. Negotiations of the Swiss Dr Jean-Marie Musy with the Reichsführer-SS on behalf of the Union of Orthodox Rabbis of the United States of America and Canada.[40]

SS-WVHA also reported on 15 January 1945 a total strength of concentration camp prisoners imprisoned in Greater Germany: 511,537 men; 202,674 women; controlled by 44,000 SS guards.[41]

The report detailed locations of imprisonment:

KL Auschwitz—Upper Silesia [now Poland]
31,746 prisoners (15,325 men, 16,421 women)
2,530 SS guards (2,474 men, 56 women)

KL Monowitz—Upper Silesia [now Poland]
35,081 prisoners (33,037 men, 2,044 women)
2,021 SS guards (2,006 men, 15 women)

KL Gross Rosen—Lower Silesia [now Poland]
77,904 prisoners (51,977 men, 25,927 women)
4,128 SS guards (3,222 men, 906 women)

KL Stutthof—West Prussia [now Poland]
48,635 prisoners (18,436 men, 30,199 women)
1,051 SS guards (943 men, 108 women)[42]

It later became known, though the order from Himmler has not been found, that in the case of an enemy approach the competent local Higher SS and Police Commander (Höhere SS- und Polizeiführer) had supreme authority over the concentration camps and had full responsibility for the timely evacuation of their prisoners.[43]

On this point, Rudolf Höss the commandant of Auschwitz concentration camp stated:

The war was nearing its end. The Russian offensive in January 1945 forced the RFSS to make a decision, whether to evacuate the camps or leave them to the enemy. Himmler orders their evacuation and return to camps in the rear. This order meant a death sentence for tens of thousands of prisoners. Most were marched on foot or sent in forcibly obtained trains with open freight-wagons in minus 20 degrees Celsius and snow, without any food provisions resulting in very few prisoners surviving these conditions. Camps where they arrived were even worse with inhuman conditions widespread. The dead could no longer be burned. But the order remained in force, camps must be cleared when the enemy approached.[44]

Tuesday, 16 January 1945

Meetings & Appointments of the Reichsführer-SS on 16.1.1945 (Forbach-Gausbach)

13:30 hrs Military briefing

14:00 hrs	SS-Obergruppenführer v.d. Bach
	SS-Obergruppenführer Jeckeln
	SS-Brigadeführer Rode
	SS-Brigadeführer [Franz] Mueller-Darss
16:00 hrs	SS-Brigadeführer Rode
18:00 hrs	Oberstleutnant Suchanek
20:00 hrs	Meal with
	SS-Obergruppenführer Jeckeln
	General [Friedrich-Wilhelm] Hauck
	SS-Brigadeführer Mueller-Darss
	SS-Hauptsturmführer Dr Groß
22:30 hrs	Military briefing
23:30 hrs	SS-Obersturmbannführer Grothmann

Wednesday, 17 January 1945

Meetings & Appointments of the Reichsführer-SS on 17.1.1945 (Forbach-Gausbach)

12:30 hrs?	SS-Obersturmbannführer Grothmann	
13:30 hrs	Military Briefing	
[Time?]	Received five sharpshooters	
	Uffz. Jakob Horn	78. V.G.D.
	Uffz. Georg Kleenburg	544. V.G.D.
	Uffz. Heinr. Lünne	6. V.G.D.
	Uffz. Alfons Ludwig	78. V.G.D.
	Uffz. Karl Maier	6. V.G.D.
14:00 hrs	Meal with	
	SS-Obergruppenführer Jeckeln	
	SS-Brigadeführer Mueller [-Darss]	
	General	
	General	
	5 sharpshooters	
16:00 hrs	Oberstleutnant Suchanek	
20:00 hrs	Meal with	
	SS-Obergruppenführer Wünnenberg	
	SS-Standartenführer Tiefenbacher	
23:30 hrs	Played cards (Doppelkopf)	
01:00 hrs	Military briefing	

Events:

In the night of 17-18 January 1945, guards of the Gestapo prison Radogoszcz (near Lodz, Poland) containing 1,000 prisoners set the building on fire. A number of the prisoners were shot before the building was set afire. Many prisoners died in the flames, others shot trying to escape.[45]

During the same night at Chelmno extermination camp, the last surviving Jewish prisoners, about forty men, were shot and their bodies burned.[46]

A secret message dated 17 January 1945 was smuggled out of Auschwitz concentration camp by two prisoners Józef Cyrankiewicz and Stanislaw Klodzinski:

> Just before the clearance of the camps started gave a foretaste of what was to come: 'Now we are experiencing evacuation. Chaos. Panic among the SS – drunks... The intentions change from hour to hour since they don't know themselves what orders they will get ... This sort of evacuation means the annihilation of at least half of the prisoners.

The note went on to describe marches on foot to Bielsko, and to Gross-Rosen Camp. Lightly sick prisoners went on a train to Hannover [i.e. Bergen-Belsen].[47]

Thursday, 18 January 1945

Meetings & Appointments of the Reichsführer-SS on 18.1.1945 (Forbach-Gausbach)

14:00 hrs	SS-Obersturmführer Lipinski (Presentation of Ritterkreuz)
14:15 hrs	Meal with
	SS-Obergruppenführer Jeckeln
	SS-Obergruppenführer Wünnenberg
	SS-Obergruppenführer Krüger
	SS-Standartenführer Klingenberg
	SS-Sturmbannführer Gwodsz (*sic* – Rudolf Gwosdz)
	SS-Untersturmführer Wegner
	SS-Obersturmführer Lipinski
15:30 hrs	SS-Obergruppenführer Jeckeln[48]
16:30 hrs	SS-Standartenführer Klingenberg
19:00 hrs	SS-Obergruppenführer Wünnenberg
20:00 hrs	Unteroffizier Anton Sattler (sharpshooter)
20:10 hrs	Meal with
	SS-Gruppenführer Kammler
	SS-Obergruppenführer Jeckeln
	SS-Obergruppenführer Wünnenberg
	SS-Obergruppenführer Krüger
	Unteroffizier Sattler (sharpshooter)
21:00 hrs	SS-Obergruppenführer Wünnenberg
22:30 hrs	Military briefing
4:30 hrs	SS-Gruppenführer Kammler

Events:

SS-Staf. Dr Brandt telegram to SS-Ogruf. Pohl:

> On January 18 [1945] Himmler spoke to Lipinsky 'about his special assignment, the extraction of gasoline from [fir tree] roots.' Pohl was instantly informed that Lipinski would report to him after leaving his [Waffen-SS] division. 'The SS Reichsführer asks you then to discuss the necessary particulars with SS Obersturmführer Lipinski and to support him in every possible way.' At the same time, Dr Brandt informed the SS Command Headquarters that Himmler had 'given Lipinsky a special assignment in his area of chemical expertise,' and for this reason he had had him transferred for the time being to the SS Economic Administrative Headquarters.[49]

In a teleprinter message from the RF-SS, SS-Ogruf. Friedrich Jeckeln was charged with assembling all the Waffen-SS replacement units in the area of HSSPF Southeast. For the duration of the crisis in the East he was to take over the tasks of HSSPF Upper Silesia.[50]

Friday, 19 January 1945

Military situation:

Lodz (Litzmannstadt) was liberated by the 1.Weißrussische Front under the command of Marshal Zhukov.[51]

Meetings & Appointments of the Reichsführer-SS on 19.1.1945

13:00 hrs	Military briefing
14:00 hrs	Meal with
	SS-Obergruppenführer Krüger
	SS-Gruppenführer Ostendorff
	Oberstleutnant Dankworth
15:00 hrs	SS-Gruppenführer Ostendorff
20:30 hrs	Departure from Forbach-Gausbach[52]
	Travel to Berlin
	Meal with SS-Obergruppenführer Krüger (W.) (?)
23:00 hrs	SS-Obergruppenführer Krüger
00:30 hrs	Oak Leaves Wearers
	Presentation of Oak Leaves by the RF-SS
	Oberstleutnant Jakob
	Oberstleutnant v. Hauser
	Oberst Wulf
	Major Weidenbrück
	Major Hilgemann
	Oberfeldw. Braun now Leutnant
	Feldwebel Arndt
	Presentation continued until 03:00 hrs.

Events:

Gauleiter and Reichsstatthalter Arthur Greiser reported by the SD to have left Posen due to the Soviet advances.[53]

Saturday, 20 January 1945

Military situation:

From the diary of Martin Bormann: "Midday: The situation in the East is increasingly menacing; evacuation of the Warthegau – [Russian] armoured spearheads in Kattowitz etc."[54]

Meetings and Appointments of the Reichsführer-SS on 20.1.1945
(Journey on Sz. Steiermark to Berlin)

14:00 hrs	Meal with
	SS-Obergruppenführer Krüger
	SS-Brigadeführer Mueller-Darss
	4 Oak Leaves Wearers
	Major Weidenbrück
	Oberst Wulf
	Major Hilgemann
	Feldwebel Arndt
17:00 hrs	SS-Brigadeführer Mueller [-Darss]
18:00 hrs	Oberführer Bender
	Oberstrichter Weinheimer
20:00 hrs	Meal with SS-Obergruppenführer Krüger
21:30 hrs	Arrived Ludwigsfelde
22:30 hrs	Departure of the Führer for Berlin
04:30 hrs	Return journey on Sz. Steiermark

Events:

Report by Hermann Müller (SD-officer at the SD office in Posen) about the evacuation of the regional capital of Posen:

On 19 January 1945, the Party and NSV offices in Posen promised the population that women and children would be evacuated. On 20 January hundreds of women and children besieged the assembly point at 17:15 hrs after an evacuation order had been announced. No vehicles were to be found. Officials of the Party and NSV offices could no longer be found after 18:00 hours. Women and children began walking 30-50 Kms. The evacuation was so rushed that that the people would not stop to take food.

As trains became available, the rush to get on was so great that the Wehrmacht had to surround the railway station. Some refugees were loaded into cattle trucks. I noticed that five young children were literally frozen. The mood was very bad – they railed in particular against the Party offices and Gauleiter Greiser who had already left Posen on Friday [19 January]. On Sunday, 21 January, I once again went through Posen to find everyone had left. The evacuation mainly took place after 2 p.m. on Saturday the 18th through to Sunday at 14:00 hours. In Pinne, treks heading in the direction of Posen were checked by Party officials and all able-bodied men pulled out.[55]

Gauleiter Arthur Greiser reported that shortly before 18:00 hours, 20 January 1945, in his Posen headquarters, a "Führer-Order called him to Berlin to take over a task of the Reichsführer SS. My Deputy [Schmalz] took over the leadership of the Gau."

Deputy Gauleiter Heinrich Schmalz reported, 20 January 1945, "that all offices of state in Posen must leave by 21:00 hrs. The Kreisleiter of Posen had orders that all Germans in the city must be evacuated by midnight."[56]

From the diary of Alfred Jodl: "Meeting with Guderian and Reichsführer SS." This may have been due to a Führer-Order issued on 20 January 1945, "Task of the Reichsführer-SS in the East."[57]

From the memoirs of General Siegfried Westphal:

On 23 January (sic – 20 January 1945) Himmler quitted the Black Forest, having been posted to the Eastern Front to command the Vistula Army Group. Paul Hausser took over the Upper Rhine Command, which once more came under von Rundstedt's orders as Commander-in-Chief West. There was naturally no question of an orderly transfer... for Himmler as Commander-in-Chief Upper Rhine, had left behind a laundry-basket full of unsorted orders and reports. That too was apparently part of his new methods of leadership.[58]

From a post-war interrogation of SS-Staf. Constantin Canaris: "On 20 Jan [1945] Prützmann was recalled [from Agram, now Ljubljana] to Berlin without having achieved his object, and in fact Himmler never had his way."[59]

Sunday, 21 January 1945

Military situation:

Grand Admiral Dönitz ordered 'Operation Hannibal' for the Polish coastal areas: "All available ships should be used to rescue Germans and save them from the Soviets. Over two million people were saved in the 'greatest evacuation by sea' and taken to the west."[60]

Meetings & Appointments of the Reichsführer-SS on 21.1.1945

07:00 hrs	Departure Berlin – Ludwigsfelde
	Journey on Sz. Steiermark to Schneidemühl
13:00 hrs	Arrival at Schneidemühl
14:00 hrs	Meal with SS-Gruppenführer Gebhardt
16:30 hrs?	Journey to Marienburg
	(RF-SS, SS-Gruppenführer Gebhardt,
	SS-Obersturmbannführer Grothmann, Major Wersig)
20:00 hrs	Arrival at Festungskommandanten Marienburg
	Meeting with
	Gauleiter Forster
	Generaloberst [Walter Weiss, 2.Armee?]

General [Karl-Wilhelm] Specht
SS-Gruppenführer Katzmann
Marinebefehlshaber Danzig-Gotenhafen [...?]
Wehrkreisarzt
—in the guest house of Gauleiter Forster

23:30 hrs	Departure from Marienburg
04:00 hrs	Arrival at Deutsch-Krone [Walcz]
	Sz. Steiermark

Events:
Teleprinter message from Adolf Hitler:

1) Reichsführer-SS assumes command of the newly forming Army Group Vistula *(Heeresgruppe Weichsel)* as quickly as possible. I will issue details via the Chief of the General Staff.

2) His mission is:

a) Located in the gap between Army Group A and Army Group Mitte to prevent an enemy break-through towards Danzig and Posen and hinder any onslaught of East Prussia, leading to security of the new force.

b) Organize a national defence on German soil behind the entire Eastern front.

3) The command staff of Army Group Vistula from the Waffen-SS and Army will be under the control of the Reichsführer-SS. Provision of signals units managed by Chief, Army Signals.[61] Headquarters Schneidemühl.

4) Army Group Upper Rhine *(Heeresgruppe Oberrhein)* taken over in the interim by the command staff, deputised by SS-Obergruppenführer and General der Waffen-SS Hausser. Army Group Upper Rhine will remain under the command of C-in-C West.[62]

On 21 January 1945, Himmler's order to the Fortress Commander Posen, Major General Ernst Mattern, called for defence of the city "to the last breath".[63]

"Blitz" teleprinter message from RSHA Amtschef I (signed SS-Oberführer Ehrlinger) to KdS Kattowitz, SS-Ostubaf. ORR Dr Thümmler:

By order of Chef Sipo SD [Kaltenbrunner], SS-Brigadeführer and Major General of Police Bierkamp is immediately attached to SS-Ogruf Jeckeln with special orders of the RFSS. SS-Brigadef. Bierkamp takes over the SS and Police leadership in Upper Silesia. Report during the course of Monday to SS-Gruf. Jeckeln in Breslau, Army Regional Office. The deputy of SS-Brigadef. Bierkamp as BdS General Government, SS-Ostubaf. Batz, will immediately take over this position.[64]

Monday, 22 January 1945

Military situation:
On 22 January 1945 the 1st Ukrainian Front reached the River Oder, north and south of Breslau.[65]

From the War Diary of the WFStab: "The evacuation of Memel has begun. The Courland spit should be held; individual forces should cross the ice there. Warships will be used as transports."[66]

Meetings & Appointments of the Reichsführer-SS on 22.1.1945 (Deutsche-Krone)

11:30 hrs	Breakfast with SS-Gruppenführer Gebhardt
13:00 hrs	SS-Obergruppenführer Demelhuber
14:00 hrs	Meal with
	SS-Obergruppenführer Mazuw
	SS-Obergruppenführer [Friedrich-Wilhelm] Krüger (F. .)
	SS-Obergruppenführer [Karl] Oberg[67]
	Deputy Gauleiter [Paul] Simon[68]
	SS-Obergruppenführer Demelhuber
	SS-Gruppenführer Gebhardt
	SS-Oberführer Ax
	SS-Obersturmführer Massell
	SS-Obersturmführer Hahn
15:00 hrs	SS-Obergruppenführer Demelhuber
17:00 hrs	General Xylander (Chef Heeresgruppe Schörner)
18:00 hrs	General Vogt Commander of the Pomeranian Position
19:00 hrs	General Kienitz Komm.General Wehrkreis II
	General Vogt
	Oberst Zitzewitz
20:00 hrs	Meal with General Kienitz
	General Voigt
	SS-Obergruppenführer Mazuw
	SS-Obergruppenführer Demelhuber
	Oberst Zitzewitz

Events:

Göring appointed SS-Gruf. Dr Ing. Hans Kammler as "Special Plenipotentiary for the implementation, development, procurement and industrial testing in the field of weapons and rocket motors" (*Sonderbeauftragten zur Durchführung der Forderung bezüglich Entwicklung, Beschaffung und Industrieerprobung auf dem Gebiet der Kampfmittel mit Raketenantrieb*).[69]

Radio signal dated 22 January 1945, to SS Signal Training Dept. 4:

SS-Ostubaf Macher, Special Train Steiermark, mentioning despatch of personnel with necessary equipment to SS GHQ SIGS REGT 503, at Deutsch Krone, reporting to SS-Stubaf Schumacher through local or railway station HQ Deutschkrone. Deutschkrone is 20 km NW of Schneidemück (*sic* – Schneidemühl), West Prussia. SS-Ostubaf Westerheide, of Special Undertaking 'GREY' ordered also 22 Jan 1945 to report to SS-Ostubaf Schumacher.[70]

On 20 January 1945, SS-Obergruppenführer Karl Oberg was telephoned at Zwickau and informed that he should report to the Reichsführer-SS Himmler in Berlin the following day. Arriving Berlin, Oberg found the Reichsführer-SS had left and given fresh instructions to report the following day, 22 January, at Himmler's special train at Schneidemühl. At their meeting, Himmler informed Oberg of the new Army Group Vistula, established to meet a "critical situation", and Oberg was appointed "Commander of the Blocking and Catching Line" (*Befehlshaber der Sperr- und Auffanglinie*) between Danzig and Glogau.[71]

Tuesday, 23 January 1945

Military situation:
Evacuation transports began from East Prussia and Danzig harbour. By the end of the war (8 May 1945) over two million refugees, soldiers and wounded would be evacuated. 14,000 people perished at sea.[72]

From the War Diary of WFStab: "The newly formed Army Group Vistula, Reichsführer-SS has been appointed Commander, takes over the section from Glogau to Elbing with headquarters in Deutsch-Krone. Taking up command expected on 25.1., 00:00 hrs. East Prussian ports have been evacuated, the ships moved to Swinemünde. The evacuation of Königsberg is underway, the evacuation of Memel will follow."[73]

Meetings & Appointments of the Reichsführer-SS on 23.1.1945 (Deutsche-Krone)
14:00 hrs? Meal with

> Gauleiter Greiser
> SS-Obergruppenführer [Felix] Steiner
> SS-Obergruppenführer [Hermann] Höfle
> SS-Gruppenführer Reinefarth
> Befehlshaber d. Ordnungspolizei Posen Gen.maj. Dr Gudewill

15:00 hrs	Gauleiter Greiser
16:30 hrs	SS-Obergruppenführer Höfle
17:30 hrs	SS-Obergruppenführer Demelhuber
	Oberst [Hans-Georg] Eismann I a Heeresgruppe Weichsel
	SS-Obersturmbannführer Grothmann
19:45 hrs	General Crasemann (Eichenlaub)
20:00 hrs	Meal with
	General Crasemann
	SS-Obergruppenführer Demelhuber
	Oberst Eismann
	Oberstleutnant [Gerhard] Wessel
	I a Heeresgruppe Weichsel [Oberst Eismann]
24:00 hrs	Military briefing
01:00 hrs	SS-Gruppenführer Gebhardt

Events:
Himmler sent to Russian Front to Stop Rot: *Front und Heimat* article broadcast 23rd January calling on soldiers to 'stand firm at any price' contained passage: 'Fuhrer sent best Army

commanders and men of iron determination such as Reichsfuhrer-SS Heinrich Himmler to focal points of the battle. They have been given complete powers and will make radical decisions and guarantee command'.[74]

District Leader (*Kreisleiter*) Dotzler wrote to Martin Bormann: "Proposals to set up a resistance movement in German eastern area occupied by the Bolsheviks."[75]

On 23 January 1945, HSSPF SS-Ogruf. and General der Waffen-SS Gutenberger in his position as Senior Commander for Prisoners in Military District VI (*Der Höhere Kommandeur der Kriegsgefangenen im Wehrkreis VII* – ref. II K2 Br.B. 352/45) issued instructions on the "Treatment of Prisoners of War":

> The Commander of the Replacement Army/Chief of Prisoner of War Matters has issued the following special directive and its basic implementation.
>
> In complete disregard to the position of the Reichsführer-SS and Commander of the Replacement Army in the treatment of foreign nationals and prisoner of war matters, a certain rabble-rousing has taken place in civilian circles which interferes with political measures, encouragement and performance increases and must, therefore, be prevented.[76]

Wednesday, 24 January 1945

Meetings & Appointments of the Reichsführer-SS on 24.1.1945 (Deutsch-Krone)

12:00 hrs	Military briefing
14:00 hrs	Oberstleutnant Remlinger
18:00 hrs	SS-Obergruppenführer Steiner
18:15 hrs	Reichsminister Speer
20:00 hrs	Meal with
	Reichsminister Speer
	SS-Gruppenführer Dr Gebhardt
	Generalarzt Walther
	Wehrkreis-Oberin [?]
22:00 hrs	Military briefing
23:00 hrs	Reichsminister Speer
00:30 hrs	General [Alfred] Toppe
	Oberst v. Rücker[t][77]

Events:

In his memoirs, Albert Speer recalled his visit to Himmler's special train in Danzig. using it as a mobile headquarters:

> ... By chance I was present at a telephone conversation between him and General [Walter] Weiss, and heard Himmler cut off all arguments for abandoning a lost position with a stereotyped reply: 'I have given you a command. You'll answer with your head for it. I'll call you to account personally if the position is lost.' But when I visited General Weiss the next day, the position had been abandoned in the course of the night. Weiss appeared unimpressed by Himmler's threats....[78]

On 24 January 1945, Himmler as Commander, Army Group Vistula, issued his instructions to 2nd Army, XI SS-Army Corps and XVI SS-Army-Corps:

1) In the area of Army Group Vistula an office will be set up:

The Commander of Blocking and Catching Lines

(*Der Befehlshaber der Sperr- und Auffanglinie*)

2) The Commander of the Blocking and Catching Lines will be under my command.

3) His primary task is to shut down the whole area on the River Oder from Glogau to its mouth on the Baltic, blocking every bridge. Also, a blocking line will be set up, running from Neusalz on the Oder to Kreuz on the Netze via Deutsch-Krone, Jastrow-Konitz and Preussisch Stargard to Danzig.

4) Members of all Wehrmacht units who want to fall back, will be intercepted without delay and brought to collection camps where the Commander for Reprocessing and New-Placement will take them. Similarly all vehicles are not allowed to cross these lines, they are to be stopped and secured.

5) Especially I would like controls on refugee and evacuation trains to clear them of stragglers.

6) Kommandos of the Commander of Blocking and Catching Lines, as far as their duties allow, will provide any support and assistance in the orderly movement of the refugee treks.

7) The Commander of the Blocking and Catching Lines operates in the regions of Wartheland, Pomerania and West Prussia, and each Region will have a Regional Commander. They will work closely with local Party and Government offices.

8) First and foremost it depends on the unrelenting and severe application of their duty by the Blocking and Catching Lines for a few days in the area of Army Group Vistula remaining quiet and there is only a stream [of people], from the homeland to the Front.

9) As Commander of the Blocking and Catching Lines I appoint SS-Obergruppenführer and General der Waffen-SS and Police Oberg.

signed H. Himmler.[79]

On 24 January 1945 the first successful launch of the A9 rocket took place at Peenemünde.[80]

Thursday, 25 January 1945

Military situation:

Army Group Vistula was joined by the 4.SS-Police Grenadier Division under the command of SS-Staf. Walter Harzer, coming from Hungary; the III SS-Corps (comprising Dutch and Norwegian Waffen-SS volunteers) was assigned to Army Group Courland.[81]

"Army Group 'Vistula' was formed on January 25th, 1945, and initially had the 9th Army, 2nd Army, three hundred Panzer-Nahbekämpfungstrupps, 'Gneisenau' and Volkssturm units of Military District II, III, XX and XXI. These were joined by the 4th SS Division, IIIrd Armoured Corps ('Nordland' and 'Nederland' SS divisions) and later by the 21st Armoured Division, the 10th SS Division, the Führerbegleitbrigade, Führergrenadierbrigade, 27th SS Division, Gen.-Kdo XXXIX Armoured Corps and Gen.-Kdo. XVIII Mountain Corps."[82]

Meetings & Appointments of the Reichsführer-SS on 25.1.1945 (Deutsch-Krone)

14:00 hrs	Meal with
	Generaloberst [Hans-Jürgen] Stumpff
	SS-Obergruppenführer Mazuw
	SS-Brigadeführer Lammerding
16:00 hrs	Generaloberst Stumpff
17:00 hrs	SS-Obergruppenführer Mazuw
18:00 hrs	SS-Brigadeführer Lammerding
20:00 hrs	Military briefing
21:00 hrs	Meal with SS-Obersturmbannführer Grothmann
	Military briefing to 24:00 hrs
	SS-Brigadeführer Lammerding
	Oberst Eismann
	Oberstleutnant Harnack
	Oberst Öhmichen

Events:

From the diary of Joseph Goebbels, which underlined Himmler's difficulties, since his "army group exists in practice only on paper."[83]

Secret report dated 25 January 1945 by Robert Schirmer, member of the International Committee of the Red Cross (ICRC) delegation in Berlin, to ICRC-Central according to a telegram dated 16 February 1945 from McClelland in Switzerland to the State Department and the War Refugee Board in Washington DC:

Schirmer and a colleague were put in touch with Obersturmbann Fuehrer De. Berndorf (*sic* – Dr Emil Berndorff) Chef Des Sicherheitsdienstes und Abwehr Fuer die Schutzheeftling whose office was located at Zimmerstrasse 19 Berlin, by a certain SS General Lieutenant Mueller. Following preliminary conversations with Schirmer, characterized as cordial, Berndorf took them to headquarters of Nazi concentration camp system at Oranienburg. Further conversations were held there with Obergruppen Fuehrer (*sic* – Gruppenführer) Glueck (*sic* – Glücks) (also a General Lieutenant in Waffen-SS) director of all concentration camps, Standartenfuehrer Dr Loling (*sic* – Lolling) head medical officer of concentration camps, and Glueck's adjutant Obersturmbannfuehrer Hoess. Explaining that Dachau near Munich was to become central assembly and clearing camp for all SH [*Schutzhäftlinge* – protective custody prisoners], these SS men seemed most willing to discuss ways and means of added ICRC relief to concentration camp inmates...

Parcels of the ICRC could be distributed to the following national groups: French, Dutch, Belgians, Greeks, Norwegians and Danes (for the moment, Poles, Czechs, Slavs and Serbs to be excluded). Although Reichsfuehrer [*Himmler*] was now willing to permit such a relief program, he could not issue blanket permission for the ICRC delegates to visit all concentration camps was explained to Schirmer by the SS.

It is most significant that, in spite of this rather important hitch, Himmler will now apparently officially permit relief for concentration camps even if only to certain categories of SH, since hitherto Berlin has categorically refused such permission and only in a small number of camps was the reception of ICRC parcels to internees tolerated. No doubt refusal to blanket visiting permission is motivated by the fact that an increasingly large number of SH are being worked in war factories at present.[84]

Telegram dated 25 January 1945 from the War Refugee Board in Washington DC (signed Mr Grew for Director Pehle), to the US Embassy in Bern, Switzerland, (for Mr Huddle) and to the WRB-Representative McClelland:

Information has reached us recently that Sternbuch has developed a plan for the release of 300,000 Jews from Germany and German occupied territory in return for payments totalling $5,000,000. The Jews are to be released at the rate of 15,000 a month and payments are to be made at the rate of $250,000 a month. It is further reported that some of $250,000 remitted from the US by Va'ad Hahatzala is now deposited in a Swiss bank in the name of Sternbuch and is to be used for payment for the first shipment of 15,000 Jews expected shortly in Switzerland… Please advise of any information you have or can obtain on the foregoing.[85]

Friday, 26 January 1945

Military situation:
Soviet units captured Tolkemit (now Tolkmicko, Poland) and cut off the Frischen Haff, then a frozen fresh water lagoon, that allowed refugees to trek from East Prussia to Danzig and the west.[86]

From the war diary of WFStab: Army Group Vistula comprises 4th Panzer Division, 32nd Infantry Division and the first unit from Army Group Courland, 227th Infantry Division is coming. Nakel (now Nakło, Poland) has been lost. The enemy is supplying his troops by air drops. Bromberg (now Bydgoszcz, Poland) is surrounded; the same situation at Thorn (now Toruń, Poland).[87]

Meetings & Appointments of the Reichsführer-SS on 26.1.1945 (Deutsch-Krone)

12:00 hrs	Military briefing
14:00 hrs	Meal with
	SS-Obergruppenführer v.d. Bach
	SS-Gruppenführer Behrends[88]
	Kommandeur Flak-Unit
	Mr Roskothen (OT – Organisation Todt)
	Mr Manke (OT)
16:00 hrs	Military briefing
16:30 hrs	SS-Obergruppenführer v.d. Bach[89]
17:30 hrs	Gauleiter Greiser
20:30 hrs	Meal with
	Gauleiter Greiser
	SS-Obergruppenführer Prützmann
	SS-Gruppenführer Behrends
	SS- Gruppenführer Gebhardt
23:00 hrs	Military briefing
01:00 hrs	SS-Gruppenführer Behrends

Events:

Order dated 26 January 1945 from IdS Düsseldorf, SS-Staf. Dr Walter Albath, addressed to Gustapo offices in Düsseldorf, Münster, Dortmund and Köln:

Subject: Special treatment (*Sonderbehandlung*) of foreign workers.

Reference: Conference of departmental heads at the office of the Inspector of Security Police, Düsseldorf, on 19 January 1945.

The head of [RSHA] department IV has confirmed my instructions whereby as a consequence of the special situation in Army Region VI, special treatment may be carried out even without a prior approval of the RSHA [Reich Security Main Office]. In such cases a retrospective report is to be rendered to the RSHA. In cases involving a considerable number of persons it is advisable to only partly carry out special treatment in public. Moreover, it can be effected without publicity and also by shooting. In future no applications for special treatment in a concentration camp will be made to the RSHA. I hereby request all concerned to act according to this instruction. Should it, in any particular case, appear necessary to carry out this special treatment against members of gangs who are German or other offenders of German nationality – as may well be the case in the present situation – an application is to be made to me accordingly. I shall put such applications before the Higher SS and Police Chief Western Zone [Gutenberger] who has received respective powers from the Reichsführer SS.[90]

(note: *Sonderbehandlung* – special treatment – was usually regarded as an euphemism for killing, as in this case)

Saturday, 27 January 1945

Military situation: Himmler's second headquarters on the eastern front was established in Robert Ley's luxurious villa complex at Falkenburg near Ordensburg Crössinsee.[91]

Meetings & Appointments of the Reichsführer-SS on 27.1.1945
(Deutsch-Krone – Falkenburg – Crössinsee)

08:30 hrs	Departure on Sz. Steiermark from Deutsch-Krone
11:00 hrs	Breakfast with SS-Gruppenführer Gebhardt
13:00 hrs	Arrival at Falkenburg
13:45 hrs	Meal aboard the train [Sz. Steiermark]
15:00 hrs	Journey continued to Ordensburg Crössinsee
15:15 hrs	SS-Brigadeführer [Heinz] Lammerding[92]
	SS-Obersturmbannführer Grothmann
17:00 hrs	SS-Standartenführer [Paul] Baumert
19:00 hrs	SS-Obersturmbannführer Grothmann
20:00 hrs	Meal with
	Gauleiter Schwede-Coburg
	SS-Brigadeführer Lammerding
	Pz.Jg. General Munzel
	Major v. Bismarck (Adjutant)

SS-Hauptsturmführer Ohlemacher
SS-Obersturmführer Schwarz van Berk
Ingenieur [...?]

22:00 hrs	SS-Obersturmbannführer Grothmann
23:00 hrs	SS-Obergruppenführer Prützmann
[Time?]	Military briefing

Events:

Bormann sent to Himmler, Dotzler's proposals as "worth reading about sabotage behind the Russian front".[93]

The Auschwitz Stammlager (main camp) and the Birkenau extermination centre were liberated by Soviet troops at 15:00 hours.[94]

Sunday, 28 January 1945

Military situation:

At Hitler's headquarters on "28.1. the Führer appointed General Wlassow as Commander of the Russian armed forces with the authority of a Commander-in-Chief. He has the right to appoint officers to Lieutenant Colonel (*Oberstleutnant*). General Wlassow also wanted to use the National Committee; but this proposal has been rejected out of consideration for the Ukrainians."[95]

Meetings and Appointments of the Reichsführer-SS on 28.1.1945 (Crössinsee)

13:00 hrs	Military briefing
14:00 hrs	Meal with
	SS-Obergruppenführer Prützmann
	SS-Gruppenführer Gebhardt
	General Melzer (XXVII. A.K.)
15:00 hrs	General Melzer (XXVII. A.K.)
17:00 hrs	General Busse (9. Armee)
18:00 hrs	SS-Brigadeführer Lammerding
20:00 hrs	Meal with
	SS-Obergruppenführer Kaltenbrunner
	General Melzer
	SS-Obergruppenführer Prützmann
	SS-Brigadeführer Lammerding
22:00 hrs	Military briefing
24:00 hrs	Generaloberst Ritter v. Greim
01:00 hrs	SS-Obergruppenführer Dr Kaltenbrunner

Events:

Secret order by Himmler (Feld-Kommandostelle):

Subject: Order of Reichsmarschall [Göring] of 26.1.1945.

   1) The Division z.V. and the Special Plenipotentiary 2 will combine with 5th Flak Division under a Commanding General.

   2) The Commanding General will have the designation A.K.z.V.

   3) Proposals for the organization of the A.K.z.V. should be presented to me by 10 February 1945.[96]

Secret order by Himmler (Feld-Kommandostelle): "I charge SS-Gruppenführer and Generalleutnant der Waffen-SS Dr Kammler with the command of A.K.z.V."[97]

Monday, 29 January 1945

Military situation:

"The enemy… has crossed the Preussisch-Holland – Königsberg road and blocking access to the sea. From Pillau 67,000 people have now been brought out."[98]

Meetings & Appointments of the Reichsführer-SS on 29.1.1945 (Crössinsee)

12:00 hrs	Military briefing
14:00 hrs	Meal with
	Reichsleiter Dr Ley
	SS-Obergruppenführer Prützmann
	Burgkommandant [Otto] Gohdes
	SS-Gruppenführer Gebhardt
	SS-Sturmbannführer Persch
	SS-Sturmbannführer [Heinz-Dieter] Gross
	SS-Hauptsturmführer Macher
15:00 hrs	Dr Ley
16:00 hrs	SS-Gruppenführer Lammerding
20:00 hrs	Meal
22:00 hrs	Oberst [Hans-Ulrich] Rudel
24:00 hrs	Military briefing

Events:

Teleprinter message from OKH to Himmler at Army Group Vistula: "The Führer has permitted a break-out by the occupiers of Fortress Thorn."[99]

   Teleprinter message from Reichsführer-SS: "The heads of all military and civilian offices must realize that leaving their place of work without orders makes them liable to the death penalty."[100]

   Heinz Macher, Himmler staff officer, in a post-war interrogation: "After leaving hospital he was sent to the Heeresgruppe at Deutsch Krone as staff officer and Special Plenipotentiary (*Sonderbeauftragter*). It was his job with a staff of two or three to go to wherever there had been an inroad by the Russians on the Eastern Front and bring it in order again."[101]

Tuesday, 30 January 1945

Military situation:

"Because of the poor weather, tailbacks at Pillau and Königsberg. At the moment, 20,000 refugees have been transported by sea. It is not possible to satisfactorily secure all ships. By the action of an enemy submarine, the steamer *Wilhelm Gustloff* carrying 5,500 people (including 3,300 refugees) was sunk. Only 200 people could be rescued."[102]

Subsequently it became known that the Soviet submarine S-13 had torpedoed the *Wilhelm Gustloff* at 21:16 hours. The steamer was carrying over 10,000 refugees. Apart from 900 cadets of the German U-Boat Lehr Division, the rest were mainly women and children. Only 1,293 people were rescued. This is probably the worst ever maritime disaster with six times as many victims as the *Titanic* sinking of 1912. Very little was known about the tragedy at the time[103]

Meetings & Appointments of the Reichsführer-SS on 30.1.1945 (Crössinsee)

13:00 hrs	Military briefing
14:00 hrs	Meal with
	Gauleiter Greiser
	SS-Gruppenführer Lammerding
15:00 hrs	Gauleiter Greiser
	General der Artillerie [...?]
20:00 hrs	Meal with
Gauleiter Greiser	
	SS-Obergruppenführer Prützmann
	SS-Gruppenführer Lammerding
	SS-Gruppenführer Gebhardt
22:15 hrs	Führer speech[104]
23:00 hrs	Military briefing

Events:

From the pocket diary of Martin Bormann: "19.15 The Führer spoke to the German nation" by radio broadcast.[105]

Order dated 30 January 1945 of Reichsführer-SS, published in all German newspapers on 8 February 1945:

1) I have degraded the former SS-Standartenführer and Police President of Bromberg, [Carl] von Salisch, due to his cowardice and forgetting his duties, and is to be shot immediately.

2.) The former Government President (*Regierungspräsident*) of Bromberg [Walther] Kühn, the former Bürgermeister of Bromberg, Ernst, were degraded and demoted due to cowardice and forgetting their duties. They come as probationary soldiers in a Probationary Battalion, after having attended the execution of von Salisch. The last two will be deployed in particularly difficult and dangerous tasks facing the Probationary Battalion.

3) The head of the Party Chancellery [Bormann] has degraded and thrown out of the Party the District Leader (*Kreisleiter*) of Bromberg, Rampf, and like Kühn and Ernst assigned to the

Probationary Battalion.

signed H. Himmler[106]

On 30 January 1945, SS-Ostubaf. Otto Skorzeny was telephoned by Himmler and given orders to "form a bridgehead east of the Oder River near Schwedt... and you will maintain this bridgehead, come what might, so that my army can launch an offensive from it." With only 2,000 men including various army, Luftwaffe, Waffen-SS stragglers and local residents, Skorzeny held the bridgehead until 23 February 1945.[107]

Tuesday-Wednesday, 30-31 January 1945

On these two days, at least 600 defenceless and unsuspecting prisoners held in Sonnenburg Prison (now Słońsk, Poland) were shot by a 200-man strong SS unit led by SS-officer Wilhelm Nickel.

Two or three days at most before 30/31 January 1945, a teleprinter message signed by Himmler was received at the offices of Gestapo Frankfurt/Oder. It was an order to evacuate Sonnenburg Prison before the Russians arrived and shoot the prisoners.[108]

Wednesday, 31 January 1945

Military situation:
"Army Group Vistula: ... Instead of General Mattern, the Reichsführer-SS has appointed Colonel Gonell as Commandant of Posen, due to his experiences in the East, with the task of continuing to block the advance of the Russians past Posen... The Waffen-SS has set-up a new Division, '30. Januar'. From the replacement Brigade 'Gross Deutschland', the Division 'Kurmark' has been built, and now fighting. From the Döberitz School the Division 'Berlin' has been established. The Reichsführer has taken over an order of Army Group Mitte (under Schörner), whereby Annihilation Troops (*Vernichtungstruppen*) act like partisans, living off the land, and carry the fight to the enemy in the flanks and in the rear."[109]

Meetings & Appointments of the Reichsführer-SS on 31.1.1945 (Crössinsee)

13:00 hrs	Military briefing
14:00 hrs	Meal with
	Gauleiter Greiser
	SS-Gruppenführer Gebhardt
	SS-Obergruppenführer Prützmann
16:00 hrs	SS-Gruppenführer Lammerding
20:00 hrs	Meal with
	SS-Obergruppenführer Koppe
	SS-Obergruppenführer Prützmann
	SS-Gruppenführer Lammerding
	Oberst Eismann

Events:

SS-Gruppenführer Dr Kammler was appointed "Special Plenipotentiary of the Führer for Jet Aircraft" (*Sonderbeauftragter des Führers für Strahlenwaffen*).[110]

For uniformity, Hitler ordered the V1 and V2 programme brought together under Kammler's leadership.[111]

A death march (*Todesmarsch*) began of at least 6,000 prisoners (mainly Jewish women) from East Prussia (from sub-camps of KL Stutthof and sub-camps of Organisation Todt: Heiligenbeil, Gerdauen, Seerappen, Jesau, Schippenbeil-Sepopol; and 947 from Königsberg). Their route was Königsberg to Palmnicken and on the march at least half of the prisoners died.

In Palmnicken it was planned to kill the prisoners in an underground mineshaft of the Bernstein-Mine 'Anna'. This was prevented by local residents (local Volkssturm unit may have been involved). Up to 200 prisoners were then murdered on the beaches of the Baltic Sea.[112]

January 1945

HSSPF Bassewitz-Behr (in Hamburg) reported: "Further, since Jan 1945, the HSSPF had to support the 'Werwolf'-organisation founded by the Reichsführer-SS, in as much as he had to back up the local Werwolf representative in his work and dealings with the Gauleiter."[113]

When Friedrich-Wilhelm Lotto, Werwolf commander in Gau Weser-Ems, faced prosecution after the war, he reported: "In January 1945 orders were given by Wehrwolf (*sic*) leadership [Prützmann via Bassewitz-Behr] to set up so-called Death Lists. In these lists should be entered the names of politically unreliable personalities who favour the enemy. These people should be keenly watched and eliminated in cases of intended betrayal."[114]

February 1945

Thursday, 1 February 1945

Meetings & Appointments of the Reichsführer-SS on 1.2.1945

01:30 hrs	Departure from Falkenburg to Birkenwald on Sz. Steiermark (changes with Wehrmacht)
11:30 hrs	Breakfast on train
13:00 hrs	Meal with SS-Gruppenführer Lammerding SS-Standartenführer Baumert
15:00 hrs	Discussions in the barracks at Birkenwald
16:30 hrs	SS-Obergruppenführer Steiner SS-Gruppenführer Lammerding
19:00 hrs	SS-Gruppenführer Lammerding
20:15 hrs	Meal with General Melzer SS-Standartenführer d'Alquen SS-Standartenführer Baumert
21:00 hrs	SS-Obergruppenführer Steiner
22:30 hrs	SS-Standartenführer d'Alquen
24:00 hrs	Fräulein [Erika] Lorenz
02:00 hrs	Military briefing

Events:

Camp Commandant KL Sachsenhausen, Anton Kaindl, when interrogated after the war:

> On 1 February 1945 I had a talk with Gestapo Chief [Heinrich] Müller. He passed onto me an order to destroy the Camp [Sachsenhausen] by artillery fire, air attack or gassing. The order came from Himmler, but implementation of it was technically impossible... Artillery fire or an air attack would become known to the local population. A gassing operation would not only affect the civilian population but also imperil the SS personnel.S
> During the night of 1–2 February the first 150 prisoners were shot. By the end of March around 5,000 had been exterminated."[1]

During the night of 1–2 February 1945, 400 Soviet prisoners of war broke out of KL Mauthausen. This resulted in a massacre of those captured by members of the Camp administration, local Volkssturm units and Hitler Youth (the so-called 'Mühlvierteler Rabbit Hunt' *Mühlvierteler Hasenjagd*).[2]

Friday, 2 February 1945

Military situation:
WFStab situation report for 3 February 1945: "From Königsberg and Gotenhafen 184,780 refugees are now fleeing."[3]

Meetings &Appointments of the Reichsführer-SS on 2.2.1945 (Birkenwald)

13:00 hrs	Military briefing
14:00 hrs	Meal with General Siebert (*sic* – Friedrich Siebert), (Wehrmachtstreifendienst)
16:30 hrs	Oberst [Fritz] Estor (Chef des Stabes Armee-Gruppe Steiner)
17:30 hrs	General [Günther] Krappe (Oder-Korps)
20:00 hrs	Meal
21:00 hrs	Military briefing
22:00 hrs	Flak-General Odebrecht

Events:
Himmler wrote to SS-Ogruf. Karl Oberg and General [Martin] Krase, Commander, Sperr- und Auffangslinie Stargard:

I wish that in any event, you will take decisive action against officers and men whose indisputable shirking and cowardice when sentenced at drumhead Courts Martial (*Standgericht*). The sentences are to be carried out before the assembled men of their Companies or Battalions.

Each evening I wish to see a teleprinter message with results of the captured officers and men, about those sent to marching battalions, of soldiers to their own Divisions after losing contact. At the same time, copy the report to Deputy Commander of the Replacement Army, SS-Obergruppenführer Jüttner, so he can take action with those scattered soldiers who through re-training can be again returned to the Army Group as soldiers.

In your daily report will you also report sentences from the Courts Martial pronounced that day, including death sentences.[4]

On 2 February 1945, the President of the International Red Cross Committee, Prof. Carl Jacob Burkhardt received a letter from Himmler, inviting him to a meeting.[5]

Saturday, 3 February 1945

Military situation:
Berlin suffered its most serious air-raid of the war. The 8th USAAF employed 937 bombers, protected by 613 fighter aircraft, and dropped 2,264 tons of bombs over Berlin. 26 B-17s and eight fighter aircraft were shot down by flak. About 2,600 people were killed. The Volksgerichtshof building was partially destroyed killing Prosecutor Roland Freisler. The RSHA building at 8 Prinz-Albrecht-Strasse also suffered damage.[6]

Meetings & Appointments of the Reichsführer-SS on 3.2.1945 (Birkenwald)

13:00 hrs	Military briefing
14:00 hrs	Meal
	General Krappe
20:00 hrs	Meal

Events:

From the diary of Martin Bormann:

> Afternoon, severe air-raid on Berlin (New Reich Chancellery, Führer's residence, entrance hall, dining room, winter garden, Party Chancellery). Battle for the Oder. (Party Chancellery at the front!).[7]

From the diary of Ursula von Kardorff: "Today, the heaviest air-attack on the city centre than has ever been. I did not think an increase was even possible."[8]

SS-Stubaf. Hans Günther spoke with the Jewish Elder (Judenältesten) Benjamin Murmelstein in Theresienstadt, in the presence of Camp Commandant SS-Ostuf. Karl Rahm, and informed him that in two days 1,200 prisoners would be taken to Switzerland.[9]

Sunday, 4 February 1945

Military situation:

Führer-Order from Hitler (4 February 1945), "The national comrades (Volksgenossen) temporarily repatriated to the Reich are to be brought to Denmark."[10]

Meetings & Appointments of the Reichsführer-SS on 4.2.1945 (Birkenwald)

13:30 hrs	SS-Obersturmbannführer Peiper
14:00 hrs	Meal with
	SS-Obergruppenführer Wolff
	SS-Gruppenführer Lammerding
	Oberst Eismann
	SS-Sturmbannführer Wanner
15:00 hrs	SS-Obersturmbannführer Peiper
16:00 hrs	SS-Gruppenführer Lammerding
	Major Wersig
20:00 hrs	General Melzer
20:10 hrs	Evening meal with
	SS-Obergruppenführer Wolff
	SS-Obergruppenführer Keppler
	Konteradmiral Hartmann
	SS-Gruppenführer Lammerding
	Fräulein Lorenz
20:45 hrs	Oberstleutnant Müller (Chef V, SS-A.K.)

21:15 hrs	SS-Gruppenführer Lammerding
	Konteradmiral Hartmann
	Oberst Eismann
24:00 hrs	SS-Obergruppenführer Wolff

Events:

Himmler issued Order No. 1 for the "Birkenwald" installation:

1. Like all field headquarter sites Birkenwald is to be kept secret. Any disclosure of its position, use etc. will be punished as high treason.

2. It is to be kept unconditionally secret when the RFSS is in residence.[11]

Post-war secretly monitored (bugged) conversation of Karl Wolff with others:

Wolff speaks:

...[Wolff] went to the Reichsfuehrer's GHQ, on 4th February [1945], and asked him what there was to be done about withdrawing. However, I received no definite information, and requested the Reichsfuehrer to arrange an interview for me with the Fuehrer so that I could make a clean breast of my difficulties and my view of the situation. I proceeded to the Fuehrer's GHQ, and made a report on the situation....[12]

In 1965, a former Order Policeman appeared before an East German court in Frankfurt/Oder. He was convicted and sentenced to 6 years' imprisonment for "Participation in hanging the Bürgermeister of Königsberg/Neumarkt for having left the city without an evacuation order and convicted in Schwedt by SS-Military Court chaired by SS-officer Skorzeny and sentenced to death" on 4 February 1945.[13]

Monday, 5 February 1945

Meetings & Appointments of the Reichsführer-SS on 5.2.1945 (Birkenwald)

12:00 hrs	SS-Obergruppenführer Wolff
13:30 hrs	General Praun
	General Melzer
	SS-Gruppenführer Lammerding
14:00 hrs	Meal with
	SS-Obergruppenführer Wolff
	SS-Obergruppenführer Winkelmann
	General Praun
	General Melzer
	SS-Gruppenführer Kammler
	SS-Standartenführer [Gebhard] Himmler
	Oberst v. Rücker O.Q.
16:00 hrs	SS-Gruppenführer Kammler

20:00 hrs	Meal with
	SS-Obergruppenführer Wolff
	SS-Obergruppenführer [Werner] Lorenz[14]
	SS-Obergruppenführer Winkelmann
	SS-Standartenführer Becher
	Fräulein Lorenz
23:00 hrs	Fräulein Lorenz
23:15 hrs	SS-Obergruppenführer Winkelmann
	SS-Standartenführer Becher

Events:

SS-Ostuf. Kriminalkommissar Franz Göring took 1,200 Jews from Theresienstadt and escorted them by train via Konstanz to the Swiss border and handed them over to the Swiss authorities.[15]

Dr Rezsö Kasztner reported: "*5. February.* Becher himself later telephoned from Himmler's headquarters. He said that 1,000 Jews as a sign of good will would be sent to Switzerland. They are already on the way."[16]

SS-Staf. Kurt Becher reported: "I think it was the end of January when I was again with Himmler. He permitted me to meet with Saly Meyer again. He told me: 'About 1,000 Jews you can again get rid of'... That was the end of January, beginning February 1945."[17]

Tuesday, 6 February 1945

Meetings & Appointments of the Reichsführer-SS on 6.2.1945 (Birkenwald)

13:45 hrs	SS-Obergruppenführer Wolff
14:00 hrs	Meal with
	SS-Obergruppenführer Wolff
	SS-Obergruppenführer Seyss-Inquart
	SS-Obergruppenführer Oberg
	General Grase
	General Rehmer [Remer?]
	Ministerialdirektor Dorsch
	General Roskothen [Generalingenieur, Organisation Todt]
	SS-Obersturmbannführer Kriebel
15:00 hrs	SS-Obergruppenführer Wolff[18]
16:00 hrs	SS-Gruppenführer Kammler
18:00 hrs	SS-Obergruppenführer Oberg
	General Grase
18:30 hrs	Ministerialdirektor Dorsch
	SS-Gruppenführer Lammerding
20:00 hrs	Meal with
	SS-Obergruppenführer Lorenz

General Decker (XXXIX. Pz. Korps)
with Chief of Staff and Adjutant
Fräulein Lorenz
21:00 hrs   General Decker
SS-Gruppenführer Lammerding

Events:
Dr Rezsö Kasztner reported: "*6 February.*1,200 Jews from Theresienstadt have arrived in Switzerland. Swiss President von Steiger spoke with Sally Meyer, the transport had been organized by former Bundesrat Musy."[19]

Wednesday, 7 February 1945

Meetings & Appointments of the Reichsführer-SS on 7.2.1945 (Birkenwald)
12:00 hrs   SS-Gruppenführer Lammerding
12:45 hrs   Departure from Birkenwald for Berlin
14:30 hrs   Arrival at Reich Chancellery, Berlin
               Lunch with SS-Gruppenführer Fegelein
15:15 hrs   Meeting with the Führer (Hitler)
16:00 hrs   Military briefing
18:00 hrs   Watched a weekly newsreel
18:30 hrs   Meeting with the Führer
20:30 hrs   Meal with
               Reichsleiter Bormann
               SS-Gruppenführer Fegelein
               SS-Obersturmbannführer Grothmann
               Meeting with
               Reichsleiter Bormann
               SS-Obergruppenführer Kaltenbrunner
               General [Bruno Ritter von] Hauenschildt[20]
               Generaloberst Guderian
               SS-Obergruppenführer Jüttner
01:15 hrs   Departure from Berlin
03:45 hrs   Arrived Birkenwald

Events:
Heinz Linge, Hitler's valet, reported in his diary:
15:25 hrs   Himmler walk
16:00 hrs   Himmler attended the military briefing
18:00 hrs   Himmler met with Gauleiter Koch, Generaloberst Guderian
               and General Wenck
18:30 hrs   Himmler attended the showing of the weekly newsreel

20:00 hrs	Himmler attended a meeting with Minister Goebbels, Oberst .Gruf. (*sic*) Dietrich, Gauleiter Koch, Obergruf. Kaltenbrunner
20:30 hrs	Himmler with Reichsleiter Bormann[21]

Martin Bormann wrote to his wife Gerda, 8 February 1945, 02:05 hrs: "Visits from Wolf (*sic* – Wolff), Koch and Heinrich H. [*Himmler*] prevented me from writing yesterday. We dined with Fegelein and then talked business until Evi [Eva Braun] came. She stayed with us for an hour and a half, and after that Heinrich had to go and see Kaltenbrunner...".[22]

Press conference of the Swiss President, von Steiger, reported in *Neuen Zürchner Zeitung*, 8 February 1945, midday: "Musy first provided information yesterday afternoon, shortly before the refugees were handed over to the Swiss authorities. He had obtained the release of these Jews from Theresienstadt camp with Himmler's personal approval. Musy must have expressed to Swiss authorities at the same time, the hope that he could possibly squeeze similar transports out on a weekly basis. The Swiss authorities have been silent about this, said Musy, due to the private character of his efforts and uncertainty of success."[23]

Telegram from Montreux to (London, 8 February 1945:

Presse agudas jisroel 53 queensdrive LN [(London] 7th february 11.45 morning just arrived first transport of 1200 jewish persons from terezin stop. this convoy was released by germany owing intervention of former conseilleur federal musy charged with the mission by us as the european council of the union of orthodox rabbis of united states of america and canada in montreux stop germany agreed to release further transports hijefs[24]

Dr Rezsö Kasztner reported: "*7 February.* Official communiqué in the Swiss Press: On behalf of Agudah and the Association of Orthodox Rabbis in the United States of America, former Swiss President Musy had a breakthrough with Himmler, and Jews will be released from concentration camps and brought to Switzerland."[25]

The Czechoslovak Representative in Switzerland, Dr Jaromír Kopecký, described the refugees as:

667 persons from Germany and Austria
432 persons from Holland
97 Czech nationals (33 men and 64 women of 6–74 years of age)
1,196[26]

Telegram No. 249 from British Ambassador, Berne (signed Mr. Norton) to Foreign Office, London:

Swiss press reports today that first convoy of 1210 civilians including 58 children from Theresienstadt arrived Wednesday 7th February at Kreuzlingen. Persons in question have been liberated through the efforts of former federal councillor Musy acting on request of European Executive Council of Union of Orthodox Rabbi's of United States of America at Montreux and Agudas Israel Organisation. State of health said to be generally good. Further convoys which are expected will be sent on from Switzerland when transport facilities permit. Refugees will temporarily be accommodated at St. Gallen for medical inspection then sent to quarantine camps elsewhere. M. Musy acting in private capacity is said to have personally obtained liberation from Himmler. Number includes 500 to 600 Dutch Jews. Further convoy of 540 French from Germany was expected at Kreuzlingen on evening of 7th February.[27]

Thursday, 8 February 1945

Military situation:
The war diary of WFStab reported a new reorganization in Courland: "On 8.2. a new Military Administration Courland (Militärverwaltung Kurland) under SS-Gruppenführer Behrends, a Latvian, as Plenipotentiary of the Reichsführers-SS was established, the military matters remain under the control of Army Group Courland, political matters remain under the control of the Reichsführer-SS."[28]

Meetings & Appointments of the Reichsführer-SS on 8.2.1945

13:00 hrs	SS-Gruppenführer Lammerding
13:30 hrs	General Busse (Commander, 9.Armee)
14:00 hrs	Meal with
	General Busse
	SS-Obergruppenführer Kleinheisterkamp
	SS-Obergruppenführer Lorenz
	SS-Obergruppenführer Demelhuber
	General Wilken
	SS-Standartenführer Giese
15:00 hrs	General Busse
16:00 hrs	SS-Obergruppenführer Kleinheisterkamp
16:30 hrs	SS-Obergruppenführer Demelhuber
18:00 hrs	SS-Gruppenführer Lammerding
20:00 hrs	Meal with
	SS-Obergruppenführer Lorenz
	Fräulein Lorenz
	SS-Obergruppenführer Kleinheisterkamp
	SS-Gruppenführer Lammerding
	Oberst Eismann
	Military briefing – meetings

Events:
German radio message decrypted by Bletchley Park on 12 February 1945, and part of the daily intelligence brief for Prime Minister Churchill: "On 12th Himmler's adjutant informed AKZV [Kammler] that Himmler was in entire agreement with V1 programme put forward on 8th."[29]

Martin Bormann wrote to his wife Gerda, 9 February 1945: "In brief – yesterday evening a conference with Becher to arrange for the supply of more horses for the North; then a talk with Kaltenbrunner, after which Giesler and I were with the Fegelein until two o'clock. Finally we went on to see Evi [Braun], where we were joined about 3 a.m. by the Chief [Hitler] and Speer… We sat on till shortly before six."[30]

Staatspolizeileitstelle Hannover wrote to the local offices of the Landrat and Army Commander in Hameln: "The Jewish Mischlinge Grade 1/Jews related by marriage, on orders of RSHA, with exceptions, should have no arrangements for working. At the end of this activity, the RFSS has ordered work closed to Jews of mixed marriages…".[31]

The *Neuen Zürcher Zeitung* reported on 8 February 1945: "Former Swiss President Musy carried out the transfer from Theresienstadt to Switzerland on the basis of a 'personal permission of Himmler'. He is confident of 'possibly arranging similar weekly transports'."[32]

Walter Schellenberg also reported on these Jewish transports in his memoirs. The first transport went through at the beginning of February and everything functioned very well. Musy acknowledged the receipt of the five million Swiss francs, which were paid to him as trustee at the end of February 1945, and also saw to it that the fact was made known to the press, as had been agreed, while an article was published by President von Steiger in Berne, and another appeared in the *New York Times*:

> Unfortunately a decoded message referring to these arrangements, which came from one of de Gaulle's centers in Spain, was brought to Hitler's notice. It was alleged in this message that Himmler had negotiated with Musy through his representative Schellenberg, to secure asylum in Switzerland for 250 'Nazi leaders,' This obvious nonsense, cunningly circulated by Kaltenbrunner, had the most uncomfortable consequences for me. Hitler immediately issued two orders: that any German who helped a Jew, or a British, or an American prisoner to escape would be executed instantly; any such attempt was to be reported to him personally.[33]

Ernst Kaltenbrunner testified at his trial before the International Military Tribunal, Nuremberg, on 12 April 1946, about the transports:

> Through this man, Becher, Himmler did the worst things which could possibly be done and brought to light here. Through Becher and the Joint Committee in Hungary and Switzerland he released Jews in exchange, first, for war equipment, then secondly, for raw material, and thirdly, for foreign currency. I heard about this through the intelligence service and immediately attempted to stop this, not through Himmler because I would have failed but through Hitler. At that moment any personal credit of Himmler with Hitler was undermined, for this action might have changed the reputation of the Reich abroad in the most serious manner.[34]

Himmler confirmed acceptance of the Dotzler proposals with Bormann, stating he had passed a copy to Prützmann and instructed him to confer with Bormann about "his special orders".[35]

Friday, 9 February 1945

Meetings & Appointments of the Reichsführer-SS on 9 February 1945

13:00 hrs	SS-Gruppenführer Lammerding
13:30 hrs	SS-Obersturmbannführer Grothmann

14:00 hrs	Meal with
	SS-Gruppenführer Lammerding
	SS-Standartenführer d'Alquen
	SS-Hauptsturmführer Schwarz van Berk (*sic* – van Berg)
	Hauptmann Hoffmann
	Oberst Müller-Hildebrandt (Chef der 3.Pz.Armee)
15:15 hrs	General Krappe
	SS-Gruppenführer Lammerding
16:30 hrs	SS-Standartenführer d'Alquen
20:00 hrs	Meal
22:00 hrs	SS-Standartenführer d'Alquen (until 01:00 hrs)
	SS-Gruppenführer Lammerding

Events:

Publication in Swedish newspaper *Svenska Dagbaldet*, 9 February 1945, of details concerning the 1,200 Jews released from Theresienstadt.[36]

Saturday, 10 February 1945

Meetings & Appointments of the Reichsführer-SS on 10.2.1945 (Birkenwald)

12:00 hrs	SS-Gruppenführer Lammerding
12:30 hrs	Report by Oberstrichter Dr Pelzeter
12:45 hrs	Departure of the RF-SS for Berlin
13:30 hrs	Lunch with Reichsleiter Bormann
	General Burgdorf
	SS-Gruppenführer Fegelein
16:15 hrs	Military briefing with the Führer (Hitler)
19:15 hrs	SS-Gruppenführer Ostendorff
19:45 hrs	SS-Obergruppenführer Berger
	SS-Obergruppenführer Heissmeyer
	SS-Gruppenführer Göhrum
20:45 hrs	Meal with
	SS-Oberstgruppenführer Dietrich
	Reichsleiter Bormann
	SS-Obergruppenführer Berger
	SS-Gruppenführer Fegelein
22:45 hrs	Departure from Berlin for Birkenwald
00:45 hrs	Arrival Birkenwald

Events:

From the diary of Hitler's valet, Heinz Linge:

| 16:00 | Briefing – RFSS [*Himmler*] |
| 19:10 | Minister Speer[37] |

From the letter of Martin Bormann to his wife Gerda, 10 February 1945: "Today I lunched with Uncle Heinrich [*Himmler*], Burgdorff and Fegelein and tonight I dined with Uncle H., Sepp D. [Dietrich], Fegelein and Berger. In the interval, between our discussions, Heinrich [*Himmler*] had a conference with the Fuehrer and at 4 p.m. had attended the main situation conference."[38]

From Bormann's diary: "Lunch with Fegelein and RFSS Himmler and Gen. Burgdorf. After the meal consulted with Himmler, then with Lammers. Evening meal with H. Himmler, Sepp Dietrich, Berger, Fegelein. Followed by discussion."[39]

In his biography, Heinz Guderian reported he was with Himmler, other military leaders and Hitler in the Reichskanzlei, Berlin, on 10 February 1945, to discuss Guderian's proposal to attack the invading Soviet armies in Himmler's military sector:

> ... I was well aware that both Hitler and Himmler would oppose these decisions of mine, since they were both subconsciously frightened of undertaking an operation which must make plain Himmler's incompetence. Himmler expressed his belief to Hitler that the attack should be postponed, since a small portion of the ammunition and fuel had not yet been unloaded and issued to the troops. I, arguing against this, produced my reasons as given above. Hitler immediately and strongly, disagreed with me... [Argument then followed over the potential military situation in Himmler's area, an argument lasting two hours] ... Suddenly Hitler stopped short in front of Himmler and said: 'Well, Himmler, General Wenck will arrive at your headquarters tonight and will take charge of the attack.' He walked over to Wenck and told him that he was to report to the army group staff forthwith.[40]

German radio message decrypted by Bletchley Park on 10 February 1945, taken at 16:27 hrs:
From: SS-Jagdverb., signed SS-Stubaf. [Alexander] Auch
To: SS-Ustuf. [Egon] Machetanz, at this time with IdS Danzig
Immediately transfer all available personnel from the course at Braunsberg to Friedenthal for a special mission ordered by Rf.SS. Immediately pull out men already on a course. Report immediately on transfer movements to senior management.[41]

On 10 February 1945, Swedish Ambassador Arvid Richert informed the German government that Sweden was prepared to receive all Jews from concentration camps, especially those from Theresienstadt and Bergen-Belsen.[42]

Sunday, 11 February 1945

Meetings & Appointments of the Reichsführer-SS on 11.2.1945 (Birkenwald)
12:30 hrs	Oberstleutnant Baumbach
14:00 hrs	Award of the Anti-Partisan Medal in Gold to
	SS-Obersturmführer Prasch
	SS-Obersturmführer Kühbandner
	SS-Hauptscharführer Ludl
	SS-Rottenführer Brauer

14:10 hrs	Meal with
	Oberstleutnant Baumbach
	SS-Obersturmführer Prasch
	SS-Obersturmführer Kühbrander
	SS-Hauptscharführer Ludl
	SS-Rottenführer Brauer
	SS-Hauptsturmführer Derichsweiler
15:30 hrs	SS-Obergruppenführer von dem Bach
	Military briefing
	General Wenck
20:00 hrs	Meal with
	General Wenck
	SS-Brigadeführer Mueller-Darss

Events:

Himmler's call to all officers of Army Group Vistula:

A few days ago I made it known that the former SS-Standartenführer and Police Director of Bromberg, von Salisch, had cowardly left his city and been shot by sentence of a court martial. Now another, Colonel von Hassenstein, had a trusted position and without orders, without any emergency, left his post and has been sentenced to death by shooting, and I have confirmed this.

I expect every officer to be a model of courage and stability before our brave soldiers. When an officer is in front, his men will not leave him. In cases of human weakness, cowardice or momentary panic when one or another falls, an officer shows himself worthy of his rank and shoulder pips.

...

My comrades, now we get to our duty, with courage and a strong heart. The Lord God has never left our people and he has always helped the brave in the greatest need. Long live the Führer.[43]

Monday, 12 February 1945

Meetings & Appointments of the Reichsführer-SS on 12.2.1945 (Birkenwald)

12:00 hrs	General Unrein
	SS-Gruppenführer Lammerding
14:45 hrs	Reichsaussenminister v. Ribbentrop
20:00 hrs	Grossadmiral Dönitz
	two Admirals
22:30 hrs	Military briefing
23:30 hrs	Reichsminister Speer
	Oberstleutnant Baumbach
	Oberst v. Below
	SS-Obersturmbannführer Skorzeny

Events:

Post-war statement of Oberstleutnant Werner Baumbach, 27 August 1946 (Nuremberg), for the International Military Tribunal:

> In November 1944 another 120-150 so-called 'Total Action Men' (*Totaleinsatzmänner*) were placed under me. There were Luftwaffe men who until then had been largely under the command of the SS, and now largely pressed into a hopeless mission that they had confirmed by their signature. They would pilot converted V-1 flying bombs and in acts of self-sacrifice, dive at enemy targets. Under SS pressure a number of these weapons were available and ready to use. Speer provided an act of salvation at the last hour. He had this weapon withdrawn from Total Action on technical grounds.
>
> Later, in the spring of 1945, when Himmler repeatedly demanded to take sole responsibility for the Total Action, with the help of Speer implementation was postponed following discussions between Speer and Himmler.
>
> Goebbels had already made a speech about 'self-sacrifice' men, but the fact is that none of these men sacrificed his life in senseless destruction.[44]

Top Secret Ultra decrypted radio message from Bletchley Park, 12 February 1945:

> From: OKH (Oberbefehlshaber der Ersatzheeres), AHA – Dept U II A, No. 75/45, signed Oberst von Bassewitz
>
> To: Wehrkreis IX [headquarters: Kassel]
>
> The Commander of the Replacement Army (*Oberbefehlshaber des Ersatzheeres*) [Himmler] has, in his capacity as Representative of the Führer for special transfers, ordered that numerous investigations for possible transfers of government offices are to be put in train immediately. Planning has been nearly completed. Exact details of strength and place of transfer can for the time being be communicated only orally. During this period officers conducting the investigations are to receive such support as they require in their tasks from departments of OKW and OKH. In cases of doubt, ring OKH, J…585. From 14/2 [14 Feb. 1945] onwards these officers conducting these investigations will carry written orders for making oral enquiries. It is necessary to send an officer immediately to OKH – AHA – Dept… Berlin 35, Bendlerstrasse 11 to 13 Room 403, on the question of the planning ordered.[45]

German radio message decrypted by Bletchley Park on 12 February 1945:

> From: SS-Hstuf. Conrad, Adjutant of Reichsführer-SS
>
> To: unnamed SS-Gruppenführer, probably SS-Gruf. Hans Kammler
>
> Gr.Fhr. Reichsführer SS is in agreement with your V-1 programme as communicated on 8/2 (8 Feb. 1945].
>
> Heil Hitler![46]

German radio message decrypted by Bletchley Park on 12 February 1945:

> From: SS-Hstuf. Conrad, Adjutant of Reichsführer-SS
>
> To: unnamed SS-Gruppenführer, probably SS-Gruf. Hans Kammler
>
> Gr.Fuehr. Reichsführer SS agrees to the direct distribution of AK ZV day reports to all distribution list as follows:

1) Gen Feldmarschall Keitel, Führer's HQ.

2) Obstltn Kleyer, Führer's HQ.

3) C in C West, Gen Feldmarschall von Rundstedt.

4) Reichsmarschall for attention of Oberst von Brauchitsch.

5) SS-Obergr.fhr. Juettner, Berlin.

6) SS-Gr.fhr. Fegelein, Führer's HQ.

Heil Hitler![47]

German radio message decrypted by Bletchley Park on 12 February 1945, taken at 18:30 hrs:

From: Chef Orpo [SS-Obergruppenführer Alfred Wünnenberg]

To: unnamed Reich Defence Kommissar

Rf.SS has ordered:

It is essential to ensure that no food ration stamps are handed to soldiers who are shirkers and deserters, instead food ration stamps be handed over to all those dispersed soldiers or find themselves on official journeys.

This order is to be strictly carried out.[48]

Tuesday, 13 February 1945

Military situation:

Extracts from WFStab War Diary:

1. Heeresgr.Weichsel [Himmler's command] ... In Arnswalde, attacks were completely rebuffed; the situation remains critical. In the Deutsch-Krone region the enemy is intensifying attacks. From 13 February, no reports from Schneidemühl.

2. In the west Baltic Sea area, losses from mines. Until this morning, 319,000 refugees and 92,000 wounded have been sent on transports.

3. For the Army Group Vistula [Heeresgruppe Weichsel], the Reichsführer has issued an order to his officers in which he calls for the toughest resistance.[49]

Meetings & Appointments of the Reichsführer-SS on 13.2.1945 (Birkenwald)

13:00 hrs	SS-Gruppenführer Lammerding
14:00 hrs	Meal with
	General Wenck
	General Toppe
	Gauleiter Stürtz
	SS-Standartenführer d'Alquen
15:30 hrs	Reichsmarshall [Göring]
17:00 hrs	Gauleiter Stürtz
19:45 hrs	Meal with
	General Decker (XXXIX Pz. Korps)
	General Thomale

                    General Wenck
                    SS-Gruppenführer Lammerding
                    Fräulein Lorenz
               Military briefing
                    General Decker
                    General Wenck
                    SS-Gruppenführer Lammerding
                    Oberst Eismann
24:00 hrs   SS-Obergruppenführer Jeckeln[50]

Wednesday, 14 February 1945

Military situation:
WFStab War Diary: "Army Group Weichsel: .... The situation in Arnswalde is now extremely serious. The Commandant of Schneidemühl, where the enemy reports 9,000 prisoners, after a 21 day defence ordered a breakthrough to the north, his task as a breakwater could no longer be carried out as little remained of the city suburbs."[51]

Meetings & Appointments of the Reichsführer-SS on 14.2.1945 (Birkenwald)
12:00 hrs   SS-Gruppenführer Lammerding
                    Oberst Eismann
14:00 hrs   Meal with SS-Obergruppenführer Lorenz
16:30 hrs   SS-Obersturmbannführer Grothmann
19:00 hrs   Frau Hanna Reitsch
20:00 hrs   Meal with
                    General Raus
                    SS-Gruppenführer Lammerding
                    SS-Obergruppenführer Winkelmann
                    SS-Brigadeführer Schellenberg
                    Frau Hanna Reitsch

Events:
On 9 February 1945, SS-Gruppenführer Dr Hans Kammler sent a radio message to Himmler's adjutant, SS-Obersturmbannführer Grothmann. Kammler had taken exception to Gauleiter Sauckel trying to reserve rooms at Golf-Hotel, Oberhof. Kammler did not have the rank to have Sauckel refrain from reserving rooms at the hotel and asked for a short note by Himmler to Sauckel.

On 14 February 1945 Himmler wrote (from his Feldkommandostelle):

Dear Party Comrade Sauckel:

Unfortunately, I am forced to take advantage of the Golf-Hotel, Oberhof, for the construction project 5 III, as ordered by the Führer. I therefore ask you to refrain from using the hotel for your purposes.[52]

German radio message decrypted by Bletchley Park on 14 February 1945, taken at 18:00 hours:

To: Waffenschule Hellerau

From: Chef Orpo

Rf.SS has ordered that SS-Brigadefhr. Schmedes will report tomorrow morning to Battle Commander at Guben, via Luebben. On arrival notify II A SS-FHA. Commander of Police Division is new in position.[53]

German radio message decrypted by Bletchley Park on 14 February 1945, taken at 2300 hours:

To: Chef Sipo and SD, SS-Ogruf. Dr Kaltenbrunner, Berlin

From: Paul Zapp, IdS Dresden

Due to heavy terror attack [British air-raid] on Dresden, headquarters of IdS, SD and Gestapo all totally destroyed. Police headquarters including those of Criminal Police very badly damaged. Personnel losses still not established. Headquarters for IdS established in offices of HSSPF, can be contacted via radio.[54]

Report of Civil Police Commander of Dresden, SS-Gruppenführer [Ludolf] von Alvensleben, to Chief of Civil Police, Luftgaukommando III:

Preliminary report: Heavy terror-raid on Dresden. Bombs dropped on Dresden from 22:09 to 22:35 hrs. In the whole city area high explosive bombs and great fires, especially in the quarter of the Inner City. Hit: Opera House, Catholic Hofkirche, Japanese Palace, Museum of Hygiene, Railway Directorates offices, several hospitals, Exhibition Palace, T-s-nberg Palace, at least 3,000 high explosive and 25,000 incendiary bombs estimated. Forces from outside called in.

Barrack Area Alberstadt: Rifle Barracks, Adolf Hitler Barracks, Army Provisioning Office, Magazine Building, Ammunition Deport. Outward communications also interrupted. Even stronger attack from 01:24 to 01:48 hrs, chiefly high explosive bombs, some of them of the heaviest calibre.

'In the raging conflagration that arose almost complete destruction of the city must be anticipated,' concluded the police commander. 'Estimated that 500,000 are homeless. Reich assistance on the greatest scale immediately and urgently required.'[55]

German radio message intercepted by Bletchley Park on 15 February 1945, taken at 05:01 hours; this radio message had originally been transmitted the previous evening at 23:15hours:

To: HSSPF Dresden

From: Himmler

Dear Alvensleben! I have received your report. The attacks were obviously very severe, yet every first air raid always gives the impression that the town has been completely destroyed. Take all necessary measures at once. I am sending you at once a particularly able S.S. Führer for your Staff, whom you may find useful in the present difficult situation. All the best.

Heil Hitler!

Yours, Himmler.[56]

Thursday, 15 February 1945

Military situation:
Soviet armies launched an assault on Himmler's field command, Army Group Vistula (Heeresgruppe Weichsel).

In Silesia, the city of Breslau was now surrounded by units of 1.Ukrainian Front. In the city itself, reports mention defenders having only 200 rifles, seven tanks and eight assault guns.

Schneidemühl has been taken by the Soviets.[57]

Bormann issued an order to all Gauleiters: "The re-location of Reich ministries and offices of state from Berlin is banned."[58]

In Ruwertal near Hermeskeil-Lampaden (south of Trier), since the Ardennes offensive two shortened versions of the "High Pressure Pump" – the V-3 – under the code name LRK 15 F 58 (Langrohrkanone – long tubular cannon) were deployed. The 1st Battery, Army Artillery Dept. 705, was in command. The installation of the first cannon lasted from 28.11.44 until 23.12.44, the second installation took more time. On 15 February 1945, SS-Gruppenführer [Kammler] ordered dismantling of the two LRK installations.[59]

Meetings & Appointments of the Reichsführer-SS on 15.2.1945 (Birkenwald)

12:30 hrs	Generaloberst Raus
13:00 hrs	SS-Gruppenführer Lammerding
14:00 hrs	Meal with SS-Brigadeführer Mueller-Darss
15:00 hrs	SS-Gruppenführer Kammler
17:00 hrs	SS-Obergruppenführer Stuckart
20:00 hrs	Meal with
	SS-Obergruppenführer Lorenz
	SS-Obergruppenführer Prützmann
	SS-Gruppenführer Lammerding
22:30 hrs	Film "Kolberg"
00:00 hrs	SS-Gruppenführer Lammerding

Events:
Himmler wrote to SS-Gruppenführer Ludof von Alvensleben, HSSPF Dresden:

My dear Alvensleben!

I received your telex of February 15.

1. Approve relocating your office but only to suburbs of Dresden. Any further out would make a rotten impression.

2. Now is the time for iron steadfastness and immediate action to restore order. You are to see to it that power, water supplies and public transport are immediately restored. I'm prepared to send you S.S. Obergruppenführer Hildebrandt to help you so that you have a comrade who can be effective for you in various other locations outside Dresden.

3. Set me a good example of calm and nerve!

Heil Hitler!

Yours, H.Himmler.[60]

Radio message from SS-Obergruppenführer von Herff to SS-Brigadeführer Walther Bierkamp in Teschen via the HSSPF Ost (Koppe), transmitted at 18:30 hrs:

> Reichsführer-SS has appointed you Deputy of HSSPF Südost [to Schmauser]. Reichsführer-SS has ordered that concurrently you will take over the responsibilities of SS-Brif. and Gen. Maj. of Police Geibel.
>
> Following taking over of both responsibilities please report to me.[61]

From a post-war interrogation of Walther Rauff:

> On 15 Feb 45 SS Obergruppenfuehrer Wolff expressed the wish to have some means of establishing contact with the Allies in Switzerland. Source [Rauff] discussed the matter with [SS-Ostuf Guido] Zimmer, and it was agreed to nominate [Baron Luigi] Parilli, whom Zimmer knew in a purely personal way from Genoa… Parilli was keen on the proposal, as he himself was interested in the preservation of Upper Italy. Wolff and [SS-Gruppenführer Wilhelm] Harster agreed to Parilli's nomination, and from then onwards the negotiations followed….[62]

Friday, 16 February 1945

Military situation:
The WFStab war diary: "Army Group Vistula: … Pressure intensified north of Küstrin. In the area between the railway and Stargard an enemy attack was launched on a broad front until 15 February, without making any significant progress. Following the occupation of Schneidemühl, until now 1,000 men have broken through the lines. Near Konitz the enemy has secured a breakthrough. Also between Tuchel and Graudenz, further enemy advances have closed the area."[63]

A counter-offensive by the 11th SS-Panzer Army (under SS-Obergruppenführer Steiner) with 4th SS-Division and 2nd Panzer Division advanced south-west of Stargard and attacked the 47th Soviet Army (under Lt. General Perchorowitsch).[64]

Meetings & Appointment of the Reichsführer-SS on 16.2.1945 (Birkenwald)

12:45 hrs	SS-Oberführer Bender
	General von Scheel
13:00 hrs	SS-Gruppenführer Lammerding
13:45 hrs	SS-Obersturmbannführer Kriebel
14:00 hrs	Award of Bar to Close Combat Award in Gold (der Goldene Nahkampfspange)

to 16 holders of this award, and award to a sharpshooter (Scharfschützen) [in Bernau]

14:10 hrs	Meal with those awarded a decoration
19:00 hrs	SS-Oberführer Bender
20:00 hrs	Meal with
	SS-Obergruppenführer Krüger
	SS-Obergruppenführer von Herff
	SS-Obergruppenführer Lorenz
22:00 hrs	SS-Obergruppenführer von Herff
	Military briefing

Events:

Teleprinter message from SS-Gruf. Lammerding to the four armies of Army Group Weichsel:

> Führer Order.
>
> When capturing towns and especially by shock troop operations do not kill prisoners close to the front, as the civilian population must remain afterwards.[65]

German radio message decrypted by Bletchley Park on 16 February 1945:

> To: SS-Brig.fhr. Bierkamp, HSSPF Südost.   Secret!
> From: Himmler
> Received information that some SS-officers and SD-officials have been taken from Glogau. Agree with the arrests, SS-Brigadefhr. Bierkamp had to make them. It is possible that these forces were in place for action against troops keeping law and order behind the new front lines. Do not hold back, the guilty should receive the harshest punishment where arrested.[66]

Top secret order distributed by IdS Düsseldorf, Dr Walter Albath, to the Gestapo chiefs (Stapoleiter) of Köln and Düsseldorf:

> The Senior SS and Police Commander West [HSSPF West] on instructions from the Reichsführer-SS will set up a group of reliable Party comrades and SS men to stay-behind and allow enemy forces to pass them, then inflict damage in the rear areas. It is necessary to enroll spirited members of the Gestapo with an intimate knowledge of left bank areas of the River Rhine. I request details of the personnel as soon as possible. Initially, these men are not to be informed. Each [Gestapo] office will name about 5 men from their left bank areas.[67]

Count Folke Bernadotte reported about the reasons behind his first wartime journey to Germany, flying directly from Sweden, 16 February 1945:

> …it was officially announced that I was going to inspect the Red Cross expedition to ascertain if it required reinforcing in order to carry out its task. The real object of my visit to Berlin was, of course, to endeavor to meet Himmler and obtain his consent to the internment in Sweden, not only of the Norwegian, but also of the Danish prisoners in Germany. Before my departure I had submitted my plans not only to the Swedish Government but also to the President of the Red Cross, Prince Charles. He had expressed the opinion that the scheme must embrace Danes as well as Norwegians. Consequently the field of operations had widened.[68]

On 16 February 1945, Roswell McClelland cabled both the US State Department and the American War Refugees Board (WRB) that a member of the International Committee of the Red Cross (ICRC) delegation in Berlin, Robert Schirmer, who had previously assisted in the efforts to rescue Hungarian Jews, on 25 January 1945 had sent the following secret report to IRCC headquarters:

> On February 11 I was informed by Nordling, the Swedish Consul General in Paris, whose forceful intercession with the German military commander in Paris resulted in the release of some four thousand political prisoners, whom the German Commander had orders to execute if they could not be evacuated at that time, that in December he had addressed a personal letter to Himmler requesting better treatment of all concentration camp inmates along the Geneva Convention lines. Even though he received no direct answer to his letter, Nordling

learned through most reliable channels that on receipt of his letter Himmler hard ordered the German Red Cross to study and report immediately on the possibility of improving the lot of Schutzhaeftlinge [SH]. The maintenance of contact with Nordling was delegated to a German industrialist named Lehrer, long a resident in France and possessing direct contact with high Nazi officials by Himmler. It is Nordling's belief that in January SS overtures to ICRC men in Berlin are at least partly due to his representation and that Himmler is definitely interested in facilitating relief to SH, for reasons which are open to considerable speculation.[69]

Saturday, 17 February 1945

Military situation:

Reported in WFStab war diary: "Army Group Vistula: ... On the [River] Oder the enemy is building up. A single attack in progress north of Arnswalde. Near the city itself, strong attacks were repulsed. General information. An order for the newly organized Army-Order Troops [Wehrmacht- Ordnungstrupen]."[70]

Meetings & Appointments of the Reichsführer-SS on 17.2.1945 (Birkenwald)

13:00 hrs	SS-Gruppenführer Lammerding
14:00 hrs	Meal with
	SS-Obergruppenführer Krüger
	SS-Obergruppenführer Lorenz
15:00 hrs	General Reinecke
16:30 hrs	SS-Obersturmbannführer Grothmann
	SS-Sturmbannführer Kiermaier
17:00 hrs	SS-Obergruppenführer Demelhuber
18:00 hrs	General Fiebig
20:00 hrs	Meal with
	SS-Obergruppenführer Lorenz
	SS-Gruppenführer Lammerding
	SS-Oberführer [Bender?]
23:00 hrs	SS-Oberführer Bender
	Bereichsleiter Bofinger [Parteikanzlei Berlin]
24:00 hrs	SS-Gruppenführer Lammerding
	SS-Obersturmbannführer Grothmann
01:30 hrs	SS-Gruppenführer Dr Klopfer

Events:

Himmler issued a secret order to HSSPF West (Gutenberger), HSSPF Rhein-Westmark (Stroop), HSSPF Südwest (Hofmann), HSSPF Fulda-Werra (Waldeck-Pyrmont) and HSSPF Nordsee (Bassewitz-Behr):

Lead the way immediately, together with military 'catching organisations' anywhere in your areas, using constant checks to grab all those who have lost contact with their units, arrest deserters and shoot them, looters and plunderers will be shot on the spot. Those more willing will be sent to the front immediately to join weakened battalions. These measures are a prerequisite for their deployment on the Western front where expected heavy attacks can be withstood... I ask that you have the closest collaboration with Gauleiters and Reich Defence Kommissars in your particular areas, as well as Regional Military Commanders, C-in-C West and commanders of army groups and armies, in the catching organisation to achieve the greatest effect.[71]

Martin Bormann wrote to his wife Gerda, 18 February 1945:
General Wenck, one of the really efficient among our Generals, hit a road obstacle with his car and will therefore be out of action for many weeks. He was on his way yesterday evening [17 Feb.] from Himmler with a report for the Führer.[72]

An account by Count Folke Bernadotte of his first meeting with German officials on 17 February 1945. He met with SS-Ogruf. Dr. Ernst Kaltenbrunner, Chief of the RSHA (that included the Gestapo), and his Chief of SD Foreign Intelligence, Walter Schellenberg, at Kaltenbrunner's villa in Berlin-Wannsee. Bernadotte expressed his desire to meet with their superior, Reichsführer-SS Heinrich Himmler and explain more fully the reasons for his visit to Germany. However Bernadotte did intimate his reasons to Kaltenbrunner:
... I told him, however, that were principally two concessions I wanted. One was the issue of exit permits for Swedish women married to Germans, and for their children, particularly for those whose homes had been bombed or whose husbands were killed or missing. The other was permission for the Swedish Red Cross to work in the Internment Camps in Germany. Oddly enough, Kaltenbrunner showed himself reasonable and understanding on these points ....[73]

Sunday, 18 February 1945

Military situation:
Reported in WFStab war diary: "Army Group Vistula: ... [The Soviet] attack is now determined. 10th Panzer Division should be withdrawn. Enemy counter-attacks towards Arnswalde. Between Konitz and Graudenz enemy pressure increasing. Graudenz becoming isolated. In Posen the enemy attacking individual railway stations and increasing his propaganda."[74]

Meetings & Appointments of the Reichsführer-SS on 18.2.1945 (Birkenwald)

12:00 hrs	SS-Gruppenführer Lammerding
13:00 hrs	General Bleckwenn
14:00 hrs	Reichsmarschall [Göring]
15:00 hrs	Meal with SS-Obergruppenführer Lorenz
16:00 hrs	General v. Hauenschildt (*sic* – Hauenschild)
20:00 hrs	Meal with
	SS-Obergruppenführer Lorenz
	SS-Gruppenführer Lammerding

| 22:00 hrs | Departure for Berlin |
| 24:00 hrs | Meeting with Fegelein |

Events:

German radio message intercepted by Bletchley Park on 18 February 1945, taken at 23:00 hrs:

> To: BdO Breslau
>
> From: Chef Orpo
>
> Subject: Transfers to the West.
>
> Rf.SS has ordered, transfer movements to the West from Wehrkreis VIII by order of Army Commander South [Oberbefehlshaber Süd], from Wehrkreis II and III given by Army Commander Weichsel (Rf.SS himself). Leaving locations without orders or permission of Army Group South, or by Weichsel, will be with immediate execution of those caught. Make known to all office chiefs.[75]

On his second day in Berlin, 18 February 1945, Count Folke Bernadotte met with German Foreign Minister von Ribbentrop, who was more concerned with improving diplomatic relations than with promoting the release of concentration camp prisoners over which he had no control or influence. Both agreed to meet again after Bernadotte had met with Himmler.[76]

Martin Bormann wrote to his wife Gerda, 18 February 1945:

> Hardly a day passes without some first-class soldier getting knocked out in a motor accident; I told you about it before. I am constantly warning Uncle Heinrich [*Himmler*] not to drive so fast. Never have I driven at the pace he usually adopts.[77]

Top Secret Ultra German radio message intercepted by Bletchley Park on 18 February 1945, and placed in the daily intercepts given to Prime Minister Winston Churchill:

> To: Chief, Naval Command West, Bad Schwalbach
>
> From: A.K.Z.V., G.O.C. [General Officer Commanding], signed SS-Gruf. und Gen.Ltn of the Waffen-SS Kammler:
>
> AKZV has for tactical reasons the greatest interest from 28/2 in getting information by the quickest possible signals route about all events in the air sector English east coast to The Hague. We request communication whether the erection of a high-lying observation post with widespread area of observation in strong point Dunkirk is possible, from which observations made can be sent to Chief Naval Command West and from there forwarded to AKZV.[78]

Monday, 19 February 1945

Military situation:

Reported in WFStab war diary: Following the vehicle accident to General Wenck, he has been replaced on Himmler's staff, Army Group Vistula, by General (Hans) Krebs, Chief of Staff with Army Group B.[79]

From the diary of Hitler's valet, Heinz Linge:

00:30 hrs	RFSS [*Himmler*]
01:00 hrs	Military briefing – RFSS
03:15 hrs	Tea
05:45 hrs	Briefing ended[80]

Meetings & Appointments of the Reichsführer-SS on 19.2.1945
(Berlin – Birkenwald)

00:30 hrs	Talks with the Führer
01:00 hrs	Military briefing
03:30 hrs	Meeting with SS-Obergruppenführer Jüttner
04:00 hrs	Meeting with SS-Obergruppenführer Kaltenbrunner
04:30 hrs	Departure from Berlin
06:30 hrs	Arrival Birkenwald
06:30 hrs	Meeting with
	SS-Gruppenführer Lammerding
	Oberst Eismann
	SS-Obersturmbannführer Grothmann (until 07:30 hrs)
12:00 hrs	Breakfast with SS-Obergruppenführer Lorenz
13:00 hrs	Military briefing
14:00 hrs	Meal with
	SS-Obergruppenführer Lorenz
	General Bleckwenn
	SS-Brigadeführer Rode
15:30 hrs	Military briefing with Chief of Staff, 11th Army, Oberst Estor
19:00 hrs	Departure for Hohenlychen

Events:

On 19 February 1945, Himmler circulated to his Generals and Division commanders in Army Group Vistula an SD study, "Soviet measures for the successful defence of Leningrad," to assist them in combatting the expected Soviet offensive.[81]

Walter Schellenberg accompanied Count Folke Bernadotte from Berlin north to Hohenlychen where Himmler had agreed to meet with them. That evening the three men had a two-and-a-half hour meeting about transferring the Danish and Norwegian prisoners held in German concentration camps to Sweden and internment there. Himmler did not agree to this plan and according to Schellenberg, a compromise formulated by him was reached:

… that these prisoners should be collected in a central camp in northwest Germany [Neuengamme concentration camp]. This was, in fact, the basis of an agreement reached between the Count and Himmler during their meeting.[82]

Tuesday, 20 February 1945

Meetings & Appointments of the Reichsführer-SS on 20.2.1945
(Birkenwald – Berlin)

11:00 hrs	Breakfast with SS-Obergruppenführer Lorenz
12:00 hrs	Military briefing (Chief of Staff, 9th Army)
14:30 hrs	Depart Birkenwald for 9th Army at Fürstenwalde
17:00 hrs	Arrived Fürstenwalde, meeting with General Busse
17:45 hrs	Departure from Fürstenwalde for Berlin
19:00 hrs	Military conference with Führer
	Meeting with SS-Obergruppenführer Kaltenbrunner
23:00 hrs	Departure from Berlin
01:00 hrs	Arrival Birkenwald
	Military briefing

Events:

From the diary of Hitler's valet, Heinz Linge:

16:00 hrs	Conference – RM [Göring], RFSS, Grossadm. Dönitz
18:00 hrs	General v. Hauenschild
19:20 hrs	Ogrf. (*sic*) Kammler
20:45 hrs	Meal ...[83]

Martin Bormann writing to his wife Gerda, 20 February 1945:

Uncle Heinrich's [*Himmler*] offensive did not succeed, that is to say it did not develop properly, and now the Divisions which he was holding in reserve have to put in on other sectors. It means constant improvisations from one day to the next.[84]

Martin Bormann writing to his wife Gerda, 21 February 1945:

Uncle Heinrich [*Himmler*] had a particularly high opinion of General von Xylander. He was telling us about him yesterday evening [20 Feb.]. Colonel Zorn was killed in Alsace when Uncle H. was Commander-in-Chief there.[85]

From a postwar interrogation of Kurt Pomme (SS-Obersturmbannführer and Oberstleutnant of the Schutzpolizei), about meeting with Himmler probably on 20 February 1945:

Pomme left Berlin the same evening (17th or 18th Feb. [1945]) and travelled by S-Bahn and omnibus to Biesenthal where in the next day or two he saw General Flade (Chef des Organisationsamt of the ORPO Hauptamt) and discussed with him the reasons for his mission. 25 Officers and 100 men (Gendarmerie), 4 vehicles and a M/C were promised. Pomme also obtained the permission that Hellwig could henceforth personally bestow the Verdienstkreuze & Wound Medals to deserving cases and Pomme was given a few hundred of these to take back with him. After this part of his mission was finished he left Biesenthal and went by car to Wandlitz (35 Km. N of Berlin) where he was picked up by the mail van going to Heeresgruppe "Weichsel" which was under the command of Himmler (S. of Prenzlau, 100 Km.N.of Berlin). Here he spoke with Himmler for a few minutes concerning the situation in the North, and also with Himmler's Adjutant Grothmann through whom permission was obtained for Hellwig to issue himself Iron Crosses (2nd Class) to all deserving cases without going through the usual channels. Pomme slept in Himmler's Personal Train that night and next morning went home to Rheinsberg for three days....[86]

Wednesday, 21 February 1945

Meetings & Appointments of the Reichsführer-SS on 21.2.1945 (Birkenwald)

12:00 hrs	SS-Brigadeführer Rode
12:30 hrs	SS-Obersturmbannführer Kempin
14:00 hrs	Award of Oak Leaves [Eichenlaubes] to SS-Standartenführer Schäfer
14:10 hrs	Meal with
	SS-Gruppenführer Lammerding
	SS-Standartenführer Schäfer
	Oberstleutnant Baumbach
	SS-Obersturmbannführer Kempin
	SS-Obersturmbannführer Grothmann
15·00 hrs	Oberstleutnant Baumbach
16:30 hrs	Departure for Hohenlychen
17:30 hrs	Tea with
	General Wlassow
	SS-Obergruppenführer Berger
	SS-Oberführer Kroeger
19:30 hrs	SS-Gruppenführer Gebhardt
20:00 hrs	Departure for Birkenwald
21:00 hrs	Meal and meeting with SS-Brigadeführer Schellenberg
23:30 hrs	SS-Gruppenführer Lammerding

Events:

SS-Gruppenführer und Generalleutnant der Waffen-SS Dr Hans Kammler met with the Führer (Hitler), in Berlin, for the second time.[87]

On 21 February 1945, Count Folke Bernadotte met with German Foreign Minister von Ribbentrop in Berlin and informed him of his talks with Himmler. Afterwards he had lunch with Schellenberg who confirmed that he and Himmler had considered his requests since their joint meeting:

... Schellenberg was authorized to inform me that Himmler had definitely given his consent to the proposals which I had submitted to him; Swedish-born women were to receive exit visas, with the reservation that if any of them had had any trouble with the Police, the case should be submitted to him personally for examination, and the Norwegian and Danish prisoners were to be assembled in a camp at Neuengamme, situated not far from Hamburg... On my side I promised to endeavor to have my Red Cross column ready at Warnemünde ten days later.[88]

Thursday, 22 February 1945

Meetings & Appointments of the Reichsführer-SS on 22.2.1945 (Birkenwald)

13:00 hrs	Military briefing
14:00 hrs	Meal
17:00 hrs	SS-Brigadeführer Rode
20:00 hrs	Meal
22:00 hrs	Military briefing

Friday, 23 February 1945

Military situation:
Fortress Posen (Commander, Generalmajor Ernst Gonell†) after a four weeks' struggle fell to the 1.White Russian Front.[89]

Meetings & Appointments of the Reichsführer-SS on 23.2.1945 (Birkenwald)

13:00 hrs	SS-Gruppenführer Lammerding
14:00 hrs	Meal
15:00 hrs	SS-Sturmbannführer [Eduard] Friedel
16:00 hrs	SS-Obergruppenführer Lorenz
	SS-Obergruppenführer Oberg
19:00 hrs	SS-Obersturmbannführer Grothmann
19:30 hrs	SS-Gruppenführer Lammerding
	Oberst Rückert
20:00 hrs	Meal with
	SS-Obergruppenführer Lorenz
	SS-Sturmbannführer Friedel
	Oberst Eismann
21:00 hrs	SS-Obersturmbannführer Grothmann
22:00 hrs	SS-Gruppenführer Lammerding

Events:
Teleprinter message (03:00 hours) from Himmler to Richard Hildebrandt:

> Generaloberst Schörner has asked me for you to join him for the duration of the heavy fighting. For this period you will be Senior SS and Police Commander (*Höherer SS- und Polizeiführer*) Silesia, since the probable death of our fine comrade Schmauser, SS-Brigadeführer Bierkamp has been there. At this time Generaloberst Schörner wants you for various tasks within the framework of his Army Group. I have immediately promised him:
>
> Accordingly I appoint you for the time being as Senior SS and Police Commander South East (*Südost*).
>
> You will be located at the location of Army Group Mitte. SS-Brigadeführer Bierkamp who was tasked with carrying out the business of this HSSPF, will be released from these tasks and remain at his post as BdS South East (*Südost*).[90]

German radio message decrypted by Bletchley Park on 23 February 1945, taken at 13:25 hours:

> To: SS-Ustuf Machetanz, via IdS Danzig
>
> From: Commander, SS-Jagdverbande [Otto Skorzeny]
>
> The Rf.SS has ordered an urgent special mission (*Sondereinstaz*) to be carried out by Sturmgeschützbrigade 275 and men training at Braunsberg. Of course it is very difficult to replace specialists with other people. I therefore request that together with Ustuf. Machetanz these men join the headquarters staff of SS-Pursuit Units (*Jagdverbände*) at Friedenthal, travelling by rail via Sachsenhausen.[91]

Saturday, 24 February 1945

Military situation:
Surprise attack by the Red Army against Himmler's poorly defended defence lines in Pomerania.[93]

Meetings & Appointments of the Reichsführer-SS on 24.2.1945 (Birkenwald)

13:00 hrs	Military briefung
14:00 hrs	Meal with
	SS-Obergruppenführer Lorenz
	SS-Gruppenführer Haltermann
	SS-Obergruppenführer v. Gottberg
17:00 hrs	SS-Gruppenführer Haltermann
20:00 hrs	Meal with SS-Obergruppenführer Lorenz
22:00 hrs	SS-Standartenführer Dr. Schlüter
23:00 hrs	Military briefing

Events:
At 09:40 hrs, Sir Victor Mallet, British Ambassador to Sweden at Stockholm, sent a secret telegram (No. 275) dated 23 February 1945, to the Foreign Office in London:

> Swedish Minister for Foreign Affairs told me to-day in confidence, asking that it should not be quoted, that Bernadotte came back yesterday having seen Himmler. While refused to allow Norwegian and Danish civilian prisoners to be transferred to Sweden[.] Himmler nevertheless agreed to place them all (amounting to at least 13,000) in two concentration camps not far from Hamburg where Swedish Red Cross officials would be allowed to supervise their welfare. Bernadotte is to return next week with the first party of these officials of whom it is anticipated about 100 will eventually proceed. Main difficulty however is the transfer of Norwegians and Danes from existing camps to the new area, and Swedes hope to be able in some way to help supervise this transfer. Minister for Foreign Affairs seemed on the whole satisfied that this new arrangement was better than nothing and would ensure that the prisoners would not be murdered by the Gestapo at the last minute.[94]

11:30 hrs, Sir Victor Mallet, British Ambassador to Sweden, sent a second secret telegram (No. 279) to the Foreign Office, London:

Following is more detailed information which has been given to me by the Swedish Ministry of Foreign Affairs:

2. Before his visit to Himmler had been arranged[,] Bernadotte was invited to call upon Ribbentrop who was also somewhere in the neighborhood of Berlin. Ribbentrop harangued him at the top of his voice for half an hour on the subject of Jewish-Bolshevik-Pluto Democracies using the familiar clichés and declaring that the only result of the war would be the spread of Bolshevism all over Europe.

3. Conversation with Himmler appears to have been purely on practical lines concerned with interned Norwegians and Danes. Bernadotte asked for those to be allowed to go to Sweden which Himmler said was impossible. After further discussion Himmler agreed in principle to all civilians, Norwegians and Danes, being moved from several camps in which they now are to a central camp at Neuengamme near Hamburg. If this camp did not suffice a further camp near-by would be arranged. Himmler questioned Bernadotte's figure of 13,000 and thought there were less. It is doubtful whether Himmler's agreement covers those undergoing sentences of hard labour or military internees.

4. Bernadotte goes back to Berlin March 3rd to meet Brigade Fuhrer (sic) Schellenberg who is the official concerned with these internees and who had made a favorable impression upon him. Himmler had pointed out that the Germans could not arrange transport of the internees to Neuengamme but agreed Bernadotte should bring to Germany a fleet of Swedish buses and ambulances and arrange for the movement of the internees as quickly as possible to their new camp where the Swedish Red Cross and medical personnel will look after them.

5. Swedish Government are satisfied that this is really a useful step in the direction of helping these internees and saving them from worse hardships and risks.[95]

At 14:00 hrs in Reich Chancellery, Berlin, Hitler attended the last meeting of all Reichsleiters, Gauleiters and senior Party officials.

Hitler: "If the German people now cross over to the enemy, it will earn them destruction."[96]

Gauleiter Paul Wegener recalled the meeting:

The only other Gauleiters meeting after that [August 1944] took place on 24 Feb 45, when Hitler called all the 42 Gauleiters to a meeting in the Reichs Chancellery. Present at this meeting were Bormann, and all the Gauleiters and Reichsleiters. In a 1½ hour session Hitler gave a picture of the political and military situation, talked about the prospective employment of new submarines, new airplanes and new divisions which were to be used on the Eastern front.

No instructions or hints on future policy were given. These, however, were always forwarded in written orders through normal channels.[97]

From the diary of Hitler's valet, Heinz Linge:

14:00 hrs	Reception – Reichsleiters and Gauleiters
14:15 hrs	Meal – Reichsleiters and Gauleiters
15:30 hrs	Speech [by Hitler]
18:00 hrs	Military conference – RM [Göring], RFSS[98]

Sunday, 25 February 1945

Meetings & Appointments of the Reichsführer-SS on 25.2.1945 (Birkenwald)

13:00 hrs	SS-Gruppenführer Lammerding
14:00 hrs	Meal with
	SS-Obergruppenführer Lorenz
	SS-Obergruppenführer Prützmann
	SS-Obergruppenführer v. Gottberg
15:00 hrs	SS-Obergruppenführer v. Gottberg
16:00 hrs	SS-Obergruppenführer Prützmann
16:30 hrs	Gauleiter Förster
18:00 hrs	SS-Gruppenführer Lammerding
18:15 hrs	General Bleckwenn
	SS-Gruppenführer Lammerding
19:00 hrs	SS-Brigadeführer Körner
20:00 hrs	Meal with
	SS-Brigadeführer [Hellmut] Körner
	Oberst Streck
22:00 hrs	SS-Gruppenführer Lammerding

Events:
German radio message decrypted by Bletchley Park on 25 February 1945, taken at 16:20 hrs, sent to Eichmann's department:

> To RSHA IV B4 Z 1.
> Your teleprinter message No. 8094 of 24.2.45:
> With visa 25, 208 without waiting to leave.
> Waiting here another 150.
> From Border Police Office, Konstanz [on Swiss border].[99]

Monday, 26 February 1945

Military situation:
Soviet troops have reached Fortress Kolberg on the Baltic Sea coast.[100]

Meetings & Appointments of the Reichsführer-SS on 26.2.1945

13:00 hrs	SS-Gruppenführer Lammerding
	General Grase
14:00 hrs	Gefreiter Jepp (sharpshooter)
18:00 hrs	SS-Gruppenführer Lammerding
20:00 hrs	General Fiebig
	General Dinter
	SS-Gruppenführer Haltermann

22:00 hrs   SS-Gruppenführer Haltermann

Events:

Decree issued by Himmler for the establishment of "Special Courts Martial to Combat Disintegration" (*Sonderstandgerichten zur Bekämpfung von Auflösungserscheinigungen*)".[101]
Radio message from SS-Ogruf. von Herff (SS-Personalhauptamt) to SS-Ogruf. Gutenberger (HSSPF West, Düsseldorf):

> Reichsführer-SS has ordered that SS-Gruppenführer and Generalleutnant of Police Wappenhans be assigned to you for support until further notice. SS-Gruppenführer Wappenhans will arrive with you from here. Report his arrival.[102]

German radio message decrypted by Bletchley Park on 26 February 1945, taken at 09:31 hours, addressed to Eichmann's department:

> To RSHA IV B/4C I.
> Further 80 Swiss arrived. No group visa, no accommodation. No courier has arrived.
> Border Police office Konstanz [on the Swiss border].[103]

German radio message decrypted by Bletchley Park on 26 February 1945, taken at 20:00 hours:

> Secret. To Rf SS personally.
> I report after talks and in agreement with Fortress Commander [Infantry General Otto Lasch in Königsberg?], since 26.1.45 troops have had no relief from the battle. Since 10.2.45 it became harder day by day, waging a bitter running fight, rising losses of the best officers and fighters resulting from massive enemy artillery salvoes and mortar attacks. Effect of our heavy weapons and artillery on recognized enemy firing positions and deployments is inadequate due to increasing lack of ammunition. So far there has been outstanding bravery, mental and physical strength with little to show. Despite facing low-value enemy infantry, they use every opportunity to charge us, but their heavy weapons can only be slowed down but not stopped.
> From Sturmbannführer [Georg] Besslein.[104]

German radio message decrypted by Bletchley Park on 26 February 1945:

> Teleprinter message of 23.2.45 on the same subject was given incomplete. Full text reads: Rf.SS has requested that Governor SS-Gruf. Dr Waechter, Chief Military Administration in Italy, to carry out...important Special Tasks (*Sonderauftrages*) in Germany for a few weeks. After seeking their agreement, today Gruf. Waechter is on the way to Rf.SS. Because of the special position in Italy for the moment I have personally taken over the tasks of Chief Military Administration during the absence of Gruf. Waechter.
> signed Wolff, SS Ogruf.[105]

In January 1945 SS-Gruppenführer Dr Wächter was originally ordered to SS-Hauptamt as Liaison Officer with General Wlassow.[106]

Tuesday, 27 February 1945

Military situation:
Marshal Zhukov launched a massive attack on Himmler's defence lines in Pomerania. Two Soviet tank armies reported in Koslin direction and on the Baltic coast.[107]

Meetings & Appointments of the Reichsführer-SS on 27.2.1945 (Birkenwald)

13:00 hrs	SS-Gruppenführer Lammerding
13:30 hrs	SS-Standartenführer [Gebhard] Himmler
14:00 hrs	Meal with
	Gauleiter Schwede-Coburg
	SS-Gruppenführer Lammerding
	General Bleckwenn
	SS-Standartenführer Himmler
	Oberst Ing. Dr Hopp
15:00 hrs	Gauleiter Schwede-Coburg
17:00 hrs	General Bleckwenn
	Military briefing
20:00 hrs	Meal with
	SS-Obergruppenführer Lorenz
	SS-Obersturmbannführer Skorzeny
	SS-Obersturmführer Phleps
21:00 hrs	SS-Obersturmbannführer Skorzeny

Events:
Notice issued by Martin Bormann, 28 February 1945:

1. RFSS Himmler told me yesterday evening, the Führer has permitted the call-up of 6,000 youths born in 1929 to strengthen his rear defence lines.

2. As well, the Führer also agreed, as I know exactly, to the trial selection for a Womens-Battalion.
   The women are to be perfectly trained as soon as possible.
   Establishing the Womens-Battalion in liaison with the Reich Womens League (Reichsfrauenführung). Should the battalion prove itself, more will be set up.[108]

German radio message decrypted by Bletchley Park on 27 February 1945, taken at 02:05 hours:

To: SS-Brigadeführer Bierkamp, deputy HSSPF Südost, Breslau.

Re. radio message SSZS No 2618 of 16.2.45, 1800 hrs.

Regional Vice President Kessler has been appointed by the Rf SS as Liaison Officer with the Reich Defence Kommissar Lower and Upper Silesia. He takes over the evacuation issues in accordance with those issued by the Rf SS on 14.12.44 and originally intended for SS-Brigadeführer Bierkamp.

Signed, Brandt, SS-Standartenfhr., Sonderzug 'Steiermark'.[109]

German radio message decrypted by Bletchley Park on 27 February 1945, taken at 07:43 hours:

> To HSSuPf. West, Obergruf. Gutenberger, Duesseldorf.
>
> I have received a large number of complaints, that during the evacuation of Kevelaer village the police behaved very badly. I ask that these complaints be investigated immediately and the guilty punished, so that we can learn in the future to avoid a mess and toughness when dealing with the populace.
>
> Signed, H. Himmler.[110]

German radio message decrypted by Bletchley Park on 27 February 1945, taken at 08:48 hours:

> To: 1) Gauleiter Sprenger, Frankfurt; 2) Gauleiter Simon, Koblenz; 3) Gauleiter Stoehr, Landstuhl.
>
> Gauleiters will have received the order from Rf.SS that a SS-Battalion for Special Purposes (SS z.b.V. Btl.) is to be established from available SS-men. Immediate call-up for the purposes only of establishing and initial training, the men will then be temporarily discharged. Examination whether immediate discharge necessary on the basis of occupation, will take place immediately after arrival.
>
> Heil Hitler!
>
> Signed, Yours, Stroop.[111]

Wednesday, 28 February 1945

Meetings & Appointments of the Reichsführer-SS on 28.2.1945 (Birkenwald)
>   Rf-SS in bed with a cold
16:30 hrs General Krebs

Events:
In his diary entry of 1 March 1945, Joseph Goebbels after meeting the Berlin Defence Council, recorded they were taking increasing measures to find more troops to defend the city. They were combing schools and conscripting army cadets:

> … looking in every nook and cranny for soldiers. We must also call-up a second Volkssturm, and may also establish Womens Battalions. I proposed that convicts with short sentences in the prisons and concentration camps be sent to tough units. As General Wlassow told me, such units performed extraordinarily well in the defence of Moscow. Stalin went so far as to ask him whether he could create a Prisoner-Division. Any brave actions would be rewarded by an amnesty. Any Convicts-Division now would need to be outstanding. Why shouldn't we create the conditions for this now?[112]

This suggestion of Goebbels was apparently picked up by Himmler as German prisoners held in concentration camps were recruited as guards.

March 1945

Beginning March 1945, date unclear

Hermann Pister, former Camp Commandant KL Buchenwald, in a post-war statement, that at the beginning of March, Himmler ordered:

> ... at the approach of the enemy, dangerous prisoners should be eliminated who could interfere with the peace and quiet [in the camp].

> ...An indication is furnished by Himmler's directive to his Chief Medical Officer (*Reichsarzt SS-und Polizei*, Dr Ernst Robert Grawitz) in early March 1945, according to which there were 600,000 inmates remaining in the [concentration] camps, of whom 120,000 were unfit for work. (Purpose of the directive, incidentally, was a belated effort to improve the health of the inmates).[1]

In addition, the Senior SS Hygienist (*Oberste Hygieniker der SS*), SS-Oberführer Prof. Joachim Mrugowsky was sent to Bergen-Belsen concentration camp on an 8-day sanitary mission.[2]

March 1945, date unclear

During March, SS-Obergruppenführer Dr Ernst Kaltenbrunner twice consulted with Himmler. The first occasion at Hohenlychen together with SS-Ogruf. Dr Gebhardt; the second occasion on Himmler's special train at Stargard.[3]

Telegram from Himmler to HSSPF Hamburg, von Bassewitz-Behr (possibly copied to HSSPF Braunschweig, Querner, and to HSSPF Stettin, Mazuw): "The Führer makes you personally responsible that no Concentration Camp prisoner shall fall into the hands of the enemy alive."[4]

From a pre-trial interrogation of Oswald Pohl at Nuremberg, 7 June 1946: Glücks and Pohl had orders to meet Himmler at his office:

> ...in March 1945; that was the last time I saw Himmler. He asked Gluecks and me on that occasion how many Jews were still left in concentration camps. We figured out there must have been about 7,000 still left. I do not recall the exact figure. It was then that he gave me the order to visit all the concentration camp commandants to tell them that they were not to touch any Jews any longer. This order I executed but I never received any general order about ceasing the extermination action.

> ...

> To be exact, I visited the commandants of the following nine concentration camps: Neuengamme, Oranienburg [Sachsenhausen], Gross-Rosen, Auschwitz (*sic*), Flossenburg, Buchenwald, Dachau, Mauthausen and Bergen-Belsen. The other two, Stutthof and Schirmeck [Natzweiler], had been overrun by Allied forces and I could not visit their commandants any longer.

Furthermore, Pohl agreed to the question that Himmler "wanted a few Jews for bargaining purposes", adding himself: "That was my impression as well as Gluecks – that he wanted to have them for bargain purposes in the peace negotiations."[5]

Oswald Pohl gave a further report on these camp visits when he was testifying in his defence at trial in Nuremberg:

> About the middle of March, 1945, I was again at Buchenwald. That was in order to execute an order by Himmler around the beginning of March 1945. Himmler ordered me to go as quickly as possible to the camp commanders which could still be reached, and to tell them effective immediately all the Jews who were still living in the camps were to be treated as good as possible. At that time I had the impression that he began to carry a firm policy all his own, and [in] this he apparently wanted to use the Jews... but neither Lolling nor Hoess were along with me. At that time I was accompanied only by my ordnance officers. It is possible that Hoess and Lolling may have been there a short time afterwards – or before – but apparently this has been mixed up here. I had to pas on this oral order of Himmler to the camp commandants, and in view of the situation I went from one camp to the next as fast as I could, and I was unable to stay at Buchenwald for any length of time.[6]

Rudolf Hoess, former Camp Commandant KL Auschwitz, in a post-war statement:

> My last and important inspection trip was with Obergruppenführer Pohl and Doctor Lolling in March 1945. We visited the following camps, Neuengamme, Bergen Belsen, Buchenwald, Dachau and Flossenburg. I went along with Obergruppenführer Pohl and Dr Lolling and visited Leitmeritz near Aussig and another big camp on the [River] Elbe. The order for this journey came from Himmler to Obergruppenführer Pohl. He had to bring an order personally to the different camp commandants that no Jew should be killed any more and everything possible should be done to stop the death rate of prisoners. The Camp Commandants also got orders regarding evacuation of certain camps. Especially Belsen was in a terrible condition. 10,000s of dead people lay about anywhere. All latrines were full and overflowing. Obergruppenführer Pohl gave Kramer the order to clear away everything. There was no possibility to get any more food, as the Landesernahrungsamt (Food Office) refused to send any more food to Belsen. I personally ordered Kramer to collect firewood in the nearby forest and burn the dead bodies. After a short time I could notice some improvement in housing but there was still no food.[7]

Thursday, 1 March 1945

Military situation:
From WFStab war diary: Reich Plenipotentiary Dr Best expected at Führer Headquarters to discuss the question of refugees in Denmark with the Führer.[8]

Meetings & Appointments of the Reichsführer-SS on 1.3.1945 (Birkenwald)

13:00 hrs	Military briefing
14:00 hrs	Meal with SS-Obergruppenführer Lorenz
20: 00 hrs	Meal with SS-Obergruppenführer Lorenz
21:00 hrs	Military briefing

Events:

Joseph Goebbels wrote in his diary, 2 March 1945:

> ... It is nonsense that there should still be Wehrmacht units under training today in Nuremberg or Bayreuth for instance. The right course is to locate them behind the front in Brandenburg or Pomerania so that, should the Soviets break through anywhere, they are ready to act. If as a result these areas necessarily become overpopulated, I would be quite prepared to reduce or even totally evacuate the civil population; our women would certainly prefer to leave their towns and villages to make room for German rather than Soviet soldiers.[9]

Himmler sent Oberst [Fritz] Fullriede to Kolberg and assist in the defence of the city.[10]

German radio message decrypted by Bletchley Park on 1 March 1945:

> To SS-Obergruppenführer [Erwin] Rösener, Laibach
> Subject: Greek Police Volunteer Battalion Poulos
> Use the small Greek Police Volunteer Battalion as you wish. Employ the men.
> (signed) Himmler.[11]

Pocket diary of Martin Bormann, (Berlin): "...afternoon talk with Obergruppenführer Prützmann... evening with Sepp Dietrich, Kaltenbrunner".[12]

Friday, 2 March 1945

Meetings & Appointments of the Reichsführer-SS on 2 March 1945 (Hohenlychen)

11:00 hrs	SS-Gruppenführer Gebhardt
11:30 hrs	General Busse
12:00 hrs	SS-Brigadeführer Rattenhuber
	Major Johannmeyer
19:45 hrs	Award of Oak Leaves with Swords (Eichenlaubs mit Schwertern)
	to General [Maximilian] Wengler
20:00 hrs	Meal with
	General Wengler
	General Melzer
	SS-Gruppenführer Lammerding
	SS-Obersturmbannführer Grothmann
	SS-Hauptsturmführer Conrad
21:30 hrs	Departure of RF-SS from Hohenlychen

Events:

File note by Ia officer in War Diary, Hinrichs, 2 March 1945: "General Kienzel (*sic* – Kinzel), commander of 327 I.D. [Infantry Division] during the indisposition of the RF-SS ordered to H.Gr... General Kienzel will join the H.Gr, tomorrow morning.[13]

The German Consulate in Geneva presented a Note to the International Red Cross Committee on the question of repatriations, 2 March 1945:

After examining the matter the Government is now ready to allow French children, women and old men located in Germany to return home in exchange for German civilian internees from France. Proposals which include the numbers to be returned home, will go to the International Committee as soon as possible. It is assumed that France also will expedite carrying out the necessary preparatory actions.

ICRC President Carl-Jacob Burckhardt responding to questions about this exchange asked by the International Military Tribunal at Nuremberg, 17 April 1946, on behalf of Kaltenbrunner:

In this context, communications now came to the International Committee of the Red Cross from the Reichsführer Himmler or one of his Plenipotentiaries [Kaltenbrunner] to the President of the International Committee wishing for a personal conversation. The conference was to take place 12 March 1945 at Feldkirch on the Liechtenstein-German border as agreed with the SD organization.[14]

Saturday, 3 March 1945

Meetings & Appointments of the Reichsführer-SS on 3.3.1945 (Hohenlychen)
There are no diary entries for this date.

Events:
Felix Kersten travelled from Sweden to Germany to treat Himmler who was ill.[15]

Diary of Joseph Goebbels, regarding a midday meeting with State Secretary Wilhelm Stuckart (Reich Ministry of the Interior), 4 March 1945, about evacuation of the populace in some areas:

Stuckart was compelled to evacuate large section of the East Pomeranian population helter-skelter and overnight. Some 800,000 people were set on the move in this area. They had to be evacuated largely by sea since the Soviets had already cut the roads as they advanced. The Reich has now become fairly constricted. We have therefore decided to carry out no more evacuations from the West. Even if the Anglo-Americans advance in the West, people must look after themselves. If we were to clear the western population out entirely, the interior of the Reich would be so congested that it would be impossible to accommodate people in practice.[16]

German radio message decrypted by Bletchley Park on 3 March 1945:

To: SS Oberabschnitt South West, Stuttgart [HSSPF Otto Hofmann].
It is incomprehensible to the Rf.SS, why with the forces of the Oberabschnitt deployed for this purpose, few or no aircraft have been shot down in spite of the large number of aircraft incursions. He wishes the use of all possible means and methods to achieve greater successes. (signed) Grothmann, SS Obersturmbannfhr.[17]

German radio message decrypted by Bletchley Park on 3 March 1945, regarding the trial of four members of the Criminal Police:

To: SS-Judge [Bender] with Rf.SS.

Subject: Personal radio message Rf.SS No. 117 to SS-Brig. Bierkamp dated 16.2.45...: Kos. Osterreicher, Ks. Milbrand, Kos. Vauenstein, Kos. Boettger immediately after judicial proceedings during a night-sitting of 27.2.45 were sentenced to death for leaving Fortress Glogau. Senior Schupo Leader South East requests Rf.SS be immediately informed of the case.

From SS and Police Court XV.[18]

Sunday, 4 March 1945

Meetings & Appointments of the Reichsführer-SS on 4.3.1945 (Hohenlychen)

	Herr Kersten
18:00 hrs	SS-Obersturmbannführer Grothmann
20:00 hrs	General Kienzel

Events:

Diary of Joseph Goebbels, 5 March 1945:

> I had a long talk with the Führer yesterday afternoon... Moreover, even Himmler is laid low with an infectious disease; but he still continues to run his Army Group from his bed, but this gives rise to numerous difficulties.[19]

Monday, 5 March 1945

Military situation:

Call-up for boys born in 1929.[20]

Meetings & Appointments of the Reichsführer-SS on 5.3.1945 (Hohenlychen)

11:00 hrs Herr Kersten

        afternoon

        General Kienzel

        Gauleiter Kaufmann, Hamburg

        SS-Gruppenführer v. Bassewitz

        General [Joachim] v. Stolzmann

        SS-Gruppenführer Lammerding

Events:

Georg Henning Count von Bassewitz-Behr, in a post-war deposition: "The next time we met was in Feb [?] 45, when I accompanied Gauleiter Kaufmann to Himmler's HQ near Stettin[?]. The third time was in the beginning of March[?]."[21]

Count Folke Bernadotte flew back to Germany for meetings with Schellenberg and Kaltenbrunner, the latter now becoming antagonistic to Bernadotte:

> *Kaltenbrunner:* I do not intend to assist you in this matter you have brought up.
>
> *Bernadotte:* And I am not going to stand one of Himmler's subordinates trying to sabotage an arrangement agreed upon between him and myself.[22]

German radio message decrypted by Bletchley Park on 5 March 1945:

To: Chief, Napola Mokritz/Oberkrain [Austria].

Teleprinter message received. RZL Napola by Führer Order (*Führerbefehl*) to join in the development of Organization Todt officer-trainees for the army and Waffen-SS. Immediately make preparations for two training courses. The RFSS has forbidden any other claims on the establishment. Implementation of the Führer Order is a wartime necessity and may not be set aside. You are personally responsible for the complete use of Mokritz.

From: SS-Ogruf. Heissmeyer.[23]

German radio message decrypted by Bletchley Park on 5 March 1945:

To: Commander, Gendarmerie Graz, with the request that it be passed to KAMA Regiment headquarters, SS-Ostubaf. Roth at Feldbach and Commander, Fortified Region Steiermark, Gen.major Jesser at Graz.

By order of Rf.SS, SS-FHA, SS-headquarters KAMA and SS-Construction Battalion KAMA together with all personnel and equipment are immediately to join with 13th Waffen-Grenadier Division der SS "Handschar".

Report transport movement to SS-FHA and Transport Office in Vienna.

From: HSSPF Laibach.[24]

Tuesday, 6 March 1945

Meetings & Appointments of the Reichsführer-SS on 6.3.1945 (Hohenlychen)

11:00 hrs	Herr Kersten
16:00 hrs	SS-Gruppenführer v. Alvensleben
17:00 hrs	SS-Standartenführer Dr Brandt
18:00 hrs	SS-Gruppenführer Kammler
	Generaloberst Raus
	General Kienzel

Events:

Diary of Joseph Goebbels, 7 March 1945, describing an evening meeting with SS-Gruf von Alvensleben, HSSPF Dresden, about the consequences of the British air-raid on the city:

…This was a real tragedy such as has seldom been seen in the history of mankind and certainly not in the course of this war. Life in Dresden is slowly beginning to emerge from the ruins. Alvensleben had visited Himmler who is sick in Hohenlychen. He had discussed the whole military and political situation with Himmler and given vent to severe criticism of Göring and Ribbentrop. Himmler had expressed a wish to speak to me as soon as possible. I got in touch with him this evening and we agreed that I should visit him some time tomorrow, Wednesday….[25]

Himmler opposed General Theodor Busse (Commander, AOK 9) by insisting that the Hitler-Youth are not deployed in units with older soldiers and Volkssturm men.[26]

German radio message decrypted by Bletchley Park on 6 March 1945:

To Police Administration, Dessau.

Rf.SS has ordered that the wife of Meister der Schupo Zunder (a suicide) be contacted in a friendly manner and the family be provided for. Report... [in accordance] with decree of 14.7.42.

From Chef Orpo.[27]

Wednesday, 7 March 1945

Meetings & Appointments of the Reichsführer-SS on 7.3.1945 (Hohenlychen)

11:00 hrs	Herr Kersten
13:00 hrs	General Kienzel
16:00 hrs	Reichsminister Dr Goebbels

Events:

From the diary of Joseph Goebbels, 8 March 1945. Goebbels and Himmler had agreed a program of intensive checks at railway stations to find soldiers doing little, and had success from the start. Goebbels travelled to the Hohenlychen clinic where Himmler was still ill:

...In the afternoon [*of 7 March*] I drive out to Himmler to have a long talk...

Himmler is in Hohenlychen under medical care. He has had a bad attack of angina but is now on the mend. He gave me a slightly frail impression. Nevertheless we were able to have a long talk about all outstanding questions. In general Himmler's attitude is good. He is one of our strongest personalities. During our two-hour discussion I established that we were in complete agreement in our estimate of the general situation so that I hardly need refer to that. He used strong language about Göring and Ribbentrop, whom he regards as the two main sources of error in our general conduct of the war, and in this he is absolutely right. But he has no more idea than I how to persuade the Führer to cut loose from them both and replace them with fresh strong personalities...

As far as the front is concerned Himmler is extremely worried, particularly about developments in Pomerania and the West. At present, however, he is even more worried about the food situation, the outlook for which is pretty gloomy over the next few months...

Himmler agrees that we should locate troops now training in barracks behind the Western and Eastern Fronts as a cushion. So far Jüttner has resisted this tooth and nail. Himmler will accordingly summon Jüttner and give him a piece of his mind. General Kleiner, Jüttner's closest associate, is the one who is calling the tune and he is in agreement with Colonel-General Fromm's policy.

I discussed the Fromm case with Himmler in detail. That morning Kaltenbrunner had taken steps to ensure that current proceedings against Fromm are conducted with greater energy than has been the case so far. During the initial stage of his trial Fromm took complete control of the proceedings.

With Himmler the atmosphere is orderly, unpretentious and one hundred percent National-Socialist, which is most refreshing. One can only rejoice that with Himmler the old National-Socialist spirit still prevails.[28]

Teleprinter from Chief of Staff, Army Group Vistula, Lammerding, to AOK 9 and Pz. AOK 3, 7 March 1945 (14:15 hours.):

The Führer has ordered:

Whoever becomes a prisoner of war without being wounded or proved to have fought to his limit, forfeits his honour. The community of decent and brave soldiers will take objection to this. Their relatives are liable for him. Any pay or support will fall on the relatives. This is to be announced immediately. Details will be regulated by Chief OKW.

By order of the Führer, (signed) Keitel, Generalfeldmarschall (WFStab/Org. No. 898/45)....[29]

General Busse referred Himmler to an agreement concluded with the Reich Youth Leader (*Reichsjugendführer*) Axmann, according to which "the Hitler Youth would go into action in their own units under the command of their HJ-commanders".[30]

Top secret report from Seyss-Inquart to Himmler, 7 March 1945: An assassination attempt on HSSPF [Hanns Albin] Rauter took place in The Hague.[31]

German radio message decrypted by Bletchley Park on 7 March 1945:

Forward via SS-Hauptamt to Rf.SS, Party Comrade Himmler, Field HQ.

Dear Reichsführer! For Army Group H, Generaloberst Blaskowitz has taken from the Volkssturm older age-groups for use with his supply train. First instalment, 1,000 men. More to follow. For Army Group B, Generalfeldmarschall Model, more Volkssturm men from Gau Essen cannot be taken.

From: Reich Defence Kommissar Essen, signed Schlessmann, Deputy Gauleiter.[32]

Thursday, 8 March 1945

Meetings & Appointments of the Reichsführer-SS on 8.3.1945 (Hohenlychen)

11:00 hrs   Herr Kersten
                          SS-Gruppenführer Lammerding
                          SS-Obersturmbannführer Grothmann

Events:

SS-Ogruf. Karl Wolff, HöSSPF Italian together with a German Army officer from Kesselring's staff crossed into Switzerland at Lugano. During the afternoon they met with American intelligence officer Allen W. Dulles in a Zürich safe-house. Wolff offered:

– cessation of all "active hostilities against Italian partisans"

– release of all imprisoned Jews

– unconditional surrender of German forces in Northern Italy (Army Group C under Generalfeldmarschall Kesselring).[33]

German radio message decrypted by Bletchley Park, 8 March 1945 (16:20 hours):

To: Personal Staff Rf.SS, for attention Hauptmann Haendel.

Chief Orpo radio message, No 143, 7.3.45, Hauptamt Orpo has received a crate containing official Diaries, etc., from Riga. If time available, please obtain decision about arrangements for the secret document detailing locations and offices, for archiving or destruction. Official seals and other useful materials from the crate have been sent here.

From: HSSPF Ostland, signed Behrends.[34]

German radio message decrypted by Bletchley Park, 8 March 1945 (19:53 hours), first part missed, including sender:

...all too many minor appeals addressed to the Führer and Rf.SS, files and opinions taken by courier to Hauptamt SS-Gericht. A pardon for Foerster is proposed. Request consent of Rf.SS for immediate hand-over to E-Batl. Dirlewanger. Good liaison with SS Obergruppenführer Kaltenbrunner, who can personally instruct the Court officials.[35]

Friday, 9 March 1945

Meetings & Appointments of the Reichsführer-SS on 9.3.1945 (Hohenlychen)

11:00 hrs	Herr Kersten
	SS-Obergruppenführer Lorenz
	SS-Obergruppenführer Jüttner
	SS-Obergruppenführer Steiner
	Oberst Estor
	SS-Standartenführer Dr Brandt
	SS-Obersturmbannführer Grothmann

Events:

From the diary of Joseph Goebbels, 10 March 1945:

Colonel-General Fromm has been sentenced to death for cowardice in face of the enemy. He thoroughly deserves this sentence. Admittedly it could not be proved that he was actually involved in 20 July; but he did not take the measures which were his duty in order to prevent 20 July.[36]

Infantry General Wilhelm Burgdorf, Chief Adjutant for the Wehrmacht with Hitler, and all offices:

By order of the Führer, Reichsführer-SS will take over construction of new Führer Headquarters accommodation in the Ohrdruf area. SS-Gruppenführer Kammler is appointed responsible carrying out the work.

...

The competent local offices in Ohrdruf area

a) Operations Staff, Oberst Streve (Major Budnick)

b) Construction Management, SS-Gruppenführer Kammler (Hstuf. Grosch).[37]

In preparation for these measures the hunting lodge and locality were inspected on 2 November 1944 by Rf.SS Himmler, SS-Gruppenführer Dr Ing. Hans Kammler and the commandant of Führer Headquarters, Oberst Gustav Streve. The hunting lodge (*Jagdschloss*) in Reinhardsbrunn (near Marienglashöhle) was rented to the Reich Chancellery on 1 February 1945.[38]

Count Folke Bernadotte went to Friedrichsruh, north of Berlin on 8 March 1945, to begin his Swedish Red Cross operations in Germany. Using their own vehicles and fuel, the Swedish Red Cross brought 2,200 Danes and Norwegian prisoners from Sachsenhausen concentration camp, 600 Scandianavian prisoners from Dachau camp and 1,600 imprisoned Danish policemen from different camps in the Dresden area and in several transports safely transferred them to Neuengamme camp near Hamburg:

> ...The transportations from Sachsenhausen were carried out in seven relays, between March 15th and March 30th. As soon as we had made sure of a supply of fuel a column of thirty-five vehicles was formed for the run to Dachau, a distance there and back of eleven hundred miles. The column left on March 19th, under the command of Colonel Björck personally, and by March 24th the task had been completed without any mishaps. At the end of March the Danish policemen had been collected from the various camps.[39]

Saturday, 10 March 1945

Meetings & Appointments of the Reichsführer-SS on 10.3.1945 (Hohenlychen)

11:00 hrs	Herr Kersten
16:00 hrs	SS-Obersturmbannführer Grothmann
	SS-Standartenführer Dr Brandt
	SS-Gruppenführer Lammerding

Events:

Letter from Himmler to SS-Obergruppenführer Pohl, Berlin; SS-Gruppenführer Glücks, Oranienburg; SS-Obergruppenführer Dr Grawitz, National Physician for the SS and Police, Berlin; and SS-Obergruppenführer Dr Kaltenbrunner, Berlin: on the same day Himmler's Adjutant, SS-Standartenführer R Brandt provided copies to SS-Gruppenführer Prof. Gebhardt, Hohenlychen, and Herr Kersten, Hohenlychen:

> It has been reported to me that at Bergen-Belsen camp, especially among the Jewish prisoners, typhus has broken out.
>
> I require that the epidemic be immediately confronted with all medical assistance. We cannot have the epidemic spreading into Germany. Neither doctors nor medicines will be spared. The prisoners themselves remain under my protection.[40]

Circular No. 128/45 g.Rs., dated 10 March 1945, issued by Martin Bormann to all Gauleiters regarding the establishing of "Werwolfes": Subject: "Carrying out Special Tasks in the rear of the enemy."[41]

> German radio message decrypted at Bletchley Park on 10 March 1945:
>
> To: Party Chancellery Berlin, for immediate forwarding to Reichsleiter Bormann and Rf.SS Himmler.

General Director Reuter has reported the common view from the Ruhr, the 43 year-old indispensable General Manager and Director, Schumacher, of "Demag" company in Benrath, in the case of occupation of his factory, as a responsible General Manager he will remain at his work. Mark this duty of an able-bodied man for the enemy as a deserter. Have the SD cause to immediately arrest General Director Reuter. General Erdmann has shown no interest in my actions. Urgent attention to industry leaders is wanted. Request immediate consultations with Party Comrade Speer for clear instructions for industry and secure indispensable forces belonging to the Wehrmacht. From: [*Gauleiter*] Florian.[42]

Sunday, 11 March 1945 (Heroes Memorial Day)

Military situation:
In this last phase of the war Generalfeldmarschall Albert Kesselring replaced Generalfeldmarschall Gerd von Rundstedt as commander of German forces in southern Germany (the West front).[43]

Meetings & Appointments of the Reichsführer-SS on 11.3.1945 (Hohenlychen)

11:00 hrs	Herr Kersten
13:?0 hrs	General [Wolfgang] Thomale
	Oberst Throtha
	SS-Obergruppenführer Schaub
	SS-Gruppenführer Lammerding
	SS-Sturmbannführer Günsche

Events:
In the diary of Joseph Goebbels, 12 March 1945, he records a long evening meeting with Hitler in the Berlin Bunker:

The Führer is very displeased with him [*Himmler*]…

I am now very forceful in my criticism to the Führer of Göring personally and the Luftwaffe in general… I ask him at least to clear up the increasing corruption in the Luftwaffe. He thinks that this cannot be done in one fell swoop but that in this case we must work slowly, trying gradually to divest Göring of his position of power and turn him into a mere figurehead. For instance he has commissioned SS-Obergruppenführer (*sic*) Kammler to organise the transport to operational bases of our fighter aircraft….[44]

Monday, 12 March 1945

Meetings & Appointments of the Reichsführer-SS on 12.3.1945 (Hohenlychen)

11:00 hrs	Herr Kersten
12:00 hrs	General Kienzel
	SS-Gruppenführer Lammerding

13:00 hrs	Generaloberst Guderian
	General Kienzel
	SS-Gruppenführer Lammerding
17:15 hrs	Tea with
	Generaloberst Raus
	SS-Gruppenführer Gebhardt
	SS-Gruppenführer Lammerding
	SS-Obersturmbannführer Grothmann
	Major v. Freitag
	SS-Hauptsturmführer Hinrichs
19:00 hrs	SS-Obersturmbannführer Grothmann

Events:

Agreement jointly signed by Himmler and his Finnish masseur, Felix Kersten, at 14:00 hours "in the name of humanity":

I hereby confirm that I made the following agreement with Medical Officer (*Medizinalrat*) Kersten [of] Stockholm:

1.) I will not pass on the order of the Führer to the concentration camps for the camps to be blown up with all inmates at the approach of the Allies and prohibit any demolition. Also, the killing of prisoners.

2.) That a concentration camp at the approach of the Allies will raise white flags and ensure an orderly hand-over.

3.) Any further killing of Jews will be forbidden and Jews will be treated like any other concentration camp prisoner.

4.) That the concentration camps will not be evacuated and prisoners will remain where they are for the time being, and all prisoners may receive food parcels from Sweden.[45]

Two reports from KL Buchenwald indicate that Reichsführer-SS Himmler did make efforts to ensure the conditions in his agreement with Felix Kersten were put into effect:

(1) Former prisoner Otto Kiep of Dresden, Block 61 hospital building:

In March [1945] a letter came from the SS-Leadership, according to which the sick should receive better treatment. Despite this letter no means were made available to carry out this better treatment.

The letter also contained a ban on shooting prisoners, from that day no lethal injections were given. According to this letter Jews should receive better treatment, fed, and equal treatment as that to Russian prisoners of war.

(2) Louis Gimnich, former Block Elder (*Blockältester*), Block 61:

In March 1945 the SS-Main Leadership Office (*SS-Führungshauptamt*) [?] called for better treatment of sick prisoners and criticized the death rate as too high – an exact reversal of an order from January 1945 – established by SS murder activities in Block 61.[46]

Negotiations between the President of the International Committee of the Red Cross (ICRC), Professor Carl J. Burkhardt, the General Secretary of the ICRC, Dr Hans Bachmann, at Winterthur (Switzerland) and with Kaltenbrunner in Feldkirch (Vorarlberg), Austria.

Kaltenbrunner reported on this meeting in a post-war statement: "…that in future the Jews will be treated in the same way as other prisoners, namely they will receive the same privileges in regard to meals, correspondence etc.".[47]

Carl J. Burkhardt also reported on this meeting with Kaltenbrunner when responding to questions asked by the International Military Tribunal at Nuremberg, 17 April 1946:

> In fact, I demanded the transfer to Switzerland of Jews held in Germany in concentration camps. Dr Kaltenbrunner took note of my wishes and said he would report positively to Reichsführer.
>
> As another possible solution in case of a negative decision, I suggested the International Committee provided for Jews in approved special camps, and I would draw the attention of the War Refugee Board to the welfare of these Jews. Dr Kaltenbrunner wanted to examine this eventuality.
>
> …
>
> Dr Kaltenbrunner said: That is just nonsense, we should release all Jews; that is my personal opinion.[48]

Tuesday, 13 March 1945

Meetings & Appointments of the Reichsführer-SS on 13.3.1945 (Hohenlychen)

11:00 hrs	Herr Kersten
13:00 hrs	SS-Standartenführer Dr Brandt
17:30 hrs	SS-Gruppenführer Lammerding
18:30 hrs	SS-Gruppenführer Kammler
	SS-Sturmbannführer Harmann (*sic* – Hartmann?)
20:00 hrs	Herr Kersten
	SS-Gruppenführer Lammerding
	SS-Obersturmbannführer Grothmann

Events:

German radio message decrypted by Bletchley Park, 13 March 1945:

> To: HSSPF Weichsel, Danzig [Katzmann]; Ostland, Libau [Behrends]; West, Essen-Kettwig [Gutenberger]; Ost, [Koppe] at Klingenthal/Sachsen.
> Secret!
> Subject: Führer Decree dated 10 December 1944 'Examination of Wehrmacht, SS and Police in the homeland exempt as soldiers for the front.'
> By order of Rf.SS, abandonment of Clause 3, Section 2, HSSPF have immediate rights of a Commander to decide on the spot, questions from the various commissions. Submission of inspection results by the HSSPF, a decision from SS FHA not applicable.[49]

Wednesday, 14 March 1945

Meetings & Appointments of the Reichsführer-SS on 14.3.1945 (Hohenlychen)

Morning	SS-Standartenführer Tiefenbacher
15:00 hrs	Departure Hohenlychen
16:00 hrs	Arrival Birkenwald
16:30 hrs	General Manteuffel
	SS-Gruppenführer Lammerding
	General Kienzel
	Oberst Eismann
18:00 hrs	General Busse
	SS-Gruppenführer Lammerding
	General Kienzel
	Oberst Eismann
20:00 hrs	Departure Birkenwald
21:00 hrs	Arrival Hohenlychen

(Note: this is the last available page of diary entries for Himmler's meetings and appointments.)

Events:

Calendar of Martin Bormann, 14 March 1945: "M.B. [Martin Bormann], R with Ruder, Mrs Forster, with Field Marshall Keitel, Dr Pawlitzky, with Müller; after with [SS-] Obergruppenfhr/ [Karl Hermann] Frank."[50]

Letter from Dr Rudolf Brandt to Hanns Johst, 14 March 1945:

> … It has not gone particularly well with the Reichsführer-SS in the last few weeks. He had too much to do and neglected himself so he caught influenza. The illness has lasted for 12 days and he took to his bed. Fortunately his conditions is now improving.[51]

Thursday, 15 March 1945

Events:

In his diary for this day, Alfred Jodl wrote of attending a conference of the Führer with Himmler, Göring and Guderian. The Führer spoke of deceptive measures that would wake-up the Russians with a surprise thrust in the south.[52]

Joseph Goebbels reported on an afternoon telephone call with Hitler, 16 March 1945:

> …In this Remagen bridge case, for instance, four death sentences have already been pronounced and carried out. Himmler had been with him in the afternoon and he [Hitler] had given him an extraordinary dressing down.....[53]

By order of German Foreign Minister von Ribbentrop, Legationsrat Fritz Hesse to sound out the Western powers about a separate peace.[54]

Start of the Swedish Red Cross transports: 2,200 Danes and Norwegians were eventually taken from KL Sachsenhausen and KL Neuengamme.[55]

Hedwig Potthast, Himmler's mistress and mother of their two children, from a post-war interrogation:

> Source states that the last time she saw Himmler was during the week ending
> 22 March 45. At that time Himmler was confined to bed in a hospital at Hohenlucchen (*sic*) near
> Berlin, suffering an attack of grippe. While visiting him there source encountered Dr (*sic*) Felix
> Kersten of Linnegatan 8. Stockholm... Dr Kersten told her to call upon him if ever she need
> any help. (A wire from source to Dr Kersten was intercepted by Allied authorities, disclosing
> source's location and leading to this interrogation).[56]

Friday, 16 March 1945

Events:

Joseph Goebbels recorded in his diary, 17 March 1945, that rumours of an armistice and peace emanated from the German mission to Sweden and given immense media coverage in Sweden and Britain:

> .... The really grotesque feature of this news coverage is that Himmler, not the Führer, is
> presented as the guarantor of peace for Germany. A powerful German clique is said to have
> offered the Führer's head as surety. Not a word of this is true, of course. All this has been
> cooked up by the British themselves. To this they reply that they require many other heads as
> well as that of the Führer...[57]

Bletchley Park intercepted a German radio message about the proposed dissolution of SS punishment camps.
Krueger, SS.Obergruf (Prag) to 11 S.S. Panzer AOK, S.S. Obergruf. Steiner, Neustrelitz, 16/3[1945]:–

> (i) It is necessary to accelerate the full powers for the plenipotentiary officer (of the Rf.SS)
> promised by telephone. Agreement of the Wehrkreise is necessary, otherwise work will be
> impossible.
> (ii) I propose that the over-filled Armed Forces Punishment Camps and SS, and Police
> Penitentiaries should to the greatest possible degree be dissolved. Sentences of death should
> be carried out, and all other personnel collected into punishment or disciplinary battalions.

Note by Dept. Of the two S.S. Obergruf's Krueger known, more probable above is F-W. Krueger, G.O.C., 5th S.S. Corps.[58]

Report by Felix Kersten:

> On this beneficial occasion I spoke with Himmler about the treatment of Jews in the
> concentration camps. In my presence he issued a special order (Sonderbefehl) in which he
> again prohibited any cruelty of Jewish prisoners and forbidding the killing of Jews.[59]

Saturday, 17 March 1945

There are no reports about Reichsführer-SS Himmler for this date.

Sunday, 18 March 1945

Military situation:
From the war diary of WFStab: Army Group Vistula: … Kolberg was evacuated. Taken away were 68,000 civilians, 1,223 wounded and 5,213 men. The City Commandant [Oberst Fritz Fullriede] left the combat zone on a Naval destroyer. An investigation is underway.[60]

Events:
Allied Intelligence source "TRUEFITT" report dated 27 March 1945:
> 2. On the morning of March 18th [1945], Himmler had a long conference at the railway station [Bregenz] with local Gestapo chief Grinner (*sic* – Griener). Later on in the day Grinner was seen in the company of Dr Alois Vogt, who is "Deputy Government Chief" of Liechtenstein. Dr Vogt seems to play an important role and receives frequent visits from Grinner.[61]

Radio message from Heinrich Himmler, 18 March 1945:
> I appoint you as responsible Senior SS. and Police Commander, with full authority, with Army Group Centre. You will deal with all matters concerning the SS. and Police and negotiate with Senior SS. and Police Cdrs. BOHEMIA and MORAVIA and ELBE, even when such matters do not lie with the sphere of SS. Main Administrative area SOUTHEAST.

Note: Name of person so appointed evidently omitted. Officer is presumably Senior SS. and Police Leader South East BRESLAU." That SS-officer was SS-Ogruf. Jeckeln.[62]

Monday, 19 March 1945

Events:
Top Secret report "Germany No. 39" dated 19 March 1945 by British Intelligence:
> Austria.
> An emissary of Kaltenbrunner has had a long preliminary conversation with a member of the Austrian Opposition here who is considered perfectly reliable – conversation probably occurred 5 or 6 days ago [13-14 March 1945].
> He said that Kaltenbrunner and other Austrian S.S. people together with Glaise-Horstenau S.D. (struck through in original) have for some months been convinced that Germany is beaten. They now only believe in one thing in the Nazi Programme, i.e. anti-Communism. Therefore they wish to offer themselves, as it were, to the Western Allied as against Russia. They might even be able to stage a Putsch in the reduit which Kesselring would back. Kesselring says he will have to withdraw into the reduit unless something like this happens.

The whole thing is interesting as information. Various indices cause me to believe that the emissary is sincere in what he says. He is in Kaltenbrunner's S.D.; he recently served on the Hungarian front [*Wilhelm Höttl?*].

He says that his group has lines to the Opposition <u>in</u> Austria, including the Austrian Communists who are <u>not</u> pro-Russian. (This sounds plausible – N.B. Austro-Marxist tradition). Kaltenbrunner has moved [*Karl*] Seitz to Bavaria so as half to liberate him and to make a gesture to the Social-Democrats.

He confirmed all that we (W.I.) have reported about the reduit where the Leib Standart (*sic*) S.S. are already stationed.

He stated that Kaltenbrunner's anti-communist programme in conjunction with the Anglo-Saxons has received positive encouragement from the Vatican.[63]

SYNOPSIS OF CHIEF [of MI 6] MESSAGES.

"General: Greek Charge, Paris, has reported statements made to him by the Secretary General of the French Foreign Office regarding France's attitude towards the San Francisco Conference (19/3[1945]). A Chinese Special Officer at Berne has received confidential information from a member of the French Embassy Staff confirming foreign rumours that Burckhardt has been entrusted by France with negotiations in Germany for the release of French Ps/W and political hostages. Himmler is said to have initiated this move by going through the Swiss Govt. a direct hint to de Gaulle who desires at San Francisco not to be tied by Allied engagements in regard to the unconditional surrender of Germany and the punishment of war-criminals."[64]

Generaloberst Heinz Guderian visited Himmler at Hohenlychen, and persuaded him to resign as Commander-in-Chief of Army Group Vistula:

> ... That same evening I proposed to Hitler that the overburdened Himmler be relieved of his command of Army Group Vistula and that in his stead Colonel-General Heinrici, at present in charge of First Panzer Army in the Carpathians, be appointed to succeed him. Hitler disliked the idea, but after a certain amount of grumbling finally agreed. Heinrici was appointed on 20th March.
>
> What could have induced a civilian like Himmler to insist on holding a military command? That he was totally ignorant of military matters was a matter of fact of which he, and indeed all of us, Hitler included, were well aware. So why did he do it? Apparently one of his motives was his measureless ambition. Above all he wanted to win a Knight's Cross.[65]

Tuesday, 20 March 1945

Events:

From a post-war interrogation of Generaloberst Heinz Guderian, describing a meeting with Himmler:

> PEACE FEELERS
>
> Due to the damage done to the railways, preparations for the attack in Hungary were lagging, and the unfavourable results of operations in the east and in the west had created a desperate situation. It seemed necessary to me to end the war immediately, in order to give the poor,

tormented people some chance of existence. Although aware of HITLER's thoughts on the subject, I explained the desperate situation at the front to Foreign Minister VON RIBBENTROP, begging him to take steps to bring about an armistice at least with the Western Powers. He coldly rejected my advice, emphasizing his loyalty to HITLER. Shortly thereafter, however, he made a vain attempt to deal with some personages in STOCKHOLM who were without sufficient influence. I then tried to win Admiral DOENITZ's support for ending the war, again without success. Finally, I got in touch with HIMMLER, who still maintained connections with foreign countries. I wanted him to act as mediator. On 20 Mar [*March 1945*] he stated that it was too early for such a step and that his unerring instincts made him feel that all would yet go well. It was unavoidable that HITLER should be informed of these dealings, and he issued a warning about commanders revealing the military situation to anyone.[66]

On 20 March 1945, Himmler telephoned SS-Obergruppenführer Karl Oberg, relieving him of his position as Commander of the Blocking and Catching Line (*Befehlshaber der Sperr-und Auffanglinie*) with Army Group Vistula. Oberg should now report to C-in-C West (Feldmarschall Kesselring) at Nauheim for a new position.[67]

Top secret Blitz teleprinter message from the Chief of Army Personnel Branch, Infantry General Burgdorf, to Army Group Vistula (sent 20 March 1945, 22:45 hours, received 21 March 1945, 01:10 hours):

The Führer has ordered:

With effect from 20 March 1945...Generaloberst Heinrici, Commander-in-Chief of Army Group Heinrici (1st Panzer Army) appointed to command Army Group Vistula.[68]

HSSPF Otto Winkelmann, in a post-war interrogation, reported:

Short meeting at the investiture of Hungarian Minister of War [Karoly] Beregfy with a German decoration by Himmler. 20 March 1945.[69]

Allied Intelligence source "TRUEFITT" report dated 27 March 1945:

1. Himmler was at Bregenz Gestapo Headquarters until March 20th, then left for an unknown destination. There has been feverish activity at this H.Q. lately.

...

3. The whole of the Bregenzerwald has been occupied by the Party. Himmler's family is at present residing at Kopfreben, in the villa Maund, the German ex-crown Prince's former shooting box (Illustrated post-card attached) [not included with this copy].

4. Fortification work is proceeding very slowly in this district, owing to lack of material and sabotage.

5. Very many new-comers are seen coming and going in the immediate neighbourhood of the Liechtenstein frontier.

6. Zuers and several adjoining localities are out of bounds and under strict surveillance.[70]

Letter from Felix Kersten to Himmler dated 20 March 1945:

I would like again to cordially thank you for your great courtesy, shown in the question of Jews and concentration camps. At the same time I would like to confirm our meetings and agreements in writing:

You declared yourself ready not to proceed with the orders of the Führer Adolf Hitler, for concentration camps to be blown up when the Allies approach the camps, and also to forbid the killing of prisoners.

2. You agreed that when the Allies approached concentration camps, white flags would be flown and the camp handed over in an orderly fashion

3. You agreed that from 6 March this year no more Jews would be shot and Jews would be treated like any other concentration camp prisoner.

4. You agreed that camps would no longer be evacuated, and prisoners would be left where they are for the moment.[71]

Wednesday, 21 March 1945

Military situation:

From war diary, WFStab, 22 March 1945: "Army Group Vistula: From Kolberg now only 800 soldiers taken away. The other 4,000 men were removed via rail, Organisation Todt etc…."[72]

Events:

Letter from Himmler (at Feld-Kommandostelle) to Felix Kersten, 21 March 1945:

Dear Mr Kersten,

First of all, with this letter I thank you for your visit. As always, at this time I appreciate that you came in friendship and for your great medical art.

In the long years of our acquaintance, we have talked about many issues and your attitude was always that of a doctor who wants the best for the individual and for humanity in general.

It will interest you, what has been achieved in the course of the last three months since last talked. In two trains, about 2,700 Jewish men, women and children have been brought to Switzerland.[73] This is a continuation of the path that my staff and I have consistently followed for many years, until the war and the onset of foolishness in the world made implementation impossible. You know that in the years 1936, 37, 38, 39 and 40 I had created an emigration organization and worked in a beneficial way with Jewish American associations. Two trains to Switzerland is a deliberate resumption of this beneficial program, despite the difficulties.

Lately, there are rumours from Bergen-Belsen prison-camp that a widespread typhus epidemic has broken out. I have urgently sent SS-hygienist Professor Dr Mrugowski (sic – Mrugowsky) with his staff. It often occurs, unfortunately, when people are transferred from the East that spotted typhus cases occur, despite controls by the best modern medical measures.

I am convinced that by excluding demagogy and appearance and our differences, despite bleeding wounds on all sides, wisdom and logic just as much as our powers, we all must want to help the human heart.

It goes without saying that I have done as I wanted in the past years, in good times and bad, and wish to share at the human level an examination of what is the right and generous decision.

With my best wishes to your honored dear wife, to your children, and especially to you.

For the sake of our ties,

Yours

H. Himmler.[74]

Letter from Dr Rudolf Brandt (Feld-Kommandostelle) to Felix Kersten at Gut Hartzwalde, 21 March 1945:

Dear Mr Kersten!

In regard to the note you gave me, let me assure you that individual wishes for orders of the Reichsführer-SS will be considered favourably. A final positive answer cannot be assured in the short time available before your departure. I will ensure that work on the various points is carried out as quickly as possible. I will advise you of the decisions taken by the Reichsführer-SS without delay.

Warm greetings,

Yours

R. Brandt.

SS-Standartenführer.[75]

Second letter from Dr Rudolf Brandt (Feld-Kommandostelle) to Felix Kersten, at Gut Hartzwalde, 21 March 1945:

Dear Mr Kersten!

I can happily advise you with news that the Reichsführer-SS intends to agree to the requests you made a few days ago.

As soon as the Norwegian painter Reidar Aulie, Princess Jean Sapieha, the Countess Ernest Fleurieu and the two Swedish subjects Heinrich and Alexander Bondy have been set free, I will let you know.

I ask that you be patient at minor delays due to the current situation. I will monitor what is happening.

At this time I can advise you that in the matter of Mr Theodor Steltzer, the issue of a pardon is being worked on.

I am, with friendly greetings,

Yours most obediently

R. Brandt.

SS-Standartenführer.[76]

Joseph Goebbels noted in his diary, 22 March 1945, that Himmler may be giving up his army command on the Vistula:

…and he should do so. Himmler's job, after all, was merely to plug a hole in the area of Army Group Vistula as best he could. Unfortunately he allowed himself to be diverted by the quest for military laurels, in which, however, he failed totally. He can only tarnish his good political reputation this way.[77]

Heinz Guderian, in his post-war memoirs, mentions a further meeting with Himmler in Berlin on 21 March 1945. Guderian found Himmler walking with Hitler in the Reich Chancellery garden. Hitler left Guderian with Himmler:

I told him bluntly what he had already known for a long time. 'The war can no longer be won. The only problem now is how quickly to put an end to the senseless slaughter and bombing. Apart from Ribbentrop you are the only man who still possesses contacts in neutral countries.

Since the Foreign Minister has proved reluctant to propose to Hitler that negotiations be begun, I must ask you to make use of your contacts and to go with me to Hitler and urge him that he arrange an armistice.' Himmler replied: 'My dear Colonel-General, it is still too early for that.' I said: 'I don't understand you. It is not now five minutes to twelve but five minutes past twelve. If we don't negotiate now we shall never be able to do so at all. Don't you realise how pitiful our situation has become?' Our conversation continued in this inconclusive vein for some time, but without result. There was nothing to be done with the man. He was afraid of Hitler.[78]

Heinz Lammerding, Chief of Staff Army Group Vistula, to the Ostministerium, for the attention of Professor von Mende, 21 March 1945:

1.) Preparations of an evasion headquarters (*Ausweichsquartiers*) for the Army Group [Vistula] Command Staff (*Oberkommando der Heeresgruppe*) requested following evacuation of the Eastern Camp at Wustrau on evening 22.3.

2.) Commander of Replacement Army [*Himmler*] informed of evacuation by Panzer Grenadier Replacement Regiment 3, sections under attack.

3.) Information about successful evacuation by 23.3. requested.[79]

Teleprinter message from the Gauleiter of Köln, Grohé, to Martin Bormann, requesting a decision by radio message about what should happen to the prisoners held in Siegburg prison, where a spotted typhus epidemic rages. There were 2,200 prisoners including 400 Germans and 1,800 French, Belgian and Dutch prisoners who had been given judicial prison sentences. About 70 Gestapo prisoners, members of a resistance movement who had not yet appeared before a court, were immediately shot.[80]

The former Gaupropaganda Leader Richard Ohling in a post-war statement:

What with the escalation of the war situation in the West, all wire and teleprinter connections failed when I got orders from Gauleiter Grohé to establish a radio station [*in Wiehl*] and connections with Reich authorities. When Köln was occupied, there was only a connection to Führer Headquarters and the Party Chancellery [*Bormann*]. It is known to me that Grohé sent an enquiry to Himmler, after prompting from the General State Prosecutor, about what should happen to the political prisoners at Siegburg prison. After the third enquiry Grohé received a reply from Himmler that under no circumstances should the prisoners fall alive into the hand of the enemy. In the presence of radio operator Wachtmeister Bertrams of Panzer Signals Dept. 26… I tore the message into shreds and burned it, without passing on the contents.

Three days later Bertrams presented me with a new message headed 'Führer Order' and signed by Bormann. This radio message was similar to the earlier mentioned secret decree of the Party Chancellery. He ordered the removal of all imprisoned political prisoners and any that could still be held. At the same time, this message ordered the hanging or shooting all those soldiers found in civilian clothes and without papers. The corpses should hang or remain laying with a placard saying: 'He refused to fight for his homeland'.

Ohling also destroyed this order.[81]

Chief radio operator Günther Bertrams from a post-war statement:

I received both radio messages after the Ruhr encirclement in March 1945. One radio message was signed by Himmler with instructions for the Gau leadership in Köln/Aachen that the inmates of Siegburg prison to be shot, especially the foreigners.

The other radio message, that I took down three days later, came as a 'Führer Order' and was signed by Bormann. He ordered the shooting or hanging of all political prisoners and those who refused to fight. The corpses should remain laying or hanging with a placard: 'He refused to fight for his homeland.'

The radio message signed by Bormann contained a footnote, the contents were to be shared with Gauleiters at Essen [*Schlessmann*], Düsseldorf [*Florian*], Westfalen-South Bochum [*Hoffmann*] and the HSSPF [*Gutenberger*]. This postscript was unique among all the radio messages received at Wiehl.[82]

Chinese intelligence report on de Gaulle–Himmler negotiations, sent by radio transmission on 21 March 1945, from Chinese Chargé in Berne to Chinese Foreign Office, Chungking. This message was intercepted and decrypted by Bletchley Park:

For the Minister. Report by Special Officer, Chu Pao-Hsien.

According to confidential information given by a member of the French Embassy Staff, the foreign rumours that Burkhardt has been entrusted by France with a request to visit Germany and negotiate with Himmler for the release of the French prisoners and political hostages are wholly in accordance with truth. It was Himmler who took the initiative by giving through the Swiss Government a direct hint to de Gaulle; neither the French Foreign Office nor the Embassy were used as a channel of communication. What is more, de Gaulle has not informed the United Nations authorities. His object is to confront them with a *fait accompli*, and then at the San Francisco conference he will not be tied by the allied engagements in regard to the unconditional surrender of Germany and punishment of war criminals.

The French Foreign Minister in view of de Gaulle's action, and in view of the fact that the agrément to Burckhardt's appointment as Ambassador to France is still under question, has shown extreme dissatisfaction. The Communist Party and others also will avail themselves of this affair to attack de Gaulle.[83]

Thursday, 22 March 1945

Military situation:

Generaloberst Gotthardt Heinrici replaced Himmler as Commander-in-Chief of Army Group Vistula on the Oder Front.

Himmler informed Heinrici in his Feldkommandostelle 'Birkenhain, near Prenzlau', he had taken steps via a neutral country to begin peace feelers with the West.[84]

Events:

Werner Grothmann, Interim Interrogation Report dated 13 June 1945:

22 March 1945 Reichsführer Himmler's Feldkommandostelle (field H.Q.) was established at Wustrau (between Fehrbellin and Neu-Strelitz). With him there were Grothmann, Oberst-Leutnant

Suchanek, Sturmbannführer Macher, Dr Brandt, Hauptsturmführer Meine (Dr Brandt's Referent), Oberstuurmführer Grieger (Ordonnanzoffizier), Oberstabsarzt Dr Müller and Major Vollmar.[85] Himmler's personal bodyguard – under Kriminalrat Kiermaier – was also in attendance.[86]

At 20:25 hrs, 27 March 1945, Sir Victor Mallet, British Ambassador to Sweden at Stockholm, sent Top Secret cypher message (No. 518, crossed out by hand, and 521 inserted) about Kersten's return from visiting Himmler to the Foreign Office, London:

Following is message which [Hillel] Storch wishes to be passed to the London offices of the Jewish Agency and the World Jewish Congress.

2. [Begins] Kersten returned March 22nd with letter from Himmler and related that Himmler promised to consider our desire kindly also prepared to release about 10,000 Jews to Sweden or Switzerland. I am invited together with Kersten to negotiations with Himmler and have been promised free conduct. The Swedish Foreign Office decided to permit the entry of 10,000 Jews, also assist with transport. The Swedish Foreign Office finds my journey important. Count Bernadotte who to-day departed Berlin to negotiate concerning interned 5,000 Danes, 8,000 Norwegians will also negotiate regarding our question but he also considered I must definitely go to Berlin. Kersten declared that he supposes Himmler wishes to procure alibi. This must be strictly confidential because Himmler declared that if this appears in the press and is interpreted as weakness on the part of Germany, he will take back his promise. Sending you these letters through British Legation here cable urgently your opinion. Our section undecided. Swedish Government prepared to permit entrance to Sweden intervened regarding release of about 8,000 [group undec. ? coming to] Palestine. Please contact Foreign Office London regarding intervention and handing over lists soonest through British legation Stockholm. [Ends].

3. You will see that as a result of conversations with the Swedish authorities Storch's scheme has now become much more precise.

4. I am keeping the United States Legation informed of all developments.

Foreign Office, London, replied to British Ambassador in Sweden, at 07:40 hrs, 6 April 1945, about his report:

Your telegram No. 518 [of 27th March: proposed release of Jews by Nazi Government]. We are not prepared to transmit this message since the proposal emanates from Himmler.

This advice was agreed by Foreign Minister, Anthony Eden, following correspondence with Prime Minister Churchill.[87]

Friday, 23 March 1945

Events:

German radio message from Himmler decrypted by Bletchley Park on 23 March 1945:

To HSSPF West, SS-Ogruf Gutenberger, Düsseldorf. Discussion recognizing assistance enabling the treks by foreigners. You are authorised to take any measures that serves the purpose of securing valuable products.[88]

Saturday, 24 March 1945

Military situation:
From the war diary of WFStab, 24 March 1945:

The huge offensive on the Rhine has begun via the Wesel, at the same time and in relation with an expected airborne landing. The enemy arrived with amphibious tanks and infantry via Rees and proceeded west along the eastern river bank at 22:00 hrs [23 March 1945]. Counter-attacks were unsuccessful. At 00:15 hrs they went south along the Wesel and fought across [the river] taking many villages and north-western suburbs of the town. At 09:05 hrs aircraft towing gliders crossed over Dünkirchen, at 10:20 hrs they had landed south of Bocholt.[89]

Events:
During the afternoon in Berlin SS-Ogruf Karl Wolff arrived at Fegelein's home and questioned by Himmler and Kaltenbrunner about his contacts with the Western powers, especially with US Intelligence Chief Allan W. Dulles, circumventing RSHA VI and Schellenberg. Wolff spoke about the possibility of an armistice in Italy.[90]

Palm Sunday, 25 March 1945

Military situation:
From the war diary of WFStab, 26 March 1945:

Churchill has seen the battles on the Wesel.... The area of C-in-C West [Kesselring] has again been extended.... General situation: After a Führer-Order all home forces should be thrown at the fronts: 'Westgoten' and 'Ostgoten' movements. The Reichsführer-SS has given up Army Group Vistula and will focus on resuming his civil duties. Tank forces were ordered to vigorously proceed against white towels were shown.[91]

Events:
German radio message decrypted by Bletchley Park on 25 March 1945:

To: Rf.SS, Feldkommandostelle.
Reichsführer!
Contents of your telephone call today, 12:50 hrs, was not understood.
Heil Hitler!
Yours Gutenberger, SS-Ogruf.[92]

Himmler orders Evacuation of 'semi-manufactured articles'.

Himmler to SS. Ogruf. Gutenberger, 25.3.45.
Dear Gutenberger,
I was unable to get through to you by telephone. I order you to press on with the following matters with the greatest energy.
        Heil Hitler.
        (sgd.) H.Himmler

(i) Intervene everywhere with ruthless severity. There must be no retreat. Signs of disintegration and softness are to be crushed.

(ii) Minister Speer will come tomorrow or the day after, to discuss with you the problem of transport by small vehicles (Kleintransportproblem).

(iii) I wish you to continue, as you have begun, to organise matters so that semi-manufactured articles (approx. 20,000 tons) are transported daily over the stretch of 100-120 km. which is blocked for traffic by the use of very small vehicles and by a system to relays, by juvenile labour and foreign workers etc. The smallest carts, horsed vehicles, hand carts and similar vehicles can be used for this. I suggest that the relay distances should be at most 10-15 km.[93]

During the afternoon of 25 March 1945, the Oberbürgermeister of Aachen was assassinated by a Werwolf unit. Joseph Goebbels noted in his diary:

It is good news that Oppenhoff, who was installed as Burgomaster in Aachen by the Anglo-Americans, was shot during the night Tuesday/Wednesday by three German partisans. I think the Vogelsang, the Burgomaster of Rheydt, will suffer the same fate in the next few days. Nevertheless I am not satisfied with the work of our Werwolf organisation. It is starting very slowly and it does not seem that there is adequate pressure behind it. At my next interview with the Führer I may well try to annex this organisation myself. I would impart more drive to it than it has at present.[94]

From a post-war interrogation of SS-Gruppenführer Wilhelm Harster (BdS Italien):

The last directive Source [Harster] had from Berlin was on the occasion of his visit to Thueringen with SS Obergruppenfuehrer Wolff on 25 Mar 45 when Schellenberg and Kaltenbrunner told them that they were not to carry on any negotiations with the Allies as any peace proposals must be considered on 'all- fronts' basis.

Source pointed out that if the front was to collapse at Bologna, there would be nothing to prevent the Allies occupying the whole of N Italy, as the R[iver] Po offered no military obstacle.[95]

Monday, 26 March 1945

Military situation:

From the war diary of WFStab:

Army Group Süd: north of Lake Balaton (Plattensee) its forces have fallen back [to defend] half the Lake.... The West – Reich territory: From the south, attacks against Vienna and Wiener Neustadt the oil-producing area of Zistersdorf, serious damage to transport.[96]

Events:

The pocket diary of Martin Bormann, 26 March 1945:

12.30 Conversation with Luftwaffe-General Schuhmacher.
Afternoon Debate with General v. Hengl.[97]
Midday M.B. R [Rücksprache? – Conversation] with RFSS.[98]

Karl-Otto Sauer in a post-war interrogation:

24-26 March 1945. Various personal and individual meetings with the Führer together with Messerschmidt, Sauckel, Bormann, Kneemeyer, Kammler on the subject of intensified power of the 262 [*new Messerschmitt jet fighter aircraft*].

...

26 March 1945. Personal information of the Führer to Göring and myself, that he had decided on Kammler for the 262 [*production*].[99]

Allan W. Dulles, from his memoirs:

After lunch [*26 March 1945*], Kaltenbrunner and Wolff drove back to Berlin. Harster was to return to Verona by car. That evening in Berlin, Wolff phoned Himmler that he had returned and was ready to report to him. Himmler was angry because Wolff had got back so late. Hitler had just ordered Himmler to leave at once for Hungary to stiffen the German resistance there. He had to catch the night train for Vienna and had no time to see Wolff. His orders to Wolff were to keep the door open to me, but not to go to Switzerland again himself.

It was after Himmler's return from Hungary that he called Wolff in Fasano and told him he had taken Wolff's family under his protection and had forbidden him any visits to Switzerland....[100]

Tuesday, 27 March 1945

Events:

From the diary of Joseph Goebbels, 28 March 1945, about a midday meeting in Reich Chancellery, Berlin, with Hitler:

...in Hungary. There we are possibly running the risk of losing our vital oilfield. Our SS formations have put up a wretched show in this area. Even the Leibstandarte is no longer the old Leibstandarte since its officer material and men have been killed off. The Leibstandarte bears its honorary title in name only. The Führer has nevertheless decoded to make an example of the SS formations. He has commissioned Himmler to fly to Hungary to remove their armbands. This will, of course, be the greatest imaginable disgrace for Sepp Dietrich.[101]

27 March 1945, Top Secret order of the Führer (also signed by Speer and Göring: "Subject: Jet aircraft." placing Kammler in complete command of jet aircraft development and production.[102]

Albert Speer, from his memoirs about events in the evening:

In the meantime Hitler had issued orders that SS Gruppenführer Kammler, already responsible for the rocket weapons, was to be in charge of the development and production of all modern aircraft. Thus I had lost my jurisdiction over air armaments. What was more, since Kammler could employ my own assistants in the Ministry, an impossible organizational and bureaucratic snarl had been created. In addition, Hitler has explicitly commanded that Goering and I accept our subordination to Kammler by countersigning the decree.[103]

Karl-Otto Saur in a post-war interrogation:

27 March 1945. Führer gives sweeping powers (Führervollmacht) to Kammler.[104]

OKW report to AOK 19, 27 March 194[5]:

In a report by the Special Plenipotentiary (Sonderbeauftragten) of the head of the Party Chancellery [Bormann], in relation to the behaviour of the German civilian population in the west, included: 'Against the hanging out of white cloth and similar appearances, providing openings for tank spearheads not manned by the Volkssturm etc., these must be addressed by draconian measures. From memory these measures could be negative in operation, not by the Party and not by the powers taken over by the Exekutive, these measures must be implemented by the Wehrmacht. I could imagine, after talking with Party comrades from the West that, for example, houses from which white flags are flown are immediately burned down and all male persons of the household shot.

Reichsführer-SS…will be asked to take police measures to prevent parts of the population raising white flags, and hinder sabotage of fortification equipment'.[105]

German radio message decrypted by Bletchley Park on 27 March 1945, taken at 18:30 hours:

To: SS-Gruf Behrend (sic – SS-Gruf. Dr Hermann Behrends).

Rf.SS is in agreement of publication of your orders for taking over the Latvian Order Police (lettischen Orpo) by the General Secretary, Interior Administration of the Latvian National Committee.

From: (signed) Grothmann.[106]

Wednesday, 28 March 1945

Military situation:

Himmler visited Army Group South in Eisenstadt, Austria. Individual meetings with Infantry general Otto Wöhler (C-in-C Army Group South), Panzer General Hermann Balck (Army Group Balck), SS-Ogruf. Sepp Dietrich (6th SS-Panzer Army) and SS-Staf. Jochen Peiper.[107]

Events:

Notes of C-in-C Army Group South: Points for discussion with Reichsführer-SS.[108]

Radio message decrypted by Bletchley Park on 28 March 1945, taken at 11:30 hours:

To: HSSPF Königsberg.

To pick up the awards quota for 20.4.45, I request a courier be sent immediately to Personal Staff Rf.SS, Berlin-Wilmersdorf, Kaiserallee 35.

From: Rf.SS Adjutant's Office.[109]

Radio message decrypted by Bletchley Park on 28 March 1945, regarded as Top Secret Ultra, and part of the daily intelligence briefing for Prime Minister Churchill:

To: C-in-C West, Chief QM/V

From: Army Group H, Chief QM/V (signed Oberst Rasch)

Ref. C-in-C West, Dept V (III) No. 30279 of 23/3.

Army corps ZBV has urgently requested release of its own repaired lorries from the M.T. Repair Park having regard to the present special task. The lorries are marked WL but are subordinated to the sphere of command of the Reichsfuehrer SS. Answer requested.[110]

Top Secret report dated 28 March 1945, possibly from S.O.E., to Anthony Haigh, Foreign Office, London:

I give you below the text of a message received last night from Denmark. The originator of the message is a Danish army officer who usually specialises in military intelligence.

'I have knowledge of three German peace feelers via Stockholm, the Pope and the Swiss Ambassador in Berlin. After the rejections Himmler has hinted that the (demand for) the deposition of Hitler was not an obstacle to an understanding even on the basis of capitulation but Himmler to remain, at all events for a time on the grounds that Himmler represents (? the German nation) and can prevent chaos on capitulation. Orders for occasion requested.

Please acknowledge receipt before 1st April.'

Perhaps we might discuss this when I come to see you tomorrow. Are we to pass it to S.I.S.?[111]

Chinese diplomatic radio message decrypted by Bletchley Park on 28 March 1945, regarded as Top Secret, and included in daily intelligence briefing for Prime Minister Churchill:

To: Foreign Office, Chungking.

From: Chinese Chargé, Berne [Switzerland]

For the Minister. I learn that the German Führer is now at Berchtesgaden holding a conference with the most important German military and administrative officials.

It is said that the German minister in Switzerland, who is very deep in the councils of the Nazi Party, suddenly and secretly returned to Germany to attend this conference.

The internal situation in Germany is such that she is on the point of plunging headlong into ruin.

To-day at the meeting of heads of allied missions here all the Ministers recognised that at no distant date there will be a great revolution.

As regards the question of the treatment of the military and civil prisoners of various nationalities in Germany, I hear that the Fuehrer still advocates severe measures but that Himmler has recently suddenly begun to advocate leniency, hoping to placate the United Nations. The conflict of opinion between the two is intense.

(signed) Jen Shi'-Hsin.[112]

Thursday, 29 March 1945

Events:

Oberst Brandstädter, Chief of Staff 19th Army, circulated an order of Reichsführers-SS about the behaviour of the German civilian population in the west:

1. At this stage of the war only the stubborn unyielding will can persevere.

2. Take drastic measures against the hanging out of white towels, any openings for tank spearheads not manned by the Volkssturm and any other happenings.

3. From any house displaying a white flag, all male persons are to be shot. Do not hesitate in taking these measures.

(Additional clause for HSSPF, SS-Obergruppenführer Otto Hofmann:
Responsible male inhabitants from the age of 14 years upwards should apply.)[113]

Jürgen Stroop reported:
When I returned from this official trip which lasted for several days the report was made to me at my headquarters that the Reichsfuehrer SS with a special train had also come to Wiesbaden, in order to stay there overnight... As long as I was the Higher SS and Police Leader that was the only time that the Reichsfuehrer came to Wiesbaden and I was not in Wiesbaden.[114]

Good Friday, 30 March 1945

Military situation:
From the war diary of WFStab, 30 March 1945: Army Group Vistula: The [*Soviet*] occupation of Küstrin has been concluded; their strength is still not known.[115]

Joseph Goebbels wrote in his diary, 31 March 1945: "...One thousand men under von Reinefarth[116] from the garrison of Küstrin have fought their way back to our lines...".[117]

Events:
German police message decrypted by Bletchley Park on 30 March 1945, taken at 1909 hours (originally transmitted at 00:15 hours):
To: Rest.feldkdo. Stelle [*i.e. Himmler*].
Führer has authorized Fortress Commandant in Breslau, in his name, to award promotions of proven non-commissioned officers to officer rank. Request same permission for parts of the Waffen-SS to eliminate adverse treatment. Radio and written requests for promotions to SSFHA have gone without reply.
From: Ullmann, SS-Brigadeführer [*Police President of Breslau*].[118]

Count Folke Bernadotte, report on his activities in Germany:
It was on Good Friday, March 30th, that I was given the first opportunity to visit Neuengamme concentration camp, where several thousand Scandinavian prisoners had already been assembled by the Swedish Red Cross... I was the first representative of a neutral humanitarian organization to visit a concentration camp....[119]

Dr Rezsö Kasztner, reported on a meeting with Himmler in Vienna:
29. March (sic – probably 30 March).
Himmler sits in front next to the driver in an open Mercedes. He came to Vienna to discuss issues relating to the defence and evacuation of 'Fortress Vienna'. I accompanied Krumey to the

headquarters building of the SS-Commandant where the meeting was held. The conference ended at 5 p.m. During the meeting the head of the Gestapo Vienna asked Himmler, 'What is to happen to the Jews of Vienna and Lower Danube area?', 'Under no circumstances may they be touched.'

8 p.m., at the reception with Wisliczeny (*sic* – Wisliceny). He confirmed Himmler's statement regarding the Jews in Austria and promises to enforce his orders with the Camp Commandants in the Provinces – where the Jews are – in a timely manner.

At 10.30 p.m. I visited Dr [*Emil*] Tuchmann, to tell him the good news. For the Jews remaining in Vienna their worst nightmare was over. At this last moment they would be neither deported nor butchered.[120]

Baldur von Schirach testifying in his own defence before the International Military Tribunal, Nuremberg, on 24 May 1946:

Himmler came to Vienna towards the middle, or the end of March [*1945*] to talk to the Commander of Army Group South. On this occasion – the Commander of Army Group South was, of course, not stationed in Vienna, he had ordered all the Reichsstatthalter of the Ostmark up to Vienna and granted them full authority to enforce martial law in the future, since Vienna and some of the other Ostmark Gaue had by that time become almost front-line zones. At this conference Himmler told his adjutant to call Ziereis in, while the papers for full powers were being typed up in the next room. That is how I came to meet Ziereis for the second time in my life.

And now Himmler did not, as Marsalek said, tell Ziereis that the Jews were to be marched on foot from Southeast Wall to Mauthausen, but he did say something else which surprised me enormously. He said: 'I want the Jews now employed in industry to be taken by boat, or by bus if possible, under the most favourable food conditions and with medical care, *et cetera*, to Linz or Mauthausen.'

I do not quite remember whether he said they should be taken to Mauthausen, but he also said to Ziereis: 'Please take care of these Jews and treat them well; they are my most valuable assets.'

From this declaration... it became clear to me that with these instructions he was following certain foreign political intentions, in the last moments of the war, in emphasizing the excellent treatment of the Jews.

What Marsalek, therefore said about making them go on foot is not correct. As I have already mentioned, Himmler, under all circumstances, wanted the best possible treatment to be given to the Jews. I gained the impression – and later on it was confirmed by other things we heard – that he wished, at the last minute, to somehow redeem himself with this treatment of the Jews.[121]

On 30 March 1945, Gauleiter Baldur von Schirach declared a state of emergency in Vienna.[122]

A meeting at KL Mittelbau chaired by the Camp Commandant, SS-Stubaf. Richard Baer, discussed an order from Himmler calling for over 40,000 camp prisoners to be exterminated in the tunnels of Kohnstein.[123]

Saturday, 31 March 1945

Military situation:

From the war diary of WFStab, 31 March 1945: "Army Group Vistula: ... 1,000 men have returned from Küstrin. Their Commandant [*SS-Gruf. Heinz Lammerding*] has been detained and an investigation underway."[124]

Events:

Radio message decrypted by Bletchley Park on 31 March 1945, late afternoon, probably from SS-Ogruf. Gottlob Berger:

> Dear Comrade Martin [*SS-Ogruf. Dr Martin, HSSPF Main*].
>
> I spoke today with the Rf.SS and the Fuehrer regarding the question of Prisoners of war.
>
> The Fuehrer stressed most emphatically the American and English P.W. Officers and N.C.O.'s should under no circumstances fall into the hands of the enemy. They will be transported away to the South. Camps are for the time being not available (remainder torn away)....[125]

Joseph Goebbels wrote in his diary, 1 April 1945:

> I am now busy organising the Werwolf radio station. Slesina is to be placed in charge of it; he has considerable experience in this field from the Saar struggle. Prützmann has not got very far with his preparations for the Werwolf organisation. It seems to me that he is proceeding far too hesitantly over this work. He complains that people in the West German enemy-occupied districts are at present apathetic and are anti-Party. But this is no reason for the work to proceed so slowly. One must now go into it with the utmost energy. I think that a powerful impulse will be given to it by the propaganda to be distributed over the new Werwolf station.
>
> ...
>
> The withdrawal our troops from Küstrin did not take place as the Führer intended. On the Führer's orders Gruppenführer Reinefarth, who was commanding there, has been arrested by Himmler. It is said that he retreated without orders.[126]

First discussions on 31 March 1945 between Dr Hans E. Meyer, representative of the International Committee of the Red Cross, and Kaltenbrunner in Berlin:

> My first discussions with General Kaltenbrunner took place on 31 March 1945 in the Foreign Office, Berlin, together with Envoys [*Ludwig Adolf*] Windecker and Schmidt of the Foreign Office and a SS-Sturmbannführer. These negotiations led to the release of French, Belgian and Dutch women prisoners from Ravensbrück concentration camp. My wish that Jews from Theresienstadt or Bergen-Belsen be taken to Switzerland could not be met for the time being, however, a visit was promised to Theresienstadt camp (confirmed by a note from the Foreign Office to the Berlin delegation of the ICRC) and supplying the camp with food and medical aid and approval of removing prisoners by the same transport that brought the supplies.[127]

End March 1945, date unclear

Franz Ziereis, commandant of Mauthausen concentration camp, in his post-war statement whilst dying. In this statement the events below took place 7-8 weeks prior to 22 May 1945 which place them at the end of March 1945, Ziereis states:

> In the presence of Baldur von Schirach, Gauleiter Reiner (*sic*), Dr Ueberreiter, Dr Juri (*sic*), I received the following order from Reichsfuehrer Himmler: The Jews who were working on the South East Wall fortifications must be put on the march from all places of the South East Border of the Ostmark after finishing their work; their destination was to be Mauthausen. According to

Himmler's order, 60,000 Jews were to come to Mauthausen. In point of fact only a fraction of this number arrived. As an example I mention a transport which left with 4,500 Jews but which arrived with 180. It is unknown to me from which place the transport originated. Women and children had no shoes – they were covered with rags and had lice. In this transport there were whole families and innumerable persons were shot on the way because of general bodily weakness.[128]

In a second statement dated 24 May 1945, Franz Ziereis reported:

In the presence of Gauleiter Rainer, Dr Uiberreiter, Dr Jury, Baldur von Schirach and others, I received the following order from the RFSS: Jews from all the 'South East' building sites must move out and travel on foot with the aim of reaching Mauthausen! 60,000 Jews to arrive at Mauthausen. But only a fraction arrived. I quote an example: a transport of 4,500 Jews arrived with only 180. I do not know where it came it from. Women and children dressed in rags without shoes, with lice. There were whole families on the transport. Many were shot on the way due to weakness. At this point, Ziereis spoke with mock indignation: 'These are the consequences of such orders.'

During the movement of 5,000 Jews from the tented camp at Mauthausen to Munzhausen camp, no less than 800 were killed, and counted on the short 4 kilometers, Mauthausen Camp–Mauthausen railway bridge. Several trucks were used to pick up the corpses. (The entire population of Mauthausen village witnessed this mass shooting.)[129]

Gauleiter Siegfried Uiberreither stated that the meeting of Himmler with the Gauleiters and the commandant of KL Mauthausen, Franz Ziereis, took place on 28 March 1945. Uiberreither himself wanted to inform the responsible District Leaders (*Kreisleiters*) of orders for an 'orderly' retreat. The west Hungarian camps had already been evacuated by 23 March 1945.

On 5 March 1946, Lord Schuster of Allied Commission for Austria (British Element), questioned Uiberreither about responsibility for the murder of 7,000 Hungarian Jews during April 1945 in southern Austria:[130]

Himmler came to Vienna and spoke with the officers of Army Group South (*Heeresgruppe Süd*). Afterwards he had a meeting in Vienna with the Gauleiters based in Austria: von Schirach, Rainer, Uiberreither, Jury and possibly Eigruber. Himmler passed on to them their summary powers. Also present was the commandant to KL Mauthausen, SS-Staf. Ziereis. Himmler wanted the return of 60,000 Jews from the South-East-Wall (*Südostwall* fortifications) from the Vienna area to Mauthausen.[131]

From a post-war interrogation of Heinz Macher:

In March 1945 Macher received an order from Grothmann to go to Wittenberg to the works of WASAG where he met Dr von Holt. Macher was accompanied by his driver, Ehm. The purpose of the visit was to enquire about the delivery of explosives and a type of hand grenade with special percussion fuse.[132]

SS-Hauptsturmführer Heinz Macher on the late evening of Good Friday [?] was ordered to attend the Commander of the Army Group [*Himmler*], whose headquarters could be found in Prenzlau near Stettin. There, Himmler ordered Macher personally to blow-up the Wewelsburg.[133]

April 1945

United Nations War Crimes Commission: List of German War Criminals holding key positions, List No. 7, April 1945: Reichsfuehrer SS Heinrich Himmler, listed alphabetically, at No. 140. Wanted for:

"Atrocities in Concentration Camps. Gestapo atrocities. Mass murders of Jews. Confiscations, evictions, denationalization. Illtreatment of foreign workers."[1]

Easter Sunday, 1 April 1945

Events:

Information given to Allen Dulles on 2 April 1945 by Baron Luigi Parilli in the presence of Max Waibel and Max Husmann (Swiss army officers):

Himmler had telephoned Wolff early on Easter Sunday morning. He had found out that Wolff had moved his family south of the Brenner Pass into an area which was under his own command. Himmler had moved them back into Austria [*Salzburg*], and had said, 'This was imprudent of you, and I have taken the liberty of correcting the situation. Your wife and your children are now under my protection.' This meant that Himmler was in a position to arrest and murder Wolff's wife and children if he chose to do so. Any man would hesitate to take action when facing such a threat.

Himmler then added that he was warning Wolff not to leave Italy; i.e. not to go to Switzerland.[2]

Peter Padfield, continued this episode:

Easter Sunday, 1 April, the day before Wolff was due back in Switzerland to continue his talks with Dulles, Lemnitzer and Airey, Himmler called him by telephone to tell him that his family was to remain at St Wolfgang; he had taken them under his personal protection, so Wolff remembered the conversation. His wife and boys had become hostages for his loyalty.[3]

During the afternoon, Himmler gave a speech in Reichsstatthalterei Hamburg before an audience of senior members of the Party, Government and Armed Forces. Among those present, Generalfeldmarschall Ernst Busch, Gauleiter and Reichsstatthalter Karl Kaufmann. Konstantin Bock von Wülfingen reported on the talk:

It is worth reporting the speech of the Reichsführer-SS of 1st April, who had nothing much to say to us other than victory was ours, since we could expect great hostility from the enemy camp because the U-boats were enjoying more and more success, and no doubt the morale and fighting spirit of German troops whose impact on the enemy cannot be stopped. He was in the presence of senior generals of the military districts and high officials of the State and

Party and spoke in detail about the construction of tank obstacles, employing the Volkssturm against tanks with their bazookas (*Panzerfaust*) and the like. His main statement was that no one should hang on to life, that we must become familiar with death. A familiarity with death was the soldier's first virtue.

No one present at this meeting told me of a belief in the explanations of the Reichsführer-SS, most people expressing disbelief that the Reichsführer-SS had dared to explain such things.[4]

From a post-war interrogation of HSSPF Otto Winkelmann:
After a telephone conversation with Himmler, he took charge of the Orpo in the South with the title CdO Sued Deutschland. This was confirmed later by a general order issued by Kaltenbrunner dtd [*dated*] 29 Apr.[5]

Radio message decrypted by Bletchley Park on 1 April 1945, taken at 19:35 hours:
To: Gauleiter Swabia [Karl Wahl], Augsburg.
Rf.SS has appointed HSSPF Ost, SS-Ogruf. Koppe, as Deputy HSSPF Süd, SS-Ogruf. Freiherr von Eberstein, who is presently ill. By order of the Rf.SS I request that you support SS-Ogruf. Koppe during his temporary assignment.
From: Chief, SS-Personalamt [*SS-Ogruf. von Herff*].[6]

Order issued 1 April 1945 (at 19:35 hours by teleprinter) from the head of the Party Chancellery, Martin Bormann, to all Reichsleiters, Gauleiters and Unit Commanders:
By command of our Führer, I order that:
The final hour to test us has arrived. The danger of a new enslavement facing our people requires a last and highest commitment. What now applies:
The fight against enemy invading the Reich is everywhere, intransigent and relentless. Gauleiters and Kreisleiters and other political leaders fighting in their Gau and Kreis, win or lose. Only a dirty coward would leave his Gau when attacked by the enemy without a written order of the Führer, who does not fight to his last breath. He will be treated as a deserter and outlawed. Raise your hearts and overcome all weakness. The only slogan now: win or lose.
Long live Germany. Long live Adolf Hitler.
(signed) M. Bormann.[7]

Easter Monday, 2 April 1945

Military situation:
The city of Vienna was declared a Defended Area.

Events:
Flight Lieutenant Ronald Seth, captured British intelligence agent of Special Operations Executive (SOE), claims he met Heinrich Himmler in Berlin.[8]

Telephone conversation between SS-Staf. Walter Schmidt, Police President of Weimar, and Himmler about the evacuation of Ohrdruf Camp:

...SS Colonel Schmidt, had left it up to the 'discretion' of SS-Captain Oldeburhuis (sic – SS-Hstuf. Gerret Oldeboershuis) Commandant of the Ohrdruf camp, to liquidate his convicts and political prisoners regarded as 'especially dangerous'.

Himmler, however, expressly ordered that nothing should happen to the Jews – a paradox that can be explained only by the curious expectations entertained by the top leadership of the SS on the international level....[9]

Bernadotte reported on his second meeting with a nervous and solemn Himmler, at Hohenlychen, in the presence of Walter Schellenberg. It lasted four hours as Himmler admitted Germany faced a critical but not "hopeless" situation:

On this occasion Schellenberg also gave me the information that Hitler had given orders that the concentration camps at Buchenwald, Bergen-Belsen and probably also Theresienstadt should be evacuated, and the prisoners compelled to cover a distance of about one-hundred-and-ninety miles [about 300 km] on foot...[10]

Cypher telegram No. 627 dated 13 April 1945, from Sir Victor Mallet, British Ambassador to Sweden at Stockholm, to Foreign Office, London:

Count Bernadotte today gave me in strict confidence some account of his interview with Himmler in Berlin last week which lasted for four hours.

2. Contrary to when Bernadotte saw him 3 weeks ago Himmler this time admitted that all was up. Bernadotte suggested the proper course was immediate surrender which would save innumerable lives. Himmler replied that he would favour this course but that Hitler refused to hear of it and he felt himself bound by his oath of loyalty to Hitler. Bernadotte suggested that his loyalty to the German people was more important but Himmler answered that he owed everything to the Fuehrer and could not desert him at the end. Himmler did not appear at all flustered but gave the impression of being completely sane and retaining his energy and organising ability. He even had time to interest himself in a book of runic inscriptions which apparently have always been a hobby of his. Himmler remarked that he knew that he was No. 1 on our list of war criminals. Bernadotte told him that it was only natural that he should be considered a war criminal because he was head of the Gestapo whose appalling cruelties had been proved... Himmler himself told him that he knew that outside Germany he was considered brutal but in fact he disliked cruelty and an entirely false picture of his character had been built up abroad. Bernadotte repeated that he must be judged by the actions of his subordinates. Himmler claimed that those acts were grossly exaggerated whereupon Bernadotte quoted to him specific and proved cases of murder by the Gestapo encluding (sic) the murder of 200 Jews in a certain hospital. Himmler denied that this murder had taken place but Bernadotte insisted and the next day when Himmler saw him again Himmler had the honesty to tell him that on making enquiries he regretted to state that the story turned out to be true. Himmler complained that he would have liked to have evacuated the Jews from Germany and actually arranged the deportation of 1200 to Switzerland and been arranged through him but unfortunately publication of the facts in the Swiss press had come to Hitler's notice and resulted in the Fuehrer giving strict orders against any repetition.

3. Schellenberg who is one of Himmler's principal assistants and believed by Bernadotte to be his intelligence officer was described by Bernadotte to me as a decent and humane man who

had been an immense help in arrangement for evacuation of Norwegian and Danish internees to Neuengamme camp. On the other hand Kaltenbrunner who is extremely powerful is universally regarded as the worst type of brute and murderer. Even Himmler appears to be afraid of him and instructed Schellenberg to warn Bernadotte that Kaltenbrunner was a most dangerous man and had made arrangements for tapping all telephones used by Bernadotte in Germany.[11]

Tuesday, 3 April 1945

Events:

Radio message decrypted by Bletchley Park on 3 April 1945:

> For personal attention RfSS. Top Secret. Reich Security.
>
> From: Concentration Camp Mauthausen, [*signed*] Ziereis.
>
> Subject: Evacuation of prisoners.
>
> From Vienna area 8,976 prisoners marching back to Mauthausen; 3,147 Jews arrived from Southeast area, 3,500 to follow. Report by [SS-] Staf. Becker (*sic* – Becher): extreme emergency by reason of surprise change in situation; otherwise turning out as planned in Vienna, that is, evacuation to take place.[12]

Order of Reichsführer-SS Heinrich Himmler to BdO Mainz [*SS-Brig. and Generalmajor der Polizei Walther Hille*] for operations of the Order Police in his area:

> 1. At this stage of the war, only a stubborn unyielding will can persevere.
>
> 2. Severe measures are to be taken against hanging out of white towels, opening of anti-tank traps, non-appearance of the Volkssturm and similar phenomena.
>
> 3. From any house which shows a white flag, all male inhabitants are to be shot. There will be no delay.[13]

BdO Hannover also distributed the same orders from the Reichsführer-SS to its regional Police offices.[14]

In his diary, Joseph Goebbels recorded that Hitler held a long discussion SS-Ogruf. Kammler in the Berlin Bunker. They discussed "the reform of the Luftwaffe" for which Kammler now had responsibility.[15]

Hitler ordered the V-weapons be armed with explosives.[16]

German radio message decrypted by Bletchley Park on 3 April 1945, taken at 22:15 hours:

> To: HSSPF SW (South West), SS-Brigf. Mueller, Stuttgart. Secret.
>
> Re your radio message today. Werwolf-Representative Rhein-Westmark, SS-Stubaf. [*Georg*] Best, via HSSPF in SS-Regional Headquarters South-West is to move for other work. Last headquarters HSSPF Rhein-Westmark, SS-Gruf. Stroop, [*at*] Göttingen-Dransfeld 231; possibly has changed.
>
> From: Office of Prützmann, I A [*SS-Ostubaf. Karl Tschierschky*][17]

Wednesday, 4 April 1945

Events:

Radio message decrypted by Bletchley Park on 4 April 1945; the message was originally transmitted at 01:10 hours and Bletchley Park intercepted a later transmission at 23:58 hours:

> To: [SS-] Gruf. Katzmann, Stutthof.
>
> 1. By exclusive order of OKH, 4th Army has taken over the entire remaining area from Nehrung to Stutthof. My area includes this and to Bodenwinkel. Meeting … at beginning of next week, previously unavailable…
>
> 2. [SS-] Ofhr. Stein placed under my command by order of Rf.SS. Request his immediate despatch.
>
> 3. Stutthof [*concentration camp*] placed under my command by order of Rf.SS.
>
> Bringing order to meeting.
>
> (signed) HSSPF [*Weichsel*], Hellwig.[18]

Anton Kaindl, Commandant of KL Sachsenhausen, met Himmler at Rheinsberg, Kreis Neuruppin, and suggested handing over the concentration camp to the International Red Cross. Himmler, however, rejected this.[19]

From a postwar interrogation of Otto Winkelmann:

> W/T [*wireless transmission*] order from Himmler to deploy police forces along existing straggler line, Drauberg-St Poelten-Krems-Bruenn (Brno), using 2 Gendarmerie Bn [Battalion] which had retreated from Hungary and had been assigned to Gen Balk's 6 Army and to 6 SS Pz Army.[20]

In Stockholm, Felix Kersten wrote to Hilel Storch, also in Stockholm, 4 April 1945:

> In reply to your letter of yesterday I can inform you as follows: I immediately contacted my secretary, Mrs Wacker, on the telephone… I have now received information from her that Dr Brandt, the personal adviser of Reichsführer-SS Himmler, has been in touch and informed that all rumours about a possible evacuation of Bergen-Belsen are untrue. On the basis of my detailed meetings with Mr Himmler about this camp he has promised me action, and I have shared this information with you. If it is necessary should the Allies approach Bergen-Belsen there will be orderly hand-over. Everything is being done to avoid unnecessary loss of life. It is the same with Theresienstadt concentration camp and others. Dr Brandt has expressly confirmed to my secretary in writing, that rigorous orders of the Reichsführer-SS have been issued. I believe that this should soothe your fears.
>
> It may interest you that Count Bernadotte, at my request, was earlier received by Himmler, and that Bernadotte has confirmed the promises made to me by the Reichsführer. Also, Dr Brandt has written to me about the attention being paid to Bergen-Belsen, and the letter will by brought by Bernadotte. I will let you know the contents as soon as I receive it.
>
> I take the opportunity to inform you that Mr Himmler is expecting our visit, again confirmed by Dr Brandt, that we will be well received and our protection is guaranteed.[21]

Top Secret telegram from the British Ambassador in Sweden, Sir Victor Mallet, to the Foreign Office, London, at 15:00 hrs:

It may not be without significance in this connexion that Storch (see my telegram No. 509) has received a message from Brandt [*Himmler's adjutant*] through Kersten's secretary in Berlin, that on April 2nd Hitler was set aside [*kalt gestellt*]. Message went on to say that scheme of releasing Jews under discussion should not go ahead without much difficulty.[22]

Postwar deposition by Dr Hans E. A. Meyer (International Committee of the Red Cross – ICRC) used in evidence at the International Military Tribunal, Nuremberg, on behalf of Kaltenbrunner:

> After negotiations in Berlin between General Kaltenbrunner, the Foreign Office and myself (on instructions of the ICRC) I was able on 4 April 1945 to bring 300 French women prisoners [*from Ravensbrück concentration camp*] to Switzerland. As a result further discussions about additional transports took place near the Swiss border.[23]

The President of the International Committee of the Red Cross, Prof. Carl Burckhardt, in evidence at the International Military Tribunal, Nuremberg, on behalf of Kaltenbrunner:

> Dr Meyer arrived in Switzerland on 9 April 1945 with 298 French women prisoners from Ravensbrück camp.[24]

The historian Jean-Claude Favez, commented on this prisoner release:

> On 5 April 1945, 299 French women and one Polish woman, prisoners from Ravensbrück arrived in Switzerland.[25]

Wednesday, 5 April 1945

Military situation:
As reported in the WFStab war diary: The Commander-in-Chief West [*Kesselring*] sent a new assignment. Schweinfurt and also the area around Nordhausen need to be kept safe, and SS-Gruppenführer Kammler charged with their defence.[26]

Events:
SS-Oberführer Hermann Pister in a postwar affidavit dated 2 July 1945: On 5 April 1945 he received a "Reichsführer-Order" [*Himmler*] that KL Buchenwald "reduce to minimum numbers".[27]

During the midday conference, Kaltenbrunner presented Hitler with the long-sought after diaries of the now imprisoned and former Abwehr chief, Admiral Wilhelm Canaris. Hitler ordered the immediate "extermination of the plotter".[28]

Top Secret letter dated 5 April 1945, from "Der Chef der Sicherheitspolizei und des SD", Berlin (signed SS-Gruf. Müller), to the Camp Commandant of Dachau, SS-Ostubaf. Weiter:

> On orders of the RfSS and after obtaining the decision of the highest authority the prisoners listed below are to be immediately admitted into KL Dachau:
> Former Generaloberst Halder
> > Former General Thomas
> > Hjalmar Schacht

Schuschnigg with wife and child

Former General v. Falkenhausen

the Englishman Best (Wolf)

Molotov's nephew Kokorin

Colonel, General Staff, v. Bonin

As I know, you have only restricted space in the camp prison [*Zellenbau*] but I ask that after examination you keep these prisoners together. However, please take steps with the prisoner Schuschnigg, who has the code-name Oyster, that he is registered under this name, is allotted a larger cell. His wife has shared his imprisonment of her own free will and is therefore not a protective custody prisoner. I request that she be allowed the same freedom she has hitherto enjoyed.

It is an instruction of the RfSS that Halder, Thomas, Schacht, Schuschnigg and v. Falkenhausen are well treated.

I request that on no account is the prisoner Best (code-name Wolf) to make contact with the Englishman Stevens who is already there.

v. Bonin was employed at Führer Headquarters and is now in a kind of honourable detention. He is still a Colonel on the Active List and expected to retain this status. I request that he be well treated.

The question of special protective custody prisoner 'Eller' [Georg Elser], has again been discussed at the highest level. The following direction [*of Hitler*] has been issued: During one of the next 'terror' attacks on Munich, or the area of Dachau, it will be alleged that 'Eller' was fatally killed. I request therefore, when such an occasion occurs to liquidate 'Eller' as discreetly as possible. I request that steps be taken to ensure very few people are involved, and must be specially pledged to silence. The notification then can be sent to me, worded as follows:

'On .... on the occasion of a 'terror' attack

on .... the protective custody prisoner 'Eller'

was fatally killed.'

After noting the contents of this letter, and after carrying out these orders, please destroy this letter.[29]

Radio message from Oranienburg (at 19:18 hrs) from SS-Gruf. Richard Glücks to Camp Commandant, KL Dachau:

By order of RF-SS [*Himmler*] from 5 April 1945 the experimental series of Prof. Schilling to be immediately broken off.[30]

Letter of Andre May and three other "prominent prisoners" to the Camp Commandant, KL Buchenwald, SS-Oberführer Pister:

We the undersigned have noted with great satisfaction the speech of the Camp Commandant [Pister] to our German fellow prisoners. At the same time, we take the liberty of speaking on behalf of the prisoners who belong to our own nationality:

During the entire period of our imprisonment we consider that you, the Commandant, have carried out your difficult task towards the prisoners in a faithful, soldierly and correct fashion. We thank you for this.

At the same time we would like to say that inspite of the understandably extreme nervousness of the prisoners[,] order and discipline are being maintained, even among the unreliable elements who are ready to listen to rumours.

We should therefore be very grateful to you, the Commandant, if you would now as in the past support our combined efforts to maintain order.

Finally we would state that in the event of our being fortunate to return home we are prepared to express our thanks for your faithful administration of Buchenwald Concentration Camp, for the benefit of the German people[,] the authorities and the public press in our countries.[31]

Friday, 6 April 1945

Events:

Radio message decrypted by Bletchley Park on 6 April 1945, taken at 01:45 hours:

To: SS. Standartenfhr. Ziereis [KL Mauthausen].

Secret Reich Matter. Radio message of 4.4.45 received.

In any case the return of prisoners. Report continually

From: (signed) H. Himmler. Tgb. Nr. 3184/45, Top Secret.[32]

At 13:30 hours Reich Minister Albert Speer had lunch with Himmler.[33]

About 15:00 hours the daily Führer Conference, in the Bunker of the Reich Chancellery. Among those present, Göring, Keitel, Burgdorf, Jodl, Winter, Krebs, Himmler, Bormann and Heinrici (commander, Army Group Vistula, who gave a presentation).

Göring: "My Führer, I put 100,000 men of the Luftwaffe at your disposal for the Oder Front. In a few days they will be at the Oder."

Himmler: "My Führer, I will provide 52,000 fighters for the Eastern front."

Hitler to Heinrici: "There are 152,000 men. They are 10 Divisions. There you have the reserves you wanted.

Heinrici: "Numerically, perhaps, but unfortunately not Divisions, but only men who have no training and no experience in ground attack and have never faced the Russians."[34]

Himmler appointed SS-Staf. Kurt Becher as "Reich Special Kommissar" [*Reichssonderkommissar*] for the camps.[35]

Radio message decrypted by Bletchley Park on 6 April 1045, taken at 02:50 hours:

To: HSSPF Hungary, SS Obergruppenfhr. Winkelmann.

Obergruppenfhr.! The Rf.SS has assigned me a new special task [*Sonderauftrag*]… I will begin my journey from here tomorrow morning and report to you in Spitz.

Heil Hitler, Obergruppenfhr.!

From (signed) Becher, SS Staf.[36]

In his report, Dr Rezsö Kasztner noted:

6.April. In an ancient castle above Spitz on the Danube, I was received by Becher. Krumey was also present.

'Now you should know,' said Becher: 'Your "big picture" has come. I now come from Himmler.' I presented a comprehensive proposal to improve the treatment of Jews as well as all political prisoners in the terms of our previous discussions. 'Himmler has accepted my proposal and appointed me as Reich Special Kommissar for the affairs of Jewish and political prisoners. With you and Krumey I want to visit all the larger concentration camps and ensure the necessary measures are in place. After the first tour we want to go the Swiss border and discuss the matter further with McClelland.'

Becher showed me the order signed by Himmler, that said as follows:

To: SS-Standartenführer Kurt Becher.

'Given the difficult sanitary and housing situation I appoint you Reich Special Kommissar for all concentration camps.'

Himmler explained that the re-organization of the concentration camp system in the 'human spirit' should proceed cautiously. He stressed that he waived any financial contribution on the part of the Jews or the Allies. What had so far been paid by us will be either repaid by the Economics Ministry or charged against improving the supplies to concentration camp inmates.

The Reichsführer will personally confirm this.[37]

Radio message decrypted by Bletchley Park on 6 April 1945:

Top Secret! The radio stations and arrangements … offices as well are away from the tasks … Rf.SS SB 2 will contact offices due to their signals operations. All offices are to give their utmost support to their commanders.[38]

Radio message decrypted by Bletchley Park on 6 April 1945:

To: HSSPF Main [Benno Martin]
From: SS-Hauptamt [Gottlob Berger]
Ref: w/t message PZ OEW No 61 of 5.4.45.

'BLITZ' wireless message of 5.4.45 not received. If the prisoners are from a special camp, they are to be taken to Flossenburg on the orders of the Rf.SS. For this purpose use the cells which became vacant as a result of the 'Anti-Kharkov' operation, as arranged with Roman 4 [RSHA IV]. If supervision is really difficult, your proposal also will be accepted. Good treatment – no 'special treatment' [S.B.].[39]

Radio message decrypted by Bletchley Park on 6 April 1945:

To: HSS PF Nordost, for attention SS-Gruf. Hellwig, Königsberg, Pillau.

1) Frontier known.

2) STEUV (sic – STEIN) has been heading towards the Reich for 3 days. Reports to Chief of Orpo [Order Police].

3) I know nothing of an order from Rf.SS concerning Stutthof. Owing to reduction in number of concentration camp prisoners, a large part of the camp personnel was sent off by me today after arrangements with the army. Adequate supervision established. The exact numbers will be reported to you in due course.

From: (signed) Katzmann.[40]

Telegram from Commandant KL Buchenwald, Pister, to WVHA Department D, Oranienburg, 22:00 hours:

> RF-SS via KdS Weimar [*Hans-Helmut Wolff*] has ordered removal of prisoners towards Flo.
> [*Flossenbürg*] and reduce numbers in the camp.
> Daily number leaving will be reported.
> How many should be sent off?
> Current camp strength 48,000.[41]

Radio message decrypted by Bletchley Park on 6 April 1945, taken at 23:15 hours:

> To: KdS, with request to be forwarded to ZFT Fuerstenberg/Mecklenburg.
> Order of Rf.SS for Buchenwald to be reduced. Pister understands, local and area police authorities instructed with movement directions. Target: Flossenbürg. Automobile prepared for Dr Thost with special guest [*probably Churchill's cousin, Major John Dodge*] to KdS Regensburg. As far as possible, instructions carried out.
> From KdS and SD Thüringen.[42]

Radio message decrypted by Bletchley Park on 6 April 1945, taken at 23:56 hours:

> Secret! To: SS-Training Course Volkswagen-Werk.
> Reichsführer has ordered the current situation in Wehrkreis Rhein requires graded unit leadership. At my command, all orders and directives to all offices and units in the area of HSSPF Nordsee will now be immediately issued from Main Departments of SSPF Nordsee. It is my sole responsibility for the correct implementation of all orders. All offices are instructed to execute only those orders issued by the Main Departments if they are re-directed via my office.
> From: (signed) Graf von Bassewitz Behr.[43]

Saturday, 7 April 1945

Events:

Radio message decrypted by Bletchley Park on 7 April 1945, taken at 03:50 hours:

> To: SS-Ogruf. Winkelmann, HSSPF Ungarn.
> Top Secret.
> Subject: Radio message of 3.4.45, Nr. 5.
> Do not constantly ask for orders, but act.
> Your activities are still too little to see.
> (signed) H. Himmler.[44]

Radio message decrypted by Bletchley Park on 7 April 1945, taken at 08:50 hours:

> To: HSSPF and SS-Oberabschnitt in Riga [*Behrends*], Demobilization Office [*Abwicklungsstelle*] Vienna, Parkring;
> HSSPF Hungary, Budapest [*Winkelmann*];
> HSSPF Donau, Vienna [*Schimana*];

HSSPF Ostsee, Stettin [*Mazuw*];
HSSPF Nordost, Königsberg [*Hellwig*];
HSSPF Südost, Breslau [*Hildebrandt*];
HSSPF Alpenland, Salzburg [*Rösener*].
Top Secret.
The radio stations and arrangements, and other offices, apart their usual tasks, are urgently needed for the special tasks of the Special Plenipotentiary Rf.SS [*Sonderaufgaben des Sonderbevollmächtigen Rf.SS – i.e. SS-Staf. Kurt Becher*].
SS-Ostubaf. Schmidt and Major Boch, of Supply Staff Rf.SS SB 2, will liaise with all necessary offices due to their signals demands. All offices are to give their utmost support to their commanders.
From: (signed) H. Himmler.[45]

Radio message, 7 April 1945, from SS-Gruf. Richard Glücks to Commandant, KL Buchenwald, transmitted at 11:50 hours:

Only about 20,000 prisoners in the other remaining camps can be transferred. The larger part, up to 15,000 men, to Dachau. The rest, 20,000, to Flossenbürg.
A further transfer is not possible as the remaining camps are overcrowded.[46]

Schellenberg claims acting on behalf of Himmler on 7 April: Although Himmler was unwilling to accede to the plan outlined above [*the evacuation of KZs*] he nevertheless agreed to Musy's proposal that no further camps, which in view of the rapidly deteriorating military situation could be expected to be overrun, should not be evacuated. In coming to this decision Himmler was also greatly influenced by Kersten who had continually urged him from Stockholm to take this course.

On 7 April 1945, Schellenberg informed Musy that it was Himmler's express wish that this decision should be transmitted without delay to General Eisenhower. That same day Musy started back for Switzerland and three or four days later informed Schellenberg that Washington had received the report and reacted favourably.[47]

Radio message, 7 April 1945, from Gottlob Berger to HSSPF Donau, Walter Schimana, in Vienna:

The 45,000 American P.O.W. at Gneixendorf (R 81) are by order of RF.SS to be despatched in a westerly direction.[48]

Radio message decrypted by Bletchley Park on 7 April 1945:

To: Rf.SS.
On receipt treat as Top Secret.
Subject: Regional operational boundaries of C-in-C South West [OB Südwest], C-in-C South East [OB Südost]. Reference: OKW West Qu. 2 OP Nr. 88532/45, Top Secret, Chiefs from 11.3.45 …

The developing situation in Croatian areas now requires, having regard to the above decree, a central command and by extension under C-in-C South West to include the existing C-in-C Southwest …. C-in-C South East still has seven severely depleted Divisions. In terms of service

C-in-C South West is somewhat older than the current C-in-C South East, and there is a danger that OKW placing C-in-C South East under C-in-C South West will fail …[signal lost] … and a new Army Group composed of new personnel under C-in-C South West, will then become a real C-in-C South. A quick clarification is now urgently required due to the tense situation.
From: HöSSPF Italy, SS-Obergruppenfhr. (signed) Wolff.
Diary No. 1253/45. Secret Army Matter. Secret![49]

Radio message decrypted by Bletchley Park on 7 April 1945, taken at 19:40 hours:
To: SS-Ogruf. Roesener, Laibach. Secret!
Immediately remove a Police Regiment as quickly as possible from Semmering. Its removal is extremely urgent. This takes precedence over other activities. Take over this task personally. Report immediately by return.
From: (signed) Himmler.[50]

Radio message decrypted by Bletchley Park on 7 April 1945, taken at 20:15 hours:
To SS-Ogruf. Winkelmann [HSSPF Hungary].
At this serious hour I expect from you a ruthless approach to eastern defences, drastic measures and organisation. You cannot wait for orders, you have only your human intelligence and belief in a concept of honour.
From: (signed) H. Himmler.[51]

Sunday, 8 April 1945

Events:
From the diary of Martin Bormann:
M.B. Discussion with Engineer Lesti (262) [Messerschmitt jet aircraft]
Military conference! Meeting of the Führer with Kaufmann and Feldm. Busch.[52]

Gauleiter Karl Kaufmann, from a postwar interrogation, when he visited the Reich Chancellery together with Generalfeldmarschall Ernst Busch:
At first Busch and I spoke personally with the Führer and Bormann. As we wanted to express our views about the difficult situation after about 5 minutes we were interrupted, and at the order of Hitler in came the military men (Jodl, Keitel, Dönitz, Himmler etc.). I told them that 680,000 women and children were in Hamburg and could not be evacuated and therefore could be no responsible defence of Hamburg. Hitler was very surly and declared that Hamburg must be defended and he did not wish a Gauleiter serve as Reich Defence Commissioner over several Gau regions. Therefore I would again be restricted to my old area of Hamburg. Then we were dismissed.[53]

Letter dated 8 April 1945 (Berlin) from Dr Rudolf Brandt to Felix Kersten:
Very dear Herr Kersten,
Further to my letter of 21.3.1945 unfortunately I still have no positive information. There are significant difficulties in establishing results as a result of the bombings and delays.

I can assure you that I continue to obtain the information with maximum speed from the competent authorities. I am sorry but I must ask that you be patient.

There is an interesting film about Theresienstadt. It is not to go unmentioned that in the Hungarian area occupied at the time by Germany alone some 350,000 Jews have been allowed back, about 80,000 to Budapest. This arrangement came about recently to eliminate the adverse comments about the forced marches.

Still, you will be interested to know that on direction of the Reichsführer-SS [*Himmler*] the International Red Cross has been given the opportunity to inspect conditions at Theresienstadt.

With friendly greetings,

Yours obediently,

R. Brandt.[54]

Joseph Goebbels in his diary:

Anglo-American journalists working in the occupied regions are giving vent to the view that the German people will never capitulate. Only Hitler, Himmler or Goebbels, they say, could conclude a peace with Germany's enemies and they are in no way prepared to do so unless this peace was in the interests of the German people.[55]

Letter dated 8 April 1945 from Major James MacLeod, War Office – London, to Commandant Pister, KL Buchenwald:

Commandant!

Transport are leaving Buchenwald. They are death-transports like the one from Ohrdruf.

The frightful tragedy of Ohrdruf must not be repeated. Dropped from the skies for special duties, we have observed over considerable distance the victims of the escorts and an agitated population with our own eyes.

Woe to Thuringia, and woe to those responsible in Buchenwald, if that is repeated. The time of Koch, the atrocious commandant has made the name of this camp horrible throughout the whole civilized world, would be repeated.

Much has been improved under your command. We know that. Like the whole country you may be in difficulties today for which you see no other way out than to send thousands of people away. Stop it! Stop it immediately!

Our tank commanders are now coming to make you account. You still have a chance![56]

Monday, 9 April 1945

Events:

Murder of Admiral Wilhelm Canaris, Dietrich Bonhoeffer and Major General Hans Oster at KL Flossenbürg.[57]

Radio message decrypted by Bletchley Park on 9 April 1945, taken at 04:30 hours:

To: SS-Ogruf Querner, HSSPF Mitte.

Letter received. Intervene wherever possible. Summon trustworthy officers and commanders and organise defence where you are able. You have full authority from me.

From: H. Himmler.[58]

Radio message decrypted by Bletchley Park on 9 April 1945, taken at 18:05 hours:

To: SA-Brigadeführer Fischer.

Request documents for the entire Steiermark [*southern Austria*] by courier as soon as possible, the RF.SS is forcing the issue.

From: SS-Hstuf. Meir. Secret![59]

Radio message decrypted by Bletchley Park on 9 April 1945, taken at 18:45 hours:

To: SS-Ogruf. Hoffmann, HSSPF Stuttgart. Secret.

Rf.SS agrees, that … [*words lost*] … will be used for building positions in the 24 Army Group [24 A.K.] area.

From: (signed) Grothmann, SS. Ostubaf.[60]

Radio message intercepted by Bletchley Park, regarded as Top Secret Ultra, part of the daily intelligence brief for Prime Minister Churchill:

On the 9th April an Obersturmbannfuehrer, in a letter to Himmler's headquarters, complaining of catastrophic conditions in Baden-Württemberg area, stated that units of the Foreign Office have begun to withdraw in numbers into the Lake Constance area so that they may save their skins by slipping across the Swiss frontier. Senior officers in Wehrkreis were described as nothing more than a Mothers' Union and they were complaining that they have had no orders for weeks. Full powers were requested to overcome difficulties created by divided responsibilities.[61]

Tuesday, 10 April 1945

Events:

Testimony of Walter Schellenberg before the International Military Tribunal at Nuremberg, 13 November 1945:

On the 10th of April 1945 when a certain Mr Musy [*son of the former Swiss President Musy*] visited me in Berlin, he told me that the concentration camp Buchenwald had actually been evacuated, which was contrary to assurances given him by Himmler. Thereupon I phoned on the one hand Himmler, and on the other hand I discussed this matter at lunch with Kaltenbrunner. Kaltenbrunner stated, however, that this was done on a directive of Hitler, and that this camp had to be evacuated on his order, and Group Leader [*SS-Gruppenführer*] Mueller added, 'You, Kaltenbrunner, told me already three or four days earlier that I should evacuated the Jews from this camp to the south.' Then Kaltenbrunner said, 'Yes, yes, that's correct. Besides, there is a general directive of Hitler to the effect that all camps should be evacuated, and that especially Jews should be regarded as hostages and be brought to the south.' Then he said, turning towards me, 'There are still enough people remaining in the camp so that you can console Mr Musy with that'.[62]

SS-Staf. Kurt Becher, as Plenipotentiary of the RFSS, visited Bergen-Belsen concentration camp.[63]

On this day (?), an order of RFSS for KL Bergen-Belsen to be surrendered to the Allies without a fight.[64]

Radio message decrypted by Bletchley Park on 10 April 1945, taken at 10:30 hours:

To: SS-FHA, for the attention of SS-Ogruf. Jüttner.

Rf.SS has charged with installing a holding-line on the Elbe, having a battle group of the Waffen-SS and given full powers. I am forced to rely on officers and NCOs of Signals Replacement Dept. IV, Stendal. Request approval.

From HSSPF Mitte.[65]

Radio message decrypted by Bletchley Park on 10 April 1945; from SS-Brigadeführer Generalmajor der Polizei Dr Eberhard Schöngarth, Commander of Security Police (BdS) Holland, addressee missing:

...150 men dropped, so far about 70 men captured. Armament consists of automatic rifles, machine pistols, MG's, light mortars, Panzerschreck hand grenades and light explosives. They belong to the S.A.S. Regiment 2 and 3. Took off from England. Groups have rations for 6 days. Troops consist partly of Frenchmen, partly of Canadians. Officers are English. P.O.W. states that their task is to make preparations for a larger air landing action in Assen...area for about 7000 men, who are waiting in England for order to take off. Air landing action is supposed to support operation of Southern Army. Captured French N.C.O. states that their task is to attack German troops in proportion to their own strength, so as to support Southern Army. Lack of troops precisely in Assen area is turning out disadvantageously. Application has been made to Rf SS for special treatment [i.e. *killing*] of the captured S.A.S. Troops. Armed Forces are inclined to treat them as P.O.W. According to agents reports, S.A.S. troops are supposed also to have task to perform acts of sabotage in area Groningen and Friesland.[66]

Wednesday, 11 April 1945

Events:

Radio message decrypted by Bletchley Park on 11 April, taken at 04:30 hours:

To: SS-Ogruf. Roesener, Laibach (Ljubljana);

SS-Ogruf. Hoefle, Laibach (Ljubljana); for information Gauleiter Rainer, Klagenfurt, and Gauleiter Uiberreither, Graz.   Secret!

Rf.SS has ordered that HSSPF Wehrkreis XVIII, SS-Ogruf. Roesener, is to be engaged exclusively in the defence of the eastern boundary of his area of authority. For this purpose, the Rf.SS has transferred all anti-partisan warfare and defence of Laibach to SS-Ogruf. Hoefle. SS-Ogruf. Hoefle will establish his headquarters in Laibach.

From: Kommandostab Rf.SS (signed) Rode.[67]

During the morning, SS-Staf Kurt Becher at the offices of SD Hamburg and sent his report on KL Bergen to Himmler; in return he received full powers from him that 'the whole area of Bergen-Belsen be promptly handed over to the English army.'[68]

Prisoner-of-war interrogation of Lt Col Eugen Sapper, Commanding Officer of 415 RR AA (Anti-Aircraft) Regiment, by First US Army:

Himmler. PW knows from reliable source that Himmler visited the Ruhr pocket on 11 April. He is supposed to have held conferences with high-ranking Party officials. PW knows that planes still arrived and left the pocket as late as 12 April. He himself forwarded a letter to his wife through one of these planes.[69]

At 15:15 hours American troops liberated Buchenwald concentration camp:
During the evening of 11 April [*1945*] American tanks had reached the [*River*] Elbe, the columns of the US 2nd Armoured Division slicing through German positions and startled defenders with immense speed. In the van of the tanks hurtling forward like cavalry, an American reconnaissance group driving at an astonishing pace swept into the suburbs of Magdeburg on the western bank of the Elbe, careering into terrified shopping crowds and jammed traffic....[70]

Rudolf Höss mentions the liberation of Buchenwald in his memoirs:
After the occupation of Buchenwald by the Americans, the prisoners armed themselves and plundered Weimar and committed rapes. This was reported to the Führer. Himmler was given orders that regardless of enemy advances all capable prisoners in concentration camps and labour camps would be evacuated.[71]

Thursday, 12 April 1945

Events:
Radio message intercepted by Bletchley Park on 12 April 1945, taken at 03:50 hours:
To: BdO Münster.
[Beginning missed] ... responsible German man, who breaches this natural national duty, loses his honour and life.
From: RfSS Reich Minister H. Himmler. Secret![72]

Chief OKW [*Keitel*], RFSS Himmler and Leader of the Party Chancellery [*Martin Bormann*], jointly signed the following order issued from OKW:
Locations at important traffic junctions. They must be defended at all costs without regard to threats or promises from peace negotiators or enemy radio broadcasts. Combat Commanders appointed in every city are personally responsible for compliance with this order. Contravention of their military duties, as with all civilian state officials who attempt to deter the Combat Commanders from performing their duties, will bring a sentence of death. Only OKW will determine exceptions to the defence of cities.[73]

A knowledge of this order is found in a postwar statement of Gauleiter Albert Hoffmann:
It is correct, that a short time later, as I recall in April, an order from Keitel, Bormann and Himmler calling for every village and every home to be defended.
To my knowledge, my Gau did not carry it out.[74]

Agreement between the Camp Commandant of Army Training Ground Bergen-Belsen and British troops for handing over the concentration camp.[75]

Friday, 13 April 1945

Events:

Himmler-Order reported in the *Hagener Zeitung*, 13 April 1945:

> The enemy attempts through deception to induce the surrender of German towns and pass
> them. Bruising encounters with armoured reconnaissance vehicles (*Panzerspähwagen*), threats
> of tank and artillery bombardment, intimidate the population when the locality is not turned
> over. By this stratagem, the enemy fails to achieve their objective.
>
> No German city is declared an open city. Every village and every town will be defended by all
> possible means. Any violation of this national duty and defensive responsibility by any German
> loses his honour and his life.[76]

From the war diary of WFStab, 13 April 1945:

> There is an order to keep the Harz. It is unclear from an apparent order of the Reichsführer-
> SS to the 11th Army [AOK 11] giving the opposite sense, that an officer brought over... The
> Reichsführer-SS in his capacity as Reich Interior Minister, has announced that no cities are
> declared open cities.[77]

Walter Schellenberg, as reported by Count Folke Bernadotte, believed Hitler was now
suffering from Parkinson's Disease (Paralysis Agitans). Schellenberg had consulted Professor
de Crinis of the Charité Hospital, Berlin, about this development then brought about a
meeting of de Crinis with Himmler and Reich Health Minister Conti:

> A few days later, it was April 13th, Himmler summoned me to his headquarters in Wustrow
> and took me for a walk in the forest, where he at last completely unburdened himself to me.
> 'Schellenberg,' he said, 'I don't think that we can let the Führer go on any longer. Do you believe
> that de Crinis was right?' I answered, 'Yes, it is true that it is two or three years since I met
> Hitler, but from what I can judge of his behaviour in recent times, I am convinced that it is high
> time for you to act.'
>
> But after a while Himmler's vacillation began again. It was clear that the breach between him
> and Hitler had commenced. Over and over he asked me what he could do...[78]

In Berlin, Minister Albert Speer held a meeting at 13:30 hrs with SS-Gruf Dr Kammler, they
did not meet again. Speer later reported on this meeting:

> .... For the first time in our four-year association, Kammler did not display his usual dash. On
> the contrary, he seemed insecure and slippery with his vague, obscure hints about why I should
> transfer to Munich with him. He said efforts were being made in the SS to get rid of the Führer.
> He himself, however, was planning to contact the Americans. In exchange for their guarantee
> of his freedom, he would offer them the entire technology of our jet planes, as well as the
> A-4 rocket and other important developments, including the transcontinental rocket. For this
> purpose, he was assembling all development experts in Upper Bavaria in order to hand them
> over to the Americans. He offered me the chance to participate in this operation, which would
> be sure to work out in my favor.[79]

From the diary of Alisah Sheck, about events at Theresienstadt:

13:00 hrs. The Danes have reached foreign shores. In the evening returned to the Jägerkaserne [*barrack block*]. Automobiles pick them up. It is like a bomb, this drunken mood gives rise to madness. 400 people, 400 young people.[80]

Himmler received information that the HöSSPF Italy SS-Ogruf. Wolff had negotiated in Switzerland with the U.S. Special Plenipotentiary Allen W. Dulles and thereby betrayed the Führer. That night Himmler made a speech, and urged Wolff to report to him immediately. Wolff replied by teleprinter message that he was otherwise engaged.[81]

In London, from the diary of Admiral Andrew B Cunningham:

During our interview the PM [*Churchill*] mentioned that Himmler appeared to be trying to show that he wasn't so bad as painted & PM said if it would save further expenditures of life he would be prepared to spare even Himmler. I suggested there were plenty of islands he could be sent to.[82]

Saturday, 14 April 1945

Events:

Extract from an order of Reichsführer-SS Himmler for Dachau and Flossenbürg concentration camps, in response to proposals from their Camp Commandants to transfer the camps into Allied hands:

On 14.4.1945.

There is no question of an hand-over.

The Camp is to be immediately evacuated.

No prisoner shall into the hands of the enemy alive.

The prisoners behaved atrociously against the civilian population at Buchenwald.

(signed) H. Himmler.[83]

Former commandant of Auschwitz, Rudolf Höss, described the problems the concentration camps faced in April 1945 when testifying before the International Military Tribunal at Nuremberg, 15 April 1945:

Let me explain. Originally there was an order from the Reichsfuehrer, according to which camps, in the event of the approach of the enemy or in case of air attacks, were to be surrendered to the enemy. Later on, due to the case of Buchenwald, which had been reported to the Fuehrer, there was – no, at the beginning of 1945, when various camps came within the operational sphere of the enemy, this order was withdrawn. The Reichsfuehrer ordered the Higher SS and Police Leaders, who in an emergency case were responsible for the security and safety of the camps, to decide themselves whether an evacuation or a surrender was appropriate.

Auschwitz and Gross Rosen were evacuated. Buchenwald was also to be evacuated, but then the order from the Reichsfuehrer came through to the effect that on principle no more camps were to be evacuated. Only prominent inmates and inmates who were not to fall into Allied hands under any circumstances were to be taken away to other camps. This also happened in the case of Buchenwald.

A young Heinrich Himmler with his older brother Gebhard. (*Fonthill Archive*)

Above left: A wartime portrait of Himmler wearing a field grey uniform. (*Fonthill Archive*)

Above right: A portrait of Himmler, probably 1939 or earlier, wearing a black uniform. (*Fonthill Archive*)

Himmler's staff officers

Above left: Werner Grothmann, Himmler's adjutant. (*Max Williams Archive*)

Above right: Paul Baumert. (*Bundesarchiv Berlin, BDC SSO*)

Below left: Dr Helmuth Fitzner. (*Bundesarchiv Berlin, BDC SSO*)

Below right: Dr Rudolf Brandt. (*Bundesarchiv Berlin, BDC SSO*)

Himmler's staff officers

Above left: Werner Grothmann. (*Bundesarchiv Berlin, BDC SSO*)

Above right: Hilmar Gutgesell. (*Bundesarchiv Berlin, BDC SSO*)

Below left: Heinrich Heckenstaller. (*Bundesarchiv Berlin, BDC SSO*)

Below right: Franz Müller-Darss. (*Bundesarchiv Berlin, BDC SSO*)

Above left: Heinz Macher. (*Bundesarchiv Berlin, BDC SSO*)

Above right: Himmler and Grothmann at Hegewaldheim headquarters. (*Max Williams Archive*)

Below left: At Birkenwald headquarters, Grothmann, Sepp Dietrich, Kiermaier. (*Max Williams Archive*)

Above left: Walter Schellenberg. (*Max Williams Archive*)

Above right: Ernst Kaltenbrunner. (*Max Williams Archive*)

Below left: Gottlob Berger. (*Max Williams Archive*)

Below right: Karl Wolff. (*Max Williams Archive*)

Above left: Udo von Woyrsch. (*Max Williams Archive*)

Above right: Otto Ohlendorf. (*Max Williams Archive*)

Below left: Hans Kammler. (*Private Collection, Germany*)

Below right: Joseph Goebbels, Minister of Propaganda. (*Max Williams Archive*)

Right: Josef "Sepp" Dietrich (*Fonthill Archive*)

Below: SS-WVHA chiefs: left to right—Glücks, Frank. Pohl, Lörner, Kammler. (*Max Williams Archive*)

Above left: Himmler presenting Hitler with a painting as a birthday gift. Karl Wolff and Sepp Dietrich standing in background. (*Fonthill Archive*)

Above right: General Rudolf Schmundt, Karl Wolff and Himmler, Wolfsschanze headquarters. Werner Grothmann standing in background. (*Fonthill Archive*)

Below: Martin Borman, General von Epp and Himmler. (*Fonthill Archive*)

Above: Himmler with his staff and SS-General Sepp Dietrich in France, 1944. (*Marc Rikmenspoel*)

Below: Himmler and his staff tasting food. (*Max Williams Archive*)

Above: Himmler visiting a Waffen-SS division. (*The Wiener Library, London*)

Below: Hitler and Himmler, Wolf's Lair meeting. (*Max Williams Archive*)

Above: Hitler and Himmler at an awards ceremony. (*Max Williams Archive*)

Below: Himmler wearing pistol, giving speech at Munich, 8-9 Nov 1944.
(*U.S. National Archives [Bayerische Staatsbibliothek]*)

Above: Himmler giving speech in East Prussia, 18 Oct 1944, to newly established Volkssturm. (*U.S. National Archives [Bayerische Staatsbibliothek]*)

Below: Himmler at an awards investiture, 5 January 1945. (*Max Williams Archive*)

Above: Tiefenbacher, Felix Kersten and Himmler. (*Max Williams Archive*)

Below left: Count Folke Bernadotte. (*Max Williams Archive*)

Below right: A modern photograph of Hohenlychen in derelict condition.

Above: Survivors at Auschwitz. (*The Daily Mirror*)

Below: Survivors at Buchenwald. (*Fonthill Archive*)

Above right: Berlin 16 March 1945, Goebbels awarding 16-year-old Willi Hübner with the Iron Cross 2nd Class. (*Fonthill Archive*)

Centre right: Hitler congratulating boy soldiers, Berlin April 1945. (*Fonthill Archive*)

Below right: Hitler's Berlin Bunker, May 1945. A Russian soldier gives British troops a view of the ruins. (*Fonthill Archive*)

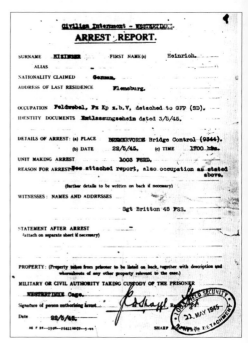

Above left: Werner Grothmann in postwar captivity, 1945. (*Ian Sayer Archive*)

Above right: Arrest Report of Heinrich Himmler using alias Heinrich Hizinger. (*The National Archives*)

Below left: Himmler's body following his suicide. (*Fonthill Archive*)

Below right: Himmler death mask.

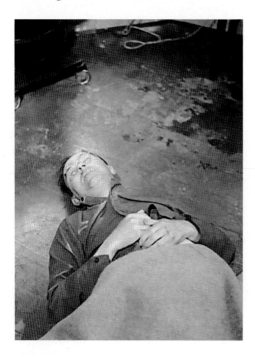

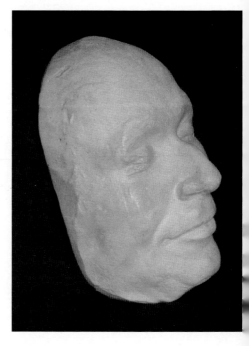

After Buchenwald had been occupied, it was reported to the Fuehrer that internees had armed themselves and were carrying out plundering in the town of Weimar. This caused the Fuehrer to give the strictest order to Himmler to the effect that in the future no more camps were to fall into the hands of the enemy, and that no internees capable of marching would be left behind in any camp.

This was shortly before the end of the war, and shortly before northern and southern Germany were cut. I shall speak about the Sachsenhausen camp. The Gestapo chief, Gruppenfuehrer Muller, called me in the evening and told me that the Reichsfuehrer had ordered that the camp at Sachsenhausen was to be evacuated at once. I pointed out to Gruppenfuehrer Muller what that would mean. Sachsenhausen could no longer fall back on any other camp except perhaps on a few labour camps attached to the armament works that were almost filled up anyway. Most of the internees would have to be sheltered in the woods somewhere. This would mean countless thousands of deaths and, above all, it would be impossible to feed these masses of people. He promised me that he would again discuss these measures with the Reichsfuehrer. He called me back and told me that the Reichsfuehrer had refused and was demanding that the commanders carry out his orders immediately.

At the same time Ravensbruck (sic) was also to be evacuated in the same manner but it could no longer be done. I do not know to what extent camps in southern Germany were cleared, since we, the Inspectorate, no longer had any connections with southern Germany.[84]

The statement above by Rudolf Hoess and the evacuation of Ravensbrück camp is confirmed in a post-war statement by former Ravensbrück Camp Commandant Fritz Suhren, who was also concerned about the fate of 75 Polish female prisoners (the so-called "rabbits") who been subjected to horrendous medical experiments at the camp:

…I believe it was in April 1945 that I was ordered to hand over some Polish nationals to the International Red Cross. At this opportunity I had a conversation with Standartenfuhrer (sic) Brandt, who was a member of the Personal staff of Himmler and suggested to him that the prisoners who had been used for experiments could be handed over to the Red Cross. Brandt told me that in this respect he could make no decision, but would talk to Himmler about it, and I was given one day later the order that these 75 prisoners were to be handed over to the Red Cross. I gave this order to Schutzhaftlagerfuhrer (sic) Schwarzhuber and also informed the representatives of these 75 women of their future disposal. As far as I know only part of these were handed over to the Red Cross because the transports from the camp were interrupted by the advance of the Russian armies. The remainder of the 75 women after the disbandment of Ravensbruck camp were evacuated with the other prisoners….[85]

In a postwar statement on oath former Buchenwald Camp Commandant Hermann Pister stated:

A report on the radio caused Himmler's change of mind. The radio reported that prisoners from Buchenwald concentration camp had been drawn to Weimar when they raped and looted. To prevent such happenings at other camps, he ordered evacuations.[86]

In a postwar Deposition on Oath former Neuengamme Concentration Camp Commandant Max Pauly stated:

A decision on the Neuengamme Main Camp had still not be taken. In his mind's eye, the HSSPF [*Bassewitz-Behr*] was looking at the island of Fehmarn. In the meantime he had had, what I took from his remarks, a meeting with the Reichsführer-SS. I was called to Hamburg and it was explained to me that in regard to incidents in Buchenwald, under no circumstances would prisoners fall into the hands of the enemy. Bassewitz-Behr now decided to search for a camp in Schleswig-Holstein or Mecklenburg.[87]

HSSPF Jürgen Stroop also held a last meeting with Himmler, he claims at Prenzlau but more probably at Wustrau. Stroop had just "a few hundred young Werwolf-fighters", including 14 year-olds moving south in the direction of the "Alpine Fortress" [*Alpenfestung*].

11 Apr [1945]

Received order to report to Himmler's office in Berlin.

12 Apr [1945]

Reported at Dienststelle des Persönlichen Stabes [Office of the Personal Staff], Kaiserallee, Berlin, where he was told to report to Himmler 14 April [1945] at special train stationed near Prenzlau (sic – Wustrau).

14 Apr [1945]

Held 20 minute talk with Himmler who convinced Stroop that Germany could still win the war. Received instructions to convey this opinion to all HSSPFs in southern Germany. Himmler gave Stroop full freedom of action.[88]

On 14 April [*1945*] a brand-new Himmler Order was intercepted and it appeared in the Intelligence Summary of the 1st Canadian Army. In it Himmler declared that field commanders who failed to hold German towns, together with civilian officials who abetted their treachery or negligence, would be punished with death, the only punishment Himmler now recognized… It is certain that many such executions took place in pursuance of the sentences of Himmler's Standgerichte….[89]

Sunday, 15 April 1945

Events:

Hitler issued a Führer-Order in regard to channels of command in separated northern and southern Germany:

On 15th April the Führer issued the Following fundamental order:

In case land communications in Central Germany are broken, I order as follow:

1. In the separated areas in which I am not present myself, a Commander-in-Chief appointed by me will conduct all military operations, and will take command of all force of the three branches of the Armed Forces in the area concerned, of all fronts, of the Reserve Army, the Waffen-SS, the Police, and other organizations attached to them.

2. If I myself should be south of the interrupted communications, *Admiral Dönitz* will be appointed Commander-in-Chief in the Northern area. An Army General Staff (Commander, Lieutenant General Kinzel), which will be kept as small as possible, will be attached to him as Operations Staff…

…

4. The Commander-in-Chief appointed for separated areas…will conduct the overall defence of the Reich in their areas, if necessary independently, should any orders and decisions, even by wireless, not reach them in time, in view of the communications position. They are personally responsible to me for exhaustive employment of their entire war potential, in the closest cooperation with the Reich Commissioners for Defence of the separated areas. Apart from this, as far as communications allow, the unified control of operations by myself personally, as hitherto, will not be altered. In particular, the duty of supplying day-to-day reports is not affected.

The High Command of the Luftwaffe, and the Reichsführer-SS, as the superior officer responsible for the military duties of the Waffen-SS, will be kept informed of decisions as quickly as the technical possibilities of communications allow.

…

6. The headquarters of the proposed Commander-in-Chief of a separated area will be sited and prepared forthwith, in agreement with the Chief of Armed Forces Signals, General of Signals Praun, and in accordance with the order by the Chief of the High Command of the Armed Forces [OKW] dated 12th April 1945, 'Establishment of subsidiary headquarters'.

…

8. Similarly, I shall appoint a Supreme Reich Commission for Defence for a separated area, under whom all authorities of the Party and State will be coordinated, and who must cooperate closely with the Commander-in-Chief of the separated area.[90]

On 15 April 1945, Hitler issued an Order of the Day, 'Soldiers of the Eastern Front':
For the last time our deadly enemies the Jewish Bolsheviks have launched their massive forces to the attack. Their aim is to reduce Germany to ruins and to exterminate our people. Many of you soldiers in the East already know the fate which threatens, above all, German women, girls and children. While the old men and children will be murdered, the women and girls will be reduced to barrack-room whores. The remainder will be marched off to Siberia.

…This time the Bolshevik will meet the ancient fate of Asia — he must and shall bleed to death before the capital of the German Reich. Whoever fails in his duty at this moment, behaves as a traitor to our people. The regiment or division which abandons its position acts so disgracefully that it must be ashamed before the women and children who are withstanding the terror of bombing in our cities. Above all, be on your guard against the few treacherous officers and soldiers who, in order to preserve their pitiful lives, fight against in Russian pay, perhaps even wearing German uniform. Anyone ordering you to retreat will, unless you know him well personally, be immediately arrested and, if necessary, killed on the spot, no matter what rank he may hold. If every soldier on the Eastern front does his duty in the days and weeks which lie ahead, the last assault of Asia will crumple, just as the invasion by our enemies in the West will finally fall, in spite of everything.[91]

Events:
Between 15:00 and 15:30 hrs Bergen-Belsen camp was handed over to British troops. They found as many as 13,000 unburied corpses on the site.[92]

On 15 April 1945, Himmler was in Wustrau and had a series of meetings with Kurt Becher, Hermann Pister, Adolf Eichmann and August Heissmeyer.

Postwar Kurt Becher was interrogated in the presence of Dr Kasztner, and stated:

I left the case of Bergen-Belsen (by Himmler), and obtained concessions for Theresienstadt and that is 100% due to me... Dr Kastner (sic) – you know that, that Himmler gave me full powers and said, also Dr Kastner, go to Theresienstadt and in the other camps [14 April 1945]. The next day [15 April], Himmler said I could not have these orders, but go to the camps and make proposals. Today I know that Mr Himmler:– 1. had not intended this, and 2. a very clear order from Hitler was there, that no prisoner may fall alive into the hands of the enemy...

On the previous evening Himmler had withdrawn his full authority from me, so on Sunday [15 April] he said I must remain true to the Führer. Tonight the Führer has issued new orders resulting in the withdrawal of Himmler's concession of powers to me... At the same time Himmler should have appointed the Commandant of Buchenwald, Pister, Inspector of Concentration Camps for the South [of Germany] (K.L.-Inspekteur fuer den Sueden), however the orders from Hitler changed his plans.

Question 44: It said?

Answer: That no prisoner will fall alive into the hands of the enemy.

Question 45: Who told you about Pister?

Answer: I was told by an Administration Officer, he was once here in the Witness Building, I believe he was called Barnewald.[93]

Question 46: He said?

Answer: That Himmler had appointed Pister as Inspector for the Concentration Camps in Southern Germany [Inspekteur fuer die K.L. fuer Sueddeutschland].

Question 47: When did you last speak with Himmler?

Answer: On 15 April 1945... He explained the reasons for withdrawing his full authority from me, saying he had had a heated discussion with the Führer and the upshot is what happened at Buchenwald – disgraceful stories in the newspapers. Then I was dismissed with authority only for Theresienstadt. He then strolled off into the woods with Obergruppenführer Heissmeier (sic – Heissmeyer), so contrary to orders I went after him and said, 'Reichsführer, I cannot be satisfied with your new instruction; on purely technical grounds it is not possible to make your proposals.' He said there is nothing you can change in this case, and that I must remain faithful to the Führer.[94]

Postwar, Dr Rezsö Kasztner described a late evening meeting at Kurt Becher's home in Berlin about the meeting with Himmler:

[Becher:] The Reichsführer has been appointed to commander on the Eastern front by Hitler [?]. He sleeps only two hours every day, and so overwhelmed by agendas that he can no longer receive people.

To my great regret I have to say that more people were dragged from camps despite instructions being given. I suspect that Kaltenbrunner had a hand in this. I was present when the Commandant of Buchenwald, Pister, gave his report to the Reichsführer. This report stated that a few days before the hand-over of the camp, 19,000 inmates went to Flossenbruck (sic – Flossenbürg) and 3,000 to Dachau. Among them about 5,500 Jews. According to the report of the Commandant, 27,000 inmates remained in the camp of whom almost 20,000 were Jews. The Commandant told Himmler that on the eve of the hand-over the Americans attacked the camp with phosphorous bombs and tank-fire. When asked by the Reichsführer why 20,000 had been transferred, the Commandant replied that leaving them in the camp would have meant more casualties from the American attack.

Elsewhere, it was reported to the Reichsführer, that Russian prisoners of war and Eastern Workers [*Ostarbeiter*] had been released in the West by the Allies, and given arms to fight against us. There are also reports that they terrorize the German civilian population in more sinister ways. It was suggested to the Reichsführer that no Russian be left alive to be released by the Allies.[95]

Kurt Becher recalled Himmler and Eichmann having a meeting at Wustrau:

I remember that I met Eichmann during mid April at Himmler's headquarters in Wustrau. Today, I can no longer remember the conversation in detail.[96]

Eichmann cleared his Berlin offices at Kurfürstenstrasse 115–116 during April (erroneously reported by him as March):

I received the order to turn over all my files to Gestapo central headquarters in Berlin who would burn them. On the day their trucks arrived, leaving iron rations in my cellar, I received orders to report to the Reichsführer. This was the case of the prominent Jews.[97]

At his trial in Israel, Adolf Eichmann recalled his last meeting with Himmler at Schloss Wustrau [*Neuruppin*]:

On 17 April 1945 there was a heavy air-raid on Brixlegg in the Tyrol. Because I might have died that day, I remember the date; therefore I know exactly, because shortly before I made my last report to the Reichsführer. We were alone; for obscure reasons the Reichsführer assessed the situation optimistically for me. He said: 'We will get a better peace than the citizens of Hubertus*, we will rustle a few feathers but this peace will be much better.' He told me that he was negotiating with Bernadotte and wanted to know about a hundred of the most prominent Jews we safely hold; I suppose he intended to 'play around' with these hundred prominent Jews... He mentioned no particular name among these hundred prominent Jews; in Theresienstadt we had a large number, also in various concentration camps, all provided with favourable conditions. Among them, I think, was Léon Blum, an Austrian General. A whole lot of people, some had been Ministers or held senior positions with international standing and for the most part Europeans. 'And I can tell you, Eichmann, that if I have to do it again I will put up concentration camps in the English pattern...'. I could not imagine what this was, because I have never run a concentration camp... This last meeting was in the old Ziethen Castle, north-east of Berlin.[98]

At his trial, Eichmann gave a second view of his last meeting with Himmler:

I was suddenly ordered to Himmler. I think his field headquarters were at that time in a castle, just east of Berlin. Himmler told me that he intended negotiating with Eisenhower, and wished me without delay to bring one hundred, two hundred, all prominent Jews from Theresienstadt and secure them in the Tyrol as hostages. I should go immediately and get the prominent figures ready to travel, then promptly meet with Hofer, Gauleiter of the Tyrol, to discuss where to take them. And with that I was dismissed.[99]

Hermann Pister, former Commandant KL Buchenwald and now the deputy of Glücks in the southern Germany, in a postwar statement describing a meeting with Himmler, possibly on 15 April 1945:

> He told me that he had orders that the prisoners from KL Flossenbürg, Mauthausen and Dachau were to be moved to a valley in the Tyrol, if no transport was available they should be moved on foot. The prisoners would have to build their own accommodation, or if necessary, foxholes.[100]

On 15 or 16 April 1945, a series of meetings were held at the offices of the Concentration Camp Inspectorate at Oranienburg. Meetings prompted by Himmler's evacuation orders. Glücks and Pister discussed the evacuation of Flossenbürg, Mauthausen and Dachau; Rudolf Höss, the evacuation of WVHA Main Office D [*Amtsgruppe D*] family members; Anton Kaindl, Commandant KL Sachsenhausen, and Paul Hoppe, Commandant KL Stutthof, discussed preparations for Wöbbelin camp to take prisoners from KL Neuengamme. Possibly WVHA-Chief Oswald Pohl was also present at these meetings.[101]

Monday, 16 April 1945

Military situation:
Beginning of the Soviet offensive on the Oder Front with 2.5 million men and over 6,000 tanks.[102]

Events:
Radio message intercepted by Bletchley Park on 16 April 1945, and part of the daily secret intelligence briefing presented by MI 6 to Prime Minister Churchill:

> To: HSSPF Main, Nuremberg, SS-Ogruf and General d. Polizei Dr Benno Martin.
> From SS WVHA, Amtsgruppe D, Oranienburg, (signed) SS-Gruf and Gen.ltn. d. Waffen-SS Richard Glücks.
> Subject: Flossenbürg concentration camp.
> Flossenbürg has fallen into the enemy's hands. In other cases the enemy has turned part of the prisoners (many of them armed) loose on the civilian population. Please take the necessary measures from your end and on your responsibility. The Jewish prisoners must at all costs be transferred to Concentration Camp Dachau.[103]

In fact, 1,700 Jewish prisoners had been transferred to the south by rail from Flossenbürg. They reached Dachau, no longer under air attack. At Flossenbürg, the SS guards fled the camp following the arrival of American troops at nearby town of Weiden.[104]

Albert Speer drafted his "Rebellious Talk", 16 April 1945. These were his thoughts about what would happen in Germany and "avoid injustice" for Germany and its people:

> 1. Prisoners of war and foreign workers will remain at their workplaces. As far as they are already on the move, they will tend to move in the direction of home.
> 2. In the concentration camps the political prisoners and also the Jews should be separated from the asocial elements. The former to remain unarmed in the camps and handed-over to the occupying troops.

3. Until further notice enforcement of punishment involving political prisoners and Jews is suspended.

…

5. The activities of Werwolf and similar organizations to cease immediately. It gives the enemy cause for reprisals and harms the conditions required to maintain peoples' rights.[105]

At the personal order of Hitler, SS-Gruf. Prof. Dr Karl Brandt was arrested for "defeatism and cowardice" and held at Goebbels' villa at Berlin-Schwanenwerder; he had sent his wife to Bad Liebenstein (Thüringen) and his staff to Garmisch (Bavaria).[106]

From 16 April 1945 until the end, Professor Theodor Morell, Hitler's personal physician, began given Hitler daily injections of "Homburg 680" against the onset of Parkinson's disease.[107]

Tuesday, 17 April 1945

Events:
On 17 April 1945, Himmler's headquarters train was to be routed from north of Pilsen to Deggendorf, 45 miles (74 km) south-east of Regensburg.[108]

Court Martial [*Standgericht*] proceedings against SS-Gruf. Prof. Dr Karl Brandt began in Goebbels' villa.

Chairman: Goebbels. Panel of Judges: Reich Youth Leader Artur Axmann, SS-Ogruf. Gottlob Berger, SA-Ogruf. Grantz and SS-Staf. Walter Huppenkothen.
Sentence of death was passed by the Court Martial because of "defeatism, lost belief in the victory and high treason". A handwritten note pleading for mercy was addressed to Hitler.

Artur Axmann wrote to Prof. Brandt: "Your way of thinking, is not our way of thinking. You will have to bear the consequences."[109]

Speer had his own view of this trial and reported in his memoirs that Brandt had left his wife and child in Thüringia where the American forces would soon appear:

.... In addition there was suspicion that he had sent secret documents to the Americans, using his wife as courier. Hitler's chief secretary of many years [Mrs Wolf] burst into tears. 'I no longer understand him.' she said of Hitler. Himmler came to the bunker and reassured the troubled entourage. Before the court-martial could take place an important witness [Professor Rostock] had to be interrogated, he told us, and added slyly: 'This witness is not going to be found'.[110]

On 16 April 1945, SS-Ogruf. Karl Wolff visited Himmler. Wolff travelled with Gebhardt to Hohenlychen, and arrived in time for lunch. Kaltenbrunner appeared for his own private meeting with Himmler. Wolff then met with Himmler to justify his negotiations with Allan Dulles. Wolff proposed a request for a Führer-Order. Himmler declined to participate, so Wolff accompanied Kaltenbrunner back to Berlin that evening, to the Reich Chancellery.[111]

Letter dated 17 April 1945 from Count Folke Bernadotte at Wisborg, Sweden, to Gillel Storch in Stockholm:

I would like to inform you, that in connection with my negotiations with Reichsführer Himmler I got clarified, that the concentration-camps for Jews in Germany will not be evacueted (sic) but these camps will intact be turned over to the concerned Allied Military authority.

Especially mentioned camps were, Theresienstadt, Bergen-Belsen and Buchenwald.

Concerning the fate of the Danish and Norwegian Jews I can today let you know, that 423 Jews are expected tomorrow [18 April 1945] to Sweden were (sic) they will remain untill (sic) the end of the war. According the information by the delegate of the Swedish Red Cross who fetched these persons in Theresienstadt, they all 423 are all the Scandinavian Jews in Theresienstadt and the neighbouring camps.[112]

Wednesday, 18 April 1945

Events:
At 03:00 hours, Kaltenbrunner and Wolff in the Führerbunker beneath the Reich Chancellery, and towards 04:00 hours received by Hitler.[113]

Hitler's desk pad, recording his meeting with SS-Ogruf. Karl Wolff "before the staff conference".[114]

From a postwar interrogation of Arthur Scheidler (Kaltenbrunner's adjutant):
... About 10 Apr 45 (sic – 18 April), Kaltenbrunner returned to Berlin for the last time to attend several conferences at the Reichskanzlei. Kaltenbrunner there three days, but before he left, Himmler gave him a wider power of attorney in writing.[115]

Himmler handed to Kaltenbrunner full command authority for southern Germany.[116]

From a postwar interrogation of SS-Staf. Anton Kaindl, Commandant KL Sachsenhausen:
On 18 April I received an order, to load them [40-50,000 concentration camp prisoners] onto barges and head for the Baltic or North Sea and in the open sea sink the barges. This was simply impossible, obtaining barges for so many prisoners would take too long, plus, the Red Army was quickly advancing...

I was left with evacuating the prisoners on foot, first in the direction of Wittstock, later towards Lübeck, where they could be loaded on ships and, as ordered, sunk at sea.[117]

From the diary of Gudrun Himmler (daughter):
Yesterday the daily order of the Führer came out. Now if must go further forward. I firmly believe in the victory.

Where we are going must remain completely secret (under false names).[116]

Thursday, 19 April 1945

Events:
From the diary of Gudrun Himmler (daughter):
Daddy and all the others are up there (near Berlin) and remain for the moment, now that the great battle in the East has begun. Daddy has found it terribly difficult with the incredible

amount of work. The Führer will not believe that the soldiers will no longer fight. Still, perhaps everything will turn out fine.[119]

Walter Schellenberg reported on bringing about an afternoon meeting between Himmler and Nazi Minister of Finance, Count Schwerin von Krosigk, at the latter's Berlin office. The Nazi Minister of Labour, Franz Seldte, was also meeting von Krosigk. Whilst Himmler saw von Krosigk privately, Schellenberg had a discussion with Seldte:

> Von Krosigk and Himmler carried on their discussion privately while I had a conversation with Seldte. Seldte felt that Himmler should seize power himself and force Hitler to read a proclamation to the German people on his birthday, announcing a plebiscite, the formation of a second party, and abolition of the People's Courts. He elaborated this thesis for almost two hours, then asked me what my opinion was of the chances for a defence of the Alpine area (known as the Redoubt). I replied that I saw no chance at all in any further military action, that only by speedy action on the political level could anything be achieved.

After the meeting with von Krosigk and Seldte, Himmler and Schellenberg returned to Hohenlychen. Schellenberg continued with the evening developments:

> … A message had come that Kersten and Norbert Masur, who had come in Herr Storch's place as representative of the World Jewish Congress, had arrived as Tempelhof airport and had gone to Kersten's estate at Hartzwalde. Therefore Himmler begged me to drive to Kersten that night and begin preparatory conversations with Masur, and also arrange a time for Himmler to meet him.
>
> I had dinner at Hohenlychen and tried to persuade Himmler to send Berger to southern Germany. I thought he would be a counterpoise to Kaltenbrunner, whom I deeply mistrusted…
>
> I excused myself shortly before midnight, just as Himmler, quite contrary to his usual custom, had ordered another bottle of champagne in which to toast Hitler's birthday at twelve o'clock.[120]

From diary of Graf Schwerin-Krosigk, 22 April 1945 entry:

> On Thursday [19 April 1945] I had a long talk with Himmler… He mentioned the deep impression my notes on 'England's guilt' had made on him… Himmler completely agreed with my judgment of the situation. He criticized our foreign policy and the Foreign Minister very sharply, but at the same time he admitted grave mistakes in the domain of internal policy. He, too, was doubtful about the automatism of a break between Russia and the Western powers. He mentioned that for two years nothing more had happened to the Jews still remaining in Germany; they were to serve as a barter in all future negotiations. But it was his belief that in questions of internal policy the Führer was not going to make concessions.
>
> …
>
> Seldte, who was with me when Himmler arrived, later on continued to put pressure on Himmler, once alone with him. He [Himmler] had to act, it was he who had to use any possible means for influencing the Führer. This was no longer something concerning individuals. It was the substance of the entire German people that was at stake.[121]

From a postwar interrogation of Hedwig Potthast:

> While she lived in Berchtesgaden, she used to receive daily telephone calls from Himmler. She presumes that the calls came from Berlin, but she is not certain. The last call from him came on 19 April 45. As usual he discussed only personal matters over the phone. Although he mentioned the fact that the situation was getting more difficult every day. Before saying good-bye he promised to call again the following day, but source states that she never spoke to him again. A letter from him arrived the same day, however, delivered by one of Himmler's staff officers. It contained the usual personal messages, but ended with another phrase about difficulties and the hope that God would protect her, the children, and Germany. The letter gave no hint as to Himmler's plans, and no directions for source. Source states positively that this was the last word, direct or indirect, which she has received from him.[122]

From a postwar interrogation of Arthur Scheidler (Kaltenbrunner's Adjutant):

> 19 [April] K[altenbrunner] left Berlin for Linz via Dresden, Prague. En route, Kaltenbrunner was also noted at Theresienstadt.[123]

Radio message from Kaltenbrunner:

> Radio message for [SS-] Gruf. Fegelein.
> Führer Headquarters.
> Via [SS-] Staf, Sansoni, Berlin.
> I request you report to the RFSS and present to the Führer, that all measures against Jews, politicals and concentration camp inmates in the Protectorate have today been personally implemented by me. The situation remains quiet, afraid of Soviet successes and hopeful of occupation by the Western enemies.
> (signed) Kaltenbrunner.[124]

On 12 April 1946, Ernst Kaltenbrunner gave testimony in his defence at the International Military Tribunal, Nuremberg. Kaltenbrunner was asked by his defence counsel, Dr Kauffmann, about a radio message he had sent to SS-Ogruf. Fegelein (document 2519-PS):

> Please report to the Reichsführer SS and inform the Führer, that all measures regarding Jews, political and concentration camp prisoners in the Protectorate, have been carried out by me personally today.

Kaltenbrunner responded:

> The wireless message was planned – the text probably was written by the adjutant who was accompanying me. I did not write it personally and as I say, it could be sent.
> On 19 April 1945 I had been given authority to act independently in accordance with the discussions with Burckhardt [ICRC Geneva] with reference for foreign civilian internees and regarding the entering of all camps by the Red Cross. On that I occasion I stated in Hitler's and Himmler's presence that my route would be via Prague and Linz to Innsbruck and that I would pass Theresienstadt. I said that there were not only Jewish prisoners there who were to be looked after by the Red Cross but also Czechoslovak political prisoners. I suggested that their release should also be carried out. That is the explanation for that wireless message. But not until 19 April at 6 o'clock in the evening was I given full powers in this connection.[125]

Notes of Jewish Council leader of Theresienstadt, Benjamin Murmelstein:

On 19.4.1945 Herr SS-Ostf. Rahm divided into two groups those destined to travel abroad, composed of prominent Jews, Jews of foreign nationality, Jews who were connected to foreign organizations and Jews with relatives abroad. The first list of 300 names will be presented on 20.4.1945.[126]

Order issued for the evacuation of KL Neuengamme main camp (near Hamburg).[127]

Schellenberg reported the arrival of Masur and Bernadotte at Berlin-Tempelhof airfield in the evening of 19 April, and together they went on to Felix Kersten's estate at Hartzwalde, north of Berlin. Schellenberg drove there for a preliminary discussion with Masur to arrrange the meeting with Himmler.[128]

Friday, 20 April 1945

Events:
Hitler's last birthday (56th).

From a postwar interrogation of Gottlob Berger:

On the 20 Apr PW [Berger] was called to Himmler's HQ somewhere near Freisack [Wustrau-Altfriesack]. Himmler told him quite vaguely that he would be getting some orders on Sunday or Monday, i.e. 22 or 23 Apr. PW pointed out that time was getting short and he still had not evacuated the staff of the SS HA [SS-Hauptamt] from Berlin. Himmler then agreed for part of the staff, those who hailed from N. Germany, including all the women, to be sent up to Flensburg. This was done.[129]

Count Folke Bernadotte requested a last meeting with Himmler before leaving for Sweden. After some delay Himmler was contacted and a meeting arranged at Hohenlychen sanatorium during the coming night. As Bernadotte left Berlin the sound of Russian artillery could be heard:

The roads were crowded with troops and with refugees, and progress was not easy. However, we got to our destination by nine o'clock the same evening, and I was informed by Professor Gebhardt that he had not yet heard from Himmler. There was nothing to do but wait.[130]

The last private meeting between Himmler and Göring, described by Göring in a post-war interrogation:

AMERICAN OFFICER: When was the last time that you personally saw Hitler alive?

GÖRING: On the evening of April 20, around half past eight. We raced away.

AMERICAN: To get away that same evening?

GÖRING: Yes, yes. Afterwards he retracted his order that I was to go South – in his usual manner – and ordered me to be at his Bunker on the following day. The room was very small. He sat at a large table and we all stood around it, about twenty of us... You should have seen him. His whole body shook violently. And he grew more vicious with every moment... Himmler said [to me] that Count Bernadotte [*a Swedish diplomat*] had come to see him [*at Hohenlychen in April 1945*]. He told me, 'You know, he must have been the man Eisenhower sent as a negotiator.'

I replied, 'I can't believe that. Don't take offence, but I doubt whether they will accept you as a negotiator.'

Then he retorted, 'Sorry to contradict you, but I have undeniable proof that I am considered abroad to be the only person who can maintain peace and order.' ... And I thought he might have more proof than I, and restrained myself; so I said, 'I just can't picture that.'

And he kept coming back to the same thing. 'If anything should happen to the Führer, and you are unable to take over – after all, that might happen – can I say such and such?' That occurred at least ten times during those two or three hours. I kept wondering, 'Why should I be unable to take over? Why should I be cut off?'

Then it suddenly dawn upon me... Popitz [*former Prussian Finance Minister, executed after the 20 July 1944 bomb plot*] already had mentioned something like that... And when I mentioned that to him [*Himmler*] he said, 'Well maybe Popitz may have said something like that. He might claim to know something. But as far as I am concerned it is an unheard-of impertinence.'

I wanted to talk with Popitz again, and was told, 'Of course, of course!' And when I asked when our talk could be arranged, they told me: 'It may not be possible to arrange it today, but the day after tomorrow'... Then I heard one day that the Führer had ordered Popitz sentenced to death.

This Himmler, he really startled me during this last conversation of ours [*on 21 April*]. He made the ridiculous suggestion that I nominate him as Chancellor upon my becoming Hitler's successor. I replied to him: 'I cannot do that, because according to our constitution the offices of Chancellor and President are combined.' Then he said, 'Sir, if anything should prevent you from becoming the successor, can I have the job then?'

There I replied, 'My dear Himmler, we'll have to wait and see... I can't see what should prevent me taking the office. What could stop me?' (And that happened in our last conversation at least ten times.)

As I sat there [*arrested at Berchtesgaden on 23 April*] I pleaded with him. All he would have to do would be to say just one word to his S.S. men and I would be free. But he dodged the question, and said that unfortunately my detention had been ordered by the Führer. He was sure it had been a mistake. Everything would be cleared up shortly. So he just let me sit there.[131]

In the afternoon of 20 April 1945, Albert Speer at the Reich Chancellery, Berlin.[132]
From the memoirs of Artur Axmann:

During the afternoon of 20 April our delegation was to be found in the garden of the Reich Chancellery. From the Bunker appeared Hitler with Dr Goebbels, Albert Speer, Heinrich Himmler and Martin Bormann. Hermann Göring was not present, he had previously been with Hitler.

As the closest aides of the Führer congratulated him, I stood near Himmler and heard his words: 'My Führer, congratulations on your birthday, and on behalf of the SS, all good wishes.' To me, this sounded cool and non-committal.[133]

From a postwar interrogation of Werner Grothmann:

He said that on 20th April Himmler's party consisted Himmler, Grothmann, Kiermeyer (of the Reichssicherheitsdienst), the drivers, and clerks of the Reichssicherheitsdienst. They arrived in the Reichskanzlei in the afternoon and left in the evening. In the Bunker there were Speer, Doenitz, Keitel, Jodl, Burgdorf, Bormann and Krebs. Asked when Doenitz had left, Grothmann said that he thought it was after Himmler and his party had left. The subject of conversation on the visit of 20/4 was only birthday congratulations.[134]

In his order of 20 April 1945, Hitler divided the remaining country into a "Northern Region" (under Grossadmiral Dönitz) and a "Southern Region" (under Generalfeldmarschall Kesselring):

The Führer.

I entrust the Commander-in-Chief of the Navy [Karl Dönitz] with immediate preparations for the complete exploitation of all personnel and materiél options for the defence of the Northern Region in the event of disruption to ground based communications in central Germany. I have given him full powers for this purpose, necessary for the issuance of orders to all offices of the State, Party and Armed Forces in this Region.[135]

Radio message decrypted by Bletchley Park on 20 April 1945, taken at 19:06 hours:

To: Rf.SS, Field Headquarters.

The Interior Minister of Baden through the Foreign Office representative in Konstanz has initiated repatriation via Switzerland of civilian workers from the West (French, Belgians and Dutch). 1200 French and 400 Belgian workers, including women and children, can be transported immediately on available trains. Removal is very desirable due to serious food situation in Konstanz. Your consent is requested.

(signed) Hofmann, SS-Obergruf. and General of the Waffen-SS and Police.[136]

From a postwar interrogation of SS-Ogruf. Friedrich Karl von Eberstein, former HSSPF Süd (Munich), who was dismissed from all his offices on orders of Gauleiter Giesler, charging him with numerous refusals to act:

Eight days [about 12 April] before my dismissal the Army Commander was thrown out, and on 20 April [1945] I was also dismissed, from all offices I held without military authority.[137]

SS-Ogruf Wilhelm Koppe was appointed HSSPF Süd, succeeding von Eberstein.[138] From a postwar interrogation of SS-Ogruf Otto Winkelmann (HSSPF Salzburg) about events on 20 April 1945:

Visited [SS-]Brigf. Rohde (sic), Himmler's C of S [Chief of Staff] in Salzburg... A W/T order signed by Grothmann, Himmler's adjutant, appointed Winkelmann HSSPF of Bavaria. He was instructed to proceed to Muenchen and relieve HSSPF von Eberstein. It was understood that Winkelmann was to continue as C d O Sued Deutschland but would give up position as HSSPF Army Group Sued.[139]

Radio message decrypted by Bletchley Park on 20 April 1945, taken at 21:31 hours:

To: Staatsminister Frank, Prag. Secret!

Rf.SS deems threat to Bohemia Region is not imminent. Takes opinion of Army Group Centre that any intended liberation of the perimeter be avoided.

(signed) Reich Minister of the Interior, Stuckart.[140]

International Committee of the Red Cross representative Otto Lehner (himself a Berliner) met with SS-Gruf. Heinrich Müller at Grossen-Wannsee, Berlin (Himmler and Schellenberg could not be reached):

> Lehner demanded that Ravensbruck and Oranienburg be handed over to the ICRC.
>
> Müller would not permit entrance into these camps, it would be up to the Reichsführer to turn them over.[141]

During 20–21 April 1945 (Friday–Saturday) most Nazi Government Ministers left Berlin. Reichministers Backe (Food), Dorpmüller (Transport), Ribbentrop (Foreign Affairs), Rosenberg (Eastern Ministry), Rust (Science, Education and Training), Schwerin von Krosigk (Finance) and Seldte (Labour) together with many Secretaries of State left Berlin for the North. Their intended destination: Council offices in Eutin, near Dönitz's headquarters. Those going south to Berchtesgaden included Reichsminister Funk (Economy), Ohnesorge (Post), Lammers (Reich Chancellery) and Reichsmarschall Göring.[142] Himmler left Berlin in the late evening, after the end of the military conference and made for Ziethen castle where Schellenberg was waiting.[143]

Schellenberg waited for Himmler at Schloss Ziethen in Wustrau- Altfriesack from 17:00 hours. Himmler was delayed by the birthday celebrations for Hitler in the Berlin Bunker and air-raids over the city, and did not arrive until 23:30 hours. The two had a discussion about Bernadotte and Norbert Masur who wanted to meet with them that night:

> Finally Himmler decided to drive to Hartzwalde and from there on the same night to Hohenlychen where he intended to breakfast with the Count at 0600 hours...
>
> At 0115 hours [21 April 1945] with a driver, Brandt and Schellenberg, Himmler left Wüstrow (sic) for Hartzwalde arriving there at 0230 hours despite low flying aircraft which had held the party up in a wood for a short time.
>
> After the customary greetings on arrival, the conference began; Himmler, Masur, Kersten and Schellenberg taking part. Himmler opened the discussion....[144]

In the period 20–24 April 1945, Heinz Macher of Himmler's Personal Staff "was engaged in blowing up bridges between Oranienburg-Berlin".[145]

Saturday, 21 April 1945

Military situation:

From the War Diary of Army Commander's Staff North, 21 April 1945:

> For the first time, on 21.4., the Russians fired artillery into the centre of Berlin. A final decision about the headquarters of OKW and WFStab has still not been made. Preparations underway for the relocation of important offices of the WFStabes by air transport to the south.[146]

Events:

From a postwar interrogation of Himmler's adjutant, Werner Grothmann:

> 21 Apr. 45 Himmler's special train (mobile H.Q.) left for Bavaria, the plan being it should await the Reichsführer either at Berchtesgaden or at Bayrisch Zell. It reached neither of these two

places, however, being held up in the neighbourhood of Pilsen owing to the bombing of the permanent way by Allied aircraft. In this train travelled the train commander (name forgotten), Major Vollmar, Oberst-Leutnant Suchanek, SS.Oberfuehrer Bender, and the members of the train personnel. Oberfuehrer Bender was SS.Richter beim Reichsführer.[147]

Count Bernadotte's account:

At half past twelve at night there was a telephone message that Himmler would arrive at Hohen-Luchen (sic) for breakfast at 6 a.m.[148]

Norbert Masur has given his own account of meeting Himmler at Kersten's farm, Gut Hartzwalde, north of Berlin, on 21 April 1945:

At exactly half past two we heard a car arriving. Kersten went outside and several minutes later, Himmler came into the room, followed by Brigadier Schellenberg, adjutant Dr Brandt and Kersten...

We sat a table laid with coffee for five. Himmler was elegantly dressed, in a beautifully cut uniform, wearing all his medals and the insignia of his rank. He looked well kempt, appeared fresh and wide awake despite the lateness of the hour. He was outwardly calm and controlled....

Himmler talked about Jews and Germany, partisans, epidemics among Jews in the East, "In order to contain the epidemic we were forced to incinerate the bodies of vast numbers of human beings who had died. That is why we built the crematoria. And now they're trying to use that against us" [emphasis in original].

Masur continues Himmler's speech: "It was my intention to hand over the camps without resistance, as promised. I handed over Bergen-Belsen and Buchenwald, but with no thanks. In Bergen-Belsen they tied up a guard and photographed him with an inmate who had just died and these pictures have been published worldwide. I even handed over Buchenwald without resistance. Suddenly shots rang out from the American tanks and they hit the hospital which was made of wood. The whole thing caught fire and burnt down and later the burnt bodies were photographed. These photographs are now being presented as evidence of a systematic programme of extermination. When I allowed 2,700 Jews out to Switzerland last year (sic), even this was misrepresented by the press and accusations were made against me personally. They wrote that I had only allowed these people to go free in an effort to gain an alibi. I only did that which I believed to be right and necessary for my people and I am prepared to stand by my actions." [emphasis in original].

Masur managed to open the discussion and reported:

A long debate on the various rescue proposals, during which Kersten backed me to the hilt. We kept on stressing the importance of allowing the release of the inmates of Ravensbrück to Sweden. I had no confidence in general undertakings given by Himmler, however, I did believe that he would keep specific promises, alone for the reason that his associates would make sure he did.

...

Himmler wanted to discuss matters with Dr Brandt, his adjutant and Schellenberg and I left the room and waited in a side room for around twenty minutes. During this time, Himmler also dictated two letters addressed to Kersten. When we returned to the gentlemen's salon, Himmler made the following statement:

"I am prepared to release 1,000 Jewish women from Ravensbrück concentration camp and you may make arrangements for the Red Cross to collect them. The release of a number of French women on the Swedish Foreign Ministry list is also approved. Some 50 Jews interned in Norwegian camps will be released and sent to the Swedish border. The case of the 20 Swedes sentenced to serve in Grini prison [Oslo] by the German courts will be reviewed as a gesture of goodwill and they will be released if possible. The same applies to a number of Norwegian hostages. A considerable number of Jews, mostly Dutch, named on the list, will be released from Theresienstadt, providing the Red Cross can collect them. But the Jewish women from Ravensbrück must not be designated as Jews: it would be better to call them Poles. This is because it is absolutely essential that not only your visit remains a secret but the arrival of Jews in Sweden must also be kept confidential.

On the question of cessation of further compulsory evacuations and the handing over of camps to the Allies, I can only say that I will do my best."

Throughout the discussions Masur reported that Himmler was soft-spoken, remaining calm even in moments of extreme agitation. However, despite this calm exterior, his inner agitation became increasingly apparent and gave vent to his hatred of the Bolsheviks, using typical phraseology of Nazi propaganda.

The meeting ended when Himmler left at 05:00 hours. Masur and Kersten left Berlin for Copenhagen by air, departing at 16:00 hrs. By midnight they had returned to Swedish soil.[149]

Himmler's meeting with Norbert Masur, representative of the World Jewish Congress, was described by the historian H. G. Adler: "Himmler appeared with his secretary Brandt on 21 April at 2 a.m. immediately after celebrating at Hitler's birthday celebrations."[150]

A second account by Masur was reported by the historian Gerald Reitlinger:

...And here is Himmler explaining to Dr Masur the reason for the crematoria and the ghettoes: 'Then the war brought us in contact with the proletarianised Jewish

masses of the Eastern countries, thereby creating new problems. We could not suffer such an enemy in our rear. The Jewish masses were infected with terrible epidemics; in particular, spotted typhus raged. I myself have lost thousands of my best SS men through these epidemics. Moreover, the Jews helped the partisans.'

To Masur's question, 'How could the Jews help the partisans when the Germans had concentrated them all in large ghettoes?' Himmler replied: 'They conveyed intelligence to the partisans. Moreover, they shot at our troops in the ghetto. In order to put a stop to the epidemics, we were forced to burn the bodies of incalculable numbers of people who had been destroyed by disease. We were therefore forced to build crematoria, and on this account they are knotting a noose for us.'[151]

Masur's own account adds a final passage of Himmler's remarks: "It was my intention to have the undefended camps handed over, as I had promised. I let Bergen-Belsen and Buchenwald be handed over, but earned no gratitude."[152]

In his memoirs, Walter Schellenberg noted that Himmler, Brandt, himself and a driver left from Hohenlychen at 01:15 hours for Hartzwalde and the meeting with Masur. Low-flying Allied aircraft in search of a target delayed their arrival until 03:00 hours:

Masur and Kersten were waiting for us and after a brief greeting their conversation began. It was conducted for the most part by Himmler who wanted to prove that he had tried to solve the Jewish question in terms of expulsion, but that this could not be done because of the outside world's resistance on the one hand, and, on the other, the opposition within the Nazi party. Masur did not embark on any long discussion on the various points, but said after about three-quarters of an hour that, although Himmler's account had been very interesting, it was not in any way conducive toward changing the situation. That, however, was his main purpose for coming here, and he wanted the following assurances: that no more Jews would be killed; that the remaining Jews – and their numbers were very uncertain – should remain in the camps and under no circumstances be evacuated. He asked for lists of all the camps in which Jews were still being held to be given to him.

On these points agreement was reached, Himmler repeating every time that he had already given such orders. He was, in fact, ready to free the Jewish women in Ravensbrueck camp and turn them over to Masur, for he had received permission from Hitler to free all the Polish women from that camp. Therefore, if there were any questions about it afterwards, he could say the Jewish women were Poles.

Schellenberg says the meeting was concluded and at 04:30 hours they drove back to Hohenlychen, arriving at 06:00 hours and in time for breakfast with Bernadotte.[153]

Count Bernadotte takes up with the breakfast and his third meeting with the "tired and weary" Himmler and the proposed "humanitarian measures":

… I again put forward the request that the Scandinavian prisoners, who were at the time being transported to Denmark, should be allowed to continue the journey to Sweden, but Himmler once more refused. Schellenberg subsequently told me that Hitler had again forbidden any concession on this point.

Himmler, however, agreed to some of my other requests. He agreed that if Denmark should become a battle-ground, the Scandinavian prisoners of war were to be transported to Sweden through the help of the Swedish Red Cross. He also showed genuine interest in my proposal that the Swedish Red Cross be allowed to fetch all French women interned at Ravensbruck concentration camp, and said that he not only agreed to this, but that he wished us to remove women of all nationalities from there, as the camp in question was shortly to be evacuated. I promised him that I would immediately give our detachments orders to this effect.[154]

From the memoirs of Albert Speer: Having been at the Reich Chancellery in Berlin for Hitler's birthday celebrations, Speer then had a meeting at 01:00 hrs with Feldmarschall Erhard Milch in the latter's hunting lodge at Neuglobsow on the Stechlinsee. Afterwards Speer travelled on to Hohenlychen (23.3 km) for a meeting with Himmler. By 16:00 hrs Speer was at Winnetou-Treffen, south of Schwerin, for a meeting with Baumbach. Later, Speer went on to Hamburg for a meeting with the local Gauleiter, Karl Kaufmann.[155]

Again, the memoirs of Walter Schellenberg: After accompanying Count Bernadotte towards Waren, they parted and Schellenberg returned to Hohenlychen. At 12:30 hours Himmler was ill in bed but they still had lunch over which they discussed the worsening military situation in Berlin:

At about four o'clock, having convinced him that it would be unwise to drive to Berlin, we drove towards Wustrow (sic). In Loewenberg we were caught in a traffic jam... Just before Wustrow we were attacked by low-flying planes...

After dinner, when we were alone again, we spoke of various problems of food supplies, the danger of epidemics, reconstruction, prisoner-of-war administration, and so on, I told him of Kaltenbrunner's blind and unrealistic attitude in insisting on the evacuation of all the concentration camps. Himmler grew very nervous when I called this a crime...

At that moment Fegelein telephoned to say that Hitler and Goebbels were raging because Berger had not remained in Berlin – he had in fact just left Berlin to fly to southern Germany in Himmler's place. He was needed by Hitler to carry out the sentence passed on Dr Brandt, Hitler's former personal physician, who just been condemned to death for smuggling his wife into the hands of the Americans in Thuringia....[156]

General Karl Koller reported: "From the Bunker, General Krebs sought contact with Himmler and could not be reached."[157]

From a postwar interrogation of Gottlob Berger, giving more details of this meeting with Himmler:

I received a telephone message on 19th April (sic) to go forthwith to the Reichsführer, who was about 60 km to the north-west of Berlin. I got into my car and drove there. I had to wait a long time but then I was invited to dinner. Obergruppenführer von Herff (PW) and Obergruppenführer Prützmann went out with me. Herff is Chief of the Personnel Branch and was already on his way to Lübeck; Prützmann was the man charged with the organizing of the so-called Werewolves. The Reichsführer said to me: 'I need you here; I must have a sensible man at my side.' He had a very nice adjutant, an Oberstleutnant Krotmann (sic – Grothmann) and a Police adjutant, Oberstleutnant Sulmaneck (sic – Suchanek). You should get hold of Sulmaneck (sic), he's important to you. Krotmann (sic) said to me: 'Separatism is already starting in South Germany. Württemberg manufacturers are already negotiating via Strasbourg with the French; in Bavaria the Monarchist Party has appeared again and is negotiating with the French and Americans via Switzerland; to say nothing of the Legitimists in Austria who are negotiating with the Russians in Switzerland.' I said: 'Good heavens, Kaltenbrunner is running loose down there.' He said: 'Yes, I was in Berlin at noon; the Führer has his doubts about Kaltenbrunner; he thinks he may be up to some very dirty game' etc. What made the Führer hit on it I cannot imagine. I had made preparations to retire with a very small staff and my documents to the colonial school at Rendsburg, which had been allotted to me long since, in order to await further developments. In the evening I was admitted to the Reichsführer and Schellenberg was there just then – the Reichsführer was trying to contact Great Britain via Sweden. It was very interesting; Count Bernadotte was present... The following day we left for Hohenlychen....[159]

From a postwar autobiographical report by Gottlob Berger, quoted by the historian Robert Kübler:

On 21 April when I was out at Seenge Teupitz in Berlin I received orders to report immediately at the Bunker on Wilhelmstrasse. I arrived at 3 p.m. where I was expected by Hitler's brother-in-law, SS-Obergruppenführer Hermann Fegelein. He told me that the Reichsführer-SS [*Himmler*] desired a meeting with me and this had been permitted by the Führer. Therefore, I promptly left for this meeting at Hohenwustrow near Altfriesack. My car arrived at 7 p.m. and I had to wait 30 minutes for the scheduled meeting to begin. When the meeting finally began, I first had a fairly heated discussion with Himmler because the American officers had still been handed over to Switzerland, contrary to a 'Führer announcement' I had initiated. However, I had learned that my actions in this respect had been prevented by another office (Bormann). On the other hand Himmler was outraged because the shooting he had ordered of Russian officers at Hammelburg prisoner of war camp I had not carried out.[160]

From a postwar interrogation of SS-Gruppenführer Otto Ohlendorf:

Things became hotter and hotter in Berlin, as the Russians had crossed the Oranienburg road on the one side and were advancing from the South-East on the other and were just near Potsdam. We were at Wannsee, 4 km. away from Potsdam. I had a telephone call put through to Himmler asking him what to do now. I was instructed to proceed North forthwith in the direction of Lübeck and to contact Dönitz. Müller was ordered to stay in Berlin as long as the Führer remained there, as he shared responsibility for the Führer's safety. Ehrlinger (?) was also to proceed North and Oberführer Pantzinger (*sic* – Panzinger), the Criminal Police fellow, was to go south.

We started off the same night. We got through all right and arrived at Schwerin, where I formed a Staff and allocated jobs to all the Security Police and SD personnel who were streaming back; in the first place I put them at Steiner's disposal for his Germanic 'Korps'. I also formed two units to keep order in the rear areas. The following day [*23 April?*] Himmler arrived; he instructed me to report to him in the presence of Gauleiter Hildebrandt and he then waited to receive Dönitz who was coming to Schwerin.

I told Himmler what I had done but only got a few disparaging remarks that I wasn't to interfere, especially not in things pertaining to 'Amt VI'. That was his personal affair, which he hoped would lead to a contact with Eisenhower via Schellenberg. He introduced me to Dönitz merely as a liaison officer. Afterwards I heard that he had designated Prützmann as his representative with Dönitz, which led me to believe Prützmann had already given up the 'Werewolf' business. I spoke to Prützmann on several occasions, at Plön as well as later at Flensburg, and I gained the impression that he was trying to find a niche for himself and beyond that had nothing more to do with the 'Werewolf' organisation. Then Himmler ordered me to proceed to Plön to join Dönitz forthwith.[161]

A postwar British secret monitoring of a conversation between SS-Ogruf. von Herff and SS-Ogruf. von Woyrsch:

WOYRSCH: You went to see the Reichsführer [*Himmler*] on the evening of 21 Apr didn't you?
HERFF: Yes, and on Sunday morning by order of the Führer – as a result of a telephone conversation between the Führer and the Reichsführer – he [Berger] went into Berlin again and on the night of the 23–24 he flew via Waren to Munich by order of the Führer.
WOYRSCH: I was with Berger on the 21st, and just then you drove up in order to go to the Reichsführer with him.
HERFF: Yes.[162]

OSS Bern/Switzerland (Allan Dulles) and directions from the U.S. Joint Chiefs of Staff:

[OSS] Bern and Caserta could not have chosen a less opportune time to close ranks in support of the surrender project [Sunrise]. With that sure touch for the ludicrous which characterized so much of Sunrise, Lemnitzer sent his encouraging cable to Dulles on 19 April. Two days later, on 21 April, the order of the Combined Chiefs arrived, demanding that the Sunrise contact be broken off immediately. Apparently all was lost and there was nothing for Caserta to do but abide by instructions while notifying the Soviets that the contact had been cut. Trying to put the best possible face on failure, Lemnitzer sent Dulles a message in which he held out the hope that if their efforts result 'in saving a single Allied life,' it would 'not have been in vain.' Such thoughts seemed as farfetched as they were ethnocentric on 21 April, because the sun had seemingly set without producing positive benefits for anyone.[163]

Radio message decrypted by Bletchley Park on 25 April 1945: SS-Brig. Wilhelm Keilhaus reported to unknown addressee that he had been at Field HQ with a small staff by order of the Rf.SS since 21 April 1945.[164]

Radio message decrypted by Bletchley Park on 21 April 1945:

From SS-Jagdverbände Operations Staff IC (signed SS-Ostuf. Dr Graf) and addressed to RFSS:
Harrassing Formation [Jagdverband] Northwest reported to Operations Staff on 20/4: The King of the Belgians has got into touch with Degrelle on German soil concerning members of the Rexist Party. Object: Degrelle is to preserve his men. Members of his Division are already being financially supported in Belgium by the Government.[165]

Telephone conversation between SS-Ostubaf. Rudolf Höss (Oranienburg) and Otto Lehner, International Committee of the Red Cross, in Berlin: 10,000 concentration camp prisoners evacuated on foot towards Wittstock, 100 km distant.[166]

Sunday, 22 April 1945

Military situation:

War Diary of Army Command Staff North (A) (*Führungsstab Nord (A)*), entry for 22 April 1945:
On 22.4. the Führer decided, he will not move south and evade his responsibilities, but will personally lead the struggle for Berlin and remain in the Reich Chancellery.
He ordered that Generalfeldmarschall Keitel, Generaloberst Jodl and Reichsleiter Bormann fly south and continue overall operations there. Implementation of this command was rejected by all three. The Führer then accepted a proposal of Generaloberst Jodl for the entire operations against the Anglo-Saxons to be turned over to OKW. After the reported departure from Dahlem to Krampnitz. Placed together there would be the entire OKW staff and parts of WFStab from Wannsee.[167]

From the diary of Martin Bormann, 22 April 1945: "The Führer remains in Bln [Berlin]! Evening, Schörner in Bln."[168]

From a postwar interrogation of Luftwaffe General Eghard Christian regarding the military briefing with Hitler in Berlin:

On 22 April Christian was present at the Lagebesprechung [military briefing] which began in the Bunker between 1600 and 1700 hours… Berlin had by then been surrounded on the North, the South and the East; the Russians were reported to have broken through to the Schlesischer Bahnhof; and a battle for the government was expected in the evening. Hitler asked Christian where the Luftwaffe troops were which had been detailed to support the Steiner attack. Christian replied that they had received no orders. The attack had not materialised. Then Hitler made the statement which to all present indicated that he had abandoned hope. He said that the 9th Army, which was cut off to the east of Berlin, must be saved, and therefore Berlin must be defended. He would stay in Berlin. Anyone else could go who wanted. (Christian explained that this was not to be taken literally: Hitler was understood to imply that anyone who did want to go was a coward). Hitler summoned Goebbels and told him to announce on the Drahtfunk (i.e. the local, wire radio which was only audible within Berlin) that he was staying in Berlin. This was about 1800 hours.

When this decision had been taken, Fegelein telephoned Himmler, and Voss telephoned Doenitz (at Eutin) to inform them of it. Himmler and Doenitz then rang Hitler and sought to dissuade him, but in vain.[169]

Events:

Walter Schellenberg and Himmler were in Wustrau on Sunday morning, 22 April. Due to the increasingly difficult military situation for Berlin, Hitler had ordered four Waffen-SS Divisions under SS-Ogruf. Felix Steiner to attack the Russian forces advancing towards Berlin:

… Himmler was convinced that this order was necessary, though both his military adjutant and I agreed that it would mean unnecessary bloodshed.

After breakfast Obergruppenführer Berger came in. He was to drive back with us to Hohenlychen and Wustrow (sic) was to be evacuated as it was threatened by the enemy.

We discussed the case of Vanamann, an American Air Force general who had formerly been Military Attaché in Berlin and was at this time a prisoner of war in Germany. Berger and I suggested that Vanamann, together with another United States Air Force colonel should be got out of Germany and flown via Switzerland to the United States to contact Roosevelt. He was to try to get supplies and conditions for the American prisoners of war, and at the same time tell Roosevelt of Himmler's desire for peace with the Western Powers. I had planned this long ago, having in mind the freeing of influential British prisoners of war so that they might work towards an understanding between their country and Germany. Hitler and Himmler, however, had given strict orders against this.

I had had long conversations with Vanamann, and we were in full agreement. As Himmler had refused his permission, I arranged with friends in Switzerland and with the United States Military Attaché in Berne, General Legg, for Vanamann to cross the border illegally. I did this on my own responsibility and arranged for a car to bring him and the Air Force colonel to the frontier near Constance.

As I had had no news, I asked Berger to attend to the matter. By this time Himmler was in agreement with the plan.

When news came at midday that Russian spearheads were now between Wustrau and Berlin, they hurriedly left for Hohenlychen. On the road, they and Wehrmacht armoured columns were constantly harrassed by Allied aircraft.[170]

In a second interrogation, Gottlob Berger continued with his days in Himmler's company:

…The following day [21 April] we left for Hohenlychen at about ten o'clock. I said: 'What am I supposed to do here, Sir?' [Reichsführer:] 'Well, stay another day. I need your advice.' Then it all came out, that all the people I thought were long since in England had only been sent off in the last few hours. Of course, they were too late.

I remained there for the night. On Sunday morning [22 April] I went to the Reichsführer at once; he said: 'Everyone is mad in Berlin; the Führer is raging, saying the Armed Forces have deceived him all along and that the SS is now leaving him in the lurch. I still have my escort 'Bataillon' here, consisting of 600 men, most of whom are wounded or convalescent. What I am to do?' I said: 'You go straight to Berlin, Herr Reichsführer, and your escort 'Bataillon', of course, with you. You haven't the right to keep an escort 'Bataillon' here at a time when the Führer intends to remain in Berlin and defend the Reichs Chancellery. During these last few days you people have sacrificed my whole 'Nordland Regiment' and I have been given just a reinforced infantry 'Regiment' from my home district to add to a 'Nibelungen Division'. It has been sacrificed in three days and nothing is left but severely wounded men.' The words failed me to voice my disgust; I was at the end of my tether. I said: 'I am going to Berlin and it is your duty to do likewise.' He telephoned Fegelein. I said: 'What sort of a Reichsführer are you? Why don't you speak to the Führer in person?' He did so. Hitler was very short with him. 'Yes, you can come to Berlin.' 'Have you any objection to Berger's coming too?' He said he had no objection; he had a job for me.

The following day we went to Berlin….[171]

From a postwar interrogation of Otto Ohlendorf:

The indecision and lack of plan [regarding the evacuation of RSHA departments from Berlin] on the part of Himmler and Kaltenbrunner became evident on 22 Apr [1945] when Himmler suddenly decided that the head of Amt IV (Mueller) should stay in Berlin, that Oberführer Panzinger and Standartenführer Spazil (sic - Spacil) should go South and Oberführer Ehrlinger and PW [Ohlendorf] go North. This decision was reached and carried out quite independently of possible future legal or illegal work by the RSHA. Himmler had no suitable man to send to the North to Doenitz and was annoyed at the "nonsensical" idea that the South German Hayler should go North and the North German Ohlendorf (PW) South, to represent the Reich Ministry of Economics.[172]

From a postwar interrogation of Werner Grothmann:

22 Apr.45 Himmler, Grothmann, Dr Brandt, SS.Standartenführer Tiefenbacher, Dr Müller and Kriminalrat Kiermaier moved [from Wustrau] to Hohenlychen (north of Oranienburg) where they remained for five or six days.[173]

From the memoirs of Walter Schellenberg, he and Himmler had further discussions with Bernadotte in the afternoon, regarding the Danish and Norwegian prisoners being transferred from Neuengamme concentration camp near Hamburg. Schellenberg left Hohenlychen at 16:30 hours heading for Lübeck "but because of enemy aircraft and the blocked roads I did not arrive late at night." Bernadotte had already reached Apenrade in Denmark and Schellenberg had to speak with him on the telephone. They arranged to meet the following afternoon at the Swedish Consulate in Flensburg.[174]

Radio message decrypted by Bletchley Park on 22 April 1945:
> From: SS-Brig. Ernst Rode to RfSS, late evening, "Reichsmarschall [Göring] at Obersalzberg since 2100/21/4 [21:00 hours, 21 April]."[175]

At 20:45 hours, Luftwaffe General Karl Koller, Göring's Chief of Staff, met with Luftwaffe General Eckard Christian, Chief of Luftwaffe Operation Staff, both still stationed in Berlin. Christian reported on various "historical events" at the Bunker. Christian also reported that Himmler had spoken to the Führer on the telephone.[176]

Radio message decrypted by Bletchley Park on 22 April 1945, taken at 21:45 hours:
> To: 1) HöSSPF with C-in-C South West, SS-Ogruf. Wolff, Verona; and
> 2) HSSPF with Commanding General Rear Army Group Area, SS-Ogruf. Roesener, Laibach.
> 1) Gauleiter Dr Rainer requests in a radio message dated 22 April 1945 to SS-Gruf. Globocnik to leave the personal command of ethnic formations that he has built up to him, he knows the mentality of these ethnic folk, and any change in leadership during this intensified combat situation seems highly dubious to him.
> 2) SS-Ogruf. Wolff and SS-Ogruf. Roesener are requested to move to an agreement on this, taking into account the command and control relationships (radio message dated 18 April 1945, Diary No. Ia 624/45, State Secret) necessary for the current situation and report back to Chief, Kommando Staff Rf.SS.
> From: Chief, Kommando Staff Rf.SS, (signed) Rode, SS-Brig., Diary No. Ia 635/45, Secret![177]

Radio message decrypted by Bletchley Park on 22 April 1945, from Himmler's adjutant, Dr Brandt, to HSSPF Nord [Norway], SS-Ogruf. Redeiss:
> Rf.SS [Himmler] has ordered release of following categories of Norwegian prisoners and internees:
> 1) Sick prisoners and those who, as a result of a lengthy period in prison, or for other reasons, are suffering from mental depression.
> 2) Older people and youths under 18.
> 3) Persons who…arrested on account of activities in which they have not taken part.
> 4) Mothers who have small children at home.[178]

Radio message decrypted by Bletchley Park on 22 April 1945, from Himmler's adjutant, Dr Brandt, marked for forwarding immediately to SS-Ogruf. Redeiss, Oslo:
> 1) The Norwegian Assistance Committee in Sweden is trying to effect an extra allotment of food to compensate for the decreased bread ration in the Grini concentration camp. The Reichsführer SS [Himmler] agrees to this if it will be possible to do it with the help of the International Red Cross.

2) The Rf.SS agrees to the release of the lawyer Kaare Borch, Oslo, and Frau Beatrice Borch nee Ramsay, Grini Concentration Camp.

3) The internees at Berg, near Koensberg, can be released provided they go straight to Sweden. List of names is attached (names – list no. 1).

The Rf.SS likewise agrees to the release and departure from the country of Swedish nationals interned in Norway, a list of whose names follows (list no. 2).

If, in either case, there should be any specially serious objections, please obtain a renewed decision from the Rf.SS.[179]

From a postwar interrogation of Werner Grothmann:

On 22nd April the same party had left Hohenlychen early in the afternoon and had all left Berlin together at 1900 or 2000 hours. They never saw Hitler, and were all the time with Fegelein. Grothmann thought that he had been with Himmler the whole time, and that Himmler could therefore not have seen Hitler either.

(*Note:* This conflicts with BERGER's statement, that he, Berger, accompanied Himmler to the Bunker, and that they both had a long session with Hitler at 8.30. But Grothmann was plainly uncertain about some of the details, and needed prompting).[180]

At about 23:00 hours, Prof. Dr med. Karl Gebhardt met with Hitler in the Bunker for 20 minutes. During which Hitler appointed him Chief of the German Red Cross.

The next day, following the suicide of Prof. Ernst Grawitz, Gebhardt was appointed his successor and President of the German Red Cross.[181]

After Gebhardt's 20 minutes with Hitler in the Bunker, he was followed by SS-Ogruf. Gottlob Berger:

They spoke about Berger's mission, about the disloyalty that was universally springing up in the south, and which would have to be investigated and suppressed. Then they spoke of Hitler's decision to remain in Berlin. Hitler explained that Himmler had made a long speech to him on the telephone, seeking to dissuade him; it was senseless, he had said, to remain....[182]

In Theresienstadt, a transport was organised, reported in the diary of Erich Kessler:

In the evening another transport of German women and children with a few SS men went off.[183]

In the unpublished diary of Eva Mändl, about events in Theresienstadt that evening:

Everyone wanted to go to Switzerland, everyone sought connections. It was only children that went, forced by their parents or people with proven visas or foreigners. Fraud is everywhere. All the prominent people went.[184]

That evening, 22 April 1945, Generalfeldmarschall Ferdinand Schörner held a three hour discussion with Hitler and afterwards informed his I a (Operations Officer), Oldwig von Natzmer: "The Führer remains in Berlin."[185]

From a postwar interrogation of Otto Ohlendorf:

During the night of 22 Apr [*1945*], PW [*Ohlendorf*] was instructed by HIMMLER to go as liaison officer to DOENITZ in the LÜBECK/EUTIN area. The other Ämter left BERLIN on the same day. PW went first to SCHWERIN where it became evident that a great number of the personnel of [RSHA] Ämter IV and VI had gone NORTH without any semblance of order and seemed already half disbanded.[186]

Monday, 23 April 1945

Events:

From a post-war interrogation of Gottlob Berger:

The following day [*23 April*] we [*Berger and Himmler*] went to Berlin [*from Hohenlychen*]; we had to drive via Nauen as considerable fighting was in progress and there was extensive ground-strafing by both sides. We must have arrived by 4.30. The Russian shells were already landing in the vicinity of the Reich's Chancellery, but one shell would land in the Wilhelmstrasse, the next on the Potsdamerplatz and the following one in the Tiergarten. You could tell their guns were being fired at extreme range in the general direction of the centre of the city. Otherwise it was comparatively quiet. We got there; a situation conference was already in full swing. The Führer didn't want anyone present except a small circle. He came in at 8.30. He was completely finished, a broken man. A few Army officers were with him. Jodl wasn't present. Burgdorf and Fegelein were.

When Himmler and Berger were finally received by Hitler, Berger was given a job by Hitler, who told him: "I have detailed reports about what is going on in Württemberg, Bavaria and Austria. Berger, you know what to do."

...Then to the second problem: his [*Hitler's*] exit out of Berlin. The Reichsführer SS explained how senseless it was to remain and spoke for a long time. I told him that was out of the question and that he couldn't betray the German people and that it was very easy – he didn't utter a word – to put a bullet through one's head or to take one of those pills or tubes issued, which work instantaneously. One couldn't desert the people after it had held out so long and so loyally. One would have to share it's fate – going, if need be, into captivity. (Imitating Hitler): 'Everyone has deceived me; no-one has told me the truth; the Armed Forces have lied to me; finally the SS has left me in the lurch' – in that vein. He went on and on in a loud voice! Then his face went blueish-purple. I thought he was due for a stroke at any minute. I had the impression that he had had a stroke already on his left side – of course they kept one in the dark. His arm, which a fortnight before used to jerk, was suddenly quiet and he never put his left foot on the ground properly. He didn't rest on the left side either, as he used to do; he only rested his right hand on the table.

...I left at 12 o'clock and was able get there [*Rechlin airfield*] by 2.30. The Reichsführer remained at the Chancellery. I assumed he was going to stay....[187]

From a second post-war interrogation of Gottlob Berger:

During the night of the 22nd and 23rd of April, I was sent to Munich...

I had reported to him for the last time during the night of 23 to 24 April (*sic*), he sent me in his own aeroplane with important documents to Munich.

I took my leave on 24 April (*sic*) at 01:30 hrs....[188]

Radio message decrypted by Bletchley Park on 23 April 1945, taken at 00:10 hours:

> To: Field Headquarters Rf.SS, SS-Ostuf. (sic) Grotmann (sic).
> 1st part unread … and the rest will be assembled in a Baupion.Batl [*Combat Construction Battalion*]. If not, where should the Battalion be sent. Hearty greetings of Lammerding.
> From: 38.SS Gren Div 'Nibelungen'.[189]

Radio message decrypted by Bletchley Park on 23 April 1945:

> From: Gottlob Berger to Reichsmarschall Göring, [in] Prague, via Staatsminister Frank (07:30 hours): I have arrived today by plane in Munich as special representative of the Rf.SS [*Himmler*] with full plenipotentiary powers. Please let me know when the Reichsmarschall is coming to this area, as there are (important) communications from Rf.SS to be handed over.[190]

Radio message decrypted by Bletchley Park on 23 April 1945:

> From: Himmler via SS-Brig. Rode to SS-Ogruf. Berger:
> Situation in Berlin remains tense. Inform the Reichsmarschall [*Göring*] immediately.[191]

Radio message decrypted by Bletchley Park on 23 April 1945:

> From: C-in-C Northwest, Chief QM (signed Oberstltn Colsmann), to A.O.K. [*Armeeoberkommando*] 25, Chief QM, QM 2 (Quartermaster departments):
> By order of the Reichsfuehrer SS, prisoners of war are not to be withdrawn from the present area but are to be handed over to the enemy with one exception of English and American Officers. These may be transported away by sea.[192]

At 15:00 hrs, Walter Schellenberg met with Count Bernadotte at the Swedish Consulate in Flensburg to discuss a further meeting with Himmler later that day:

> Schellenberg lost no time in letting off his bombshell. Hitler was finished. It was thought he could not live more than a couple of days at the outside…[*and, according to Schellenberg*] Himmler has decided to bring about a meeting with General Eisenhower to inform him that he is willing to give orders to the German forces in the West to capitulate. Would you [*Bernadotte*] be prepared to take this message to General Eisenhower?[193]

Schellenberg himself added more details in his memoirs:

> Schellenberg and Bernadotte spoke for about an hour then Schellenberg telephoned Himmler's special train to ask him [*Himmler*] to come to Lübeck. Brandt answered, and said that Himmler could not be reached at the moment but promised to call me back… Brandt called me back at six o'clock and said that Himmler would be glad to meet Count Bernadotte at Lübeck at ten o'clock that night, and that he wished me to be present.[194]

From the War Diary of the Army Command Staff North (A), 23 April 1945:

> 15:00 hours. Military conference in the Reich Chancellery with Chief OKW [*Keitel*], Oberstleutnant Brudermüller, Oberstltn. von John [*and Hitler*].
> After the return to Krampnitz immediate departure necessary as the Russians had crossed the Niendorfer Canal and forged south with tanks. A journey at night via Nauen-Ber, an hour

later enemy tanks broke through at Neu-Roofen Camp south-west of Fürstenberg. They arrived 04:00 hours [*24 April 1945*].

...

Teleprinter message from Reichsmarschall Göring to the Führer, to Oberst von Below, Generaloberst Jodl (for Generalfeldmarschall Keitel) and to Foreign Minister von Ribbentrop, in which he considered himself successor of the Führer. Due to the developing military situation in Berlin he wants the succession from 23.4.45, 22:00 hours, unless the Führer responds to the opposite.

By radio message, the Führer severely prohibits any such steps of the Reichsmarschall and Feldmarschall Keitel sent a radio message to Reichsmarschall Göring with the current situation.[195]

Radio message from Himmler (Berlin) to HöSSPF Karl Wolff (Headquarters, Fasano/Italy):
It matters now, more than ever, that the Italian front holds and remains intact. Not the slightest regard is to be paid to local considerations.[196]

Radio message (timed at 16:58 hours) from SS-Ogruf Dr Ing Hans Kammler, sent from Munich, to SS-Stubaf Volkmar Grosch, Bauinspektion (Construction Inspection) of the Waffen-SS and Police Bohemia-Moravia in Prague, to be forwarded to SS-Ostuf Schürmann in Berlin:
Immediately blow-up V I equipment at Berlin.
SS-Ostuf. Schürmann immediately travel to Message-Centre Munich-Oberföhring, Muspillistr. I 9.[197]

At KL Mauthausen (Austria), the representative of the International Committee of the Red Cross, Charles Steffen, was able to remove 183 French prisoners from the concentration camp.[198]

Start of the evacuation from KL Dachau of 137 "special prisoners" and the so-called "Prominent Prisoners" from 17 nations, taken in several vehicles to the Pustertal, South Tyrol.[199]

Events during the night of Monday–Tuesday, 23–24 April 1945

SS-Ogruf Hans Prützmann accompanied Himmler to Lübeck. In the Swedish Consulate at Lübeck Himmler and Count Bernadotte held peace talks.[200]

For the late night meeting of Himmler and Count Bernadotte, Schellenberg and Count Bernadotte drove from Flensburg south to Lübeck and all met in the Swedish Consultate. On arrival at 23.00 hours, a severe air-raid on the city began and all took shelter in the Consulate cellar, electric power was lost and the meeting resumed under candle-light around midnight:

A great deal of time was taken up in deciding how the declaration or surrender should be transmitted to the Western Powers... Eventually they agreed that Himmler should write a letter to His Excellency Christian Günther, the Foreign Minister of Sweden, begging him to give his kind support to Himmler's communication, handed to him through Count Bernadotte. Himmler briefly discussed the wording of the letter with me and then drafted it himself by candlelight.

The Count would fly to Sweden the following day, 24 April; Schellenberg would set up at Flensburg to act as liaison between Bernadotte and Himmler. Himmler and Schellenberg left the Consulate at 01:30 hrs, Himmler driving his own vehicle to the nearby headquarters of Police General Wünnenberg [*Hotel Danziger Hof, Lübeck*] where the two men had a 30 minute discussion on how the meeting had gone.[201]

Top Secret telegram dated 25 April 1945 (No. 711) from Sir Victor Mallet, British Ambassador to Sweden in Stockholm, to Foreign Office, London:

> Swedish Minister for Foreign Affairs asked me and my United States colleague to call upon him as 23 hours 24th April. Boheman and Count Bernadotte of Swedish Red Cross also present.
>
> 2. Bernadotte had returned from Germany via Denmark tonight. Himmler who was on the eastern front had asked him to come from Flensburg where he had been on Red Cross work to meet him urgently in North Germany and Bernadotte suggested Lubeck where the meeting took place at 10 o'clock this morning 24th April. Himmler though tired and admitting Germany was finished was still calm and coherent.
>
> 3. Himmler said that Hitler was so desperately ill that he might be dead already and in any case would be so in two days time. General Schellenberg of Himmler's staff told Bernadotte that it was haemorrhage of the brain.
>
> 4. Himmler stated that while Hitler was still active he would not have been able to take the step he now proposed, but as Hitler was finished he was now in a position of full authority to act. He then asked Bernadotte to forward to the Swedish Government his desire that they should make arrangements in order to arrange for him to meet General Eisenhower in order to capitulate on the whole Western front. Bernadotte remarked that such a meeting was not necessary as he could simply order his troops to surrender. He was not willing to forward Himmler's request to the Swedish Government unless Norway and Denmark were included in this capitulation. If this were the case there might be some point in a meeting because special technical arrangements might have to be made regarding how and to whom the Germans there were to lay down their arms. Himmler replied that he was prepared to order the troops in Denmark and Norway to surrender to either British, American or Swedish troops.
>
> 5. Himmler hoped to continue resistance on the Eastern front at least for a time which Bernadotte told him was scarcely possible in practice and not acceptable to the Allies. Himmler mentioned for instance that he hoped that the Western allies (*sic*) rather than the Russians would be the first to enter Mecklenburg in order to save the civilian population.
>
> 6. Schellenberg is now in Flensburg near the Danish border eagerly waiting to hear something and could ensure immediate delivery to Himmler of any message which it might be desired to convey. Bernadotte remarked to us that if no reaction at all was forthcoming from the Allies, it would probably mean a lot of unnecessary suffering and loss of human life.[202]

U.S. Minister Johnson reported from Stockholm that he had met Bernadotte in Stockholm, 25 April 1945, and discussed his meeting the day before with Himmler:

> The United States Chiefs of Staff wish you [*the British intelligence liaison officer in Washington – A.M.S.S.O.*] to have a copy of the following message just now sent to General Eisenhower:

This meeting took place at one o'clock in the morning April 24 [*at Lübeck*]. Bernadotte reports that Himmler, although tired and admitting that Germany was finished was calm and coherent. Himmler told him that Hitler was so ill that he might be already dead or could not be expected to live more than two days longer.

(General Schellenberg, Himmler's Confidential Staff Officer, told Bernadotte that Hitler was suffering from brain hemorrhage.) Himmler said that while Hitler was still active he would not have been able to take the step he now proposed to take but as Hitler was finished, he, Himmler, is in a position of full authority to act.[203]

Tuesday, 24 April 1945

Events:

Himmler's handwritten letter dated 24 April 1945 to the Swedish Foreign Minister Günther:

> Excellency!
>
> I have asked Count Bernadatte (*sic*) to inform you of a number of problems which I had the opportunity of discussing with him today. Please accept in advance my genuine appreciation for your kind attention to these matters.
>
> With the expression of my highest respects,
>
> I remain Your Excellency's,
>
> very devoted,
>
> H. Himmler.[204]

A report of the US Ambassador in Sweden, Herschel V. Johnson, to the U.S. Department of State, Washington DC, sent on 25 April 1945 at 03:00 hrs:

Summary of message:

> (1) Count Bernadotte met Himmler at Lubeck (sic) at 1 o'clock the morning of April 24, at Himmler's request.
>
> (2) Himmler said that Hitler was so ill he might already be dead and could not live more than two days (General Schellenberg, Himmler's confidential staff officer said Hitler was suffering from brain hemorrhage (*sic*), and that he, Himmler, was therefore in a position of full authority.
>
> (3) Himmler asked Swedish Government to arrange for him to meet Eisenhower in order to arrange to capitulate on the whole Western front (including Holland). Bernadotte asked if Norway and Denmark were included in the capitulation. Himmler agreed to order his troops in Norway and Denmark to surrender to American, British or Swedish troops.
>
> (4) Himmler said he hoped to be able to continue to fight on the Eastern front and stipulated that his offer was for the Western Allies only.[205]

From a post-war interrogation of Otto Ohlendorf:

> Two days after PW [Ohlendorf] had arrived at Schwerin, Himmler turned up and summoned him to an interview. He expressed satisfaction at PW's measures to keep order. He especially forbade him to interfere in any way with Amt VI (Schellenberg). Himmler had appointed a number of Obergruppenführer to deal with all problems arising. Together with their unemployed staffs they were all concentrating in this small area.

Himmler ordered PW to go immediately as his chief liaison officer to Doenitz. PW alleges that the interview with Himmler lasted only five minutes and that he received no directives as to his duties, the future of the RSHA or the SD. PW instructed Oberführer Erlinger (*sic*), the head of Amt I, to carry on with his plans for keeping order. After three days in Schwerin he left for Malente.[206]

Gebhard Himmler was the older brother of Heinrich Himmler. In 1945 Gebhard Himmler was SS-Standartenführer working in SS-Führungshauptamt, Berlin.
During 22-24 April 1945 the offices were evacuated from Berlin to Lübeck, travelling via Schwerin:

> …Whilst on the road to Schwerin Gebhard Himmler encountered his brother Heinrich travelling by car with his SS-escort and accompanied by his driver SS-Hptstufü Lukas and SS-Stubafü Kiermeier. The two brothers spoke only briefly and discussed no important topics owing to the others present; this was the last time Gebhard and Heinrich ever met….[207]

Radio message intercepted by Bletchley Park on 24 April 1945, taken at 14:53 hours:

> To: RF.SS Special Train 'Steiermark' from HSSPF Northwest, signed SS-Brig. Dr Schoengarth:
>
> Situation in Fortress Holland is becoming daily more difficult. Amn [*ammunition*] supply is not assured. Food for civilian population available only until 10/5 [*10 May*]. In territories not occupied by the enemy, the customary acts of terrorism and sabotage. Police units always employed as crucial points, and have been partly wiped out. At present re-organisation is in progress. On instructions from C in C Blaskowitz I have moved the Battle HQ to The Hague. Am forming SS and police strong-points here. The morale and fighting spirit of the Armed Forces and the Reich Germans is bad. They regard resistance as senseless. SS and police are resolute to the last. Landstorm Division is fighting outstandingly. Landwacht is unreliable and has in part been disarmed by me.[208]

Himmler returned to Hohenlychen after the late night discussions with Count Bernadotte in Lübeck. At 15:00 hours, Albert Speer in a Fieseler Storch aeroplane landed at Rechlin airfield and went to see Himmler at Hohenlychen. At 17:00 hours Speer left Rechlin airfield in the Fieseler Storch.[209]

In his memoirs, Speer reported on this meeting with Himmler during which he informed Himmler of "Hitler's treatment of Goering" and Goering's resignation. Himmler then explained his thinking of Germany's future governance in his hands:

> The world in which Himmler was still moving was fantastic. 'Europe cannot manage without me in the future either,' he commented. 'It will go on needing me as Minister of Police. After I've spent an hour with Eisenhower he'll appreciate that fact. They'll soon realize that they're dependent on me – or they'll have a hopeless chaos on their hands.' He spoke of his contacts with Count Bernadotte, which involved transfer of the concentration camps to the International Red Cross. Now I understood why I had seen so many parked red Cross trucks in the Sachsenwald near Hamburg. Earlier, they had always talked about liquidating all political prisoners before the end. Now Himmler was trying to strike some private bargains with the victors. Hitler himself, as my last talk with him had made apparent, had put such ideas far behind him.

Finally, Himmler after all held out a faint prospect of my becoming a minister in his government. For my part, with some sarcasm I offered him my plane so that he could pay a farewell visit to Hitler. But Himmler waved that aside. He had no time for that now, he said. Unemotionally, he explained: 'Now I must prepare my new government. And besides, my person is too important for the future of Germany for me to risk the flight.'

The arrival of Keitel put an end to our conversation. On my way out I heard the Field Marshal, in the same form voice with which he so frequently addressed high-blown sentimental declarations to Hitler, now assuring Himmler of his unconditional loyalty and announcing that he was entirely at his disposal.[210]

Twenty-five years after publishing his memoirs, Speer gave a slightly different version of this meeting with Himmler to Gitta Sereny:

Speer remembered his meeting as somewhat between Grimm's *Fairy Tales* and a painting by Hieronymus Bosch. Himmler told him that he was extremely busy setting up his future government. Europe, he said, would need him as Minister of Interior; Eisenhower would understand this as soon as they had spent an hour together. The fact of Hitler's dismissal of Göring was immaterial; for the people, he said, Göring was the successor, and he and Göring had a long-standing agreement that Himmler would be his premier. He was in the process of organizing his cabinet; he had already been in touch with various people; Dönitz had been to see him, and Keitel was on his way. Wouldn't Speer, too, like to join his government? he asked; that would surely be the best thing for his future.[211]

During the afternoon of 24 April 1945, Kaltenbrunner met with the General Secretary of the International Committee of the Red Cross, Dr Hans Bachmann, and an ICRC delegate, Dr Hans E. A. Mayer, at the offices of the Commander of the Security Police [KdS] in Innsbruck, Austria. On 11 April 1946, Dr Bachmann gave a deposition for the International Military Tribunal at Nuremberg in the case against Kaltenbrunner:

I can confirm that during the Innsbruck meeting Dr Kaltenbrunner assured us about carrying out the repatriations, in particular on the same day he telephoned the commandant of Mauthausen concentration camp [Ziereis] and ordered him to release prisoners being collected by a vehicle of the ICRC, he also promised to look at transporting prisoners from concentration camps in the north [of Germany] via Lübeck to Sweden. To do this he would need to make radio contact with the Naval staff. It is correct that Dr Kaltenbrunner assisted us with transport routes, providing the necessary information, and promised competent officers to get through the frontlines.

…

Dr Kaltenbrunner asked us to organize aid shipments to 14,000 Jews located at Gunskirchen near Wels (Austria) and to offload the consignment at the school house in the village.

…

It is correct that Dr Kaltenbrunner allowed us to use the roads of South Tyrol.

He also spoke without giving details, of the evacuation of 35-50 Allied Jews from a camp at Bozen (Bolzano). Concerning the evacuation of 200 Italian Jews from the same camp, as well as 400 Hungarian Jews also in Bozen, Dr Kaltenbrunner put us in contact with Obergruppenführer Wolff. The ICRC delegation in northern Italy would need to raise the question with Wolff.[212]

Wednesday, 25 April 1945

Events:

War Diary of Army Command Staff South (B) (*Führungsstabs Süd (B)*):

> Request to the Reichsführer SS for a Liaison Officer, in particular SS-Sturmbannführer Göhler, previously with the office of SS-Gruppenführer Fegelein, Representative of the Reichsführer-SS with the Führer.[213]

From a post-war interrogation of Werner Grothmann:

> In answer to further questions, Grothmann said that on one day, date uncertain, probably about 23rd or 24th April, at about midday, Himmler had moved his H.Q. from Wustrow to Hohenlychen, as the Russian advance was threatening Wustrow. During the night of the same day Himmler arranged a meeting with Fegelein, to take place next morning. Fegelein came from Berlin by car for this meeting. On the same day on which Fegelein arrived from Berlin, Himmler sent Dr Gebhardt to Berlin to persuade Hitler to leave the Reichskanzlei. At the same time he also sent his Begleitbattaillon (*sic*) to Berlin to put itself at Hitler's disposal and to escort him out of Berlin, if he should be persuaded by Gebhardt's arguments. Himmler had intended that Fegelein should lead the Begleitbattaillon (*sic*) to Berlin, but Fegelein arrived too late, having been delayed on the way, and the Begleitbattallion (*sic*) had to set off without him, under Ostubaf. Persch. Fegelein returned to Berlin the same day.[214]

H. R. Trevor-Roper also mentions Fegelein's travels outside Berlin on this day:

> Fegelein had left Berlin by car, with SS Hstuf. Bordholdt of the SS Escort Unit (*Begleitkommando*) to visit Ogruf. Juettner, head of the SS *Führungs-hauptamt,* at Fuerstenberg. On April 25th return by car was impossible, and Fegelein had flown back, leaving Bornholdt at Fuerstenberg. (Statement of Bornholdt.) Fegelein's last words to Juettner had been 'I certainly don't intend to die in Berlin' (Juettner).[215]

J. P. O'Donnell also mentions Fegelein's travels:

> On Wednesday, April 25 … Fegelein had left Berlin at dawn that morning for Hohenlychen, Heinrich Himmler's headquarters … General Fegelein was chauffeur-driven in his staff car. After the short visit in Hohenlychen, he set out for several headquarters in the same area – Field Marshal Keitel at Waren, General Jodl at Krampnitz, and the SS headquarters at Fuerstenberg. Some time during that afternoon, the road back to Berlin was cut off… Fegelein had to take to the air… But now from Rechlin, the airbase in the same area, Himmler sent him a Junkers-52, with pilot, for the journey back to Berlin. It was too dangerous to fly the slow, lumbering Junkers-52 by daylight. Fegelein thus waited at Rechlin until around 9:00 p.m. He was then flown to Berlin, landing at Gatow. The pilot took off back to Rechlin, his home station.[216]

Radio message decrypted by Bletchley Park on 25 April 1945:

> From: Himmler to Berger:
>
> In the Bayerische Staatsbank in Munich there are documents deposited by Frau [*Ilse*] Hess which concerns the Führer and which are linked with the development of the Party. Please make sure

of them. The deposit certificate 7346, is made out to Frau Ilse Hess, with of the Reichsminister, Munich-Harlaching, Darthauser Str 48, and is held by Frau Hess. The case is bound and sealed. Size 399, 79 CDM, Munich 15.8.42 (B% catalogue) No. 53940 of the deposit certificate.[217]

British summary of German radio messages decrypted on 25 April 1945:

Berger goes S. of Reich to represent RF SS in capacity of Ob.d.E.

(a) Berger to C. in C. Centre, 0200[*hours*]/25/4[*1945*] (extract):-

RF SS has ordered me to the South of the Reich as his representative in his capacity as Ob.d.E. Present Battle H.Q. SS Junker School Toelz.

(b) Berger, to Field H.Q. RF SS, Staf. Dr Brandt, 0215[*hours*]/25/4[*1945*]:

The numerous delegations of full powers, supposedly underwritten by RF SS, are turning out to be intolerable and obstructive for the Command. I request order from RF SS that full control (Gesamtregelung) in this area is to be carried out by me.

(c) Berger, to RF SS and Ob.d.E., 1800[*hours*]/25/4[*1945*]:–

Reichsfuehrer: After I have tried in vain for 2 days to reach SS Ogruf Kaltenbrunner I receive today information of an order of SS Ogruf K. dated 23/4[*1945*], according to which my activity in this area is not possible.

Wording: 'Contrary orders of RF SS for employment of SS Ogruf Berger have not come to my knowledge, (and will ?), to avoid confused relationships, not be carried out so long as I have not received contrary orders from RF SS.' The remaining form and nature of the order is not such as has hitherto been customary among SS officers. Kesselring's view is that I represent RF SS in his capacity as Ob.d.E., apart from the special task which RF SS personally gave me.

(d) F.H.Q. Staff RF SS to RF SS, 1530[*hours*]/25/4[*1945*]:

SS Ogruf Berger requests explanation: apart from his plenary powers, SS Ogruf Dr Kaltenbrunner also possesses the same plenary powers. Which plenary powers are valid?[218]

Personal and Top Secret telegram dated 25 April 1945 from Prime Minister Churchill to Marshal Stalin:

The telegram in my immediately following telegram [*Stockholm telegram No. 711, 25 April*] has just reached me from the British Ambassador in Sweden. The President of the United States has the news also. There can be no question as far as His Majesty's Government is concerned of anything less than unconditional surrender simultaneously to the three major Powers. We consider Himmler should be told that German forces, either as individuals or in units, should everywhere surrender themselves to the Allied troops or representatives on the spot. Until this happens the attack of the Allies upon them on all sides and in all theatres where resistance continues will be prosecuted with the utmost vigour.

Nothing in the above telegram should affect the release of our orations on the link-up.[219]

Personal and Top Secret telegram (No. 16, 25 April 1945) from Prime Minister Churchill to President Truman:

You will no doubt have received some hours ago the report from Stockholm by your Ambassador on the Bernadotte-Himmler talks. I called the War Cabinet together at once and they approved the immediately following telegram [the telegram from Mallet in Stockholm] which we are sending to Marshal Stalin and repeating through the usual channels to you. We hope you will find it possible to telegraph to Marshal Stalin and to us in the same sense. As Himmler is evidently speaking for the German State, as much as anybody can, the reply that should be sent him through the Swedish Government is in principle a matter for the triple Powers, since no one of us can enter into separate negotiations. This fact however in no way abrogates General Eisenhower's or Field Marshal Alexander's authority to accept local surrenders as they occur.[220]

Personal and Top Secret telegram No. 14, 25 April 1945, from President Truman to Prime Minister Churchill:

I have today sent the following message to Minister Johnson, Stockholm:
Replying to your message of April 25, 3 a.m., inform Himmler's agent that the only acceptable terms of surrender by Germany are unconditional surrender on all fronts to the Soviet Government, Great Britain and the United States. If the above stated terms of surrender are accepted the German Armed Forces should surrender on all fronts at once to local commanders in the field. In all theaters where resistance continues the attack of the Allies upon them will be vigorously prosecuted until complete victory is attained.
(signed) Truman.[221]

Premier J. V. Stalin to Mr Prime Minister W. Churchill dated 25 April 1945:

I thank you for your communication of the 25th April regarding the intention of Himmler to surrender on the Western Front.

I consider your proposal to present to Himmler a demand for unconditional surrender on all fronts, including the Soviet front, the only correct one. Knowing you, I had no doubt that you would act just in this way. I beg you to act in the sense of your proposal, and the Red Army will maintain its pressure on Berlin in the interests of our common cause.

I have to state, for your information, that I have given a similar reply to President Truman, who also addressed to me the same enquiry.[222]

1,000 French, Belgian and Dutch women and almost 4,000 Polish women, all prisoners at Ravensbrück concentration camp for women, were released to the Swedish Red Cross for transport to Sweden.[223]

Thursday, 26 April 1945

Events:
Top Secret telegram dated 26 April 1945, from His Majesty's Minister in Stockholm, Sir Victor Mallet, to the Foreign Office in London:

Sir,
With ref. to my tel. No. 709 of the 24th April, I have the honour to enclose herein the translation of a strictly confidential report prepared by M. Masur on his visit to Germany to negotiate with Himmler for the release of certain Jews and others at present imprisoned in various

concentration camps in Germany. You will observe that M. Masur made it perfectly clear that he had undertaken his visit to Germany as a private individual and that although he belonged to the Swedish section of the World Jewish Organisation, the Swedish section had no authority to speak on behalf of the Central Organisation in America.

[quotes the Masur report]

In connection with various conversations between Herr Storch of the World Jewish Congress Relief and Rehabilitation Department in Stockholm and Dr F. Kersten, Herr Storch handed over to Dr Kersten in March [1945] a list of our wishes with regard to the Jewish internees in Germany. Dr Kersten was to visit Germany and submit these wishes to the German authorities, primarily Himmler, together with a list which he had received from the Swedish Ministry for Foreign Affairs. Himmler granted certain of Dr Kersten's demands but Dr Kersten proposed that the execution of the plan as a whole be discussed with a Jewish representative from Stockholm. Himmler agreed and through Dr Kersten invited a representative, whose safe-conduct was guaranteed.

On the morning of Wednesday 19th April I was informed that the negotiations with Himmler would take place on Friday 20th (sic). As Germany's military position had in the meantime become very critical I wondered if the journey was still of any value. I was told on telephoning to M. Engzell, however, that the Swedish Ministry of Foreign Affairs considered that the journey was still of value and that I should therefore travel with Dr Kersten if possible. The Ministry had once again provided a list of its various wishes regarding Jewish internees, Swedish citizens and a number of Dutch, French and other internees. The Ministry of Foreign Affairs has been fully informed in advance of all preparatory negotiations. The Allied representatives in Stockholm have also been informed in advance.

On Friday morning I had an exhaustive conversation with General Schellenberg at Dr Kersten's estate outside Berlin. I first made it clear, for transmission to Himmler, that I had come as a private individual, and that although I belonged to the Swedish section of the World Jewish Congress, the Swedish section had no authority in this matter, as the authority lay with the central organisation in America. The latter has not been informed, however, because it could not on account of the war take any decision regarding a journey to Germany. I therefore came purely as a private individual as Dr Kersten had previously indicated. I then went through our various demands with Schellenberg. He expressed his full agreement with all that we demanded and promised to support all our demands when they were submitted to Himmler.

The conversation with Himmler took place on the night of Friday and Saturday, 20th and 21st April. Our general demands were as follows:

All Jews still alive in Germany should be allowed to remain where they were and there should be no more compulsory evacuation.

If evacuation to a neutral country by the Red Cross or other neutral organisation was possible, such voluntary evacuation should be permitted.

Camp commandants should be ordered to treat Jews well and to hand over the camps to the Allies (American, Soviet or British Armies) if the fronts reached any camp.

We also handed over the Ministry of Foreign Affairs detailed list of persons whose release was desired. The negotiations lasted 2½ hours. It transpired that a few days earlier a camp at Flossenbirk (sic) near Plauen had been evacuated because American panzer (sic) forces were approaching. The internees had been moved elsewhere and we were told on the following day by an official that some were taken to Dachau and some to other camps near Innsbruck and the southern frontier of Bavaria. With regard to the camps in Germany, Himmler stated that during the last few weeks Bergen-Belsen with 50,000 Jews and Buchenwald with 6,000 Jews had been handed over to the Allies. There are the following camps still under German control:

Mauthausen by Linz with 20/30,000 Jews.

Ravensbrück, about 100km north-west of Berlin, with about 20,000 Jewish women.

Theresienstadt with about 25,000 Jews.

Himmler said that he did not know what other camps existed but I learned on the following day from Schellenberg's closest associate, Franz Göring, that there are a number of small camps in south Germany and near Innsbruck.

The result of the negotiations was as follows:

1. 50 Norwegian Jews on the Ministry's list have been liberated and conveyed by the German authorities in Norway to the Swedish frontier.

2. The release of Swedish citizens who, according to the Ministry's list, are held at Grini and elsewhere in Norway will be favourably considered and permitted if possible.

3. 1,000 Jewish women and some French women on the Ministry's list, interned at Rawensbrück (sic), are to be released and immediately fetched by the Swedish Red Cross.

4. The release from Theresienstadt of a number of persons specified by name on a list from the Dutch Legation is permitted but it is unlikely that it can be put into effect.

5. A definite pledge that no Jews will be shot.

6. A pledge that if possible there will be no compulsory evacuation even if the fronts approach the camps.

7. Food and medical supplies can be sent through the Red Cross to all internment camps.

8. Persons specified by name on various other lists will be searched for but in the present circumstances the task is almost certainly an impossible one.

9. One condition – that our visit and conversation with Himmler remain absolutely secret and nothing is published about the arrival in neutral countries of Jews or non-Jews who have been released.

With regard to point 9 I wish to mention that I learned from persons in close association with Himmler that Hitler is still absolutely against the release of any Jews from Germany. He was furious when he learned a few months ago about the 2,700 Jews who had been released to Switzerland. Even if Himmler is at the moment stronger than Hitler it is to be feared that Himmler will stop releasing these persons if Hitler learns about it through the press.

On Saturday morning we had a talk with Franz Göring, Schellenberg's closest associate, who was most closely concerned with the evacuation to Sweden and Switzerland. He stated that the Swedish Red Cross transport column should be in Friedrichsruh and was about to return to Sweden. He was sure that he was entitled – even if he was not successful in meeting Count Bernadotte who was then in North Germany – to send the column direct to Ravensbrück to fetch the thousand women. He appeared most efficient and Monsieur Engzell stated on Saturday morning that the Legation in Berlin had reported on Saturday evening at Count Bernadotte's request that the transport column was on its way to Rawensbrück (sic). It is to be expected that this transport with 1,000 women will reach Sweden on Wednesday.

If the column succeeds in bringing home the thousand women from Rawensbrück (sic) we are confident that – if there is still time – more women will be released and can be fetched. When the transport column from Sweden and Copenhagen returns to Rawensbrück (sic) it is of the utmost importance that it should take with it food and medical supplies. These will be important even if the camp has been occupied by Allied armies. There is most certainly an extreme shortage of food and medical supplied in these camps.

It would be useful if the Swiss could fetch as many Jews as possible from the camps which can be reached most easily from Switzerland – Bieberach in Württemberg, Mauthausen near Linz, and some camps near Innsbruck and in southern Bavaria. We believe that the Swiss can obtain permits for the purpose. The Ministry has therefore promised to suggest this to the Swiss authorities concerned through the Swedish Legation in Berne in order that the necessary steps can be taken.

I wish only to mention one particular feature of the conversation with Himmler to which he attached particular importance:

Himmler said that the surrender to the Allies of the concentration camps at Bergen-Belsen and Buchenwald had been ill-rewarded by reports in the press of conditions in these camps which he described as *Greuelmärchen*. This made him doubtful as to whether it was advisable to continue on the course that he had adopted. I told him frankly that it could not be denied that gross misdeeds had been committed and that the press in a free land, like its government, could not be silenced. It is possible that these reports may stimulate Himmler and his associates to eliminate all traces by evacuating or exterminating whole camps instead of handing them over to the Allies. On Saturday we saw columns of prisoners from the concentration camp at Oranienburg [Sachsenhausen] marching northwards.

To sum up, I would like to make the following remarks. Himmler's word is of course nothing to rely on. In his conversations with us he told many obvious untruths. It appears however that he wants to do something now at the last moment and I therefore believe that he will issue the orders he has promised. On the other hand his whole trend of thought is concerned with the impending catastrophe. If Nazidom is to fail as many as possible in Europe and the rest of the world shall share its fate. It is not inconceivable that Himmler or some other Nazi leaders, if the power slips from their hands, might give an order for the murder of all Jews. It is therefore extremely important to evacuate somehow as many Jews as possible to neutral countries or behind the Allied lines, even if it is believed that liberation by the armies is now impending. The danger to non-Jews is much less and it is scarcely conceivable that Nazi leaders would dare to order the mass murder of non-Jews belonging to the countries hostile to Germany.

The negotiations were conducted with Schellenberg, Franz Göring and Dr Brandt, Himmler's secretary, were very valuable. It is these persons who in the first instance execute Himmler's orders. They are young men who want to live. They say that they are fully aware that any deed of violence – even against Jews – is a crime against the Germany of the future. We are of the firm opinion that they will sabotage any orders to commit deeds of violence which Himmler may issue. Such sabotage on their part is easy to commit and cannot be discovered because disorganisation is already such that communication between towns in most parts of Germany is so poor that any order can disappear on the way without the reason being discovered.

The above mentioned negotiations and the results achieved would have been inconceivable without the active and whole-hearted cooperation of Dr Kersten and I am most grateful to him for accompanying me on this dangerous journey of humanitarian salvation without regard to his own safety.[224]

Radio message decrypted by Bletchley Park on 26 April 1945, taken at 08:45 hours:

To: BdS Berlin.

Immediately send Geheimrat [Hermann] Buecher, Amtsgericht Berlin, to Landrat Ploen/Holstein, for special task of Rf.SS. For Buecher ... travel to Friesack, and telephone [from there].

From: RSHA VI [Schellenberg].[225]

Radio message decrypted by Bletchley Park on 26 April 1945:

Addressee not quoted, message from SS-Brig. Keilhaus.

By order of the Reichsführer SS, Signals Transport Abt 4, strong Signals Platoon (mot.) with O.C. for the Reichsführer SS. They are to report to local town major's office in Guestrow. Notify me of time of their departure.[226]

Radio message decrypted by Bletchley Park on 26 April 1945, taken at 13:30 hours:

From Himmler to Kaltenbrunner

(1) Liaison with known persons Switzerland (word or two garbled).

(2) Children of Belgian King to Switzerland needs authorisation from Fuehrer.

(3) As I see things there are no objections of any sort to the reforming of the Slovakian Government.

(4) Organise the production of ammunition (word or two illegible) with all forces.[227]

Radio message decrypted by Bletchley Park on 26 April 1945, taken at 15:15 hours:

To: SS-Ogruf. Dr Kaltenbrunner, Salzburg.

Ogruf., reporting, That I am currently in Gau Swabia on the basis of personal instructions of Rf.SS and consulting with SS-Ogruf. von Eberstein, for using Special Kommandos (Sonderkommandos) with specifics tasks. Gruf. Ebrecht has made use of me in Lindau. Orders can reach me via SS and Police radio.

From: SS-Gruf Stroop, Headquarters Hohenschwangau-Füssen.[228]

Radio message decrypted by Bletchley Park on 26 April 1945, taken at 16:00 hours:

From: SS-Staf. Brandt to SS-Obergruppenfuehrer Dr Kaltenbrunner, Salzburg:

Reichsfuehrer SS is on his way. I inform you by way of precaution that SS Obergruppenfuehrer Berger has been sent to the South with definite full powers. As I do not want to trouble Reichsfuehrer SS, I suggest we have a full discussion and come to some arrangement.[229]

Radio message decrypted by Bletchley Park on 26 April 1945, taken at 16:35 hours:

To: Stapo Innsbruck, for immediate forwarding to Oberfhr. Kroeger, Staff of General Wlassow.
Make known immediately to General Wlassow, the following instructions of Rf.SS:
'Ensure that Gen. Wlassow with a small staff gets to Panzerkorps I, 15 Km south of Maehrisch-Ostrau, as action with 600 Infantry Div. imminent. Yours Himmler.'
From: SS-Gruf. Stroop.[230]

Radio message decrypted by Bletchley Park on 26 April 1945:

From: SS-Hstuf. Gutgesell (Himmler's staff) to SS-Staf. Baumert, Swabia:
On order of Rf.SS, I am with SS-Ostubaf. Grothmann. By order of Battle Group Mohnke, the members of the Personal Staff have been given up.[231]

Radio message decrypted by Bletchley Park on 26 April 1945, taken at 17:00 hours; four days later it was included in the intelligence material passed by "C" (chief of MI6) to Prime Minister Churchill:

From: SS-Staf. Baumert to Himmler's adjutant, SS-Ostubaf. Grothmann:
I am flying to Wittstock [west of Neustrelitz] at 2200 hours tonight. Please have me fetched. It is urgent for me to go to the Chief [i.e. *Himmler*].[232]

Radio message decrypted by Bletchley Park on 26 April 1945, taken at 17:15 hours:

To: Rf.SS and Chief of the German Police, Chief Order Police, Berlin.
Secret!
On 25.4.45 from 11.12 hrs to 14.13 hrs, air-raid on Reichsgau Upper Austria (*Oberdonau*). 650 to 700 aircraft in 27 waves. Point of concentration Linz railway station and Wels. Strafing attacks in the region. During the attack on Linz, SS and Pol. Leader Oberdonau, SS.Obfhr. Dr Piffrader (*sic* – Pifrader) and Chief of Gestapo Linz, SS.Oberstbf. Dr [*Leopold*] Spann killed.
From: Commander of Gendarmerie Oberdonau.[233]

Radio message decrypted by Bletchley Park on 26 April 1945, taken at 17:20 hours:

Secret State Matter! To: Party Chancellery:
C-in-C Army Group Vistula [*Heinrici*] has ordered the hand-over of positions on the Oder [*River*], Fortress Stettin to the Randzow position on 25.4.45 without a fight. Great confusion among troops and population. Orders should have been given by the Führer. Further withdrawal orders for positions in the rear have been issued. Request information and rules of conduct (continuation unread).
From: Gauleiter Schwede-Koburg (*sic* – Coburg).[234]

Radio message decrypted by Bletchley Park on 26 April 1945, taken at 19:00 hours:

To: HSSPF Süd [Munich]. with request for forwarding to Rf.SS, Field Headquarters.

Rf.SS!

Further work on the western borders of Gau Swabia, for the moment I am at Hohenschwangau near Fuessen.

From: SS-Gruf. Stroop.[235]

Friday, 27 April 1945

Military situation:

Hitler attended the last military conference in Berlin, where he commented on reports that some Party Leaders whose districts were facing Allied armies were not passing on his orders for destroying facilities:

> Failure to comply with an order given me, means for a Party Leader immediate death and a kick into nothingness... I cannot imagine that a Party Leader who has my order, understands but does nothing.[236]

Events:

The War Diary of Army Command South (B), recorded an order by Hitler "for the dissolving the post of Commander of the Replacement Army" [*a position held by Himmler*].[237]

"...On the 27th [April 1945] Himmler sent the last of his 'Führerbefehle' which by-passed the High Command. It was addressed to the 25th Panzer Grenadier Division which was to join Holste's Army Corps because Hitler had lost faith in Steiner." SS-Ogruf. Steiner, a Waffen-SS commander, held command of a poorly equipped army that Hitler was expecting to attack and throw-back superior Soviet armies surrounding Berlin. [238]

From a post-war statement of SS-Staf. Kurt Becher about events at KL Mauthausen:

> On the occasion of my visit to Mauthausen concentration camp on 27 April 1945, at 09:00 hrs in the morning, the Camp Commandant SS-Standartenführer Ziereis informed me, under the strictest secrecy: 'Kaltenbrunner had given me instructions, that in Mauthausen on a daily basis at least 1,000 people must die.'[239]

On this date, the delegate of the International Committee of the Red Cross, Louis Haefliger, arrived at KL Mauthausen with a column of 19 trucks. At first the Camp Commandant refused them admittance before allowing them into the camp accommodation. Above all Ziereis wanted the inmates of Gusen I and II camps brought out before the destruction of the aircraft factory.[240]

From a post-war interrogation of Werner Grothmann:

> Grothmann said that about 27th April Fegelein again came from Berlin to Himmler, this time by air. He came to Fuerstenburg (*sic*), and was seen by Grothmann. He returned to Berlin the same day. Grothmann knew nothing of the fate of Fegelein.[241]

From the memoirs of Wilhelm Keitel:

On 27th April, towards midday, Grand Admiral Dönitz put in an appearance at our camp at Neu-Roofen; he had also radioed Himmler to attend. The four of us, including Jodl, discussed the situation privately, after both our guests had sat in on the war conference. It was obvious to us that the Führer was determined to stand fast and fight in Berlin, and that our duty would be not to abandon him so long as there remained any chance of backing him out....[242]

From the diary of Luftwaffe General Karl Koller:

I learned that OKW [staff] could be found in a forester's house among woods near Fürstenberg [Neuroofen] so I made my way there...

The briefing was underway when I arrived, also late were Dönitz and Himmler. I spoke to Himmler about Göring, who said: 'There is a really unhappy history with the Reichsmarschall.' I replied that Göring could not be otherwise when I was interrupted by Keitel. Himmler mentioned that he would talk to me later, unfortunately a discussion did not later follow. Himmler later said he had no time, having brought forward other meetings he first wanted lunch. Then he will come back to me...

Today at the briefing, Dönitz and Himmler occupied Hitler's place. They sat side by side and made a few meaningless comments. Jodl and the various experts explained...

Afterwards I tried to reach Himmler, but the 'Reichsheini' had gone, as now a [Russian] tank alarm was given for the forester's house (movement readiness 2 hours). At Prenzlau, Russian tanks have broken through, and advancing on Lychen and Woldegk.[243]

In his memoirs, Karl Dönitz recorded:

On April 27 I went from Plön to Supreme Headquarters in Rheinsberg [Neuroofen]... The roads from Plön to Rheinsberg were choked with fleeing refugees and lorries full of wounded soldiers and civilians, all moving westwards. British and American fighter aircraft were shooting up the congested traffic...

When I reached Supreme Headquarters I found that Himmler was also there. After the conference he turned the conversation to the question of Hitler's successor in the event of the latter being killed in Berlin and asked whether, if Hitler entrusted the control of the State to him, I would place my services at his disposal. To this I replied that the only thing that now mattered was to prevent a reign of chaos which would inevitably lead to further bloodshed, and that I was therefore prepared to serve under any legally constituted Government.[244]

From a secretly monitored post-war conversation of Generalleutnant Dr Walter Dornberger in Britain:

Himmler had a persecution mania. He had me arrested on 27 Apr [1945], for not carrying out orders. I only got away thanks to Kammler, who was also to be arrested. We both drove off to Garmisch.[245]

Radio message decrypted by Bletchley Park on 27 April 1945, taken at 19:30 hours:

From: Himmler to SS-Ogruf Berger in Munich:

I earnestly ask you and Kaltenbrunner to get into touch with one another, and to work together in the closest cooperation, thus removing by discussion any possibility of friction. Your full powers, in practice the putting together of SS Main Administrative Districts (OA) South, South-West and the remains of Main, as also the control of prisoners of war, cover a different sphere from that in which Kaltenbrunner has full powers.[246]

Radio message decrypted by Bletchley Park on 27 April 1945:

From: Rf.SS Headquarters Staff, signed SS-Brif Rohde (*sic* – Rode), to HSSPF Bohemia and Moravia, Prague:

Subject: Rendering of returns and reports.

Ref.: Order of Rf.SS No. 108/43 of 21 June 1943, and Rf.SS Chief of Anti-Partisan Formations, No. IA/1635 of 15 Oct 1944.

1) For orientation of Rf.SS with immediate effect a short report on the situation in the whole sphere of command will be presented daily.

Contents:

   1) Situation at the front.

   2) Werewolf situation

   3) Attitude of the population, resistance movement.

   4) Economic, transport and labour situation.

2) The order of Rf.SS, Chief of Anti-Partisan Formations No. IA/1635 of 15 Oct 1944 goes out of force with immediate effect owing to changed situation.[247]

Radio message decrypted by Bletchley Park on 27 April 1945, sent in the late evening to an unknown address (this section of the message was not intercepted), and signed by SS-Staf. Brandt, Rf.SS Field Headquarters:

Subject: Leaving behind of prisoners of war and Eastern civilian workers in enemy hands.

English and American prisoners of war are to be brought back at all costs. Female Eastern workers can be left to the enemy. A decision about leaving Eastern prisoners will be given on 28/4 [28 April].[248]

From the diary of Martin Bormann:

The Divisions coming to our relief were stopped by Himmler – Jodl!

We will stand or fall with the Führer: faithful unto death.

Other believe "from higher insight" then act on them, they sacrifice their Führer and disloyalty – ugh, Devil! – looks like their "sense of honour"![249]

And from a memorandum (*Aktenvermerk*) of Martin Bormann:

One might have expected that H.H. [*Heinrich Himmler*], at least once he received my letter of April 25, would had addressed a fiery appeal to his SS – 'SS men, our honour is our loyalty' [*this was the motto of the SS*]. But H.H. kept silent!! While Old Father Keitel drove around out there raging and roaring to raise help for us in time, H.H. tucked himself away at Hohenlychen! And Steiner's SS force, which was supposed to move off first, just marched on the spot from the word go – it just play-acted – and this was the force that H.H. should have appealed to first and foremost: 'SS men, rally to your Führer! For our battleflag, fluttering ahead on high, let's take the oath we all swore, Our loyalty is our honour.' No, H.H. just kept quiet. How are we to interpret

170

that? And what are we to make of the question he radioed to General Burgdorf, whether the Führer might not be judging Göring's intentions too harshly? Obviously H.H. is wholly out of touch with the situation. If the Führer dies, how does he plan to survive!!?

Again and again, as the hours tick past, the Führer stresses how tired he is of living now with all the treachery he has had to endure. Were one to ignore the heroism of even the women and children, one could only agree with the Führer. How many disappointments this man has had to suffer unto the very end.[250]

Count Bernadotte received the answer to Himmler's conditions for surrender in the west:

…During the evening of April 26th… I at once went to the American Legation [in Stockholm, Sweden], where I found Mr. Johnson and Boheman. The telegram [from President Truman] read: 'A German offer of surrender will only be accepted on condition that it is complete on all fronts as regards Great Britain, the Soviet Union as well as U.S.A. When these conditions have been fulfilled, the German forces must immediately on all fronts lay down their arms to the local Allied Commanders. Should resistance continue anywhere, the Allied attacks will be ruthlessly carried on until complete victory has been gained.'

M. Boheman and I, on leaving the American Legation, went on to the residence of the [Swedish] Minister for Foreign Affairs, who pointed out that the answer from the United States was anything but unexpected… On April 27th I flew to Odense, where I met Brigadeführer Schellenberg, to whom I presented the Western Powers' reply to Himmler's offer of capitulation.[251]

Schellenberg met Bernadotte at Odense airport, and together they travelled to Apenrade to discuss the negative response from the Allies toward Himmler's offer:

Not only had our plans come to nothing, but the Allied press had published an account of the matter. My position with Himmler would therefore be a rather delicate one, and I was very glad to have the Count come to Lübeck with me. We arranged to meet at four the next morning and to drive there together.

I returned to Flensburg and tried to get in touch with Himmler, but was only able to speak to Brandt, who asked very excitedly what the results were. I said that they had been negative, but the Count wanted to come to Lübeck to discuss the question of the German armies in the Scandinavian area. This proposal was sharply rejected; I was to report to Himmler alone.

This conversation place just after midnight… I was to meet Himmler… to the south of Lübeck… This was on the morning of April 28.[252]

From the memoirs of Field Marshal Montgomery:

On the 27th April [1945] I received a report from the War Office that on the 24th Himmler had made an offer of capitulation through the Swedish Red Cross.

Himmler stated that Hitler was desperately ill and that he (Himmler) was in a position of full authority to act. I did not pay much attention to this report. So far as I was concerned the oncoming Russians were more dangerous that the stricken Germans. I knew the German war was practically over. The essential and immediate task was to push on with all speed and get to the Baltic, and then to form a flank facing east….[253]

Saturday, 28 April 1945

Military situation:
War Diary of Army Command Staff Nord (A): 'The inner defence ring around Berlin is broken. The fight for the city has begun.'[254]

Events:
"An SS report dated 28 Apr [underlining in original], addressed to HIMMLER, stated that on account of the military situation and of amn (*sic* – ammunition) and food difficulties, the dismissal of the Croats and all other foreigners from the armed forces and the Legion divs was under consideration." Since 1944 the Waffen-SS had created Legions and Brigades from ethnic minorities deemed acceptable to join the aryan Waffen-SS. In April 1945 these units had no munitions and limited food supplies. At this very late stage of the war, decisions were being made to re-assign these units into the Wehrmacht.[255]

German radio heard the morning news from Radio Stockholm, quoting a Reuter's despatch by reporter Paul Rankine:

> The Reichsführer-SS Himmler has offered capitulation to the USA and Great Britain. However, the Anglo-Americans have rejected this, for total capitulation with the involvement of the Soviet Union.[256]

Radio message from Bormann to Grossadmiral Dönitz at 04:05 hrs:

> Foreign press reports about a new betrayal. The Führer expects that you will act instantly with hard steel against all traitors in the North German region. Without distinction. Schörner, Wenck and others must prove their loyalty to the relief of the Führer.[257]

Letter from Martin Bormann and Generaloberst Krebs [*Chief of the General Staff*] to General Wenck:

> Dear General Wenck!
> From the enclosed messages RFSS Himmler has agreed to make an offer that would unconditionally hand our people to the plutocracies.
> A change can only be brought about by the Führer himself. Only by him.
> As a precondition, the Wenck Army without losing its liaison with us, leaves the Führer free for internal and foreign political freedom of action.[258]

Radio message decrypted by Bletchley Park on 28 April 1945, taken at 16:00 hours; it is signed by SS-Ogruf Berger and addressed to Himmler:

> Owing to the mutiny of an Interpreter Coy the Bavarian Freedom Party was proclaimed and a transmitter at Munich was seized. After the arrest of the Gauleiter [*Giesler*] had failed, Christian Weber was relieved of office and put out of the way at 0930 hrs. I went to the Gauleiter [*Giesler*] at once. Measures laid on with the Waffen-SS and the G.A.F. [*Wehrmacht*]. The police were not used anywhere as there were none.
> Old Party members also took part in the conduct of the revolt, for instance Major Erb, holder of the Blutsorden (*sic*) and former leader of the Beamtenbund Munich and OB ZAY (*sic*). The

Werwolf was laid on against the latter. I had a detailed discussion with Gauleiter Giesler. We came to full agreement, Gauleiter Giesler wants to remain in Munich under all circumstances although the town cannot be defended as there are no forces for this. The advance in the south is so rapid that Munich probably from the south and southeast [*are likely to be attacked*].

Ritter von Epp was wakened about midnight by the rebels and asked to cooperate. He refused but failed to inform the Gauleiter [*Giesler*] of this. There is naturally great unrest. Junker School Tölz is on the move and will block in the Murnau area. I am remaining for the moment in Tölz.[259]

A second radio message from Berger to Himmler was decrypted by Bletchley Park:

Obergruppenfuehrer Berger, on instructions from Himmler of 25th, had by 28th redeemed documents concerning Hitler and the development of the Party, deposited in the Bayerische Staatsbank, Munich, in name of Frau Hess, Munich-Harlaching, Darthauser Strasse 48. Documents then at Berger's house. Berger was for time being leaving with Frau Hess at Oberdorf near (slight indications Hindelang, C 98), House Buergle, what was saved from the Harlaching house when it was bombed 'long ago'.

The message then stated that Berger had "also received to-day from the German Reichsbank 12 small bags for R.F.S.S. They are being brought here too."[260]

War Diary of Army Command Staff North (A):

16:50 hrs: Conversation with Grossadmiral [*Dönitz*]. (Appendix 3)

Grossadmiral asked whether foreign reports are known, that the Reichsführer SS has made a capitulation offer to the Anglo-Americans and only a total capitulation including the Soviets is acceptable.

Answer: Information here unknown. Will be clarified, if needs be with enemy statements.

17:20 hrs: Reichsführer SS verbally agreed:

a) of the liaison and information. given by Generaloberst Krebs,

b) of the call from Munich-Erding,

c) of the alleged capitulation offer the Reichsführer SS made and the reply for the Anglo-Saxons.

Reichsführer SS will inform Grossadmiral Dönitz that these reports are false. Ignore any enemy statements broadcast on the radio.[261]

From a post-war interrogation of Himmler's adjutant, Werner Grothmann:

28 Apr. 45 Himmler's party (as above) [*Himmler, Grothmann, Dr Brandt, Kiermaier, Tiefenbacher, Dr Müller*] moved on again to a villa near Krakow (Mecklenburg) where they stayed for a day or two.[262]

Radio message decrypted by Bletchley Park on 28 April 1945, sent at 17:30 hours, from Himmler to SS-Obergruppenführer Dr Kaltenbrunner:

Your letter of 26/4 [*26 April*] is to hand. You did well to bring Gauleiter Hofer into line. Eberstein was turned down by Giesler as weary and apathetic, therefore Berger was actually sent down to pull together the South-West, South and remaining elements of Main. Apart from this Berger is absolutely necessary there for the English and American POW. Surely it should be possible to

avoid all friction by making immediate contact and a thorough and clear discussion.
Heil Hitler![263]

Radio message decrypted by Bletchley Park on 28 April 1945; from Himmler to Kaltenbrunner:
"The Führer urgently requires a report on the situation in South Germany."[264]

Radio message decrypted by Bletchley Park on 28 April 1945; from Himmler to SS-Ogruf.
Berger: "See to it that all records[,] offices and documents at Dachau camp are destroyed."[265]

Radio message decrypted by Bletchley Park on 28 April 1945; from SS-Ogruf. Gottlob Berger
to Himmler:

Dear Reichsfuehrer,

(By what the eminent) in this area are doing is unimaginable and so incomprehensible that I must
request you to release me from my task so that least the honour of the SS is saved. Orders that
I gave are nullified by counterorders (sic) from within the SS. Not even the physical backing of the
people...can be obtained in this way. Everything perfectly O.K. with the prisoners of war and the
International Red Cross.

Heil Hitler.

Your ever-faithful and grateful

Gottlob [Berger].[266]

Radio message decrypted by Bletchley Park on 28 April 1945; from SS-Gruppenführer
Konstantin Kammerhofer, HSSPF Croatia to Reichsführer-SS Himmler:

1) On account of the military situation and of amn [ammunition] and food difficulties[,] the
dismissal of the Croats and all other foreigners from the Armed Forces (and the) Legion Divs is
under consideration. Request orders as to whether I may act similarly in respect of the Police
and SS Div Handschar if Gen Oberst Loehr gives orders to this effect.

2) I request you, Reichsführer, to give me orders regarding my course of action, should the
necessity arise, in the event of all communications with your H.Q. being interrupted. If possible
I ask that after my tasks in Croatia have been completed I may be put at the disposal of
Reichsgau Styria [Austria] for the final struggle.

Heil Hitler.[267]

From the diary of Martin Bormann, entry dated 28 April 1945:

Our RK [Reich Chancellery] is a pile of rubble: 'at dagger's point the world stands'. Treason and
high treason − unconditional surrender − will be announced from abroad. Fegelein degraded
− cowardly tried to get away from Berlin in civilian clothing.[268]

At Dachau concentration camp, International Committee of the Red Cross delegate Victor
Maurer negotiating for the camp to be handed over.[269]

The journalist William L. Shirer, writing in San Francisco, 28 April 1945:

Great excitement in this country from coast to coast tonight following a phony A.P. [Associated
Press] report from San Francisco, quoting 'a high United States official,' that Germany had

surrendered unconditionally and that an announcement was expected officially. The official was Senator Tom Connally and it seems he did tell an A.P. reporter that he expected 'momentarily' a statement that Germany had surrendered. But if the Associated Press had a greater sense of responsibility, it would at least check such a momentous piece of news in Washington, where it would have been received before transmission to San Francisco...

Late this evening President Truman issued an official denial that Germany had surrendered. But it can only be a matter of days or even hours. What seems to be fact is that Himmler offered through Sweden a German surrender to Great Britain and the United States, but was told the offer would have to be made to Russia too. Thank God we didn't let the Nazis split the victorious Allied coalition this early in game![270]

Count Bernadotte on the events of the day; he had stayed overnight at the home of a Danish official in Aabanraa. In the morning Schellenberg appeared to arrange the next meeting with Himmler:

This was on April 28th. When later in the afternoon I sat listening to the so-called 'Atlantic Sender's' news report, I heard my name mentioned. This was followed by the announcement that according to reports from London and New York I had opened negotiations with the Head of the S.S., Reichsminister Himmler, for a German capitulation. My first thought was that this had spoilt everything, and there was no further possibility of negotiations.[271]

From a pre-trial interrogation of Walter Schellenberg at Nuremberg, 13 November 1945:

When on the 28th of April 1945 I returned from Copenhagen to Luebeck from my discussions with Count Bernadotte after the refusal by the Allies of Germany's capitulation only to the Western Powers, my section chief of VI C, Dr Rapp, informed me that the refusal of the capitulation of Germany to the Western Powers was constantly broadcast over the radio and that this refusal had resulted in Hitler's (sic) issuing an order of arrest against Himmler, and at the same time it was announced over the Radio that Himmler had been deprived of all his offices, so Dr Rapp told me. I didn't hear it myself.[272]

Schellenberg's memoirs reveal a different and self-protective view. He imagined that his relationship with Himmler might be jeopardized or even become fatal:

... I therefore arranged for an astrologer [Wulff] from Hamburg to accompany me [to Lübeck]. Himmler knew the man personally, and thought very highly of him. He could never resist having his horoscope read, and I felt this would soften his reaction to the disappointment.

The first part of my talk with Himmler need not be described here. It was not easy, and looking back on it I cannot understand why it turned out so well.

For a long time we discussed the grounds of the Allies' rejection. Himmler was bitterly disappointed, and particularly annoyed that the facts had been published in the world's press. He feared that his letter to the Swedish Foreign Minister would now be published as well. We then discussed the problem of Denmark and Norway. The fact that Himmler held me responsible, as the instigator of his peace move, for its failure, which could have such fatal consequences for his relationship with Hitler, did not seem to offer a very good basis for my plans to save the Scandinavian countries. However, with the aid of the astrological gentleman, I was able to persuade him to accept my view and, after thinking the matter over for an hour, he gave me permission to discuss with Count Bernadotte the end of the German occupation of Norway and the internment in Sweden of the German occupation forces for the remainder of the war. Himmler stated that he was prepared to arrange a similar solution for Denmark, but that this should be finally decided later on....[273]

SS-Gruppenführer Hermann Fegelein was shot in the grounds of the Reich Chancellery between 23:00 hrs and midnight.[274]

Christa Schröder, one of Hitler's secretaries still in the Bunker at the time, recalled a briefcase of Fegelein's papers found in the Bunker:

In the briefcase were found papers relating to negotiations of the Reichsführer [*Himmler*] with Switzerland (1944) and Sweden. The court martial then met and pronounced the death sentence, carried out immediately in the Tiergarten.[275]

Sunday, 29 April 1945

Events:

Order issued at 14:20 hrs by Chief OKW, Keitel, on employment for evacuated civilians:

1. In agreement with the Reichsführer SS I order for the north German region:

a) With the evacuation of the civilian population areas threatened by the enemy, none of them will be forcibly employed.

b) As far as the population will voluntarily evade this movement this is still Party led and the Wehrmacht will support them in this respect.

c) OKH, Army Group Vistula, C-in-C North West and 12th Army will determine special roads for the refugee treks.

d) Army units keeping order will advise accordingly.

e) Grossadmiral Dönitz is asked to instruct the Gauleiters and Reich Defence Commissioners.

2. Appropriates directives for the southern region will – if necessary – be requested through Deputy Chief, WFStab (Gen. Lt. Winter) and the Leader of the Party Chancellery [*Bormann*].[276]

Order issued by Chief, Naval War Staff [*Admiral Wilhelm Meisel*]:

Rumours about the formation of a Bavarian Freedom Committee and an offer of capitulation by Reichsführer Himmler or an armistice on the Western Front are the products of enemy agitation. The Führer is in Berlin in the midst of the fateful struggle. It is necessary more than ever only to accept order from ones (*sic*) appointed superiors, to obey these unreservedly and to follow instructions of the Supreme Command to the last.[277]

War Diary of Army Command Staff North (A), entry dated 29 April 1945:

19:00 hrs: Departure from Neuroofen by forest tracks to Dobbin.

19:31 hrs: radio message arrived from General Krebs and Reichsleiter Bormann for Feldmarschall Keitel.

The foreign press is spreading a new betrayal. The Führer expects from you, that you will act instantly with hard steel and without distinction.

From Wenck, Schörner and others the Führer expects that they demonstrate their loyalty to him in the quickest way.[278]

Diary of Martin Bormann, entry of 28 April 1945:

Night 28/29.4. – foreign press reports on the offer of surrender of the Reich by H. Himmler. Marriage of Adolf Hitler + Eva Braun.

The Führer dictated his political and private wills.

The traitors Jodl, Himmler and their comrades would leave us to the Bolsheviks.

Again constant [*artillery*] barrage.

From enemy reports the Americans have penetrated Munich.[279]

Hitler: "My Political Will" Part I, dated 29 April 1945, 04:00 hrs:

I have no doubts that if the nations of Europe are again to be regarded as mere shares to be bought and sold by international conspirators in money and finance, and who will be saddled with the responsibility, the real criminal in this murderous struggle: Jewry! Furthermore I left no one in doubt that this time not only would millions of children of Europe's aryan people die of hunger, not only would millions of grown men suffer death, and not only hundreds of thousands of women and children be burned and bombed to death in the towns, without the real criminal having to atone for his guilt...

After six years of war, which in spite of all setbacks will one day go down in history as the most glorious and heroic manifestation of a people's will to live, I cannot forsake the city which is the capital of this Reich. Since our forces are too small to withstand any longer the enemy's attacks on this place, and since our resistance will be gradually worn down by an army of blind automata, I wish to share the fate that millions of others have accepted and to remain here in this city. Further, I will not fall into the hands of an enemy who required a new spectacle. exhibited by Jews, to divert his hysterical masses. I have therefore decided to remain in Berlin, and there to choose death voluntarily at the moment when I believe the residence of the Führer and Chancellor can no longer be held...

Many of the most courageous men and women have decided to unite their lives with mine until the very last. I have begged and finally ordered them not to do this, but to take part in the further battle of the Nation. I beg the heads of the Army, the Navy, and the Air Force to strengthen by all possible means the spirit of resistance of our soldiers in the National-Socialist sense, with special reference to the fact that also I myself, as founder and creator of this movement, have preferred death to cowardly abdication or even capitulation.

Second Part of the Political Testament:

Before my death I expel from the Party the earlier Reichsmarschall Hermann Goering and deprive him of all rights which he may enjoy by virtue of the decree of June 29th, 1941; and also by virtue of my statement in the Reichstag on September 1st, 1939, I appoint in his place Grossadmiral Doenitz, President of the Reich and Supreme Commander of the Armed Forces.

Before my death I expel the earlier Reichsführer-SS and Reich Minister of the Interior Heinrich Himmler from the Party and all offices of State. In his place I appoint Gauleiter Karl Hanke as Reichsführer-SS and Chief of German Police and Gauleiter Paul Gieseler as Reich Minister of the Interior.

Göring and Himmler, by their secret negotiations with the enemy, without my knowledge or approval, and by their illegal attempts to seize power in the state, quite apart from their treachery to my person, have brought irrefutable shame on the country and the whole people.

In order that the German people may have a government of honourable men who will continue the war by all methods. I appoint the following members of the new Cabinet as leaders of the nation:

There then follows a list of nineteen men nominated by Hitler to his successor, Grand Admiral Dönitz, now appointed Reich President and Minister for War. In his turn, Dönitz took no notice of those nominated for him.[280]

Radio message decrypted by Bletchley Park on 29 April 1945, taken at 15:30 hours, from Himmler to Kaltenbrunner in Salzburg:

Situation in Berlin very strained. Situation on Eastern Front w.[west] of Prenzlau very difficult.

Reports on the enemy wireless are malicious perversions of a conversation that I had with Bernadotte.

It is clear that to fight is the only possibility, since the other side is at present absolutely at one against us.

Equally malicious and untrue is the other assertion, that I, with [Werner] Naumann, have prepared a detailed declaration concerning the Führer's death 'Eine Botschaft Ueber Den Tod Des Führers Ausgearbeiter Habe' [A message about the death of the Führer has been worked out]. Naumann is in Berlin. I am outside. We have not spoken to each other for a fortnight.[281]

From a post-war interrogation of Otto Ohlendorf:

HIMMLER before dismissal from Party and Government.

Himmler considered himself to be the first man after Hitler. Bormann intrigued with Hitler against Himmler. In March [1945] the Berlin government ceased to function as the constant air raids made all serious work impossible. It was then decided that Hitler should go to the Southern redoubt with part of the government and Himmler should remain somewhere in North or North West Germany. Hitler seems to have been persuaded by Bormann to reside in Berlin after Himmler had left for N.W. Germany. From that moment Hitler's distrust of the Reichsführer was fanned into hatred by Bormann.

HIMMLER dismissed by Führer.

In N.W. Germany Himmler proceeded to negotiate with the Allies first through Bernadotte, latter attempts were made to contact Eisenhower through Schellenberg and Montgomery through Jodl. Bormann apparently heard of this and persuaded the Führer to dismiss Himmler from the party (sic) and the government. Some sort of message with the Führer's signature seems to have reached Himmler.

HIMMLER after his Downfall.

Ohlendorf claims that for years Himmler had paid little attention to him [Ohlendorf], but after his fall made him and Schellenberg his chief confidants. "He was no longer the same man. He asked me the queerest questions and made the most absurd proposals and plans. I could no longer understand him. He seemed to have lost his self-confidence, his aim and ambition.[282]

Radio message intercepted by Bletchley Park on 29 April 1945, taken at 18:15 hours, from K. H. Frank (Prague) to Himmler:

If something happens to (B% [sic] the Führer, the Government, administration) and the executive feels themselves to be no longer bound by the oath. For the situation in the Protectorate also it will then be of decisive importance whether a successor has already been designated or whether such designation in good time is to be counted upon. I request immediate information so that I can guide the current political measures accordingly.[283]

Radio message intercepted by Bletchley Park on 29 April 1945, taken at 19:00 hours, from K. H. Frank [*Karl Hermann Frank in Prague*] to Hitler and copied to Himmler:

My Führer,

In view of the latest Reich situation, I request immediate reply giving freedom of action in domestic and foreign policy for Bohemia and Moravia in order still to exploit all opportunities offering themselves for the rescue of the Germans here from Bolshevism.[284]

Radio message intercepted by Bletchley Park on 29 April 1945, taken at 21:00 hours, shows Himmler responding to Frank:

Ref. yours of 1900 hours.

What do you mean by freedom of action in domestic and in particular foreign policy.[285]

Radio message intercepted by Bletchley Park on 29 April 1945, from Wilhelm Stuckart [*Secretary of State, Ministry of the Interior*] to K. H. Frank:

You have been informed several times that there comes into question, for removal of German population from the Protectorate, the bordering western (C% Gaues)… Sudetengau, Bavarian … Upper Danube. These areas were already envisaged for the repatriation movements from Silesia which run through the Protectorate. The setting in motion of repatriation measures should be reported solely to Reichsführer SS in good time.[286]

Radio message intercepted by Bletchley Park on 29 April 1945, from Himmler to Kaltenbrunner:

Wireless Transmitting Centre South Rf.SS is in the Bad Tölz area. If the situation demands it, to order its transfer to the Tirol.[287]

Further developments concerning Count Bernadotte's negotiations with Himmler came from his meeting with Schellenberg on 29 April. Himmler had reacted quite badly to the Allied publicity of his partial surrender offer. However Himmler eventually turned calmer:

…The next moment he had proposed that both he and Schellenberg should place themselves under General Schörner's orders and attack the enemy on the Eastern front at the head of a battalion. Schellenberg succeeded in calming him down, and after a couple of hours' discussion Himmler declared himself prepared to allow the German troops in Norway to capitulate, and also to allow the Germans in Denmark to lay down their arms to the British forces.[288]

At Ploen, Grossadmiral Dönitz received the wounded and new Commander in Chief of the Luftwaffe, Feldmarschall Ritter von Greim.[289]

In the course of the afternoon, the OKW Command Post then at Himmler's headquarters, moved to Dobbin/Mecklenburg. A radio message intercepted by Bletchley Park on 29 April 1945, taken at 23:30 hrs, that was included in the daily intelligence material for Prime Minister Churchill, confirmed the move:

> Main body of OKW/Armed Forces Ops Staff at Wismar…
>
> Extremely small advance party of key operational personnel (Führungsspitze) will probably be at Dobbin by midday tomorrow. RFSS Himmler also here. Next HQ is supposed to be Eutin area. Dethleffsen has been Chief of Staff Vistula from today. Heinrici and old Chief of Staff no longer commanding.[290]

From the memoirs of Wilhelm Keitel:

> We drove on to our new operational headquarters at Dobbin, the estate of the famous Dutch oil magnate Deterding (who had died in 1939).
>
> When we arrived we met Himmler, he planned to move out with his staff early next day, so the sleeping quarters provided for us were cramped and crowded. But at least we were in wireless communication again, and we at once took over the radio office, which almost immediately began furnishing us with signals….[291]

War Diary of Army Command Staff Nord (A):

> 23.30 hrs: Relieving of Commander and Chief of General Staff Army Group Vistula, Generaloberst Heinrici and General v. Trotha, by Generalfeldmarschall Keitel. They will be replaced by Generaloberst Student and General Dethleffsen.[292]

War Diary of Army Command Staff South (B):

> Passing on a report from C-in-C West [Kesselring], that of the Munich mutineers 200 were shot or hanged.[293]

Monday, 30 April 1945

Events:

Himmler set up his headquarters at Schloss Kalkhorst on the road between Klütz and Dassow.

From a post-war interrogation of Werner Grothmann:

> 30 Apr. 45 Himmler's party left for another villa in the neighbourhood of Klütz [*Schloss Kalkhorst*] (Lübeck district). On the evening of the same day they moved once again to Admiral Dönitz H.Q. at Plön (between Lübeck & Kiel) where they spent a couple of days. There they saw Ribbentrop for the last time, and before they left Plön Himmler received a telegram from the Führer in Berlin in which Hitler said that he was remaining in Berlin until the end and that Doenitz was to take his place as Führer. On the 1st May news came through that Berlin was completely cut off, and it was accordingly presumed that Hitler had died in the capital.[294]

From a second post-war interrogation of Werner Grothmann:

Grothmann said that the statement ascribed to him in his previous interrogation report, that on 30th April Himmler, at Ploen, received a telegram from Hitler in Berlin in which Doenitz was named as his successor, was inaccurate. The telegram had been sent to Doenitz, who showed it to Himmler. Himmler received no communication from Hitler, and had heard, through a telephone conversation with Berlin, that Hitler had received the news of his dealings with Count Bernadotte very badly.[295]

Radio message decrypted by Bletchley Park on 30 April 1945 (at 13:00 hours), regarded as Top Secret Ultra, and part of the daily intelligence brief for Prime Minister Churchill:

...to Reichsfuehrer SS Himmler

Since according to Czech interpretation the Reich can no longer defend the Protectorate, the Government organisations and population of the Protectorate now consider that they are responsible on their own account and are making political as well as constitutional demands, underlined by strikes, disturbances and refusal of German currency. I have already arrested various personalities including a minister and two National Bank governors. With regard to internal politics, the situation may at any hour lead to developments in respect of which [I] must [have full powers] in order to extract from the situation what is best for the Reich and Germanism. With regard to foreign policy, the possibility exists of interesting the Western Powers in the Bohemian-Moravian area by activating the Czech problem (like the Polish problem), of creating new material for conflict in order to break up the enemy coalition and thus of preserving 5,000,000 Germans from Bolshevist chaos. Immediate action is necessary. Since Feldm[arschall] Schoerner turns a deaf ear to political possibilities, it is necessary to have a conference with you in Prague this very day in consultation with Schoerner and SS Obergruppenfuehrer Hildebrandt who joins in this request. Please acknowledge receipt. Heil Hitler. Yours ever, Frank.[296]

Karl Dönitz on the surprising message from Berlin and its aftermath:

On April 30 I received a radio signal in the naval cipher from the Chancellery in Berlin: 'Fresh treachery afoot. According to enemy broadcast Himmler has made offer to surrender via Sweden. Führer expects you to take instant and ruthless action against traitors.' – Bormann.

... I invited Himmler to a meeting for I wanted to know what game he was playing. We agreed to meet at the police barracks in Luebeck.

About midday, as I was about to set out, Admiral Meisel, the Naval Chief of Staff, and Gauleiter Wegener came to see me and told me that they feared for my personal safety if I went to visit Himmler. I did my best to allay their anxieties...

When I reached the police barracks in Luebeck I found that every available senior SS leader had apparently been summoned to the meeting. Himmler kept me waiting. He seemed ready to regard himself as head of the state. I asked him whether the report was true that he had sought contact with the Allies through the medium of Count Bernadotte. He asserted that it was not true, and that in his opinion it was essential, in these last days of the war, that discord among ourselves should not be allowed to create further chaos in the country. We parted amicably.[297]

Radio message decrypted by Bletchley Park on 30 April 1945, signed by Himmler and counter-signed by Stuckart; addressed to Reich Defence Commissioners in Schwerin, Kiel, Dresden, Reichenberg, Linz, Salzburg, Innsbruck, Klagenfurt, Graz and SS-Ogruf. Werner Best in Copenhagen:

(C5 in the event of direct) enemy (C% threat) by troops of the Western powers the local authorities are to hand over all fit male members of their staffs to the Armed Forces or to the Volkssturm in so far as they can be employed in these. With the personnel remaining at their disposal the local authorities are to maintain an emergence administration. All secret material and also files and documents which may be of interest to the enemy and his democratic mentality which is filled with hatred for National Socialism are to be destroyed. This not applicable to card indexes of offices for economics and food, such items of equipment as are necessary for ensuring that the authorities can continue their work are to be left intact. Supply goods are as far as possible to be distributed to the population and what is left is to be preserved.

2) In the event of a direct enemy threat by Soviet troops the authorities are to cease to function as soon as the possibility of carrying on their work ceases to exist, at the same time the administrative apparatus necessary for the maintenance of life is to be maintained to the last. Administrative personnel who do not go into the Armed Forces or Volkssturm may withdraw with the population. Files and documents and also card indexes of the offices for economics and food are to be completely destroyed. He who fails to do this endangers the population, supply goods which are suitable for distribution among the population are to be distributed in good time.[298]

Radio message decrypted by Bletchley Park on 30 April 1945, Naval Chief Command North informed authorities under its command of the following order from the Naval War Staff:

Rumours about the formation of a Bavarian Freedom Committee and an offer of capitulation by Reichsführer Himmler or an armistice on the Western Front are the products of enemy agitation. The Führer is in Berlin in the midst of the fateful struggle. It is more necessary than ever only to accept orders from ones (sic) appointed superiors, to obey these unreservedly and to follow out the instructions of the Supreme Command to the last.[299]

Another telegram, timed at 18:07 hrs. from Bormann to Dönitz:

Instead of the previous Reichsmarschall Göring, the Führer appoints you, Herr Grossadmiral, as his successor. Written power of attorney on its way to you. Now you have all the necessary measures for the current situation.[300]

Karl Dönitz from his memoirs:

Shortly after our surrender I learned that he [Himmler] had lied to me when he denied having started negotiations.

By about six o'clock on the evening of April 30 I was back in Ploen ... my aide-de-camp, Commander Luedde-Neurath, handed me a radio signal in the secure naval cipher, which had just arrived from Berlin:

Grand Admiral Doenitz.

The Führer has appointed you, Herr Admiral, as his successor in place of Reichsmarschall Goering. Confirmation in writing follows.

You are hereby authorized to take any measures which the situation demands.

Bormann.

... On the evening of April 30, shortly after the receipt of the telegram, I told my ADC to telephone Himmler, from whom I had parted in Luebeck only a few hours before, and ask him to come to Ploen forthwith. To my ADC he retorted with a blunt refusal, but when I myself spoke to him and told that his presence was essential, he eventually consented to come.

At about midnight he arrived, accompanied by six armed SS officers, and was received by my ADC, Luedde-Neurath. I offered Himmler a chair and myself sat down behind my writing desk, upon which lay, hidden by some paper, a pistol with the safety catch off. I had never done anything of this sort in my life before, but I did not know what the outcome of this meeting might be.

I handed Himmler the telegram containing my appointment. 'Please read this,' I said. I watched him closely. As he read, an expression of astonishment, indeed, of consternation spread over his face. All hope seemed to collapse within him. He went very pale. Finally he stood up and bowed. 'Allow me,' he said, 'to become the second man in your state.' I replied that this was out of the question and that there was no way in which I could make use of his services.

Thus advised, he left me at about one o'clock in the morning [1 May 1945]. The showdown had taken place without force, and I felt relieved. I was, of course, by no means sure that Himmler would not take some action to oppose my orders in the days ahead. But so far at least we had avoided that open conflict which I had feared and which would have had such disastrous effects on internal order and our efforts to save lives.[301]

Radio message decrypted by Bletchley Park on 30 April 1945; from SS-Hauptsturmführer Kriminalrat Heinecke to the Reichsfuehrer SS:

After 5 days' arrest by the Gestapo in Salzburg I have been released on...28/4... with instruction of Chief of Security Police and of Security Service Obergruppenfuehrer Kaltenbrunner to report, after fulfilling my most urgent duties, to Ergaenzung's Bn of Waffen S.S, at Hallein... Request order whether I have to place myself as disposal again of the Reichsmarschall [Göring] with my available 10 men, or whether I am relieved of my task of ensuring the safety of the Reichsmarschall.[302]

May 1945

Events:

From Schellenberg's memoirs; he had been delayed getting back from Copenhagen to Flensburg, arriving at night on 30 April 1945. From his timetable of events it was around midnight or shortly afterwards, on 1 May 1945, where he heard astounding news. Kaltenbrunner had dismissed Schellenberg as Chief of RSHA VI, replacing him with Wilhelm Waneck. He had a telephone conversation with Himmler then drove towards Lübeck with one of his political advisers, SS-Stubaf. Dr Wirsing:

> ... Our journey which was only thirty miles, took us three and a half hours because the roads were completely blocked by troops streaming back from the Mecklenburg area. We arrived at four o'clock in the morning of May 1, and I was conducted to Himmler's new quarters at Kalkhorst, near Travemuende, by one of his adjutants.
>
> As Himmler had not gone to bed until three o'clock, I went to Brandt, who told me the startling news that Hitler had committed suicide and Admiral Doenitz, not Himmler, had been made his successor.
>
> ... Himmler and Admiral Doenitz, the new chief of the German Reich, had met at Ploen and conferred late into the night on the immediate future policy that was to be adopted. Himmler had prevailed upon Doenitz to proclaim, as his first act, the removal of Ribbentrop and the appointment of Count Schwerin von Krosigk as foreign Minister. But the Admiral and his entourage, consisting wholly of Wehrmacht officers, had shown no understanding of Himmler's political moves towards the Western Powers, and consequently the Reichsfuehrer was in the worst possible mood. He was playing with the idea of resigning, and was even talking of suicide.[1]

From a post-war interrogation of HSSPF Georg Henning Graf von Bassewitz-Behr:

> When Busch transferred his HQ from Reinbek nr Hamburg to Flensburg, he asked me to do the same. In the night of 30/4 to 1/5 1945 I was summoned to Himmler's HQ (a farm house near Ploen) for 6 a.m. by the Chief of the Security Police, Brigadeführer Bierkamp. Evidently due to the attitude to a speedy cessation of hostilities, and not defending Hamburg, I was being watched by the security police, because the next morning it was not I, but Bierkamp who was admitted to see Himmler first. As a result Himmler ordered me not to return to Hamburg, but only to remain with Feldmarschall Busch in my evacuated HQ in Schleswig.[2]

Radio message timed at 01:22 hrs from Grossadmiral Dönitz to Hitler:

> My Führer,
> My loyalty to you is unalienable. From here I will attempt further operations to relieve you in Berlin.

If destiny forces me to succeed you and lead the German Reich, I will bring this war to an end, a requirement of this unique battle of heroes from the German people.[3]

The final meeting of Léon Degrelle, the Belgian Rexist leader then serving with a Belgian SS unit:

...Degrelle drove through the night among the milling refugees and in the small hours of the morning of 1 May he reached the hideous late-Victorian castle on the road from Luebeck to Wismar, where Himmler had his 'field headquarters'. During the morning Himmler arrived from Ploen, pale and unshaven, but only to spend a few minutes at the castle before removing his staff to the neighbourhood of Admiral Doenitz. Himmler left word for Degrelle that he was to assemble his men at Bad Segeberg, west of Luebeck. Late in the afternoon, after the announcement of Hitler's death, Degrelle received a personal summons to Himmler's presence. He was to be next day at Malente near Ploen.[4]

In his memoirs Walter Schellenberg details the breakfast meeting with Himmler at 9.00 a.m. in Himmler's headquarters at Kalkhorst. Here Schellenberg made his report about the meeting with Bernadotte, Swedish government representative von Post and Dr Werner Best:

... He was very nervous and distracted, and told me that he was no longer capable to taking action in the matters I had discussed with them... Himmler wanted to take me to Doenitz right away, so that I could act as von Krosigk's assistant on questions of foreign policy. It would also be an advantage if I could report to the Doenitz government on my efforts regarding Denmark and Norway...

At eleven o'clock that morning we set out to drive to Ploen to see Doenitz. We went by way of Lübeck and, after a difficult journey, arrived at two in the afternoon....[5]

Radio message from Bormann in Berlin to Grossadmiral Dönitz, sent at 07:40 hours, received at 10:53 hours:

Will ['Testament'] in force. As soon as possible I will come to you. Until then I think that publication be put back.[6]

Radio message decrypted by Bletchley Park on 1 May 1945, to RFSS from the 19th Army [AOK 19], signed Hauptmann Reich, NS Political Commissar, possibly on station in Austria:

In the Gau Tirol-Vorarlberg large non-fighting groups of the Waffen-SS, Security Service and Gestapo are staying in the valleys. Detachment Commanders do not comply with orders to join in the fighting as they all allege that they have a special task of the Reichsführer SS. Request orders from Reichsführer SS to AOK 19.[7]

Radio message intercepted by Bletchley Park on 1 May 1945, addressed to Reichsführer Himmler, no sender was noted:

In the defence of the Fortress Tyrol-Vorarlberg the political attitude of the local population acquires great importance. Everything that helps to prolong the war is rejected. Slogans of the Viennese opposition government and of the clergy are being followed. However nowhere else do the terrain as well as they political atmosphere provide more favourable pre-requisites for the continuation of a lasting resistance than in the Tyrol. Various interests of Allies or neutrals come into conflict here. A skilful political game and military energy (B% in the Tito manner) will make more acute the conflict (B% of the others) among themselves and preserve German (C% existence). Clear (B% slogans) for such a ... of the Tyrol, must ... as the Army 'A' has rations and amn [ammunition] for only 10 days more, victuals and amn (C% must) ... must be promoted by our political skill. A man must be (C% appointed), who, in every situation (B% in the spirit) ....[8]

"Personal and Top Secret" telegram from Prime Minister Churchill to Field Marshal Sir Harold Alexander [*later Lord Alexander of Tunis, Supreme Allied Commander Mediterranean Theatre*] marked "Through C [*Major General Sir Stewart Menzies, Head of Britain's Secret Intelligence Service – MI 6*]":
Churchill was confident they were "perhaps only a day or two from surrender on all fronts through [*Heinrich*] Himmler". He continued stating that he would be sorry if this overshadows "Italian events"; assuming that Alexander will broadcast his announcement [*of the surrender of German forces in Italy*] at noon GMT the next day.[9]

Radio message timed at 14:46 hours from Goebbels (and possibly Bormann) to Donitz (receipt entered at 15:18 hours):
FRR Grossadmiral Dönitz.
Secret State Matter – only via officer –
Führer passed away yesterday 15:30 hrs. Testament of 29.4. transfers to you the Office of Reich President, Reich Minister Goebbels the Office of Reich Chancellor, Reichsleiter Bormann the Office of Party Minister, Reich Minister Seyss-Inquart the Office of Reich Foreign Minister. The Testament was announced to you by the Führer, to Feldmarschall Schörner and for security taken out of Berlin. Reichsleiter Bormann is attempting to come to you today, and inform you of the situation. The form and date of the announcement to the public and the armed forces is left to you.
Acknowledge receipt.
Goebbels.[10]

Schwerin-Krosigk noted in his diary:
On Tuesday came the expected, and after the shock that we survived, came even more shocking tidings – how can one fight it – that the Führer is no longer alive and the surprising news that that he had appointed Grand Admiral Dönitz as his successor. Not Himmler but Dönitz. I went from Eutin to Dönitz's headquarters [*at Plön*] and spoke with Speer....[11]

From the diary of Albert Speer:
Information from Berlin –
Dönitz appointed Leader.
Schwerin-Krosigk will be Foreign Minister...
Decree; Paralysis and destruction are stopping.[12]

From the post-war interrogation of Dr Giselher Wirsing:

> 1 May 1945 @ 0900 hrs, Kalkhorst.
>
> Schellenberg met with the RfSS for a few minutes to discuss the situation re the Allies now the Führer's death announced. Then RfSS and Schellenberg, with Wirsing following in a second car, drove over to Plön where the RfSS met with Dönitz around 12 noon.[13]

From a post-war interrogation of Dr Rudolf Brandt: '1 May 1945: Himmler's Party moved by car to a village [*Neverfelde near Malente*] near Ploen [*Plön*].'[14]

During the afternoon, Schwerin von Krosigk visited Himmler at his SS-Command Post between Eutin and Plön.[15]

From a post-war interrogation of Otto Ohlendorf:

> Relations with Doenitz.
>
> After Hitler had bestowed his mantle upon the Grossadmiral, Himmler changed his plans and action (sic). He did not attempt to assert his claim to the succession of the Nazi Führership, but placed himself unreservedly at the disposal of Doenitz. To Ohlendorf and others he revealed his hope that he would become Doenitz's prime minister [*Ministerpräsident*] at Ploen. The admiral (sic) declined Himmler's offer of service under him and did not include him in his government, although Ohlendorf was given a post in it. Himmler had to eat humble pie and spent much time in vain, waits in the new Führer's ante-chambre (sic). Ohlendorf, who had been neglected, now became H.[*immler*]'s father-confessor. Ohlendorf did not see him during the last few days of his life but believes that his two ADC's or Adjutanten were constantly with him to the end. One ADC was Rothmann (sic - Grothmann)…[16]

From a later post-war interrogation of Otto Ohlendorf:

> Meanwhile Ogruf Prützmann arrived at Doenitz's HQ as Himmler's representative, with instructions to assume command of all troops and police units in unoccupied North Germany. In practice however all staffs were already in process of disbandment.[17]

Radio message decrypted by Bletchley Park on 1 May 1945, from Himmler to SS-Ogruf. Berger:

> Collect the FS (sic – SS) units militarily under your command and lead them yourself. Defend the entrances to the Alps for me.[18]

Radio message decrypted by Bletchley Park on 1 May 1945, from SS-Ogruf. Berger to Rf.SS in the field:

> … The measures at Dachau which ran counter to the Reichsführer's orders have had disastrous consequences. An SS Officer from Dachau and an Officer of the Security Service whose names, unfortunately, are not known, reported to the International Red Cross and the Swiss Legation and, unsolicited, made the most monstrous statements.[19]

British intelligence report, based on decrypted radio message:

> On 1 May [*underlining in original*] Frank, Senior SS and Police Commander of Bohemia and Moravia informed Himmler that the delegate of the Red Cross had proposed the transfer

of the responsibility for Theresienstadt to the International Red Cross. Frank advocated the adoption of this proposal in view of the extraordinary role played by Theresienstadt in world opinion and the unforeseeable consequences of disorders breaking out there.[20]

On 1 May 1945, KL Dachau main camp still held 31,432 prisoners. About 4,000 lay in the camp hospital (Revier), 6,000 needed medical support, 400 cases of typhus and 800 cases of tuberculosis.[21]

On 1 May 1945 at 22:26 hours there was a radio broadcast announcing the death of Hitler:

From Führer headquarters it was reported that our Führer Adolf Hitler had died fighting for Germany against Bolshevism earlier this afternoon at his command post at the Reich Chancellery.[22]

Hermann Voosen. a German Jew who survived deportation to Latvia, made a report about his release from captivity:

Together with a group of 86 Jewish women and girls and 64 Jewish men, the remnants of a group of 1,400 [deported to Riga], who had been interned since November, 1943. I was rescued by the Swedish Red Cross from the Labour and Training Camp at Kiel-Russee on the 1st May 1945. The following day, we stood on Swedish territory.[23]

Heinz Samuel who was also in the same rescue, has slightly different details:

But then the unbelievable happened. On May 1st, 1945, the Danish Red Cross fetched us out of this hell [Kiel] and brought us back to freedom.[24]

Wednesday, 2 May 1945

Events:

Radio message decrypted by Bletchley Park on 2 May 1945, taken at 09:00 hours; from Himmler to Generaloberst Rendulic, copied to Generalfeldmarschall Kesselring:

I am with the Gross Admiral [Dönitz], to whom I have, of course, subordinated myself, faithfully and loyally.

During the past days greatest intrigue by M.B. [Martin Bormann] from Berlin (Durch M.B. aus Berlin heraus).

The Schoerner – Rendulic area is now of decisive importance, and must be held at all costs.[25]

From a post-war interrogation of Hanna Reitsch:

...On the 2nd of May [1945] the new government was called to Plön. Greim and Reitsch, to receive orders from Doenitz as to immediate Luftwaffe activities, had the additional purpose of meeting Himmler and confronting him with the betrayal story.

Himmler's Capitulation Explanation: Himmler arrived late so that all the others were in the conference room, leaving Reitsch alone when he walked in.

'One moment, Herr Reichsführer, a matter of the highest importance, if you can spare the time?' Reitsch asked. Himmler seemed almost jovial as he said: 'Of course.'

'Is it true, Herr Reichsführer, that you contacted the Allies with proposals of peace without orders to do so from Hitler?'

'But of course.'

'You betrayed your Führer and your people in the very darkest hour? Such a thing is high treason, Herr Reichsführer. You did that when your place was actually in the bunker with Hitler?'

'High treason? No! You'll see, history will weigh it differently. Hitler wanted to continue the fight. He was mad with his pride and his 'honor'. He wanted to shed more German blood when there was none left to flow. Hitler was insane. It should have been stopped long ago.'

'Insane? I came from him less than thirty-six hours ago. He died for the cause he believed in. He died bravely and filled with the 'honor' you speak of, while you and Göring and the rest must now live as branded traitors and cowards.'

'I did as I did to save German blood, to rescue what was left of our country.'

'You speak of German blood, Herr Reichsführer? You speak of it now? You should have thought of it years ago, before you became identified with the useless shedding of so much of it.'

A sudden [aircraft] strafing attack terminated the conversation.[26]

From the diary of Grand Admiral Karl Dönitz:

10:30 Hrs, Plön. Grand Admiral [Dönitz], Graf Schwerin v. Krosigk, Gauleiter Wegener.
Discussion on principle political questions.
The military situation is hopeless. At this stage the main objective of the Government must be to save as many German people from annihilation by Bolshevism. As far as the Anglo-Saxons stand in the way of our goal, we must continue the fight against them.
…
11:50 hrs: Meeting on the Bohemian question.
Participants as above [*Dönitz, Keitel, Schwerin von Krosigk, Wegener*], in addition Reichsführer-SS. Military situation is good, region is only dependent on 3 weeks supplies and munitions.
…
13:10 hrs: Meeting with Reichsführer-SS [*Himmler; with Dönitz*].
…
20:00 hrs: Move to new headquarters in Flensburg.[27]

From the memoirs of Albert Speer:

…the next day he [*Himmler*] turned up unannounced at Doenitz's headquarters. It was around noon, and Doenitz invited Himmler and me to dine with him – though not out of any special friendliness. However much he disliked Himmler, Doenitz would have regarded it as discourteous to treat a man who had so recently held so much power with contempt. Himmler brought the news that Gauleiter Kaufmann intended to surrender Hamburg without a fight. A leaflet addressed to the populace was now being printed. Himmler said, to prepare the way for the impending entrance of British troops into the city. Doenitz was angry….[28]

War diary of Army Command Staff North (A):

> Teleprinter message to Battle Commander Hamburg, C-in-C North West and Gauleiter Kaufmann that it is not intended to defend Hamburg. Approval given to an English offer of 3 May 1945, 8.00 hours in the morning, for a peace negotiator to be sent.[29]

Himmler and Ohlendorf moved to an estate at Neversfelde (part of Malente). On 2 May 1945, also present were SS-Ogruf. Prützmann and the BdS Hamburg, SS-Brig. Bierkamp.[30]

In Malente, Himmler was surprised by the British breakthrough. Leon Degrelle. commander of the 5.SS-Sturmbrigade "Wallonien", found that Himmler had flown his headquarters, a farm. It was three in the afternoon:

> As I came to the back of Eutin on a country road I saw a spectacle that Dante remembered of hell. Hundreds of refugee waggons, hundreds of military trucks, all burning away. Low-flying aircraft in groups of six came down like vultures... We came to the junction at Bad Segeberg. Suddenly I saw a long black car emerging from a side road. A vigorous man with a pale face beneath a leather helmut sat at the steering wheel. I knew him. It was Himmler.[31]

From a post-war interrogation of Heinz Macher:

> He [Macher] retreated with the Army Group and eventually arrived in Flensburg. He then became commander of about 15 men who had been chosen to act as a personal guard to Himmler. Previously he had only been a staff officer.[32]

From a post-war interrogation of Dr Rudolf Brandt, that on 2 May 1945 Himmler's staff moved to a village near Flensburg.[33]

From a post-war interrogation of Werner Grothmann:

> 2 May 45 Himmler and his retinue moved [from Plön] to Flensburg by car, and on arrival established themselves at C.H.Q....
>
> While in Flensburg Himmler discussed with Dönitz the possibility of an armistice with the Western Allies, and there was also a long debate as to whether it would be wise for Himmler to remain a member of the German Government.
>
> Before leaving Flensburg, Himmler changed into civilian clothes, removed his glasses & placed a black patch over one of his eyes, while Grothmann, Macher, Dr Brandt and Kiermaier discarded their official uniforms in favour of the hybrid dress in which they felt it would be best to continue their journey. Dr Müller, however, remained in uniform.[34]

After his arrest, SS-Gruf. Otto Ohlendorf had a conversation with a British Army Office in London:

> I left Plön for Flensburg at the same time as Dönitz... When we got to Flensburg I also arranged billets for Himmler, outside the town...[35]

During the day, Himmler was observed in an armoured personnel carrier (*Kübelwagen*) in Market Square, Bad Bramstedt*, with SS-Panzer-Grenadier Training and Replacement Battalion 12, SS-Division "Hitlerjugend".[36]

[*Bad Bramstedt lays to the east of Hamburg and already occupied by Allied forces; Bramstedtlund, 11 Kms. west of Flensburg may have been meant.*]

SS-WVHA senior officials Glücks, Maurer, Sommer, Burger and Lolling and a few others from *Amtsgruppe D*, travelled together in many vehicles from Oranienburg to Flensburg.[37]

SS-Ogruf. Dr Werner Best described a journey south from Plön to Flensburg during the night of 2-3 May 1945:

> The last time I saw Himmler was during the night of 2–3 May 1945. I had an appointment with the new head of state, Dönitz, at his headquarters in Plön.
>
> When I got there it was already on the move to Flensburg. I met Himmler who asked me to join him in his car so we could talk together. He drove the car. Due to an air attack we drove around Kiel on side roads and in the morning came to Himmler's destination near Flensburg.
>
> When I put the question to him, why it had come so far, he answered in these words: 'In recent times the Führer is no longer the same.' ... Then he told me of the increasing change in Hitler, how Himmler's opponents, particularly Bormann and the OKW used their influence against him; he was transferred to military commands only for him to take the blame. In regard to the situation at the moment, he said: 'If I could just talk to Eisenhower for two hours. Then I would convince that together we need to go against the Russians.' ...
>
> During that night of 2–3 May, I found Himmler very nervous and really absent-minded. Moody and quite despondent. One could say that he had an exciting and exhausting time behind him. And before him he saw a way out – but no job.
>
> Possibly he did not have in mind becoming a prisoner with the task of defending a lost cause. I am sure that if we had been surprised that night by enemy troops, by my side he would have taken poison. By the end his nerves and intentions had moderated...[38]

During the night, Himmler knocked on the bedroom window of Johannes Festesen, in the village of Esgrus, about 12 km east of Ausacker (both locations east of Flensburg):

> Himmler stood on the lawn in front of our house and greeted me with words: "You want to take me in...". The next morning [3 May] he disappeared just as secretly as he had come.[39]

Radio message from Chinese Military attaché, Berne, to Chinese General Staff, Chungking, intercepted and decrypted by Bletchley Park:

> 1. As far as fighting between the various United States armies and the Germans is concerned, hostilities may now be said to have terminated and the present scattered fighting in other sectors has no significance.
>
> Himmler's surrender negotiations in Sweden, through the medium of the Vice-President of the Red Cross Society, have been going on for some time; the main issue, apart from a desire to save themselves, was that the defeated German armies must be handed over to the British and Americans and not to the Russians. The Russians however were early aware of this stipulation and, while themselves maintaining absolute silence, are closely watching British and United States reactions. The United States was in favour of accepting the German offer but the British advocated working together with the U.S.S.R. While the issue was still unsettled, Stalin telegraphed to Molotov suggesting that the request for surrender should be accepted but pointing out that Himmler was not empowered to take the lead in surrendering. The mopping-up process accordingly continues...
>
> 2. Intelligence from French sources.

Himmler has accepted the British-United States proposal to address his request for surrender to the Soviet also (*sic*). The Soviet has demanded of Himmler that the Wehrmacht must simultaneously come forward in the same sense after which the general surrender can be settled.[40]

The American journalist, William L. Shirer, reported:

The Germans in Italy have surrendered... Moscow says Berlin fell at three p.m. today... Himmler told Bernadotte that Hitler was suffering from a brain hemorrhage and 'might already be dead but could not live more than two days at best'.[41]

Thursday to Monday, 3 to 7 May 1945

Post-war interrogation of Wilhelm Walther, Himmler's bodyguard:

...accompanied them to the farm of Lorenzen, vic. [*vicinity*] Ausacker, approx. 10 Kilometers SE of Flensburg which Walter identified as Himmler's hq. and the place where he had buried the files. Extensive digging as well as subsequent high-pressure interrogation of farmer Lorenzen and his daughter produced neither the documents nor any leads as to how they disappeared: they did admit – though reluctantly – that Himmler had been living at their farm from 3 May to 7 May 1945.[42]

The journalist Holger Pieneing:

A few kilometers [*from Flensburg*] in Hüholz camped out senior SS-officers and concentration camp commanders.[43]

Thursday, 3 May 1945

Events:

From the post-war interrogation of Dr Rudolf Brandt: "3 May, Himmler's Party moved to Flensburg."[44]

From the post-war interrogation of Werner Grothmann: "On 3 or 4 May it [*the HQ*] arrived at Flensburg."[45]

From the post-war interrogation of Heinz Macher:

He retreated with the Army Group and eventually arrived in Flensburg. He then became commander of about 15 men who had been chosen to act as personal guard to Himmler. Previously he had only been staff officer.[46]

Chief of the Ordungspolizei (Chef Orpo), General of Police Alfred Wünnenberg moved from Lübeck to Felsburg-Harriesleefeld, setting up his headquarters in a fireman's training school (*Feuerwehrschule*). It was probably two days later when Himmler and his staff arrived [*3 May*].

Himmler met with the Police President of Flensburg, SS-Staf. Hans Hinsch, to discuss the situation, and Wünnenberg who acknowledged that any defence was now futile.[47]

From the diary of Grand Admiral Karl Dönitz:

09:30 hrs: Meeting on the Bohemian Question. Reich Protector [?], Minister of State Frank, Reich Foreign Minister [*Schwerin von Krosigk*], Feldmarschall Keitel, Generaloberst Jodl, Gauleiter Wegener, Reich Minister Speer.

Bohemia remains on the verge of revolution. In the long run, the Protectorate can be kept neither militarily nor politically…

As a side issue, the appropriateness of Bohemia was discussed as an alternative territory for the Government. Contrary to the advice of OKW and the Reichsführer-SS the Grand Admiral has concerns that abroad Bohemia has uncertain political relations.

…

18:30 hrs: Special Order for Schellenberg. Reichsführer-SS, Foreign Minister, Gauleiter Wegener, Gruppenführer Schellenberg.

Proposal to resolve the Norwegian question through Sweden.

Schellenberg has orders to clarify further possibilities, however, no authority for the conclusion of negotiations.

20:00 hrs: Reichsführer-SS.

23:00 hrs: Generaladmiral von Friedeburg back from Montgomery's headquarters. Report on the course of the negotiations.[48]

From the memoirs of Karl Dönitz:

At one of our conferences with Terboven and General Boehme on Norway, Himmler unexpectedly appeared, accompanied by Gruppenführer Schellenberg, the Chief of the German Foreign Security Service. General Boehme reported that Norway was quiet…

Schellenberg suggested that we should offer to surrender Norway to Sweden and ask at the same time that the German army of occupation should be allowed to enter Sweden and be interned there. In this way, he pointed out, our troops would escape becoming prisoners of the British or the Americans. In the course of the discussion it was disclosed that through Schellenberg, Himmler had sometime before raised this question with Sweden and that the country had expressed, in confidence, its willingness to agree to the internment of these troops on its territory.

I viewed with suspicions both the motives which had actuated these unofficial negotiations and the success that had attended them. Apart from the dubiousness of the motive, it seemed to me that to take a step would, of itself, be a mistake.

On Graf Schwerin-Krosigk's advice I therefore confined myself to agreeing that Schellenberg should ascertain whether Sweden's acquiescence had been obtained with British concurrence, which implicit or definitely expressed. But I certainly did not give Schellenberg the right to conclude any formal agreement.[49]

Schellenberg gave Count Bernadotte his view of this meeting, described in his memoirs:

Schellenberg gave us some other interesting information. In Murwik, in the neighbourhood of Flensburg, he had had a long meeting with Dönitz, Schwerin von Krosigk and Himmler, at which were also present General Field-Marshal Keitel and General Jodl. On this occasion Schellenberg said that he had been able to persuade the Government to order the capitulation of all German troops in Holland, North-west Germany and Denmark. The only one who had violently opposed this was Keitel....[50]

Rudolf Hoess remembered his last meeting with Himmler, on 3 May 1945:

We report for the last time at Flensburg, where the Reichsführer SS had withdrawn with others members of the government. There was no more talk of fighting. Every man for himself was now the order of the day...

Glücks was already half-dead. We carried him to the naval hospital [Flensburg] under another name...

On May 3rd, 1945, I met Himmler for the last time. What remained of the Inspectorate of Concentration Camps had been ordered to follow Himmler to Flensburg. Glücks, Maurer and myself duly reported to him there. He had just come from a conference with the surviving members of the government. He was hale and hearty, and in the best of humour. He greeted me and at once gave the following orders:'Glücks and Hoess are to disguise themselves as non-commissioned officers of the army to make their way across the green frontier to Denmark as stragglers, and hide themselves in the army. Maurer and what is left of the Inspectorate of Concentration Camps are to disappear into the army in the same way. All further matters will be dealt with by Standartenführer Hintz (sic – Hinsch), the police president of Flensburg.' He shook each of us by the hand. We were dismissed!

He had with him at the time, Professor Gebhardt and Schellenberg of the Reich Security Head Office. Like Gebhardt, Glücks said that Himmler intended to go into hiding in Sweden.[51]

From a postwar British interrogation of WVHA, Amtsgruppe D, personnel:

According to Sommer, who has been interrogated, the head of the party (who was apparently Glücks) and Maurer had an interview with Himmler who told them that he was getting in touch with Field Marshal Montgomery to arrange an armistice with the Western Allies in order to carry on the war against Russia and advised them to go underground for some weeks by which time all grievances would be forgotten. All members of the party then obtained false papers from the naval camp at Murwik and each member went on his own way.[52]

The historian Jan Erik Schule:

The personnel of [WVHA] Amtsgruppe D for example, in the first days of May, received naval uniforms and pay-books in Flensburg then sent in the direction of Sylt.[53]

Friday, 4 May 1945

Events:

Generalfeldmarschall Ernst Busch with his 350 officers and men set up his headquarters staff as C-in-C North West in the village of Kollerup (100 inhabitants – today, Grossolt parish), taking over the farm of Johannes Christiansen and adjacent yards. The village was completely sealed off.

Also SS-Reichsführer Heinrich Himmler came to Kollerup from his Hüholz headquarters near Kappeln. Nervous and exhausted he wanted a service record book (*Wehrpass*) that could be used. This was denied him by Busch.[54]

From a postwar interrogation of Otto Ohlendorf:

> When we got to Flensburg I also arranged billets for Himmler, outside the town. Himmler was very depressed. The second morning there [4 May] he sent for me and kept on asking the same question: what was he to do? Should he commit suicide or give himself up? ... Gebhardt was present during our conversation but didn't utter a word and only after a minute or so, when the whole atmosphere was deep gloom, did he say to Himmler that something would have to be done, that three medical organizations were still functioning and he wished Himmler would see that he (Gebhardt) became head of the whole medical service and of the medical profession generally, a most embarrassing thing for me to have to listen to.[55]

From the diary of Karl Dönitz:

> 09:00 hrs: Report by Friedeberg over the negotiations with Montgomery. Friedeberg, Foreign Minister, Keitel, Jodl, Lt.Col. Brudermüller.
>
> ...
>
> 12:25 hrs: Reichsführer-SS, Foreign Minister, Reich Kommissar for Holland [Seyss-Inquart]: Discussion on surrender questions and further steps. Return journey of Reich Kommissar Holland hindered by the weather. Thus concrete orders given him on 4th [May] have lapsed. He should return to development of an armistice for his region...[56]

Postwar statement of Oberstleutant Werner Baumbach, for IMT Nuremberg:

> When Himmler again appeared at Flensburg, he spoke to him [Speer] about his [Himmler's] duty, when British troops took over... After this day, Himmler disappeared.[57]

Albert Speer recalled that Admiral Dönitz refused to leave the Flensburg area, despite rumours that British forces would soon occupy the town. Himmler reportedly was thinking of fleeing to Prague where he had a power base.

> Himmler then began pressing Baumbach, who had been placed in charge of the government air squadron, to provide him with a plane so that he could escape to Prague. Baumbach and I decided that we would land him on an airfield already held by enemy. But Himmler's intelligence service was still functioning: 'When you fly in your planes,' Himmler snarled at Baumbach, 'they don't know where they're going to land.'[58]

From the memoirs of Walter Schellenberg: On 3 May 1945 Schellenberg held a meeting with Swedish Foreign Office officials in Copenhagen. He made a difficult car journey back to Mürwik via Flensburg, arriving at 17.00 hours of 4 May. Minutes later he attended a meeting with Foreign Minister von Krosigk and Himmler. Schellenberg later briefed Dönitz on his talks before having dinner that evening with von Krosigk, Keitel and Jodl. This was the last meeting of Schellenberg and Himmler.[59]

The viewpoint of Count Bernadotte to Schellenberg's meeting in Copenhagen:

> ...On the evening of May 4th, M. von Post, who had returned to Stockholm on the previous evening, informed me that Schellenberg had returned to Copenhagen. And there Schellenberg had reported some sensational events. In the first place, Grand Admiral Dönitz had decided to surrender with all German forces in Holland, North-west Germany and Denmark. Secondly,

Schellenberg was to reach Stockholm the following morning with authority from Dönitz to arrive at an understanding regarding a German surrender in Norway....[60]

At 18:30 hours, 4 May 1945, at Montgomery's headquarters on the Lüneburg heathlands, Admiral Hans-Georg von Friedeburg signed the surrender document. This agreed to a capitulation of all German forces in Holland (Generaloberst Blaskowitz), North-West Germany including the islands (Generalfeldmarschall Busch) and in Denmark (Generaloberst Lindemann).

The signature of Admiral von Friedeberg signaled the capitulation would come into force on 5 May 1945 at 08:00 hours. Troops of Army Group Vistula (Generaloberst Student) had been given the possibility of retreating westward to the British lines and come into British captivity.[61]

Radio message intercepted by Bletchley Park on 4 May 1945, taken at 20:15 hours; from Himmler to HSSPF Oslo, SS-Ogruf Redeiss:

Schellenberg will possibly pass to you in the next few days directives and orders. These directives are being issued in the name of Gross Admiral Doenitz, and with my full concurrence. They are then to be carried out without fail.[62]

That evening at 20:30 hours, a speaker on BBC Danish service broadcast news of the German capitulation in north-west Germany, Holland and Denmark. Everywhere in Denmark joyous rallies took place. The illegal Danish resistance army came out publicly with blue-white-red armbands: more than 43,000 men.[63]

Generaloberst Lindemann, C-in-C German Army in Denmark, assumed command of the entire Order Police (Orpo) in Denmark that evening, after the difficulties with Orpo in Copenhagen. HSSPF Günther Pancke and BdS Otto Bovensiepen, SS security police commanders in Denmark, disappeared from Copenhagen during the evening.

Establishment of a provisional Danish Government.[64]

That night, at a meeting with Reichsleiter Bohle, Himmler made it clear he wished to keep all his offices:

While maintaining the leadership of the Waffen-SS, the Reichsführer-SS Heinrich Himmler has taken over responsibility for the maintenance of law and order.[65]

Saturday, 5 May 1945

Events:
At 08:00 hours the capitulation of all German forces in Holland, northwest Germany including the island, and Denmark.[66]

Formation of an "Executive Government" in Germany under Graf Schwerin-Krosigk.[67]

From the memoirs of Walter Schellenberg: morning of 4 May 1945, Schellenberg is appointed Envoy (Gesandter) with plenary powers and provided with papers signed by Dönitz for his official journey via Copenhagen to Sweden. Before he left Flensburg, Schellenberg had his last meeting with Himmler.[68]

From the diary of Karl Dönitz:
> 13:00 hours: Report about the armistice signatures with Montgomery.
> Konteradmiral Wagner, Foreign Minister, Keitel, Jodl, Reichsführer-SS, Gauleiter Wegener...
> The Wehrwolf (sic – Werwolf) is forbidden because its activities in the present situation is a burden when implementing political intentions.[69]

Radio message intercepted by Bletchley Park on 5 May 1945, from Chief OKW, signed Keitel:
> Subject: Treatment of PWs.
> In agreement with Reichsfuehrer SS, the following is ordered:
> All PWs, foreign workers and persons detained in concentration camps are to be handed over to the enemy under a small guard when areas are evacuated. They may no longer be brought back nor may camps be moved. All orders to the contrary are hereby cancelled.[70]

Radio message intercepted by Bletchley Park on 5 May 1945, from Himmler to HSSPF Oslo, Redeiss: "Report any information from Schellenberg at once to me."[71]

Himmler's last staff conference with his SS-Obergruppenführers and SS-Gruppenführers, held in Flensburg:
> The conference was held at Flensburg on 5 May 1945. According to PW B [SS-Ogruf. Maximilian von Herff], it lasted only 45 minutes at the most.
> Those present were: Gen d Pol. SS-Ogruf Wünnenberg   (Main Office, Orpo); Ogruf von Herff (PW B) (Head of SS-Personnel Main Office); Ogruf Werner Lorenz (VOMI); Jüttner (Head, SS-Leadership Main Office, and chief of staff to Commander of Replacement Army); Ogruf Prützmann; von Woyrsch (PW A) HSSPF Wehrkreis IV; Demelhuber (Inspector of Training under Jüttner); Ogruf von Gottberg (Kommander der Ordnungs-truppen with FM Busch); Gruf Gebhardt; Ohlendorf; Bassewitz-Behr (HSSPF Hamburg); Behrends (HSSPF Kurland); Katzmann (HSSPF Danzig). Also present were two adjutants of the RfSS: Staf. Dr Brandt; Ostubaf. Grothmann.
> a) Himmler gave an exposé in the form of a situation report.
> b) Himmler informed the conference that he had been admonished (probably by Bormann) for having initiated peace parleys with the Western Powers without the authority of the Führer.
> c) Himmler stated that it was his intention to establish, if possible, a reformed (or newly formed) government in Schleswig-Holstein whence it could conduct peace negotiations with the Western Powers on what approximated to its own territory. Himmler gave orders that members of the police detailed for duty in this area should be specially selected for their smartness, soldierly appearance etc.
> d) Several of the Ogrufs present were allotted definite tasks, among them:
> (i) PW B [von Herff] was to carry on as Head of the SS Personal-hauptamt and be responsible for the disbandment of the Waffen-SS; for this he was to liase with the HPA [Heerespersonalamt? – Army Personnel Office?] in Mürwik

(ii) Gen. Wünnenberg was told to carry on with his duties as Chef d Orpo

(iii) Ogruf Jüttner was entrusted with the duties of Stellvertreter BdE [*Deputy Commander of the Replacement Army*] with HQ at Kappeln

(iv) Ogruf Prützmann was ordered to hold himself at the disposal of Himmler as Stabschef des RfSS z.b.V. [*Chief of Staff to RfSS for special purposes*].

According to PW B [*von Herff*], the results of the meeting were regarded as quite inconclusive. All were unanimous in their opinion Himmler was unduly optimistic in his estimate of future events and quite out of the picture as regards the actual situation.

It would appear that at the later stages of the meeting, and after the Grufs. had left, Himmler went into conference with the Ogrufs. As far as can be gathered from PW B's statements, this conference also yielded nothing fresh.[72]

SS-Ogruf von Herff and SS-Ogruf Gottlob Berger, in British captivity, were the subject of secret monitoring (bugging):

BERGER: What did the Reichsführer say at Schleswig?

HERFF: He said that he still saw political possibilities, even if they were only slight. That it would probably come about that Schleswig would remain as a refuge where the government could at least work in an extremely small area. The SS should then be used as a police force and show what they were made of, so that their worth should be acknowledged by the English etc. We were with the Reichsführer as late as the 3rd May ... spoke to our 'Gruppenführer' who were still up there. The 'Obergruppenführer' only – the other 'Gruppenführer' were sent out – spoke to him alone afterwards. I can tell you, the possibilities of which the Reichsführer was told: 'Reichsführer, we really must view things quite soberly now!'

BERGER: What 'Obergruppenführer' were up there?

HERFF: Wünnenberg and Prützmann, who's said to be dead; I caused Prützmann to remain there and play his part. There was also Jüttner, Demelhuber and Werner Lorenz.[73]

SS-Ogruf. Hans Jüttner was interrogated in British captivity, just three weeks after the conference:

PW [Jüttner] saw Himmler last on 4 or 5 May at Rendsburg when Himmler stated that he had no intention to commit suicide or be killed, but that he was on the contrary full of vitality and plans. All he wanted now was an interview with Field Marshal Montgomery. PW and some of the SS-Obergruppenführer present (Prützmann, Lorenz and others) got the impression that Himmler intended to strike some sort of bargain with the Western Allies, in order to save his own life. They also had the impression that he was quite sure to succeed with his plans.[74]

When interrogated SS-Gruf. Otto Ohlendorf put forward his views of the conference:

All these men [*the Obergruppenführer*] were equally disillusioned that, as senior SS officials with the responsibility, they had been given no instructions and had no idea what to do. There was no leadership at all. Afterwards – it must have been after he'd lost all his offices[?] – Himmler called a meeting of all these leaders; at the end we [*Gruppenführers*] were turned out and the 'Obergruppenführer' remained alone with him. However, nothing came of that either. I spoke to Obergruppenführer Prützmann about it afterwards; Himmler gave them no instructions and they had nothing whatever to go by. That is the cause of all the wavering in the SS. They all remained in the area and, as far as I know, they were all taken away as prisoners.[75]

On 5 May 1945, Rudolf Höss received his false papers:

On the next morning [5 May] we received paybooks under false names and were equipped as such. I took for myself the name of Franz Lang, Bootsmaat, Navy. To my best knowledge the following persons took the following names:

Sturmbannführer Burgur (sic – Burger] – Wolff

Maurer – the girl's name, which I don't remember (?)

Glücks – Sonnemann

Lolling – Dr Gerlach

The remainder of the Amtsgruppe were not supposed to take false names as they were not so much in danger. Maurer, Burger and I received marching-orders to Rantum on Sylt. The other paybooks and marching-orders were not yet ready and should be made out only in the course of the 5th May.[76]

From the diary of Count Folke Bernadotte:

… At ten o'clock in the morning on May 5th Schellenberg, who had been nominated envoy, arrived at Stockholm by special plane, and immediately a meeting took place at my residence between him, M. von Post and myself. Schellenberg presented his credentials, signed by Dönitz, and stated that the new German Minister for Foreign Affairs, Count Schwerin von Krosigk, had asked him to endeavour to arrange a meeting with General Eisenhower for the discussion of a general German surrender.[77]

Saturday or Sunday, 5 or 6 May 1945

Events:

From a postwar interrogation of Otto Ohlendorf:

The secret departure of HIMMLER from FLENSBURG without leaving any instructions, during the night of 5/6 May, led PW to regard the SD and all other depts of the RSHA as finally disbanded. HIMMLER's plan to go underground with BUSCH's help failed. His reappearance two days later made no difference to PW's measures for disbandment and HIMMLER disappeared again as before.[78]

In a postwar interrogation report, Heinz Macher reported:

On about 5/6 May Macher saw a letter written by Himmler to Montgomery which was to be handed over to either Keitel or Jodl for delivery by a courier to Montgomery. The general contents were that Himmler recognised the fact that Montgomery was the conqueror and Himmler the conquered and that there remained many things to be done in re-establishing order in Germany. In view of these things and the possible help that Himmler could give a meeting was suggested. The letter was dispatched about the 8 May.[79]

In a postwar interrogation, Werner Grothmann also reported:

> According to Grothmann, Himmler wanted to speak to Field Marshal Montgomery about an alliance between the Western Powers and Germany against Russia. He intended putting the Waffen-SS at the disposal of the Field Marshal for the fight against the USSR.[80]

Himmler was on the move:

> From Hüholz, Himmler made for Kollerup where Army C-in-C Nord [Generalfeldmarschall Ernst Busch] had set up his headquarters at the Christiansen farm.[81]

Sunday, 6 May 1945

Events:

Radio message decrypted by Bletchley Park on 6 May 1945, taken at 01:00 hours; from Himmler to Kaltenbrunner via SS-Brig. Rothe (*sic* – Rode) in Salzburg:

> 1. The King of the Belgians with his family is to be set free, and his journey to Switzerland assured.
> 2. I have still not received answers to my communications.[82]

From the diary of Karl Dönitz, Flensburg:

> 13:40 hrs: dismissal and leave-taking. Gauleiter Lohse
> 17:00 hrs: dismissal, Reichsführer-SS [*Himmler*]
> The Grand Admiral dispensed with his service as Minister of the Interior, Chief of the Replacement Army and the Police, and considered all ties between him and the current Government hereby dissolved.[83]

Interrogation of Otto Ohlendorf and Himmler's dismissal:

> Anyhow the conversation [*with Schwerin-Krosigk*] ended on a very unpleasant note and, either that afternoon or the afternoon afterwards, Himmler went to see Dönitz again, who finally persuaded him to resign from the government and hand over all his offices.
>
> That happened...around 6th [*May*]. I remember the date so well because it was the worst night I ever spent, because everything was in a state of dissolution. Himmler went to see [*Ernst*] Busch that night. I was firmly convinced that he wanted only to keep in contact, but to disappear and go underground himself. Without saying a word to me, after having been in the habit of visiting me twice or three times a day and discussing everything with me, he disappeared. The thing which annoyed me most – and here I must mention some embarrassing details – was that Himmler still had a relatively large staff around him, considering the circumstances. Whenever he went anywhere he went with four cars to protect him and he had a staff of about 150 people around him, a WT 'Zug' [*radio truck*] of his own and heaven knows what else, and now, after I had never anything to do with any of that crowd and had met only rebuffs from them, some Obersturmführer or other turned up and three in the morning and said the head of this staff requested me to see that they were put up somewhere. Suddenly I was landed with the responsibility for the whole staff.[84]

During the evening of 6 May 1945, Generaloberst Jodl arrived by aircraft at Reims, General Eisenhower's headquarters, for the signing of the total capitulation of all German armed forces.

Jodl later informed Major General Rooks that he had last seen Himmler shortly before his flight to Reims. Himmler wanted his advice on the question of what he should do next; whether he should fly by night-fighter aircraft to southern Germany where most of his SS troops were deployed.[85]

In a postwar interrogation, just four days after the events, Rudolf Brandt stated: "6 May 1945 Himmler's Party moved to a village near Flensburg."[86]

Another member of Himmler's staff, Wilhelm Walter, when interrogated:

Walter then recounted how on 6 May 1945 the leader of these twenty-four men, Ostubaf (sic) Macher from Chemnitz, had given them instructions which presumably came directly from Himmler: To go to Bavaria and from there to the Russian-British and Russian-American occupation borders and spread Nazi propaganda and incite Russian troops against British and American troops.[87]

Sunday or Monday, 6 or 7 May 1945

From a postwar interrogation of Werner Grothmann, just a month after the events he described:

6 or 7 May 45 Himmler, Grothmann, Dr Müller, Macher, Dr Brandt and Kiermaier left for a farm near Satrup (just to the south of Flensburg) which as close of General Feldmarschall Busch's H.Q. [Kollerup]. From there members of the party paid flying visits to Flensburg in search of news. During the first two days Himmler went alone, but afterwards Grothmann & Brandt took it in turns to make the journey.[88]

Monday, 7 May 1945

Events:
At 02:01 hours, headquarters of General Eisenhower in Reims, Generaloberst Alfred Jodl signed the total capitulation document on behalf of the German armed forces.[89]

Tuesday, 8 May 1945

Events:
Grand Admiral Dönitz broadcast a radio statement on *Flensburger Sender* about the capitulation.[90]

From the postwar interrogation of Heinz Macher:

About 8 May, after a discussion in the Feuerwehrschule Flensburg, Himmler gave the order that troops under his command should surrender to the Western Allies. This was passed to Grothmann for onward transmission to all the troops under Himmler on the Western front.[91]

At this time Himmler still had an escort unit (*Begleitungskommando RF-SS*), consisting:

Kiermaier, Josef, Stubafü. <u>Begleitsoffizier</u> and O.C. of Unit.

Müller, Max, Scharfü. NCO belonging to Unit.

Schmid, Erhard, Member of the Unit.

Böttcher, Rudolf, Uscha. <u>Ordonnanz</u> to RFSS.

Lorenz, Nikolaus, U/Stufü. Member of the Unit.

…

Dr med. Artur Müller, Senior Field Dr, Feldkommandostelle (RfSS).

…

Members of Special Unit Macher:

Macher, O.C.

Ehm, Erhard, U/Stufü. Driver of O.C.

Haushalter, Heinz, U/scha. MG [*Machine Gun*] No. I and clerk to O.C.

Ehrt, Heinz, Mach/Hpt/Gefr vehicle mechanic

Queisser, Willi, U/Scha. Runner of O.C.

Baumann, Otto, U/Scha. 2 i/c to Macher.

On 8 May 1945, Himmler reduced his motorcade to four vehicles and now shaved off his moustache.[92]

Wednesday, 9 May 1945

At 00:01 hrs the total surrender of German armed forces on all fronts came into effect.[93]

From a postwar interrogation of Werner Grothmann:

On the day of the armistice they moved out of town [*Flensburg*] and stayed for a short while in several places in the neighborhood. Himmler had given General Jodl a letter addressed to Field-Marshal Montgomery and Jodl had promised to deliver it to a liaison offr [*officer*] of the Field-Marshal's.

…

According to Grothmann, Himmler wanted to speak to Field Marshal Montgomery about an alliance between the Western Powers and Germany against Russia. He intended putting the Waffen SS at the disposal of the Field Marshal for the fight against the USSR.[94]

Albert Speer, in his memoirs:

…as soon as communications with Field Marshal Montgomery had been established, Himmler gave Jodl a letter asking him to have it passed on to Montgomery. As General Kinzel, the liaison officer to the British Forces, told me, Himmler asked for an interview with the British Field Marshal under a safe-conduct. Should he be taken prisoner he wanted it established that by the laws of war he had a right to be treated as a high-ranking general – since he had been Commander in Chief of the Vistula Army Group. But this letter never arrived. Jodl destroyed it, as he told me at Nuremberg.[95]

From the memoirs of Field Marshal Montgomery:
> Himmler left Flensburg on 9 May, using a false name, with the intention of wandering the country for several weeks, until the hustle and bustle of victory had subsided. Then he hoped to get an interview with me and promote his view of the situation.[96]

From a postwar interrogation of Heinz Macher:
> On the 9 or 10 May 1945 Macher received orders from the RFSS [Himmler] personally to go with him on a journey to the Harz as a bodyguard.[97]

SS-Ogruf. Dr Ing. Hans Kammler committed suicide (Czechoslovakia).[98]

Thursday, 10 May 1945

From a postwar interrogation of Heinz Macher:
> About the 10 May, Macher is unsure of exact dates, Himmler and his staff left Flensburg in 3 or 4 PKW [automobiles]. Previously arrangements had been made that any answer to his letter should be brought by personal courier to Himmler at Friedrichskoog. Macher can give no reason why Himmler should leave Flensburg except to gain time until the reply came.
>
> The party left by night and put up in the woods at Kollerup ... Here they stayed two or three days and were issued with false identity cards. They had already dressed themselves in a variety of civilian and military clothes.[99]

From a postwar interrogation of Werner Grothmann:
> On a day between the 9 to 12 May (Grothmann is not very sure of the dates of his recent movements) as no reply had been received by Himmler he decided to move out of the Flensburg area in order to remain at liberty and to be able to talk to the Field Marshal [Montgomery] as a free man, and not as a captive.
>
> According to Grothmann, Himmler wanted to speak to Field Marshal Montgomery about an alliance between the Western Powers and Germany against Russia. He intended putting the Waffen-SS at the disposal of the Field Marshal for the fight against the USSR.
>
> Fourteen men accompanied Himmler on his journey. The only members of the party personally known to Grothmann are Sturmbannführer Macher..., Dr Brandt..., Police Major Kiermaier and Oberfeldarzt Mueller.[100]

From a postwar interrogation of Otto Ohlendorf:
> Himmler – Famous Last Words.
> Ohlendorf was with his leader almost to the end. Apparently Himmler never lost the illusion that he could justify himself, that he had done his best for the German people, a good ruse. On 10 or 11 May Himmler sent a letter to Montgomery which seems to have been left unanswered or to which a curt reply was received. (O.[hlendorf] was too excited in his recital of events to be coherent. He may be more lucid when next this is discussed with him.) O. tried to persuade Himmler to ... [last line of page is missing] through Schellenberg 'who had excellent

and numerous international connections.' O. is not certain of the results of this last attempt to save the German people.[101]

Ohlendorf was re-interrogated on this point ten days later:

Letter to Montgomery.

On 10 or 11 May 1945 Himmler wrote a letter to Montgomery, as correctly related in the previous report. This letter was to be transmitted to the British F.M. [*Field Marshal*] by Jodl. Himmler requested an interview with Montgomery. He wished to discuss with him the German concentration camps and felt that he could justify himself and his actions with Montgomery. He also wished to explain to the F.M. just what role he had played in the Reich. Apparently no reply was received. Himmler told Ohlendorf that he believed in Jodl and that he had forwarded the letter. Ohlendorf opined that Jodl had not been a man of his word.[102]

At his own trial, Otto Ohlendorf testified before a U.S. Military Tribunal on 8 October 1947:

Himmler 'had been of the belief that via his officer Schellenberg the Allies might negotiate with him and he might be used as a confidence man within Europe. From there these conversations with Schellenberg via Bernadotte, the chief of the Red Cross in Sweden, with Churchill and the British government, Himmler really believed in it, until the day of his escape, even until the day before his death. Even after he escaped he sent me ordinance reports every day by which manner he tried to find out whether Schellenberg had returned from Sweden or whether Field Marshal Montgomery had answered the letter which he had sent on the 9th of May [*1945*].'

Ohlendorf was asked, 'Were you in daily contact with Himmler following May 8?'

Ohlendorf answered, 'Yes... at least until the 19th of May. I believe it must have been until the 21st, by ordinances. He had camouflaged himself and was living in a disguise under which he then was delivered into a prisoner of war camp.'[103]

On 10 May 1945, Himmler's party left Flensburg and began their journey south, two days later they arrived at Marne on the western coast of Schleswig-Holstein. En route 'they slept either out in the open or inside railway stations'. A few miles further on was the mouth of the River Elbe.

Josef Kiermaier reported on this journey:

At length on 10 May, Himmler and his remaining entourage left Flensburg and set out for Marne at the Dicksander Koog on the east coast of Schleswig Holstein... In addition to Kiermaier, the group still included Brandt, Ohlendorf [*this is an error, Ohlendorf was not present*], Karl Gebhardt, Waffen S.S. Colonel Werner Grothmann and Major Macher.[104]

SS-Gruf. Richard Glücks committed suicide (cyanide), Marinelazarett Mürwik II, at 15:00 hours.[105]

Thursday–Friday, 10–11 May 1945

From a postwar interrogation of Dr Rudolf Brandt:

10/11 May: Himmler's Party moved to another village near Flensburg. Shortly after this the whole party disguised themselves as follows: Himmler in Mar Art [*Marine Artillery*] uniform; Grothmann,

Brandt, in Mar Art Uffz [*Unteroffizier*] uniform; Macher in Mar Art Gefr [*Gefreiter*] uniform; Dr Mueller, Schmidt, S/Scharfue Mueller, Lorenz, Kirmaier (*sic*) all in green police uniforms. Brandt is unable to state what disguises the other members of the party were wearing.[106]

Friday or Saturday, 11 or 12 May 1945

From a postwar interrogation of Gebhard Himmler:

Gebhard Himmler arrived at the Feuerwehrkaserne in Flensburg to find ...the RFSS Personal Staff Officers Baumert, Diefenbach (*sic* – Tiefenbacher), Gutgesell and SS-Stubafü. Faelschein and the Police Officers Wuenenberg (*sic* –Wünnenberg) & Rogalski.

From the members of the RFSS Personal Staff Gebhard Himmler heard that the RFSS was no longer quartered there but was on the move accompanied by SS-Stubafü. Grothmann and SS-Stafü. Brandt.[107]

Friday, 11 May 1945

From a postwar interrogation of Werner Grothmann:

11 May 45: The six men [*Himmler, Grothmann, Dr Müller, Macher, Dr Brandt, Kiermaier*] made their way [*from Satrup, near Flensburg*] to Friedrichskoog where they remained until the 15th [*May*]. Their object was to wait for favourable weather in which to cross the Elbe estuary in a fishing boat to the small town to Neuhaus. Their plan, at this time, was to reach the sanctuary of the Hartz Mountains where, it was felt, Himmler could safely remain in hiding for a considerable time. As soon as the hue and cry had died down somewhat, he proposed making his way to the Alps, for he was determined to keep out of Allied hands for as long as possible.

Note: Grothmann swears that Himmler had no particular hiding place in view and declares that the Reichsfuehrer had no intention of making any sort of military stand in the Alpine Regions.[108]

From a postwar interrogation of Wilhelm Walter:

Walter was told by a Frau Christiansen at Adolf Hitler Koog* that Himmler and his entourage had stayed in three houses (including her own) on their way from Flensburg to Lueneburg, and that several months ago, a message had reached her that the ones who had stayed at her home were well and safe.

[*Adolf Hitler Koog* is now Dieksander Koog, Friedrichskoog municipality*][109]

From the diary of the Karl Dönitz:

At midday Dönitz, Foreign Minister Schwerin-Krosigk and Keitel had a meeting. Point 3 on the agenda:

The Waffen-SS as part of the Germany Armed Forces (Wehrmacht) continues to be handled and looked after. The Wehrmacht has nothing to do with other formations of the SS and SD, and is not responsible for them.[109]

Saturday, 12 May 1945

Himmler's party left their four vehicles in Marne, north of the River Elbe, and went to the coast on foot. They found a fisherman who, for 500 Reichsmarks, took them over the river to Neuhaus on the south coast of the river estuary.[110]

Saturday-Sunday, 12-13 May 1945

Himmler's strong boxes:

a) In May 1945 Himmler stored two strong-boxes in the house of W/SS Stubaf Heinrich Adolf Springer. One contained gold, jewellery and other personal articles, amongst which were a valuable pearl necklace, diamond watches etc. The other strong-box contained a considerable amount sum of money in various foreign countries.

b) When Springer was arrested on 27th of May 1945, SS-Ostuf Dürring, former 2nd Adjt to Himmler) was also in the house but was not questioned as to his identity. Springer was later told by his wife that Dürring left the place immediately afterwards and went into hiding. A few days later a man visited Frau Springer in the middle of the night bringing greetings from Dürring and from other officers of Himmler's personal staff. The man said he had been sent to collect the strong boxes and Frau Springer allowed him to take them away.

c) The above information was obtained from Springer during interrogation in Jan 1947, but Springer has since repeated it to Generalmajor Keilhaus in internment, adding that the boxes were collected from Frau Springer on the night of 12/13th May 1945 by a man unknown to her.

…

2. Fräulein Doris Mähner. She was reported in August 1946 as living at Eberhausen near Munich (Isesthal). She was issued with the papers of a Wehrmachtshelferin at Murwik near Flensburg…

3. A woman called Hintze, is reported as 'second secretary' and is stated to have accompanied Mähner. The two women and various staff officers of Himmler's Headquarters are said to have spent some nights at Springer's home in Lutzhoft (*sic* – Lutzhöft) near Flensburg.[111]

Sunday, 13 May 1945

Report by Major Bessler at a Ministerial meeting with Reich Foreign Minister, Schwerin-Krosigk, at 10:00 hrs:

The American press report the arrested of State Secretary Hayler and Reichsführer Himmler handed over by Grand Admiral Dönitz.[112]

Sunday–Monday, 13–14 May 1945

From a postwar interrogation of Heinz Macher:

On the night of the 13/14 (date uncertain) Macher left in a car along with Himmler, Grothmann and a Feldwebel, whose name Macher gives as Lungen [*Siegfried Lüngen*], though he is unsure of this. Macher was driver. They took all the side roads that they could and made for Friedrichskoog… They had set off about 2230 hrs and arrived about 0630 hrs the next day.

...

Their papers were checked on the journey Flensburg to Friedrichskoog four times and their false papers accepted and they were also checked several times later.

...

They found a hut there which so far Macher knows was not a previously reconnoitered position and there awaited the courier. They had brought tinned food with them.[113]

From a postwar interrogation of Dr Rudolf Brandt:
13/14 May: Himmler's Party moved to village near Melldorf (sic – Meldorf). Vehicles abandoned.[114]

Tuesday, 15 May 1945

From the diary of Major Norman Whittaker, Lüneburg:
First customer for No. 31a. No less a figure that Pruetzmann (SS-Obergruppenfuhrer) and chief organiser of the Werewolf movement. Truly an evil looking type. But he jumped up quickly enough when I entered the room. Is never to be left without escort.[115]

Top Secret minutes of a meeting held that morning in London, between the Chiefs of Staff and the Joint Intelligence Committee (signed V. Cavendish Bentinck and addressed to Sir Orme Sergeant):
Stop Press. Since dictating the above [*minutes*] I have spoken to Major-General Strong, D.M.I. at SHAEF, who informs me that Himmler and Rosenberg have offered to surrender in the vicinity of Flensburg provided they are assured of a fair trial. Instructions have been returned that the surrender is to be unconditional, and that it will not matter if they are killed resisting capture.[116]

Night of Tuesday and Wednesday, 15–16 May 1945

Historian Holger Piening:
Fisherman Willi Plett of Friedrichskoog, took unknown German troops together with refugees, for about 500 Reichsmarks, across the Elbe in his fishing boat to Otterndorf.[117]

From a postwar interrogation of Heinz Macher:
After two days [*in Fredrichskoog*] and no courier, they began to feel their position a little insecure owing to the increased no. of troops in the area, so Himmler decided to head South first for the Harz and then to Bavaria, always with the idea of gaining time.
They then set off on the night of the 15/16 (date uncertain) on a small fishing boat and crossed over the Elbe somewhere near Neuhaus... Here the Feldwebel [*Siegfried Lüngen*] left them and Himmler, Macher and Grothmann continued on foot, making their way South and keeping to side roads as much as possible.[118]

From a postwar interrogation of Dr Rudolf Brandt:
15/16 May: Entire party changed into civilian clothes; Himmler wearing a patch over one eye.[119]

From a postwar interrogation of Werner Grothmann:

> 15 or 16 May 45: They succeeded in crossing the Elbe to Neuhaus in a small fishing boat fitted with an auxiliary motor. Grothmann states that the boat was loaned to them, and that the fishermen who provided it had no idea whom they were assisting.
>
> From Neuhaus they proceeded on foot via Lamstedt & Bremervörde to the neighbourhood of Meinstedt. Brandt, Müller and Kiermaier left the party to go into town of Bremervörde with a view to having their 'Ausweise' stamped by the British Town Major, but unfortunately did not return, so Himmler, Grothmann and Macher entered Meinstedt alone. There they were arrested by three Russian soldiers.[120]

Wednesday, 16 May 1945

Secret message dated 16 May 1945 (ref. FWD-21666) from SHAEF Forward to EXFOR MAIN [*Expeditionary Force, Main*]:

> On query SHAEF Control Group OKW[,] Admiral Doenitz denied knowledge whereabouts Himmler. General Jodl subsequently stated he had last seen Himmler in north after the formation of Doenitz Government when he had advised him to fly south, as his continued presence in northern area would be prejudicial to new government. Jodl does not believe took his advice but denies all knowledge of his present whereabouts. Danish underground reports Himmler and staff with 170 armed SS located 15 kilos [*kilometers*] S E Flensburg between Sudersee and Satrup... You are to conduct search for Himmler in your area including area Flensburg enclave and if discovered effect his arrest. If search of Flensburg enclave is necessary please coordinate with counterintelligence representative on OKW Control Group Lieutenant Colonel Marshall. If arrested Himmler should be sent under escort to Ashcan.[121]

In London, in answer to a Parliamentary Question dated 16 May from Commander Locker-Lampson, asking if the Prime Minister has any information on the whereabouts of Himmler, Churchill says he does not, but that he expects Himmler will 'turn up somewhere in this world or the next, and will be dealt with by their appropriate authority'. Churchill added that 'the latter would be more convenient to HMG'.

On the file cover a handwritten note dated 15 May: 'Now dead – in every sense!'[122]

In Lüneburg, Major Norman Whittaker noted 'Pruetzmann taken away this morning at 1100 hrs.'[123]

In Rendsburg (Schleswig), SS-Staf. Gebhard Himmler was arrested by British forces. From his later interrogation report:

> On 16 May arrangements were made for a conference to be held between Gen. Lindemann, Gen. Mueller, and Juettner concerning the SS-Concentration area; the conference never materialized since 2100 hrs 16 May Juettner, his adjutant, Graessler and Gebhard Himmler were ordered to a conference with a British General in Schleswig; the 3 Germans were taken by car by a British Officer to Schleswig and there placed under arrest.[124]

Thursday, 17 May 1945

From the diary of Karl Dönitz:
> 12:30 hrs: State Secretary Wegener.
> The President of the German Red Cross, until now located in Flensburg, is no longer available for work, the entire Officer Corps who belonged to the SS, have been arrested by the occupation forces. The Executive President, Prof. Dr Gebhardt, has not been confirmed.[125]

From the diary of Major Whittaker, Lüneburg:
> I heard this morning that Pruetzmann has committed suicide – poison concealed in a cigarette lighter. Thank God he didn't do it while in my charge.
> At 2000 hrs Karl Daluege who is another SS-Obergruppenfuhrer and a General of Police. Apparently he was directly under Himmler, was brought in together with Dr [*Otto*] Meissner, who was Hitler's personal secretary.
> After the Pruetzmann episode I was taking no chances so I had them stripped and their clothes thrown out on the landing and gave them blankets to wrap themselves in.
> Meissner didn't like being stripped – said that he shouldn't be treated in the same manner as Daluege – he wasn't a criminal and shouldn't be classed as one.
> He was Secretary of State to Hindenburg and apparently stayed on quite gladly when Hitler 'came to the throne'. So with these thoughts I made him take off his clothes – and with his clothes off he looked the same as any other Nazi!!!
> I would give more than a penny for his [*stress in original*] thoughts – I bet he knows a thing or two![126]

Thursday or Friday, 17 or 18 May 1945

From a postwar interrogation of Heinz Macher:
> Subject states that all personalities mentioned in a/n [above noted] Corps letter travelled together as far as a farm NE of Bremervörde… This they reached about 17-18 May 45. He states that this farm was not mentioned in his interrogation report of 5 Aug, as 'he did not wish to involve the family resident there'. From this point, Kiermaier, Schmid, and others of whom subject is uncertain, were sent into Bremervörde to seek assistance from Mil.Gov. in the matter of transport, permission to travel, etc. Up until this date, the group had travelled together, and had no contact with other SS personnel [?], or members of the entourage of the RFSS. After the separation at Bremervörde, the Himmler-Grothmann-Macher group proceeded independently until arrested.[127]

Friday, 18 May 1945

On 18 May 1945, Foreign Office official Mr C. E. King in company with Mr Murphy visited Flensburg:
> …Mr. Murphy and I paid a short visit to the O.K.W. offices, which confirmed what we had been told about the futility of that organisation. We then met Admiral Dönitz in General Rook's

office...Two significant points are: (a) Dönitz's statement that he assumed power as head of the State in obedience to direct instructions issued from Hitler's Headquarters in Berlin on the 30th April, and (b) his insistence on the necessity and urgency of setting up a central German Government capable of deal with the food problem and thus saving western Germany from communism. He denied any knowledge of the whereabouts of Himmler, saying that he had last seen him in Flensburg on the 5th or 6th May.[128]

Historian Marlies G. Steinert:

The Himmler group stayed at the farmhouse outside Bremervörde (Waldstrasse 165) of Hinrich Dankers and his family. Only Mrs Dankers and her son, Heinrich, were at home. According to the then nine-year old Heinrich Dankers, the Himmler party was 5–6 men, still in uniform. He recalls Himmler wearing an eye-patch.

English forces occupied the house next door, where the grandparents lived, and watched as Himmler's group pulled off onto the dirt road to the farmhouse.

Himmler was caught either on the Osterbrücke, over the River Bever, in Bremervörde or at Kirchtimke.[129]

From the diary of Major Norman Whittaker, Lüneburg: "Daluege and Meissner taken away at 1100 hrs, having been re-clothed!!!"[130]

Saturday, 19 May 1945

From a postwar interrogation of Dr Rudolf Brandt: "19 May: Party moved into two houses outside Bremervoerde."[131]

Sunday, 20 May 1945

From the "Interim Report of the Interrogation of SS-Standfue. Dr Rudolf Brandt":

Introduction.
On 20 May 45 Brandt was with Himmler's party which consisted of the following:
Sturmbannfue. Kiermaier, i/c Himmler's personal guard;
O/Sturmbannfue. Grothmann, Chief Adjutant to Himmler;
Sturmbannfue. Macher, apparently a former officer of Himmler's Escort Btl;
O/Feldarzt Müller, M.O. to Himmler's Feldkommandostelle;
O/Sturmfue. Schmidt   )
O/Scharfue. Müller   )   ...attached to Kiermaier
U/Sturmfue. Lorenz   )
U/Scharfue. Haushalter   )
U/Scharfue. Erdt   )
U/Scharfue. Queisser   )   ...attached to Macher

U/Sturmfue. Baumann)
U/Sturmfue. Ehm)
U/Scharfue. Rudolf (?), Ordonnanz Offizier.

At about 10 o'clock in the morning Kiermaier and [Dr] Müller went to see the Landrat [Wilhelm Dohrmann] in Bremervoerde in the hope of obtaining authority for the party to travel to the area of Lueneburg. Müller intended to describe them as a party of discharged wounded soldiers. It was hoped that this authority could be obtained from the British military authorities with the help of the Landrat. At Midday, as the two had not returned Himmler, Grothmann and Macher decided to leave the main party and make their own way southwards.

About one hour later a British lorry containing three or four armed British soldiers stopped before the two houses where the party was quartered. The soldiers entered the houses and ordered all the occupants to enter the lorry which thereupon proceeded to a British H.Q. in Bremervoerde. After a short interrogation here the party was sent by lorry the same evening to Westertimke where they were again interrogated, and Brandt eventually admitted his identity.

The whole of Himmler's party was in civilian clothes with the exception of the following who were in green police uniforms: Kiermayer (sic), Lorenz, Schmidt and both Müllers.

Dr Rudolf Brandt was arrested by British forces in Bremervörde.[132]

Monday, 21 May 1945

Interim interrogation report of Werner Grothmann:

On 21 May 1945 Reichsführer Heinrich Himmler, his principal adjutant Werner Grothmann, and his assistant adjutant Sturmbannführer Macher were arrested near Meinstedt (between Wesermünde and Hamburg) by three Russian soldiers attached to a British security control. Himmler was wearing civilian clothing and had a black patch over one of his eyes, whilst Grothmann & Macher were dressed half in uniform (tunics & greatcoats without badge of any kind) and half in civilian clothing. In view of this disguise, they were not recognised by the Russians, who handed them over to the occupants of a British army car. In this vehicle they were driven to a camp at Seelos (sic – Seedorf) near Bremervörde where their captors still failed to recognise them. Grothmann says that this was not surprising, since Heinrich Himmler in civilian clothing and without his glasses appears as an ordinary type of middle-class German and was definitely difficult to identify.[133]

From a postwar interrogation of Heinz Macher:

They had been on the way for about 7 days when in the vicinity of Zeven they were arrested by British troops at Meinstedt.[134]

Notice of the arrest of Himmler: Himmler taken prisoner

On Monday, 21 May 1945, a guard patrol consisting of three English and two Russian soldiers under Corporal Morris (73rd Assault Regiment) were based in the village of Meinstedt, 5 km north-east of Zeven, stopped suspect persons (for the purpose of examination).

They examined a group of three men dressed in civilian clothing; the papers of the last one were not in order, they were arrested and brought to the guardhouse at Seedorf Camp.

After questioning they spent the night in the cells of the guardhouse at Seedorf, 21-22 May, then the group were brought under escort to Bremervörde.

On the basis of subsequent investigation one of them was definitely found to be Himmler.

Surnames of the two Russian guards: Gubarev and Sidorov.

(signed) Lt. Col., [no name]. Seedorf, Prisoner of War Camp.[135]

From the memoirs of Field Marshal Montgomery:

In the days that followed the surrender, the general attitude of the Germans, both civilians and soldiers, was on the whole correct. They were willing to carry out whatever orders were issued to them, their chief fear being that they might be handed over to the Russians. The arrest and interrogation of Himmler is of interest in this connection. He left Flensburg of the 9th May [1945] under an assumed name, intending to roam the country for some weeks until the tumult of victory had died down. He then hoped to obtain an interview with me so that he could expound his views on the situation. He was, however, arrested by a British patrol on the 21st May and taken to an internment camp where he eventually disclosed his identity. He needed no encouragement to speak. He said that before leaving Flensburg he had called off all German resistance movements and that for some time before then he had been urging the conclusion of peace with the Western Allies. His purpose in seeking an interview with me was to stress that sooner or later there would be another war to stop the march of the Asiatic hordes into Western Europe, led by Russia. Now that Germany was beaten, Britain was left alone to face the Asiatic onslaught. It was essential to save the fighting man-power of Germany from falling into Russian hands, since it would be needed to fight with the British against the Russians in the near future – such a war, in his view, being inevitable. This attitude of mind as expounded by Himmler was general throughout the civilians in the British Zone. Subsequently, while being searched to ascertain if he carried poison, Himmler bit on a concealed phial and committed suicide.[136]

Tuesday, 22 May 1945

From a postwar interrogation of Werner Grothmann:

On the following day, 22 May, the three men were taken to another camp at Bremervörde where they were briefly interrogated. Their disguise, however, remained unpenetrated, the British interrogating officers supposing them to be either German civilian refugees, or deserters from the Wehrmacht. At this interrogation Himmler gave his name as <u>Hitzinger</u>, whilst Grothmann assumed the identity of his elder brother, Eduard Grothmann.[137]

On 22 May 1945, the Arrest Report of Heinrich Hizinger was issued by 1003 Field Security Detachment at Westertimke Cage. It shows that Himmler had been arrested at Bremervorde Bridge Control at 17:00 hrs that day by 1003 FSRD. The Arrest Report also shows that Himmler was questioned by Sgt. Britton, 45 FSS (Field Security Section) and that Himmler was claiming the rank of Feldwebel with a 'Panzer Company for Special Duties (Pz Kp z.b.V.) detached to GFP (SD)'. It was also noted that he had been demobilized on 3 May 1945.

Note: The Arrest Report mentions an 'attached report' but this has not been found.[138]

From the diary of Major Norman Whittaker, Lüneburg:

> Told to get enough accom [accommodation] for 40 important prisoners so got four houses outside Lüneburg. They can be isolated and we can surround them with armd [armoured] cars, which have spotlights. These can be switched on all night or we can post guards in each room. The party may come to-morrow but they may not come at all – all depends on the weather. Told that the people are Doenitz, Jodl and company who are to be arrested at Flensburg to-morrow.[139]

In Italy, British interrogators issued their report on Marga and Gudrun Himmler (wife and daughter) who had been captured there.[140]

Wednesday, 23 May 1945

On 23 May 1945 'all members of the self-styled acting German Government, as well as all members of the German High Command in Flensburg had been taken into [British] custody as prisoners of war. Those arrested had included about three hundred officers and an unstated number of other ranks and also civilians.'[141]

From a postwar interrogation of Werner Grothmann:

> On 23 May the three prisoners were transferred to another camp at Westertimke where, as before, they remained unrecognised. From Westertimke they were taken on the same day to the P/W camp [Kolkhagen] at Lüneburg, and there Himmler finally resolved to admit to his identity.
>
> When the British camp authorities realised who their three prisoners were, they immediately separated the men, and Grothmann saw Himmler and Macher for the last time on the evening of 23 May.[142]

Historians Manvell and Fraenkel interviewed former Gauleiter Karl Kaufmann:

> …During the morning of 23 May, Kaufmann along with Brandt and other prisoners stood at the barbed-wire fence of Camp 031 at Kolkhagen, near Nienburg on the river Weser. They were watching lorries from Fellingbosdel (sic – Fallingbostel) Camp (Lüneburg Heath) driving up. Among those who got out was Himmler, minus his moustache and with a patch over one eye. He stood in the right wing of the group, wearing boots, field grey trousers and some sort of civilian jacket. He did not recognize Kaufmann and the others, but they saw him suddenly disappear behind a rhododendron bush, where he removed the eye-patch. He reappeared almost instantly putting on his glasses; he was immediately recognizable. This was the time he decided to give himself up, in Kaufmann's opinion. A few minutes later there was quite a commotion; extra guards with tommy-guns and machine-guns appeared; extra sentries were posted at the gate. Soon the cause of the excitement was being passed through the grapevine of the camp. The British soldiers seemed overjoyed that Himmler was among their prisoners.[143]

Secret Report dated 23 May 1945 by Capt. C. A. Smith, Chief Interrogation, 031 Camp:

Subject: Identification of HEINRICH HIMMLER.

To: GSO 2 I (b) Ops and Policy HQ 2 Army Main

1. At 1840 hrs today twenty German civilian and military prisoners arrived at 031 Civilian Interrogation Camp [*Kolkhagen near Barnstedt*] from the internment camp at Westertimke.

2. While they were being searched, I was informed that one of them wished to speak urgently with the Camp Commandant. I went to the camp office and saw the man who had made the request. His arrest report gave his particulars as: Uffz Grothmann Eduard, a suspected member of the GFP; arrested by 1003 FSRD on 22 May 45 at Bremervorder (*sic*).

3. Grothmann said that he was a member of the SS and that he, and two others would like to speak privately with me. I took him apart with the other two men whose arrest reports showed them as: Feldwebel Hizinger, Heinrich, and Obergfr. Macher Horst. The details of arrest were the same as for Grothmann.

4. The man who called himself Hizinger then told me that he was Reichsfuehrer SS Heinrich Himmler, and that the other two were officers of his staff. He wished to speak to an officer on the staff of Field-Marshal Montgomery.

5. I asked the other two men their real names, and they gave them as follows:

Obersturmbannfuehrer Werner Grothmann and

Sturmbannfuehrer Heinz Macher.

The three men were immediately taken into a room and a guard was posted, while I advised you of their arrival by 'phone.

6. Himmler was immediately searched with the utmost thoroughness by Capt. [*Thomas*] Selvester, Lieut. Findlay and myself. He was made to strip entirely and don a complete change of ~~clothing~~ underwear which was examined minutely beforehand. His other clothes were also carefully examined, and all his effects, which were contained in a rucksack.

7. The only unusual article we found was a small glass phial containing a colourless liquid and enclosed in a small metal tube. Himmler explained that he suffered from cramps in the stomach, and the phial contained a medicinal remedy. I handed the phial ~~contained~~ to you later on in the evening.

8. The three men were dressed in a miscellaneous assortment of German army uniform and civilian clothes. Himmler wore horn-rimmed glasses, and on his arrival at the camp had a black patch over his right eye. He removed this patch on his first being searched.

9. Himmler and the other two men were kept in the room under constant supervision until you arrived with Major Rice.

BLA

Signed C A Smith Capt.

Chief Interrogator

031 Camp[144]

Statement by Captain T. Selvester, Commandant of 031 Civilian Interrogation Camp, near Luneburg (undated):

On the 23rd May 1945, I was the Commandant of 031 Civilian Interrogation Camp, near Luneburg.

About 2-0 p.m. on that day, a convoy arrived at the Camp with a party of suspected persons, who I understood had been arrested at a check point on a bridge near Bremervorde. At that time, large numbers of German troops were endeavouring to make their way home, and were carrying in most cases documents issued by senior officers of their respective regiments. These troops were being stopped, and placed in ordinary P.O.W. cages, but if there was any doubt as to their identity they were sent to my Camp for further interrogation. On arrival at my Camp, the drill was for such prisoners to be paraded outside my office, and then allowed to enter singly, when it was my duty to obtain from them their names, addresses, ages, and any documents carried. I was also responsible for the searching of the prisoners, and the listing of the personal property in their possession.

It will be appreciated that such procedure took some little time, and somewhere about 4-0 p.m. it was reported to me that the troops guarding the prisoners outside the offices were having some little trouble with three men in the party, who were insisting on seeing me immediately. This was most unusual, as normally these prisoners were most apprehensive, and only too anxious to please, and as a result I ordered that they be brought before me one at a time. The first man to enter my office was small, ill-looking and shabbily dressed, but he was immediately followed by two other men, both of whom were tall and soldierly looking, one slim, and one well built. The well built man walked with a limp. I sensed something unusual, and ordered one of my Sergeants to place the two Tall (sic) men in close custody, and not allow anyone to speak to them without my authority. They were then removed from my office, whereupon the small man, who was wearing a black patch over his left eye, removed the patch and put on a pair of spectacles. His identity was at once obvious, and he said 'Heinrich Himmler' in a very quiet voice. At that time only myself and a Sergeant were present in the room, so I ordered the sergeant to notify Captain Smith of the Intelligence Corps that I would like to see him in my office, and arranged for an armed guard to be posted outside the room to prevent any person entering.

On Captain Smith's arrival, I told him what had transpired, (but I don't think he needed to be told the identity of our prisoner), and he asked Himmler to sign his name in order to compare with a copy we had in our possession. Himmler was most reluctant to write his name, and was under the impression that we wanted it as a souvenir, but eventually agreed on condition that the paper was torn up immediately.

The next step was to search the prisoner, & this I carried out personally, handing each item of clothing as it was removed to my Sergeant, who re-examined it. Himmler was carrying documents bearing the name of Heinrich Hizinger, who I think was described as a postman. In his jacket I found a small brass case, similar to a cartridge case, which contained a small glass phial. I recognised it for what it was, but asked Himmler what it contained, and he said, 'That is my medicine. It cures my stomach cramp.' I also found a similar brass case, but without the phial, and came to the conclusion that the phial was hidden somewhere on the prisoner's person. When all Himmler's clothing had been removed and searched, all the orifices of his body were searched, also his hair combed and any likely hiding places examined, but no trace of the phial was found. At this stage he was not asked to open his mouth, as I considered that if the phial was hidden in his mouth and we tried to remove it, it may precipitate some action would be regretted. I did however send for thick bread and cheese sandwiches and tea, which I offered to Himmler, hoping that I would see him if he removed anything from his mouth. I watched him closely but did not notice anything unusual.

In the meantime, information had been sent to 2nd Army Headquarters, and whilst we were waiting for Senior Intelligence Officers to arrive, I arranged for clothing to be provided for the prisoner. The only clothing available of course was British Army uniform, and on seeing it Himmler refused to put it on, with the exception of the shirt, underpants and socks. He seemed to be under the impression that we would photograph him in the uniform, and use it for Press purposes. He was then provided with a blanket to wrap on top of the underwear.

If memory serves me correctly, it would be about 7-30 or 8-0 p.m. when Colonel Murphy arrived at the Camp to interrogate the prisoner, and I was present during that interrogation. I have no knowledge of the actual conversation, as I was still obsessed with the thoughts of the missing phial, and watched Himmler closely. I had informed other Intelligence Officers of my fears regarding the poison, and they had been in touch with senior medical officers to try and discover if there was any method of giving Himmler a drug to make him lose consciousness and enable us to search his mouth. We were told that it was impossible to administer a drug to any person which would act so quickly that the person would be unaware that he had been drugged, so the idea was abandoned. During the interrogation, Himmler was again asked to sign his name, this time by Colonel Murphy, and he did so, but again he tore the paper into small fragments after the signature was examined. During the course of the evening, the prisoner was again served with sandwiches and tea, and none of the five or six officers present saw him make any unusual move.

About midnight Colonel Murphy issued orders for Himmler to be removed to 2nd Army Headquarters, and he was escorted there by Intelligence Officers. I have no further knowledge of later events.

During the time Himmler was in my custody he behaved perfectly correctly, and gave the impression that he realised things had caught up with him. I was rather surprised when I heard of his death so soon after leaving my camp, but as I said earlier, although I have no knowledge of what transpired when he was interrogated by Colonel Murphy, I did gain the impression that he was quite prepared to talk, and indeed at times appeared almost jovial. He looked ill when I first saw him, but improved tremendously after a meal and a wash (he was not permitted to shave). He was in my custody for approximately eight hours, and during that time, whilst not being interrogated, asked repeatedly about the whereabouts of his 'Adjutants' (Grothmann & Macher?), appearing genuinely worried over their welfare. I have no reason to believe that Himmler was successful in passing any check points prior to being detained at Bremervorde. His simple disguise was extremely effective, but once the eye patch was removed his identity was obvious. I found it impossible to believe that he could be the arrogant man portrayed by the Press before and during the war.[145]

Colonel Michael Murphy, in 1964, gave his recollections of Himmler's last hours:
Murphy reached Westertimke Camp about 20:00 hrs, had Himmler stripped and searched, noting that it 'was clear to me that it was still possible for Himmler to have poison hidden about him, the most obvious places being his mouth and his buttocks. I therefore told him to dress, and wishing to have a medical search conducted, telephoned my second-in-command at

my headquarters and told him to get a doctor to stand by at a house [*Uelzenstrasse, Lüneburg*] I had had prepared for such men as Himmler.

Colonel Michael Murphy travelled with Himmler from Barnstedt (Westertimke) to Lüneburg, arriving 22:40 hrs.

On arrival at the house the doctor, Captain C. J. L. Wells, was already there and Himmler again stripped off for a bodily examination. Ears, armpits, hair, buttocks and then his mouth. The doctor asked him Himmler to open his mouth, inside the mouth immediately he saw a small black knob sticking out between a gap in the teeth on the right hand side lower jaw. Wanting to take a better look, the doctor put two fingers into Himmler's mouth, Himmler bit hard on them, hurting the doctor and breaking the phial, releasing the cyanide poison. Immediately Murphy threw Himmler to the ground and turned him on his stomach to prevent swallowing. Murphy recollected shouting for a needle and cotton, which arrived with remarkable speed. 'I pierced the tongue and with the cotton threaded through held the tongue out.' To no avail, Himmler died fifteen minutes later.[146]

On Himmler's journey from Westertimke to Lüneburg his escort consisted of Lt.Col. Murphy (driver), Lt.Col. B A. Stapleton and Major M. A. C. Osborn; the latter's report of Himmler's last hours adds more information:

…While preparations were being made for his removal [*from Westertimke*] he said he had voluntarily surrendered to the Camp Commandant and made the following statement:
'On the 8th May, 1945, I wrote a letter to Field-Marshal Montgomery and gave it to General Kinsel (*sic*) for delivery. This letter asked for an interview to expound my views. On 9th May I decided, however, not to embarrass Admiral Doenitz with my presence and therefore I left Flensburg with a small party under the assumed name of Feldwebel Heinrich Hizinger. My intention was to roam about the country for a few weeks until the tumult of victory had died down and circumstances were more favourable for an interview…'.

His purpose is seeking an interview with Field Marshal Montgomery was to discuss future events explaining that sooner or later there would be another war to stop the intrusion of Asiatic hordes into Western Europe. 'Germany had to go to war because she could not tolerate an enemy in superior numbers within 150 miles of her capital. Germany was not an island with natural sea defences. Furthermore, Russia's birth- rate far exceed that of Germany and the menace was growing daily. Most of the German war effort was concentrated on the Eastern front.' … Now that Germany was beaten, Great Britain was left alone to face the Asiatic onslaught. It should be noted, said Himmler, that he had never attacked England in any of his speeches, in fact he had always hoped an understanding could be reached. Most of his S.S. men had died… Was this not proof of their honesty of purpose and loyalty to the cause of civilisation? Inside Germany, too, great changes had been made. In order to prevent the birth-rate from dropping, in his capacity as Police President, prostitution was abolished and heavy punishments were inflicted for abortion and unnatural offences.
'One should distinguish… between a few isolated facts in regard to concentration camps and propaganda. There may have been excesses committed by some misguided people here and there, but they were neither planned nor ordered…'.

Himmler said he would have preferred to speak to Field-Marshal Montgomery as a free man but this was no longer possible.[147]

The diary of Major Norman Whittaker, Lüneburg:

The doctors left at 1100 hrs and during the afternoon I learn that Doenitz, Jodl and Coy are not coming to Luneburg but flying straight on.

But at 2100 hrs another flap started. Jack Ashworth rang and said that Himmler was at Camp 031 and was going to be my guest for the night – My word, I do get 'em!! Got hold of Doc Wells from Rear Army HQ to conduct a bodysearch. Whilst waiting we discussed all the places where poison might be concealed – won't give all the details here!!

At 2245 Himmler was brought in. He was wrapped in a blanket. No arrogance about him. He was a cringing figure who knew that the game was up. We took him into the front room and the doctor began the search. He made him wash his hands and feet (in case he had poison underneath his nails).

And then he came to the moment. Himmler wouldn't open his mouth wide so I shone the standard lamp into it. And then I heard the doc say 'My God! it is in his mouth – he has done it on me.'

Himmler gave a shake of his head (the doc told me afterwards that he had bitten his finger). Himmler pitched forward immediately at once I smelled cyanide and knew that it must be a very strong dose.

And we immediately upended the old bastard and got his mouth into the bowl of water which was there to wash the poison out. There were terrible groans and grunts coming from the swine. Col Murphy and I were taking it in turns to get hold of his tongue. But have you ever tried to keep hold of a slippery tongue? All this time the doc was working on artificial respiration and calling for cardiac stimulant, which Keith was vainly trying to get by telephone to Rear HQ! But the telephone wouldn't function.

So I sent Mac down to Rear HQ. Afterwards Mac told me that he appeared in a very disheveled state in a doctor's party and when he gasped 'Must have cardiac stimulant' they thought it was a huge joke and said 'Come and have a drink, old man.' And it took him at least five minutes to convince them that he really did want cardiac stimulant. Of course, it was then too late.

We had now procured a needle and cotton to fix his tongue, but the first thing we did was to get the needle through his lip so we had to get it out. But finally we got his tongue fixed. But it was a losing battle that we were fighting.

And this evil thing breathed its last at 2314 [hrs].

We turned it on its back, put a blanket on it and came away.

The Brig A/Q and B.G.S. [Brigadier Williams] came to the office and we told them about the suicide. They didn't seem unduly disturbed. They had a drink.

And when the they had gone, Jimmy the dentist badly wanted to take a couple of teeth out as souvenirs – but I said 'No!'[148]

From the War Diary, British Second Army Defence Company:

2100 hrs: Informed by G 1(b) that Heinrich Himmler (Reich Minister of Interior, Chief of German Police, Reichsführer SS, and Head of the Home Army) had been detained, and was to be brought to Second Army Defence Company guard room. All arrangements were made for him to be guarded, and Capt. C. J. L. Wells (RAMC) was summoned from Rear Army HQ to make the necessary medical search.

<u>2245 hrs</u>: Himmler arrived and was immediately taken to a room in No. 31a, Uelzenerstrasse and Capt. Wells commenced the medical search. Poison was suspected and all possible hiding places were searched. When the doctor began to examine Himmler's mouth, he only half-opened his mouth, and the doctor demanded that the mouth should be opened wide, and at the same time requested that a light should be shone more closely. The doctor perceived a blue object between Himmler's right lower teeth and gum, and attempted to get it from his mouth. But Himmler gave a shake of his head bit the doctor's finger and crushed this object, which proved to be a phial of poison between his teeth. He dropped almost immediately to the floor and every effort was made to get the poison from his mouth, including turning the patient upside down with his mouth in a bowl of water. Artificial respiration was attempted but it was of no avail, and Himmler died at 2314 hrs.

Present in the room at Himmler's death were Col. L. N. [Michael] Murphy (Col. G (I)), Major N. [Norman] Whittaker (O.C. Defence Coy), Capt. C. [Clement] J. L. Wells (RAMC), Medical officer – Rear Army HQ, and CSM [Company Sergeant Major] [Edwin] Austin (CSM Defence Coy). In the hall of the house at the time were Major K. Randall (G 2 1(b)) and Major S. [Storm] Rice (G 2 1 (b)0. These two officers had accompanied Col. Murphy with Himmler from the Interrogation Centre.[149]

After the war, Captain Clement J. L. Wells gave an account of his body search of Himmler to the Oxford Medical Society:

In doing this he [Himmler] threw his head a little backwards and away, but only in the same way that many other people do when asked to show their teeth. There was nothing exaggerated in the movement. I can see the mouth now. They were goodish teeth. But what I did see was a small blue tit-like object sticking out of the lower sulcus of his left cheek [the space between the jaw bone and the inner cheek]. That was something abnormal. That more than likely was it. What on earth was I going to do now?...

We struggled for a moment. He wrenched my hand out of his mouth, swung his head away and then with almost deliberate disdain faced me, crushed the glass capsule between his teeth and took a deep inhalation. His face immediately became deeply suffused and contorted with pain. His neck veins stood out, and his eyes stared glassily, and he crashed to the ground...

There was a slowing series of stertorous breaths, which may have continued for half a minute, and the pulse for another minute after that.[150]

Request from Allied Force Headquarters, Italy, dated 23 May 1945, to SHAEF for G-2 officer:

Unconfirmed reports indicate Himmler in custody 21 Army Group. Can you confirm or deny as we are interrogating Mrs Himmler to determine his whereabouts. Cable reply.[151]

Thursday, 24 May 1945

War Diary, British Second Army Defence Company:

<u>1700 hrs</u>: Press Conference held by Col Murphy, and the Press were shown Himmler's body.[152]

Diary of Major Norman Whittaker, Lüneburg:

At 1700 hrs Col Murphy held a Press Conference. What a party – Himmler cannot have been photographed so much before.

He does seem to be the central figure in that room to-day!!!

...

Today at various off moments I have been able to piece together some particulars of Himmler's last days, notably from conversation with Cols [Colonels] Murphy and Stapleton and Major Rice and Randall.

Himmler and two of his adjutants were detained because their papers were not in order at the bridge at Bremervorde which is between Bremen and Hamburg, and were then sent to the Corps Camp at Westetimke (sic) where they were interrogated. Himmler was wearing his glasses with a black patch over his right eye and had shaved off his moustache. He was travelling under the name of Hizzinger (sic).

The people at the Corps Camp were not satisfied and so the party was sent to Camp 031 which is South of Lüneburg. Here, having removed his black patch, he requested an interview with the Camp Commandant and announced 'I am Heinrich Himmler.'

And then telephones, including mine, commenced to ring.!!!

Storm Rice was really the last person to have a conversation with the Reichsfuehrer SS, Himmler. Of course, he had been trying to negotiate an armistice with the Western Allies through Sweden. It now appears, by his last conversation, that he was windy of the Russians and preferred to surrender to us. His main idea was to see somebody of high rank and said that he would be willing to talk, – In fact, he said that he would talk quite freely – can you beat the mentality of these Nazis? – cheeky devils right up to the last! This fellow, Himmler, must have more murders to his credit than anybody since the Borgias.

I suppose he must have had just a faint hope that he might make some sort of bargain with the Field Marshal – maybe trading his information about the Werewolves for his miserable skin? And then when he was stripped and treated as he should be treated – as a criminal – one of the biggest criminals of all time – the most hateful man in the Nazi Party; the bully became the coward.

...

The poison phial must have been in his mouth before his last interview with the Camp Commandant of Camp 031.

Bernard Stapleton told me that he sat beside Himmler on his journey from Camp 031 to Lüneburg and he certainly didn't put anything into his mouth during the journey. And he was well watched by 031 fellows and also by us from the time of his arrival.

There was a rather humourous incident during that journey from Camp 031. At one point Col. Murphy was not quite sure of the road and he turned to Bernard [Stapleton] to inquire and to their amusement Himmler replied 'You are on the road to Lüneburg.'

I wonder when he made the decision to follow his fuehrer (sic)? I suppose at the instant that the doctor went for his mouth and his mind said 'Now or Never?' and replied at the same time 'Now!'

During the search I never looked away from him. His eyes were not the eyes of an arrogant man – they were those of a man who was frightened. And I think that I know why he was frightened – he had been hoping all along to keep that phial concealed and he knew that it would not be discovered. The time for Heinrich Himmler to face his Maker had come!

He must die!![153]

The BBC broadcast "The Death of Himmler" from Lüneburg with reporter Chester Wilmot taking an eye-witness report from Sergeant Major Edwin Austin.[154]

During the evening a statement was issued by 2nd British Army:

> The commissars of Marshal Zukov, for questions relating to fulfillment of the conditions of the German surrender, Colonel Gorbusin, Lt. Col. Ievlev and Captain Kucin, saw the corpse [of Himmler] at 18.15 hrs today, 24 May 1945, and have been given relevant photographs and reports.[155]

Historian Peter-Ferdinand Koch:

> The news of Himmler's suicide came through the ether a few hours later. In Eichbuhl, Bavaria, Oswald Pohl heard it and immediately informed Hedwig Potthast then living at Achensee. Hedwig Potthast seemed cool about the news. The day after the death of the father of her children, on 24 May 1945, she returned from the Tyrol to Bavaria. Himmler's children had stayed with Pohl's wife, Eleonore. She was on her way to Pohl's wife when two US jeeps stopped in front of her small house. When asked if she was Hedwig Potthast, she nodded. Politely she was asked to accompany them. The jeeps returned to Munich. For a week Hedwig Potthast was questioned.[156]

The American journalist, William L. Shirer, writing in New York, 24 May 1945:

> Himmler, next to Hitler, the most evil of the Nazi barbarians, has escaped the Justice of this world. The British reveal he was picked up on Monday at a bridge at Bremervoerde, northeast of Bremen, but was not immediately recognized, having shaved off his mustache, donned civilian clothes and tied a black patch over his right eye. Recognized as the killer Gestapo chief during a check-up at a prisoner-of-war camp yesterday, he bit a small vial of poison concealed in his mouth as he was being stripped. He was a dead Nazi fifteen minutes later, at eleven four p.m. yesterday. Wonder if the British are just as satisfied to be rid of him this way? The Foreign Office, at least, does not appear enthusiastic about the prospect of trying the Nazi war criminals.[157]

Radio message from (British) 2 Army Main to 21 Army Group Main (signed, Major and a signature):

> 176, TOPSEC, for CoS from CoS, please give orders for disposal of body of Himmler.[158]

US Military Intelligence issued the Preliminary Interrogation Report on Hedwig Potthast.[159]
British Military Intelligence issued the Preliminary Interrogation Report on Heinz Macher.[160]
British Military Intelligence issued the Preliminary Interrogation Report on Werner Grothmann.[161]

Friday, 25 May 1945

From the diary of Norman Whittaker, Lüneburg:

> Various doctors and dentists came to take measurements and various things. What a good job I didn't let Jimmy take out those teeth. Message from Col Murphy telling me to put the body under the earth in the morning. As few as possible to know the location.[162]

From the War Diary, Second Army Defence Company:

> 1100 hrs: D.D.M.S. arrived with Medical and Dental Officers to take certain measurements, impressions, etc.[163]

Major G R Attkins signed his "Report on Dentition" after examining Himmler's mouth:

> "Cadaver examined at 11.00 hrs to 13.15 hrs on 25 May 45 at 31a Uelsenerstrasse (sic), Lüneburg."[164]

Death mask and fingerprints of Himmler were taken by two criminal police officials from Lüneburg, Max Musgiller and Wichmann.[165]

Newspaper editor Ursula von Kardorff, compared Himmler's death to the executions that followed of people connected to the July 1944 bomb plot against Hitler:

> Himmler is dead. Cyanide, the English doctors could not prevent it. The people of 20 July [1944] did not die so easily. It was awful to hear of his death. Everyone meets the same fate. But I can longer hate him.[166]

Saturday, 26 May 1945

From the diary of Major Norman Whittaker, Lüneburg:

> Took the body [of Himmler] out in a truck for its last ride. Hell of job to find a lonely spot. Anyhow! we did find one and threw the old bastard into the hole which we had dug.
>
> Present were only four of us. We had wrapped the thing in a camouflage net.
>
> The Press are still asking when we are going to have the funeral.
>
> On my return to the office am told by Sgt Foweather that we may have to dig the body up as Himmler's other brother has been caught and it may be necessary for him to identify the corpse. Anyhow! it is a false alarm. Kid brother (Gebhardt Himmler) arrived at 2000 hrs – a harmless looking individual (a Captain).[167]

War Diary, Second Army Defence Company:

> Himmler's body was buried in an unknown grave without a religious ceremony. Those present at the burial were Major N. Whittaker, CSM Austin, Sgt W. Ottery and Sgt R. Weston. These four were the only people who knew the location of the grave. Subsequently the Map Reference of the location was handed by O.C. Defence Coy to Col. G (I), HQ, Second Army.[168]

War Diary, Second Army Defence Company:

> 2000 hrs: Gebhardt Himmler, Himmler's brother taken into custody.[169]

Sunday, 27 May 1945

From a postwar interrogation of Werner Grothmann:

> Grothmann was brought [from Barnstedt] to Det. C.S.D.I.C. prison camp for detailed interrogation on 27 May 1945. He as yet knows nothing of Himmler's fate and precautions have

been taken to prevent him from learning the news. The story of Grothmann's life and activities as obtained from him by interrogation at Det. C.S.D.I.C. may now be set forth as follows....[170]

Second Army Troops News journal, No. 350, 27 May 1945:

Unmarked Grave for Himmler.

Himmler was buried yesterday [26 May] in a wooded area not far from the house at Second Army H.Q. in which he committed suicide on Wednesday last.

Before this took place British Army surgeons took casts of his features and removed the brain and parts of the skull. The body was then wrapped in a blanket and conveyed in an army lorry to the site chosen for his burial.

There was no religious service, and the few soldiers present at the act of burial in unconsecrated ground are sworn to secrecy as to the whereabouts of his grave.[171]

War Diary, Second Army Defence Company:

1600 hrs: Gebhardt Himmler taken away under escort.[172]

SS-Stubaf Heinrich Springer arrested by British forces.[173]

Saturday, 2 June 1945

The Illustrated London News journal, 2 June 1945:

Himmler, Gestapo Chief and the most sinister figure in Germany, is dead. He committed suicide by taking poison, just after 11 p.m. on May 23 at the British Second Army H.Q. at Lüneburg. Heinrich Himmler, disguised with a black patch over one eye, and with his moustache shaved off, was arrested at Bremervörde, north-east of Bremen, detained, searched and questioned as a nearby internment camp, and finally transferred to General Dempsey's H.Q. There he was stripped for the fourth time in order to make certain he was not concealing poison. The medical officer asked him to open his mouth, but not being able to see efficiently well, took the prisoner over to the window and told him to open his mouth again. It was as the doctor was putting a finger in Himmler's mouth that he saw the German bite on a black dot, which proved to be the top of a phial contained cyanide of potassium. Every effort was made to save Himmler's life, but without success. A message was then sent to Flensburg asking the Supreme H.Q. control party there to send representatives of the U.S. and Russian Armies to view the body.

Saturday, 14 July 1945

Il Giornale del Mattino journal (Rome); article "A Tragic Woman" by Ann Stringer, United Press, in discussion with Margherita (sic) Himmler:

She tells me finally the last events which she saw in Germany. No instruction had been given to her by her husband when the American troops were seen to be advancing on Munich. In fear that the city would be turned into a field of battle, she left the Bavarian capital in an automobile with her daughter [Gudrun], a sister and an aunt. She took refuge in a place in Alto Adige where she was captured by the Allies. She does not know what happened to her sister and an aunt.[174]

30 July 1945

Himmler's secretary, Erika Lorenz, was arrested by US security forces at Zell am See and taken to "Salzburg jail" (Austria).[175]

21 Aug 1947

Death certificate issued by Registrars' Office (Standesamt), Lüneburg, for Heinrich Luitpold Himmler, "death by suicide (poison)".[176]

26 September 1964

A report by the Moscow newspaper, *Izvestia* dated 26 September 1964, about the arrest and death of Himmler; translated and published in the German newspaper *Frankfurter Allgemeine Zeitung* dated 28 September 1964:

From a military archive in Moscow a report by a Soviet officer has been found showing that the Reichsführer-SS was captured by two Soviet soldiers, and not, as previously assumed, by an English patrol. They were Wassili Gubarev and Ivan Sidorov.

According to the newspaper report, the two had shortly before been released from a German prisoner of war camp and brought them to an assembly point; the following day they were on patrol in vicinity of Meinstedt village near Bremervörde. The report continued, while the British drank tea, the two Russian maintained their patrol: "Five hundred meters off the road, three Germans appeared out of the woods. We noticed, and got behind them. When we were two hundreds meters distant, we called on them to stop. One stopped, the two other went further on. We then called loudly: 'stop'. raised out rifles and brought all three to a stand still. We asked: 'Soldiers?' One answered: 'Yes!' To our question: "Have you identity cards?' One answered with: 'Jawohl!' They showed us one identity card. It had neither stamp nor signature. They wore officers' coats and boots. One of the Germans, later found to be Himmler, had civilian shoes and a hat. His left eye was covered by a black bandage, he had no mustache. He carried a stick.

We led the detainees into the village and handed them over to the English soldiers. The three Germans told the English they had recently been released from hospital. One had been injured in the eye and foot. The English patrol wanted to let them go. But we insisted they should not be released and be brought to the camp. Together with two English soldiers we took the detainees. At the camp an English officer-interpreter received us. He took over the detainees and sent them to the guard house.

A few days later we heard that a British officer and interpreter were looking for us. They asked: 'Where are the Russians who captured the three Germans on 21 May? What badges did they have?' We asked them: 'Do you know if they have been arrested?' 'No,' the interpreter explained. 'You arrested the head of the Gestapo, Himmler, right-hand man of Hitler.' Then the Englishman added that Himmler had taken poison."

That is the report of soldier Gubarev. *Izvestiya* added the report of the Soviet Major [*Godlevski*]. The Major had dealt with the repatriation of his liberated countrymen from the assembly point at Meinstedt. He describes how Himmler and his two bodyguards spent the night in the guardhouse of Camp 619 at Bremervörde, and the following morning passed onto the administration unit. In the presence of two former Russian prisoners of war, an English interpreter spoke to the detainees. We searched them and took away watches, compasses and maps. Later, an ampoule containing a solution was found on them. Himmler declared that it was a stomach medicine and it was given back to him. The interpreter reported to the Russians, after the detainees had been examined in the administration unit, that the man with the bandaged eye was Himmler and the other two his bodyguards. During the medical examination, a doctor tried examining Himmler's mouth whereupon Himmler bit the doctor's fingers and crushed the phial in his mouth, fatally poisoning himself. The Soviet Major, according to *Izvestiya*, had the incident confirmed in writing by the English commandant, a Lieutenant Colonel.[177]

Once Admiral Dönitz asked Himmler to resign all his offices on 6 May, Himmler must have realised that his dreams of postwar power were at an end. His letters for interviews with Eisenhower and latterly with Montgomery went unanswered. After the German surrender, Himmler and a small staff left the German-occupied areas of Flensburg and headed south, ever hopeful of couriers bringing positive news from the Allied side about a meeting with Montgomery. None came. Once Himmler and his men crossed the River Elbe there was no return with Germany now under Allied control and Himmler's capture by the occupying Allies became inevitable.

The suicide of Adolf Hitler and then of Heinrich Himmler were probably the most significant events indicating the end of the Nazi regime. They were followed by the International Military Tribunal at Nuremberg who prosecuted most surviving former Nazi government ministers; Ernst Kaltenbrunner deputizing for Himmler. Their trial began on 20 November 1945 and the verdicts passed on 1 October 1946. Of the twenty-one defendants still in the dock to hear their sentences, eleven heard a sentence of death by hanging. There would be no reprieve; ten went to the gallows and Göring avoided his death sentence by committing suicide by poison in his prison cell. Three received Not Guilty verdicts; the rest served prison sentences.

History will show Heinrich Himmler forever associated with the role of the Gestapo as an instrument of state terror against a civilian population, concentration camps and the factory killing of millions of unarmed defenceless Jews and countless other political and ethnic victims of National Socialism. Many of these victims are buried in unmarked graves, a fate shared by Heinrich Himmler.

Endnotes

JANUARY 1945

1. Interrogation report, CSDIC SIR 1725, 11 Sept. 1945, TNA, KV 2/106.
2. "Termine des Reichsführers-SS 1944/1945", BAB, NS 19/1793, with all the desk calendar entries from 1 January–14 March 1945.
3. "Sz.", Sonderzug: Himmler's private train was Sonderzug Steiermark.
4. Today, Dillweissenstein, southern suburbs of Pforzheim.
5. In all the desk diary entries Ostendorff is incorrectly spelled Ostendorf.
6. Yehuda Bauer, *Jews for Sale*, p. 230.
7. Telegram 2 Jan. 1945 from Foreign Office, London, to Rome, TNA, FO 371/46764.
8. H. R. Trevor–Roper (ed.), *The Bormann Letters. The Private correspondence between Martin Bormann and his Wife from January 1943 to April 1945*, p.158.
9. Twice incorrectly spelled "Piepkorn".
10. Himmler's Notes for a speech before the commanders of Heeresgruppe Oberrhein in Sasbachwalden (Baden), BAB, NS 19/4018; Geheimreden, p. 277.
11. KdS Radom [Joachim Illmer] to Aussenstellen, 3 Jan.1945, BAB, R 70/Bd. 81; publ. in *Nacht über Europa*, Poland, p. 327, footnote 2.
12. SS–Ostubaf. Ekkehard Albert, 14 Jan.1945, Chief of Staff – XIII. SS–A.K. under SS–Gruf. Max Simon; Kurt Mehner, *Die Waffen–SS und Polizei*, p. 134.
13. message CX/MSS/C.400, TNA, HW 5/705
14. Citation by SS–WVHA for the award of Deutschen Kreuzes in Silver to SS–Gruf. Richard Glücks, p. 1, 13 Jan.1945, BAB, BDC, SSO Richard Glücks.
15. Facsimile in: Johannes Tuchel, *Inspektion der Konzentrationslager*, Doc. 9.3, p. 61.
16. Percy E. Schramm (ed.), *Kriegstagebuch des Oberkommandos der Wehrmacht 1944–1945*, Teilband II, p. 1305.
17. Jan Erik Schulte, "Hans Jüttner. Der Mann im Hintergrund der Waffen-SS," in Ronald Smelser/Enrico Syring, *Die SS: Elite unter dem Totenkopf*, p. 285.
18. CIRO/PEARL/ZIP/GPD 4041 (message 11), TNA, HW 16/43.
19. Prof. Werner Osenberg, Planungsamt des Reichsforschungsrates.
20. WHW – "Winter-Hilfswerk", an annual voluntary monetary collection to provide less fortunate Germans with provisions etc during the winter months,
21. Götz Persch was the last commander, RfSS Escort Battalion (Begleit-Bataillon); H R Trevor-Roper, *The Last Days of Hitler*, p. 171.
22. Walter Jenschke, born 15 Dec.1924, awarded Ritterkreuz on 18 Dec.1944 when serving with 23.SS-Freiwilligen-Panzergrenadierdivision "Nederland"; Ernst-Günther, *Die Ritterkreuzträger der Waffen-SS*," p.802.
23. http://www.geocities.com/~orion47/SS-POLIZEI/SS-Gruf_H-N.html

24. Statement on oath by Kurt Becher, 1 March 1948, p. 1; T/37 (235) = T/689 = PdI 774, MF 12.

25. Interrogation of Kurt Becher in presence of Dr Kasztner, 7 July 1947, p. 19 f; T/37 (235) = T/689 = PdI 774, MF 12.

26. Interrogation of Werner Grothmann, 12 April 1948 by Mr. Barr, also present Kurt Becher, US NARA, FC 6083 = BAK, 838 K, p. 1.

27. Percy E. Schramm (ed.), *Kriegstagebuch des Oberkommandos der Wehrmacht 1944–1945*, Teilband II, p. 1648.

28. Original copy at British Library, Newspaper Section.

29. Top Secret note by Botschaftsrat Hilger for Ribbentrop, 11 Jan.1945; publ. in ADAP, Serie E, Vol. VIII, Doc. 335, p. 629 f.

30. Kasztner-Report, p. 152, T/37 (237) = T/113 = PdI 900, MF 14.

31. Albert Speer, *The Slave State*, p. 237.

32. Hillgruber/Hümmelchen, *Chronik des Zweiten Weltkrieges*, p. 258.

33. Heinz Höhne, *Order of the Death's Head*, p. 555.

34. Interim Report on the Interrogation of SS Standfue. Dr Brandt, Rudolf, 10 June 1945, p. 3, US NARA, RG 319, Entry MLR 134B, Box 85, folder XE 000632.

35. Maximilian v. Herff to HSSPF Südost Schmauser, 30 Jan.1945, BAB, BDC, SSO Fritz Arlt.

36. Letter Himmler to SS–Ogruf. Hermann Höfle, 14 Jan.1945, BAB, NS 19/3312.

37. Himmler's report [Rf/Br.], 18 Jan.1945, BAB, BDC, SSO Kurt Becher; BAB, BDC, SS-HO 5912; facsimile in Werner Maser, *Nürnberg. Tribunal der Sieger*; Alexandra–Eileen Wenck, *Zwischen Menschenhandel und "Endlösung": Das Konzentrationslager Bergen-Belsen*, p. 295, footnote 619.

38. Walter Schellenberg, *The Labyrinth*, p. 379.

39. H. G. Adler, *Der Kampf gegen die "Endlösung der Judenfrage"*, p. 104; Alexandra-Eileen Wenck, *Bergen–Belsen*, p. 363.

40. BAB, NS 19/2776.

41. BAK, Collection Schumacher/329; Martin Broszat, "The Concentration Camps 1933–1945," in *Anatomy of the SS-State*, p. 504.

42. Bundesarchiv Abteilungen Potsdam, Microfilm Nr. 14428; http://www.flossenbuerg.de/infozentrum/ [Täter]; Prisoner Reports, 1 Jan. and 15 Jan.1945, BAB, NS 3/439; facsimile in: Johannes Tuchel, *Inspektion*, p. 212f.

43. Martin Broszat (ed.), *Kommandant in Auschwitz*, p. 145, footnote 1, quoting statement by Oswald Pohl dated 3 April 1947 (NO-2736) and his former Ordonnanzoffizier (NO-1565), for the date, see NO-1876, for the evacuation order of KL Stutthof, see NO-3796.

44. Martin Broszat (Hg.), *Kommandant in Auschwitz*, p. 185.

45. Adalbert Rückerl, *NS–Vernichtungslager*, p. 287.

46. *Ibid*.

47. Danuta Czech, *Kalendarium*, p. 967; Ian Kershaw, *Hitler 1936–1945*, p.767.

48. On 18 January Jeckeln was replaced as HSSPF Ostland und Rußland Nord. His successor, SS–Gruf. Dr Hermann Behrends was appointed on 30 January 1945; Ruth Bettina Birn, *Die Höheren SS– und Polizeiführer*, p. 337; http://www.islandfarm.fsnet.co.uk/SS-Gruppenf%FChrer%20und%20Generalleutnant%20der%20Polizei% 20Dr%20jur.%20Hermann%20Behrends.htm

49. BAB, NS 19/758; Albert Speer, *The Slave State*, p. 149.

50. BAB, BDC, SSO Friedrich Jeckeln, handwritten note on his Stammkarte.

51. Hillgruber/Hümmelchen: *Chronik des Zweiten Weltkrieges*, p. 267.

52. Departure with Otto Skorzeny from the Black Forest to the East given as 23 Jan.1945 is incorrect, quoted in Fraenkel/Manvell, *Himmler*, p.207.

53. SD-A Lüneburg to RSHA III, 10.02.1945, BAB, R 58/976, p. 105.

54. Lew Besymenski, *Die letzten Notizen von Martin Bormann*, p. 104.

55. SD–Abschnitt Lüneburg to RSHA III D 5, 10 Feb.1945, with report of SD-Chief Hermann Müller about the evacuation of Posen, BAB, R 58/976, p. 105f.

56. Jürgen Thorwald, *Die große Flucht*, p. 71.

57. Diary of Alfred Jodl, 21 Jan.1945; cited in Walter Warlimont, *Im Hauptquartier der deutschen*

Wehrmacht 1939 bis 1945, Vol. 2, p. 533; Führer Order, 21 Jan.1945, appendix to circular sent by Bormann R 21/45gRs "Task of the Reichsführer-SS in the East" (Auftrag des Reichsführers–SS im Osten), 23 Jan.1945, BAB, NS 6/354.

58. Siegfried Westphal, *Heer in Fesseln*, Bonn, 1950, p.289, quoted in Gerald Reitlinger, *The SS. Alibi of a Nation 1922-1945*, p. 399.

59. Second Detailed Interrogation Report on SS-Staf. Canaris, Constantin, CSDIC/CMF/SD 53, 8 Aug.1945, TNA, WO 204/12806.

60. "Die verdrängte Tragödie", in: *Der Spiegel*, Nr. 6, 4 Feb.2002, p. 194.

61. General d. Nachrichten-Truppen Albert Praun, since 11 Aug.1944.

62. BA–MA, RH 19 XV, p. 3f.

63. Jürgen Thorwald, *Die große Flucht*, p. 73.

64. RSHA Amtschef I, Ehrlinger, to KdS Thümmler, 21 Jan.1945, BDC, SSO Walther Bierkamp.

65. Hillgruber/Hümmelchen, *Chronik des Zweiten Weltkrieges*, p. 261.

66. Percy E. Schramm, *Kriegstagebuch des Oberkommandos der Wehrmacht 1944-1945*, Teilband II, p. 1033; Percy Ernst Schramm (Ed.), *Die Niederlage 1945. Aus dem Kriegstagebuch des Oberkommandos der Wehrmacht*, 2. Edition, p. 95.

67. SS–Ogruf. Oberg on 24 Jan.1945 appointed "Befehlshaber der Sperr– und Auffanglinie", from 20 Feb.1945 it became "Befehlshaber der Auffanglinien I".

68. Deputy Gauleiter of Pomerania (Pommern.).

69. Dietrich Eichholtz, *Geschichte der deutschen Kriegswirtschaft*, Vol. III, p. 204; Jan Erik Schulte, *Zwangsarbeit und Vernichtung: Das Wirtschaftsimperium der SS*, p. 413.

70. message CX/MSS/T442/31, TNA, HW 1/3491

71. French interrogation of Karl Albrecht Oberg, 9 Dec.1945, TNA, KV 2/1668.

72. Hillgruber/Hümmelchen, *Chronik des Zweiten Weltkrieges*, p. 262.

73. Percy E. Schramm, *Kriegstagebuch des Oberkommandos der Wehrmacht 1944-1945*, Teilband II, p. 1035; Percy Ernst Schramm, *Die Niederlage 1945*, p. 98 f; Hillgruber/Hümmelchen, *Chronik des Zweiten Weltkrieges*, p. 262.

74. Telegram 24 Jan.1945 from Foreign Office, London, to Rome, TNA, FO 371/47674.

75. Kreisleiter Dotzler to Bormann "Vorschläge zum Aufbau einer Widerstandsbewegung in den von Bolschewisten besetzten deutschen Ostgebieten"; BAB, NS 19/832; Arno Rose, *Werwolf*, p. 108, 241.

76. TNA, HW 5/706.

77. Generalmajor Alfred Toppe, General Quartermaster of the Army, July 1944-1945; Oberst von Rückert was Chief of Provisions Department under Toppe.

78. Albert Speer, *Inside the Third Reich*, p. 434.

79. Inserted into Top Secret teleprinter message by Chief of Gen–Staff, Obkdos der Heeresgruppe "Weichsel", i.V. Oberst Eismann, to AOK 2, Gen.Kdo. XI. SS–A.K. and Gen.Kdo. XVI. SS–A.K.

80. David Irving, *Die Geheimwaffen des Dritten Reiches*, p. 343.

81. Percy E. Schramm, *Kriegstagebuch des Oberkommandos der Wehrmacht 1944-1945*, Teilband II, p. 1041; Schramm, *Die Niederlage 1945*, p. 105.

82. Roger James Bender and Hugh Page Taylor, Uniforms, Organization and History of the Waffen-SS, Vol. 2, published by the authors, 1971, USA, p. 25.

83. Diary of Joseph Goebbels, entry for 26 Jan.1945; cited in Ian Kershaw, *Hitler 1936–1945*, p.1018, footnote 17.

84. Unsigned report (confidential) and undated, Strategic Services Unit, War Department, in: Dwork/Duker Papers, US NARA, RG 200, box 10, doc. 99; cited in: Shlomo Aronson, Theresienstadt im Spiegel amerikanischer Dokumentation, in *Theresienstädter Studien und Dokumente 1994*, p. 25.

85. Dwork/Duker Papers, RG 200, box 29, #36; cited in Shlomo Aronson, Theresienstadt im Spiegel amerikanischer Dokumentation, in: *Theresienstädter Studien und Dokumente 1994*, p.22.

86. Hillgruber/Hümmelchen, *Chronik des Zweiten Weltkrieges*, p. 262.

87. Percy E. Schramm, *Kriegstagebuch des Oberkommandos der Wehrmacht 1944-1945*, Teilband

II, p. 1046; Schramm, *Die Niederlage 1945*, p. 112.

88. SS–Gruf. Dr Hermann Behrends appointed HSSPF Kurland, serving until the end of the war.
89. Erich von dem Bach took over 26 Jan. to 10 Feb.1945 as Commanding General of X. Waffen–Armee–Korps der SS (estn.[Estonian]); Kurt Mehner, *Waffen–SS und Polizei*, p. 127.
90. Top Secret letter from IdS Düsseldorf SS–Staf. Dr Albath to the Staatspolizei(leit)stellen Düsseldorf, Münster, Dortmund and Köln, 26 Jan.1945; BAB, BDC, SS-Hängeordner Nr. 14, SS-1442; copy in, TNA, WO 235/530.
91. Manvell & Fraenkel, *Himmler*, p. 211.
92. Himmler's Chief of Staff in H.Gr. Weichsel (Army Group Vistula); Heinz Höhne, *Order of the Death's Head*, p. 556.
93. BAB, NS 19/832; Arno Rose, *Werwolf*, p. 241.
94. Danuta Czech, *Kalendarium*, pp. 994-995.
95. Percy E. Schramm (Hg.), *KTB/OKW 1944/1945*, Vol. II, p. 1431.
96. BAB, NS 19/2719.
97. *Ibid.*
98. Schramm, *Die Niederlage 1945*, p. 126.
99. Teleprinter message from OKH to Himmler, 29 Jan.1945, in KTB HGr. Weichsel; David Irving, *Götterdämmerung*, p. 527, footnote 14.
100. Teleprinter message of Reichsführer–SS, 29 Jan.1945, inserted in Schnellbrief des Generalbevollmächtigten for the Reichsverwaltung to the higher offices of the State, 1 Feb.1945, Appendix to Bekanntgabe 61/45 Bormann, 8 Feb.1945; BAB, NS 6/353.
101. Preliminary Interrogation Report 031/Misc 20 of Heinz Macher, 24 May.1945, TNA, WO 208/4431.
102. Schramm, *Die Niederlage 1945*, p. 129, quoting a very low. early estimate.
103. "Die verdrängte Tragödie", in: *Der Spiegel*, Nr. 6, 4 Feb.2002, p.192f, 199f.
104. Hitler's last radio speech. The speech was broadcast at 19:15 hours, and repeated at 22:00 hours. See entry in Martin Bormann's pocket diary; Ian Kershaw, *Hitler 1936–1945*, p.773.
105. Lew Besymenski, *Die letzten Notizen von Martin Bormann. Ein Dokument und sein Verfasser*, p. 105.
106. Order of Reichsführer–SS, 30 Jan.1945, inserted in a Schnellbrief of the Generalbevollmächtigten für die Reichsverwaltung to the higher government offices, 1 Feb.1945, Appendix to Bekanntgabe 61/45 Bormann, 8 Feb.1945; BAB, NS 6/353. – The Himmler-Order was published in all German newspapers on 8 Feb.1945; *Hagener Zeitung*, 8 Feb.1945.
107. Glenn B. Infield, *Skorzeny: Hitler's Commando*, pp. 101-104.
108. Prof. MR. C. F. Rüter, Dr D. W. de Mildt unter Mitwirkung von L. Hekelaar Gombert, (Eds.) *Justiz und NS-Verbrechen. Sammlung deutscher Strafurteile wegen nationalsozialistischer Tötungsverbrechen 1945-1999*, Vol. XXXVI, pp. 1-70, LfD. Nr. 758, trial of Heinz Richter and Wilhelm Nickel for complicity in murder; in 1971 both men were acquitted.
109. Percy E. Schramm, *Kriegstagebuch des Oberkommandos der Wehrmacht 1944-1945*, Teilband II, p. 1062; Schramm, *Die Niederlage 1945*, p. 131f.
110. BAB, BDC, SSO Dr Hans Kammler; Rainer Karlsch, *Hitlers Bombe*, p. 184.
111. OKW teleprinter message, 31 Jan.1945 (Nuremberg doc. NOKW-460); Gregor Janssen, *Das Ministerium Speer*, p. 206.
112. Karin Orth, *System der nationalsozialistischen Konzentrationslager, p. 282 f.*
113. *Deposition on oath Georg Henning Graf von Bassewitz-Behr, 20 April.1947, p. 6, TNA, WO 309/408.*
114. *Charges before Oldenburg County Court against Friedrich–Wilhelm Lotto, 3 June 1948, BAK, Z 42 IV/1160, p. 22.*

FEBRUARY 1945

1. Interrogation of SS-Staf. Anton Kaindl in pre-trial custody before the Sachsenhausen-Trial,

Berlin, 1947; extract in *SS im Einsatz*, p. 200.

2. Hans Marsalek, *Geschichte des Konzentrationslagers Mauthausen*, p. 255-263.

3. Percy E. Schramm, *Kriegstagebuch des Oberkommandos der Wehrmacht 1944-1945*, Teilband II, p. 1067; Schramm, *Die Niederlage 1945*, p. 138.

4. BA–MA, RH 19 XV/2, p. 34.

5. Jean-Claude Favez, *Warum schwieg das Rote Kreuz?* p. 488, 585.

6. Hillgruber/Hümmelchen, *Chronik des Zweiten Weltkrieges*, p. 264; Tuchel/Schattenfroh, *Zentrale des Terrors*, p. 108, 297

7. Lew Besymenski, *Die letzten Notizen von Martin Bormann*, p. 106.

8. Ursula von Kardorff, *Berliner Aufzeichnungen*, entry of 3 Feb.1945, p. 212.

9. Miroslav Kárný, "Geschichte des Theresienstädter Transports in die Schweiz," in *Judaica Bohemiae* XXVII/ 1991, p. 4.

10. Führer-Order (Führerbefehl), 4 Feb.1945, BA–MA, RW 4/v. 754; cited in Ulrich Herbert, *Best*, p. 397.

11. IWM London, H/1/202; Peter Padfield, *Himmler*, p. 564.

12. Report CSDIC/CMF/X 169, 26 May 1945 (conversation bugged on 21 May 1945), TNA, WO 204/10182.

13. http://www.jur.uva.nl/junsv/ddr/files/ddr1063.htm.

14. February-May 1945: Commander of Ordungstruppen (order troops) in rear area of Army Group "Weichsel."

15. H. G. Adler, *Der Kampf gegen die "Endlösung der Judenfrage"*, p. 104.

16. Kasztner-Report, p. 152, T/37 (237) = T/113 = PdI 900, MF 14.

17. Interrogation of Kurt Becher, 2 March 1948, p. 3 f; T/37 (235) = T/689 = PdI 774, MF 12.

18. Afterwards Wolff travelled to Berlin for a meeting with Hitler and Ribbentrop in the Reich Chancellery. Wolff argued together with Foreign Minister Ribbentrop, that a political solution should run parallel with a military solution. Perhaps they could get their enemies to stand against each other. Hitler did not explicitly reject the proposal: see, Jochen von Lang, *Der Adjutant*, p. 263.

19. Kasztner-Report, p. 160, T/37 (237) = T/113 = PdI 900, MF 14.

20. Generalleutnant Bruno Ritter v. Hauenschildt, January–March 1945 Kampfkommandant for Berlin. See, OKW Situation Report, 2 Feb.1945: "For the defence of Berlin, General von Hauenschildt is appointed, and reports directly to the Führer…His appointment includes control of Flak operations for Berlin." (Schramm, *Die Niederlage 1945*, p. 135).

21. Hitler's Appointment Diary, kept by SS-Hstuf. Heinz Linge, IfZ, MA-147.

22. H. R. Trevor–Roper (ed.), *The Bormann Letters*, p. 178.

23. *Neue Zürcher Zeitung*, 8 Feb.1945, Mittagsausgabe; H.G. Adler, *Der Kampf gegen die "Endlösung der Judenfrage"*, p. 104f.

24. Miroslav Kárný, "Geschichte des Theresienstädter Transports in die Schweiz," in *Judaica Bohemiae* XXVII/ 1991, p. 6.

25. Kasztner-Report, p. 160, T/37 (237) = T/113 = PdI 900, MF 14.

26. Miroslav Kárný, "Geschichte des Theresienstädter Transports in die Schweiz," in *Judaica Bohemiae* XXVII/ 1991, p. 6.

27. TNA, FO 371/46788.

28. Percy E. Schramm (Ed.), *KTB/OKW 1944/1945*, II, p. 1430.

29. TNA, HW 1/3518.

30. H. R. Trevor-Roper (ed.),*The Bormann Letters*, p. 180.

31. Marlis Buchholz, *Die hannoverschen Judenhäuser*, Doc. Nr. 6, p. 276.

32. *Neue Zürcher Zeitung*, 8 Feb.1945, Klaus–Dietmar Henke, *Die amerikanische Besetzung Deutschlands*, p. 886

33. Walter Schellenberg, *The Labyrinth*, pp. 357-358.

34. IMT, Bd. XI, p. 371.

35. BAB, NS 19/832; Arno Rose, *Werwolf*, p. 241.

36. Yehuda Bauer, *Jews for Sale?* p. 243.

37. Hitler's appointments diary, kept by SS-Hstuf. Heinz Linge, IfZ, MA-147.

38. H. R. Trevor–Roper (ed.), *The Bormann Letters*, p. 181.

39. Lew Besymenski, *Die letzten Notizen von Martin Bormann. Ein Dokument und sein Verfasser*, p. 107.

40. Heinz Guderian, *Panzer Leader*, pp. 413-415. – Guderian's incorrect date of "13.02.45" was accepted by various publications: see, Fraenkel/Manvell, *Himmler*, p. 212; John Toland, *Adolf Hitler*, p. 1053, and Jürgen Thorwald, *Die große Flucht*, p. 202. Correct date of 10 Feb.1945 in David Irving, *Götterdämmerung*, p. 407.

41. CIRO/PEARL/ZIP/GPD 4010 transmitted 10 Feb.1945 (message 90): TNA, HW 16/43.

42. Yehuda Bauer, *Jews for Sale?* p. 243; Steven Koblik, *The Stones Cry Out*, p. 125.

43. BA-MA, RL 7/535, p. 391f.

44. Statement of Oberstleutnant Werner Baumbach, Nuremberg, 27 Aug.1946, IMT, Vol. XLI, p. 537f.

45. TNA, HW 1/3521.

46. TNA, HW 1/3534.

47. *Ibid.*

48. CIRO/PEARL/ZIP/GPD 4011 transmitted 12 Feb.1945 (message 23), TNA, HW 16/43.

49. Percy E. Schramm, *Kriegstagebuch des Oberkommandos der Wehrmacht 1944-1945*, Teilband II, pp. 1094-1096.

50. On 17 Feb.1945 Jeckeln replaced Friedrich–Wilhelm Krüger as Commanding General of V. SS–Freiwilligen–Gebirgskorps in Breslau area: BAB, BDC, SSO Friedrich Jeckeln.

51. Percy E. Schramm, *Kriegstagebuch des Oberkommandos der Wehrmacht 1944-1945*, Teilband II, pp. 1096-1097.

52. BAB, NS 19/763; Abb. Thüringer Allgemeine 1995. - http://www.gtgj.de/script/news/index.php?shownews=276

53. CIRO/PEARL/ZIP/AT 1531 transmitted 14 Feb.1945 – extract from GPD 4009, TNA, HW 16/70.

54. CIRO/PEARL/ZIP/GPD 4009 transmitted 14 Feb.1945 (msg 146), TNA, HW 16/43.

55. Report of Civil Police Commander of Dresden to Chief of Civil Police, Luftgaukommando III: extract from Ultra file GPD 4009, 14 Feb.1945, decrypt (English translation); SHAEF file, 'Dresden Attack,' ca. March 1945, document No.506.55a (Maxwell AFB: USAF Historical Division Archives).

56. CIRO/PEARL/ZIP/GPD 4009 transmitted 14 Feb.1945 (message 152), TNA, HW 16/43; Walter F Angell Jr., 'Historical Analysis of the 14–15.02.1945 Bombings of Dresden.' (USAF Historical Division Archives), p. 25.

57. Percy E. Schramm, *Kriegstagebuch des Oberkommandos der Wehrmacht 1944-1945*, Teilband II, p. 1099, 1102; Hillgruber/Hümmelchen, *Chronik des Zweiten Weltkrieges*, p. 266.

58. Circular by Bormann to the Gauleiters, R 81/45g, 15 Feb.1945, BAB, NS 6/354.

59. http://www.lostplaces.de/lampaden/

60. Himmler to von Alvensleben, 15 Feb.1945 (US NARA, film T175, roll 40, p. 550, 553).

61. BAB, BDC, SSO Walther Bierkamp.

62. Interrogation report CSDIC/SC/15AG/SD 11, 29 May 1945, of Walther Rauff, TNA, KV 2/1970.

63. Percy E. Schramm, *Kriegstagebuch des Oberkommandos der Wehrmacht 1944-1945*, Teilband II, p. 1102.

64. Hillgruber/Hümmelchen, *Chronik des Zweiten Weltkrieges*, p. 266.

65. Teleprinter message from Army Group Vistula (SS–Gruf. Lammerding) to 2., 9., 11. und 3. Pz. Armies and Oderkorps, US NARA, film T 311 roll 168 frame 9677.

66. CIRO/PEARL/ZIP/AT 1572 transmitted 16 Feb.1945 – extract from GPD 4022, TNA, HW 16/70.

67. HStA Düsseldorf, RW 34/31, p. 61; Arno Rose, *Werwolf*, p. 301.

68. Count Folke Bernadotte, *The Fall of the Curtain*, p. 20.

69. Randolph Braham, *The Politics of Genocide. The Holocaust in Hungary*, Vol. 2, p.1060;

Unsigned report (confidential) and undated, Strategic Services Unit, War Department, in: Dwork/Duker Papers, RG 200, box 10, doc. 99; Shlomo Aronson, "Theresienstadt im Spiegel amerikanischer Dokumentation," in *Theresienstädter Studien und Dokumente 1994*, p. 25.

70. Percy E. Schramm, *Kriegstagebuch des Oberkommandos der Wehrmacht 1944-1945*, Teilband II, p. 1105, 1107.

71. BAB, NS 6/354, p. 81f. – Possibly in March 1945 regarded as the "Catastrophe Order".

72. H. R. Trevor-Roper (ed.), *The Bormann Letters*, p. 183; Fraenkel/Manvell, *Himmler*, p. 213.

73. Count Folke Bernadotte, *The Fall of the Curtain*, p.13.

74. Percy E. Schramm, *Kriegstagebuch des Oberkommandos der Wehrmacht 1944-1945*, Teilband II, p. 1107.

75. CIRO/PEARL/ZIP/GPD 4019 transmitted 18 Feb.1945, Addendum II, message 123, TNA, HW 16/43.

76. Count Folke Bernadotte, *The Fall of the Curtain*, pp. 17-18.

77. H. R. Trevor-Roper, *The Bormann Letters*, pp. 184-185.

78. TNA, HW 1/3534.

79. Percy E. Schramm, *Kriegstagebuch des Oberkommandos der Wehrmacht 1944-1945*, Teilband II, p. 1110; Schramm, *Die Niederlage 1945*, p. 193.

80. Hitler's appointments diary, kept by SS-Hstuf. Heinz Linge, IfZ, MA-147.

81. Heinz Höhne, *Orden unter dem Totenkopf*, p. 500 (not in English edition).

82. Walter Schellenberg, *The Labyrinth*, pp. 384-385.

83. Hitler's appointments diary, kept by SS-Hstuf. Heinz Linge, IfZ, MA-147.

84. H. R. Trevor-Roper, *The Bormann Letters*, p. 189.

85. *Ibid.*

86. Interrogation report 030/095 of Kurt Pomme, 12 Nov.1945, US NARA, RG 498 Box 49.

87. Heinz Linge daily diary, IfZ München, MA 147; Rainer Karlsch, *Hitlers Bombe*, p. 238.

88. Count Folke Bernadotte, *The Fall of the Curtain*, pp. 29-30; Professor Seip, Rector of Oslo University.

89. Hillgruber/Hümmelchen, *Chronik des Zweiten Weltkrieges*, p. 267.

90. BAB, BDC, SSO Walther Bierkamp.

91. CIRO-PEARL/ZIP/GPD 4027 transmitted 23 Feb.1945 (message 105); TNA, HW 16/43.

92. TNA, FO 371/48046.

93. John Erickson, *The Road to Berlin*, p. 522.

94. TNA, FO 371/48046.

95. *Ibid.*

96. Lew Besymenski, *Die letzten Notizen von Martin Bormann*, p. 145; Toland, p. 1061; Von Lang, p. 308; Martin Broszat, *Nach Hitler. Der schwierige Umgang mit unserer Geschichte*, p.53.

97. Interrogation report CCPWE #32/DI-22 of Paul Wegener, 3 July 1945, TNA, FO 371/46779.

98. Hitler's appointments diary, kept by SS-Hstuf. Heinz Linge, IfZ, MA-147.

99. CIRO-PEARL/ZIP/GPD 4036 transmitted 25 Feb.1945, TNA, HW 16/43.

100. Gerd R. Ueberschär/Rolf Dieter Müller, *Deutschland am Abgrund*, p. 87; John Erickson, *The Road to Berlin*, p. 522.

101. Schramm, *Die Niederlage 1945*, p. 470; Hillgruber/Hümmelchen, *Chronik des Zweiten Weltkrieges*, p. 268.

102. BAB, BDC, SSO Waldemar Wappenhans.

103. CIRO-PEARL/ZIP/GPD 4034 transmitted 26 Feb.1945 (message 34), TNA, HW 16/43.

104. CIRO-PEARL/ZIP/GPD 4034 transmitted 26 Feb.1945 (message 14), TNA, HW 16/43.

105. ULTRA/ZIP/GPDR 50 transmitted 26 Feb.1945, SS Ogruf WOLFF to Kdo. Heer Gen.Qu.Abt. Kriegsverw. Berlin (message 55), TNA, HW 16/49.

106. BAB, NS 19/732.

107. John Erickson, *The Road to Berlin*, p. 522.

108. Notification by Martin Bormann, 28 Feb.1945; see *Der zweite Weltkrieg. Dokumente. Ausgewählt und eingeleitet von Gerhard Förster und Olaf Gröhler*, Doc. 130, p. 367.

109. CIRO-PEARL/ZIP/GPD 4035 transmitted 27 Feb.1945 (message 109), TNA, HW 16/43.

110. CIRO-PEARL/ZIP/GPD 4035 transmitted 27 Feb.1945 (message 2), TNA, HW 16/43.

111. CIRO-PEARL/ZIP/GPD 4035 transmitted 27 Feb.1945 (message 15), TNA, HW 16/43.

112. H. R. Trevor-Roper, *Final Entries 1945. The Diaries of Joseph Goebbels, p.10.*

MARCH 1945

1. *Klaus Drobisch, Widerstand in Buchenwald,* Berlin (Ost) 1985, p. 180.

2. *Buchenwald-Report,* p. 58; Eugen Kogon, *The Theory and Practice of Hell,* p.39.

3. Final Interrogation Report FIR No. 7, 11 July 1945, of SS-Ostubaf. Arthur Scheidler (adjutant of Kaltenbrunner), TNA, WO 208/4478.

4. Himmler telegram to Bassewitz Behr, March 1945, cited in Affidavit of Georg Henning Graf von Bassewitz-Behr, 14 Feb.1946, US NARA, RG 238, D-681, facsimile in *1945. The Year of Liberation,* p. 98. Bassewitz's statement was also confirmed by a witness [Hermann Kaienburg, *Das Konzentrationslager Neuengamme 1938-1945,* p. 306].

5. *Nazi Conspiracy and Aggression,* Supplement B (Red Series), publ. U.S. Government Printing Office, Washington, 1948, pp. 1593-1596.

6. U.S. Military Tribunal, Case 4 (WVHA/Pohl trial), trial transcript (English language), pp. 1408-1409 (19 March 1947).

7. Deposition of [Rudolf] Franz Ferdinand Hoess – alias Franz Lang, OC 92 Field Security Section, 14 March 1946, p. 6, TNA, WO 309/217.

8. Percy E. Schramm, *Kriegstagebuch des Oberkommandos der Wehrmacht 1944-1945,* Teilband II, p. 1138.

9. H. R. Trevor-Roper, *Final Entries 1945,* pp. 17-18.

10. Jürgen Thorwald, *Die große Flucht,* p. 238 ff.

11. ULTRA/ZIP/GPDR 55 transmitted 1 March 1945 (message 11), TNA, HW 16/49.

12. Jürgen Thorwald, *Die große Flucht,* p. 147.

13. BA–MA, RH 19 XV/7a, Bp. 59.

14. Answer supplied by Minister Burckhardt to questions asked by the International Military Tribunal, 17 April 1946; publ. as Document Kaltenbrunner-3 in IMT, Vol. XL, p. 308 f.

15. Highly confidential letter from Felix Kersten to Hillel Storch, 24 March 1945, TNA, FO 371/51194, p. 22.

16. H. R. Trevor-Roper, *Final Entries 1945,* p. 33.

17. ULTRA/ZIP/GPDR 52 transmitted 3 March 1945 (message 2), TNA, HW 16/49.

18. CIRO/PEARL/ZIP/GPD 4088 transmitted 3 March 1945 (message 2), TNA, HW 16/43.

19. H. R. Trevor-Roper, *Final Entries 1945,* pp. 41-42.

20. *Der Große Ploetz,* p. 2366.

21. Deposition on oath of Georg Henning Graf von Bassewitz–Behr, 20 April 1947, p. 3, TNA, WO 309/408.

22. Count Folke Bernadotte, *The Fall of the Curtain,* pp. 33-34; Kaltenbrunner role in Gerald Reitlinger, *The Final Solution,* p. 503.

23. CIRO/PEARL/ZIP/GPD 4042 transmitted 5 March 1945 (messages 22 and 183), TNA, HW 16/43.

24. CIRO/PEARL/ZIP/GPD 4042 transmitted 5 March 1945 (message 5), TNA, HW 16/43.

25. H. R. Trevor-Roper, *Final Entries 1945,* pp. 66-67.

26. Arno Rose, *Werwolf,* p. 114.

27. CIRO/PEARL/ZIP/GPD 4044 transmitted 6 March 1945 (message 43), TNA, HW 16/43.

28. H. R. Trevor-Roper, *Final Entries 1945,* pp. 73-75.

29. BA–MA, RH 19 XV/7b, p. 21.

30. Arno Rose, *Werwolf,* p. 114.

31. Secret message Seyß–Inquart to Himmler, 7 March 1945, facsimile in *Nederland in Oorlogstijd. Orgaan van het Rijksinstituut voor Oorlogsdocumentatie,* Nummer 1, March 1949 (32 S), p. 27; TNA, WO 208/5209.

32. CIRO/PEARL/ZIP/GPD 4041 transmitted 7 March 1945 (message 11), TNA, HW 16/43.

33. Heinz Höhne, *Der Krieg im Dunkeln,* p. 462.

34. CIRO/PEARL/ZIP/GPD 4087 transmitted 8 March 1945 (message 189), TNA, HW 16/43.

35. CIRO/PEARL/ZIP/GPD 4087 transmitted 8 March 1945 (message 152), TNA, HW 16/43.

36. H. R. Trevor-Roper, *Final Entries 1945*, p. 93.

37. BA-MA, RH 2/306, p. 96; facsimile in Dieter Zeigert, *Hitlers letztes Refugium?*, p. 40; Franz W. Seidler/Dieter Zeigert, *Die Führerhauptquartiere*, p. 310.

38. http://www.gtgj.de/archiv/indexa.html?kammler_leb45.html

39. Count Folke Bernadotte, *The Fall of the Curtain*, p. 34.

40. Photostatic copy of a letter from Himmler to Pohl, Glücks, Grawitz and Kaltenbrunner, and for information to Gebhardt and Kersten (prepared for Kersten), 10 March 1945, TNA, 371/51194; copy also, in ZStL, Versch. Ordner Nr. 151, Bild 5. – The document accompanied a communication from British Legation Stockholm to the Refugee Department, Foreign Office (London) on 17 June 1945 with the commentary: "The document is a piece of repulsive hypocrisy and may be of historical interest." also in Alexandra-Eileen Wenck, *Bergen–Belsen*, p. 367.

41. Circular by Bormann, Nr. 128/45 g.Rs., to the Gauleiters, 10 March 1945, BAB, NS 6/354, p. 90 + R.

42. CIRO/PEARL/ZIP/GPD 4043 transmitted 10 March 1945 (message 12), TNA, HW 16/43.

43. http://www.dhm.de/lemo/html/biografien/KesselringAlbert/

44. H. R. Trevor-Roper, *Final Entries 1945*, pp. 105-106, 110.

45. Agreement between Felix Kersten and Heinrich Himmler, 12 March 1945, The Wiener Library, London, MF Documents 054, roll 2/46 (Fleming Papers); Felix Kersten, *Totenkopf*, p. 343; Karin Orth, *Das System der nationalsozialistischen Konzentrationslager*, p. 302; Hillgruber/Hümmelchen, *Chronik des Zweiten Weltkrieges*, p. 271; Klaus-Dietmar Henke, *Die amerikanische Besetzung Deutschlands*, p. 889.

46. David A. Hackett (Hg.), *Der Buchenwald–Report*, p. 360, 363.

47. Date 12-13.03.1945 in Deposition of Dr Hans E. A. Meyer, Zürich 11 April 1946; publ. as Document Kaltenbrunner-4 in IMT, Vol. XL, p. 322. Date 12-14 March 1945 in Leni Yahil, *The Holocaust*, p. 650; Yehuda Bauer, *Jews for Sale?*, p. 249; Favez, *Kreuz*, p. 495 f; Karin Orth, *Das System der nationalsozialistischen Konzentrationslager*, p. 302.

48. Answer supplied by Minister Burckhardt to questions asked by the International Military Tribunal, 17 April 1946; publ. as Document Kaltenbrunner-3 in IMT, Vol. XL, p. 317 f.

49. CIRO-PEARL/ZIP/GPD 4050 transmitted 13 March 1945 (message 6), TNA, HW 16/43.

50. Lew Besymenski, *Die letzten Notizen von Martin Bormann*, p. 158.

51. Dr Rudolf Brandt to Hanns Johst, 14 March 1945; Helmut Heiber (Ed..), *Reichsführer*, Dok. 386, p. 310.

52. Diary, Alfred Jodl, entry for 15 March 1945.

53. H. R. Trevor-Roper, *Final Entries 1945*, p. 153.

54. Hillgruber/Hümmelchen, *Chronik des Zweiten Weltkrieges*, p. 271.

55. Count Folke Bernadotte, *Das Ende*, p. 52 (not in the English edition).

56. Interrogation report SAIC/X/5 dated 24 May 1945, Hedwig Potthast, Reichsführer Himmler's Mistress, TNA, WO 208/4474.

57. H. R. Trevor-Roper, *Final Entries 1945*, p. 156.

58. Summary Report No. 976, dated 22 March 1945, TNA, HW 13/42.

59. Alexandra-Eileen Wenck, *Bergen–Belsen*, p. 359, footnote 84.

60. Percy E. Schramm, *Kriegstagebuch des Oberkommandos der Wehrmacht 1944-1945*, Teilband II, p. 1182.

61. Report No. 6216/A, p.55, Source "Truefitt", 27 March 1945, TNA, WO 208/4474.

62. Summary Report No. 978, dated 24 March 1945, TNA, HW 13/42.

63. TNA, FO 371/46783.

64. Summary Report No. 978, dated 24 March 1945, TNA, HW 13/42.

65. Heinz Guderian, *Panzer Leader*, p. 421f.

66. [US] Seventh Army Interrogation Centre: SAIC/FIR/12 dated 26 July 1945, "A History of Germany's Campaigns in World War II by GenObst (Col Gen) Heinz Guderian. Final Interrogation Report.": TNA, WO 208/3151.

67. French interrogation of Karl Albrecht Oberg dated 9 Dec. 1945, TNA, KV 2/1668.

68. BA–MA, RH 19 XV/8, p. 198.

69. Final Interrogation report No 20, SS-Ogruf Gen d Pol Otto Winkelmann, 17 Aug. 1945, Annex No III: "Meetings with Kaltenbrunner", US NARA, RG 165 Entry 179 Box 737.

70. Report No. 6216/A, dated 27 March 1945, Source "Truefitt", TNA, WO 208/4474.

71. Felix Kersten to Himmler, 20 March 1945, ZStL, Versch. Ordner Nr. 151, Photograph No. 7; Alexandra-Eileen Wenck, Bergen–Belsen, p. 367, footnote 120.

72. Percy E. Schramm, Kriegstagebuch des Oberkommandos der Wehrmacht 1944-1945, Teilband II, p. 1190.

73. 1,648 Jewish prisoners from Bergen-Belsen and 1,210 from Theresienstadt in February 1945, in Klaus-Dietmar Henke, Die amerikanische Besetzung Deutschlands, p. 886.

74. Letter Himmler to Kersten dated 21 March 1945; facsimile in Felix Kersten, Totenkopf und Treue. Heinrich Himmler ohne Uniform, p. 358 f; copy in TNA, FO 188/526; Eichmann–Doc. T 1277 [MF 110].

75. Photocopy of a letter from Dr Rudolf Brandt (Feld-Kommandostelle) to Felix Kersten (Gut Hartzwalde), 21 March 1945, TNA, FO 371/51194.

76. Ibid.

77. H. R. Trevor-Roper, Final Entries 1945, p. 199.

78. Heinz Guderian, Panzer Leader, p. 426.

79. BA–MA, RH 19 XV/8, p. 215.

80. Volksstimme journal, 16 Dec.1949.

81. Interrogation of Richard Ohling, dated 15 July 1949, HSTA Düsseldorf, NW 34/19, p. 180 f.

82. Interrogation of Günther Bertrams, dated 22 July 1949, HSTA Düsseldorf, NW 34/19, p. 109 R.

83. TNA, HW 12/311, message 142728.

84. Hillgruber/Hümmelchen, Chronik des Zweiten Weltkrieges, S. 273; Peter Padfield, Himmler, p. 572; Fraenkel/Manvell, Himmler, p.222. t

85. Major Vollmar, Adjutant for the Replacement Army on staff of Himmler.

86. Interim Interrogation Report in the case of Werner Grothmann, 13 June 1945, TNA. WO 208/4474.

87. TNA, FO 371/51194.

88. CIRO/PEARL/ZIP/GPD 4064 transmitted 23 March 1945 (message 6), TNA, HW 16/43.

89. Percy E. Schramm, Kriegstagebuch des Oberkommandos der Wehrmacht 1944-1945, Teilband II, p. 1196 f.

90. Jochen von Lang, Der Adjutant, p. 272.

91. Führerbefehl dated 25 March 1945; Percy E. Schramm, Die Niederlage, p. 463, footnote 45.

92. CIRO/PEARL/ZIP/GPD 4062 transmitted 25 March 1945 (message 69), TNA, HW 16/43.

93. Summary Report No. 988, dated 3 April 1945, TNA, HW 13/42.

94. H. R. Trevor-Roper, Final Entries 1945, p. 268.

95. Interrogation report CSDIC/SC/15AG/SD 5, dated 20 May1945, of Wilhelm Harster, TNA, WO 204/13005.

96. Percy E. Schramm, Kriegstagebuch des Oberkommandos der Wehrmacht 1944-1945, Teilband II, p. 1202.

97. General der Gebirgs-Truppen Georg Ritter von Hengl, Chief of the NS-Leadership Staff at OKH.

98. Bormann-Kalender, p. 177.

99. "Report by Saur on various new weapons and types of ammunition, 28 June 1945", Imperial War Museum, London, F.D. 3049/49 folder f 8.

100. Allan Dulles, The Secret Surrender, pp.135-136.

101. H. R. Trevor-Roper, Final Entries 1945, p. 246.

102. Facsimile in Tom Agoston, Teufel oder Technokrat? p. 106 f.

103. Albert Speer, Inside the Third Reich, p. 450.

104. "Report by Saur on various new weapons and types of ammunition, 28 June 1945", Imperial

War Museum, London, F.D. 3049/49 folder f 8.

105. OKW to AOK 19, 27 March 1945, BA-MA, H 12-19/202; Manfred Messerschmidt, "Krieg in der Trümmerlandschaft. 'Pflichterfüllung' wofür?" in *Über Leben im Krieg. Kriegserfahrungen in einer Industrieregion 1939- 1945*, (Ed.) Ulrich Borsdorf und Mathilde Jamin, p. 175.

106. CIRO-PEARL/ZIP/GPD 4082 transmitted 27 March 1945 (message 3), TNA, HW 16/43.

107. Danny Parker, *Jochen Peiper*, Chapter 17, p. 52 [unpublished manuscript].

108. *Ibid*, p.96.

109. CIRO/PEARL/ZIP/GPD 4074 transmitted 28 March 1945 (message 51), TNA, HW 16/43.

110. TNA, HW 1/3565.

111. TNA, FO 371/46783.

112. TNA, HW 12/311.

113. BA-MA, H 12-19/202; BA/MA, RH 20-19/196.

114. USFET, CI Intermediate Interrogation Report (CIIIR) No. 20, dated 18 Oct.1945, by Jürgen Stroop, TNA, WO 208/4508.

115. Percy E. Schramm, *Kriegstagebuch des Oberkommandos der Wehrmacht 1944-1945*, Teilband. II, p. 1209 f; Schramm, *Die Niederlage 1945*, p. 317.

116. SS–Gruf. und Generalleutnant d. W–SS und Polizei Heinz Reinefarth, from 20 April 1944 to January 1945 HSSPF Warthe; and from 1 Feb.1945 commander of Fortress Küstrin; Ruth Bettina Birn, *Die Höheren SS– und Polizeiführer*, p. 344.

117. H. R. Trevor-Roper, *Final Entries 1945*, p.295.

118. CIRO/PEARL/ZIP/GPD 4071 transmitted 29 March 1945 (message 178), TNA, HW 16/43.

119. Count Folke Bernadotte, *The Fall of the Curtain*, p. 41.

120. Kasztner-Report, p. 170, T/37 (237) = T/113 = PdI 900, MF 14.

121. Testimony of Baldur at his trial, IMT Nuremberg, Vol. XIV, pp. 439-440, 484;

122. Michael Wortmann, *Baldur von Schirach*, p. 226.

123. Camp Doctor Dr Alfred Kurzke, quoted in, Manfred Bornemann, *Geheimprojekt Mittelbau. Die Geschichte der deutschen V-Waffen-Werke*, p. 138.

124. Percy E. Schramm, *Kriegstagebuch des Oberkommandos der Wehrmacht 1944-1945*, Teilband II, p. 1212; Schramm, *Die Niederlage 1945*, p. 321.

125. TNA, HW 5/706.

126. H. R. Trevor-Roper, *Final Entries 1945*, pp. 302, 304-305.

127. Deposition Dr Hans E. A. Meyer,11 April 1946, IMT, Vol. 40, Doc. Kaltenbrunner–4, p. 321f.

128. IMT, Vol. XIV, p. 484f; Doc. Vol. IX, p. 283 (3870-PS).

129. "Niederschrift des Verhöres des SS-Standartenführers Ziereis Franz, ehemaliger Lagerkommandant des Konzentrationslagers Mauthausen" (24 May 1945), Dokumentationsarchiv des Österreichischen Widerstandes (2721) http://www.mauthausen-memorial.gv.at/Geschichte/menu-o.05.03.html.

130. Elenore Lappin, *Die Todesmärsche ungarischer Juden durch Österreich im Frühjahr 1945*, p. 46; http://www.gedenken.org/german/archive_text_hg2.htm,

131. IMT, Vol. XIV, p. 484f; Doc.Vol. IX, p. 283 (3870-PS).

132. Interrogation Report 031/G.0915/I of Heinz Macher, 10 Nov.1945, TNA, WO 208/4431.

133. *Wewelsburg 1933 bis 1945*, p. 104; Stuart Russell/ Jost W. Schneider, *Heinrich Himmlers Burg, Das weltanschauliche Zentrum der SS*, p. 184.

APRIL 1945

1. TNA, FO 371/51020.

2. *Allen Dulles, Secret Surrender*, p. 129.

3. Peter Padfield, *Himmler*, p. 577.

4. Kurt Detlev Möller, *Das letzte Kapitel. Geschichte der Kapitulation Hamburgs. Von der Hamburger Katastrophe des Jahres 1943 bis zur Übergabe der Stadt am 3. Mai 1945*, p. 55f; Heinz Höhne, *Orden unter dem Totenkopf*, p. 528; Report by Konstantin Bock von Wülfingen on the basis of his pocket diary, 20.05.1945, in Archiv Forschungsstelle für Zeitgeschichte in

Hamburg, 292–299, p. 6 [copy courtesy of Frank Bajohr].

5. Final Interrogation Report No 20, SS-Ogruf Gen d Pol Otto Winkelmann, 17 Aug. 1945, Annex No II: "Winkelmann's Activities 1 Apr-8 May 1945", US NARA, RG 165 Entry 179 Box 737.

6. CIRO-PEARL/ZIP/GPD 4057A transmitted 1 April 1945, Addendum III, message 157, TNA, HW 16/43.

7. Announcement of the chief of the Party Chancellery, Martin Bormann, to all Reichsleiters, Gauleiters and Unit Chiefs, 1 April 1945, teleprinter message sent 19:35 hours, BAB, NS 6/353, p. 151; facsimile in Franz W. Seidler, *Deutscher Volkssturm*, p. 347f; with covering note by Obersten SA–Führung, SA–Ogruf. Jüttner dated 5 April 1945, publ. in Jochen von Lang, *Der Sekretär*, p. 491.

8. TNA, HS 9/1345, p. 33.

9. Eugen Kogon, *Theory and Practice of Hell*, p. 264 (German edition, p. 355); David A. Hackett, *Der Buchenwald-Report*, p. 130. – Eugen Kogon had received this information from his SS superior, SS-Stubaf. Dr Ding-Schuler.

10. Count Folke Bernadotte, *The Fall of the Curtain*, pp. 48-49. On p. 49 makes an error in mentioning Hitler, when he meant Himmler.

11. TNA, PREM 3/197/16.

12. CIRO/PEAR/ZIP/AT 1726 transmitted 3 April 1945 – extract from GPD 4053, TNA, HW 16/71.

13. *JuNSV*, Vol. XVI, Case 492, p. 392; Vol. XVII, Case 513, p. 565; Chronik 1945, p. 60 – see entry for 29.03.1945.

14. CIRO-PEARL/ZIP/GPD 4053 transmitted 3 April 1945 (message 60), TNA, HW 16/43.

15. H. R. Trevor-Roper, *Final Entries 1945*, p. 324.

16. Gregor Janssen, *Das Ministerium Speer*, p. 207.

17. CIRO/PEARL/ZIP/GPD 4053 transmitted 3 April 1945 (message 93), TNA, HW 16/43.

18. ULTRA/ZIP/GPDR 61 transmitted 4 April 1945 (message 99), TNA, HW 16/49.

19. Statement on oath Anton Kaindl, 16 July 1946, BAK, All. Proz. 3/Pelckmann 27; Karin Orth, *System der nationalsozialistischen Konzentrationslager*, p. 322.

20. Final Interrogation Report No 20, SS-Ogruf Gen d Pol Otto Winkelmann, 17 Aug. 1945, Annex No II: "Winkelmann's Activities 1 Apr–8 May 1945", US NARA, RG 165 Entry 179 Box 737.

21. Felix Kersten to Hilel Storch, 4 April 1945, in Eberhard Kolb, *Bergen-Belsen*, p. 224 f; Gerd R. Ueberschär/Rolf Dieter Müller, *Deutschland am Abgrund*, p. 125.

22. TNA, FO 371/51194.

23. Deposition Dr Hans E. A. Meyer, 11 April 1946, IMT, Vol. 40, Document Kaltenbrunner–4, p. 321.

24. Answer supplied by Minister Burckhardt to Questions asked by the IMT, 17 April 1946, IMT, Vol. 40, Document Kaltenbrunner–3, p. 310 f.

25. Jean-Claude Favez, *Warum schwieg das Rote Kreuz*, p. 498.

26. Percy E. Schramm, *Kriegstagebuch des Oberkommandos der Wehrmacht 1944-1945*, Teilband II, p. 1225; Schramm, Die Niederlage 1945, p. 336f.

27. IfZ-Archiv, Nuremberg document NO-254; Klaus-Dietmar Henke, *Die amerikanische Besetzung Deutschlands*, p. 892, footnote 552.

28. Heinz Höhne, *Canaris*, p. 563f.

29. Captain S. Payne Best, *The Venlo Incident*, photostatic copy between pp. 208-209.

30. Radio message Glücks to Camp Commander KL Dachau, 5 April 1945; facsimile in *Konzentrationslager Dachau 1933–1945*, Nr. 326, p. 143. For details of Prof. Claus Schilling's malaria experiments at Dachau by an eyewitness, see Ernst Klee, *Auschwitz, die SS–Medizin und ihre Opfer*, p. 123: "The experiments ended on 30 March 1945."

31. Interim Report on the Interrogation of SS Standfue. Dr Brandt, Rudolf, 10 June 1945, Appendix "B" (2), US NARA, RG 319, Entry MLR 134B, Box 85, folder XE 00 06 32.

32. CIRO/PEARL/ZIP/GPD 4068 transmitted 6 April 1945 (message 10), TNA, HW 16/43.

33. BAB, R 3/1661, p. 8.

34. Jürgen Thorwald, *Die Große Flucht*, p. 269, 272, 274, 276.

35. Gerd R. Ueberschär/Rolf-Dieter Müller, *Deutschland am Abgrund*, p. 118; *Kriegsende 1945*, p. 88.

36. ULTRA/ZIP/GPDR 56 transmitted 6 April 1945 (message 1), TNA, HW 16/49.

37. Kasztner-Report, p. 171 f, T/37 (237) = T/113 = PdI 900, MF 14.

38. ULTRA/ZIP/GPDR 56 transmitted 6 April 1945 (message 30), TNA, HW 16/49.

39. ULTRA/ZIP/RAT/13 transmitted 6 April 1945, TNA, HW 16/73.

40. ULTRA/ZIP/GPDR 56 transmitted 6 April 1945 (message 21), TNA, HW 16/49; and, ULTRA/ZIP/RAT 14, TNA, HW 16/73.

41. Telegram Pister to Amtsgruppe D, Oranienburg [6 April 1945], ITS Arolsen, Historische Abteilung, Buchenwald Nr. 6, p. 139; Klaus Drobisch, *Widerstand in Buchenwald*, p. 184; facsimile in: Johannes Tuchel, *Inspektion*, Dok. 37.5, p. 214; Karin Orth, *System der nationalsozialistischen Konzentrationslager*, p. 307. – IMT, trial testimony of Ernst Kaltenbrunner on 11 April 1946, IMT, Bd. XI, p. 284.

42. CIRO/PEARL/ZIP/GPD 4068 transmitted 6 April 1945 (message 204), TNA, HW 16/43.

43. CIRO/PEARL/ZIP/GPD 4068 transmitted 6 April 1945 (message 214), TNA, HW 16/43.

44. CIRO/PEARL/ZIP/GPD 4059 transmitted 7 April 1945 (message 4), TNA, HW 16/43.

45. CIRO/PEARL/ZIP/GPD 4059 transmitted 7 April 1945 (message 5), TNA, HW 16/43.

46. Radio message Glücks to KL Buchenwald [11:50 hours], 7 April 1945; ITS Arolsen, Historische Abteilung, Buchenwald Nr. 6, p. 135; ZStL, Ordner 311 d; facsimile in Johannes Tuchel, *Inspektion*, Doc. 37.5, p. 215; Klaus Drobisch, *Widerstand in Buchenwald*, p. 185; Karin Orth, *System der nationalsozialistischen Konzentrationslager*, p. 308.

47. Reinhard R Doerries, *Hitler's Last Chief of Intelligence: Allied Interrogations of Walter Schellenberg*, p.172.

48. TNA, HW 5/706.

49. ULTRA/ZIP/GPDR 60 transmitted 7 April 1945 (message 93), TNA, HW 16/49.

50. CIRO-PEARL/ZIP/GPD 4059 transmitted 7 April 1945 (message 57), TNA, HW 16/43.

51. CIRO-PEARL/ZIP/GPD 4059 transmitted 7 April 1945 (message 61), TNA, HW 16/43.

52. Bormann Notizen, p. 179; Generalfeldmarschall Ernst Busch was C-in-C North West.

53. Interrogation of Karl Kaufmann, 14 May 1949, denazification file of Paul Wegener, BAK, Z 42 IV/1716, Vol. I, p. 207+R – Kaufmann incorrectly dated the audience with Hitler as 3 April 1945.

54. Letter Rudolf Brandt to Felix Kersten, 8 April 1945, The Wiener Library, London, MF Documents 054, roll 2/46 (Fleming Papers). The contents of the letter indicate Brandt had not been informed of the meeting of 6 April 1945 between the Deputy Chief Delegate of the ICRC in Berlin, Dr Otto Lehner, and the Swiss ICRC Delegate Paul Dunant.

55. H. R. Trevor-Roper, *Final Entries 1945*, p. 336.

56. Interim Report on the Interrogation of SS Standfue. Dr Brandt, Rudolf, 10 June 1945, Appendix "B" (1), US NARA, RG 319, Entry MLR 134B, Box 85, folder XE 00 06 32.

57. Klaus–Dietmar Henke, *Amerikanische Besetzung Deutschlands*, p. 876; Hillgruber/Hümmelchen, *Chronik des Zweiten Weltkrieges*, p. 277.

58. CIRO/PEARL/ZIP/GPD 4070 transmitted 9 April 1945 (message 2), TNA, HW 16/43.

59. CIRO/PEARL/ZIP/GPD 4070 transmitted 9 April 1945 (message 116), TNA, HW 16/43.

60. CIRO/PEARL/ZIP/GPD 4070 transmitted 9 April 1945 (message 162), TNA, HW 16/43.

61. TNA, HW 1/3695.

62. *Nazi Conspiracy and Aggression*, Supplement B (Red Series), publ. U.S. Government Printing Office, Washington, 1948, p.1622.

63. Ueberschär/Müller, *Deutschland am Abgrund*, p. 120 f; *Kriegsende*, p. 91.

64. Ueberschär/Müller: *Deutschland am Abgrund*, p. 126.

65. CIRO/PEARL/ZIP/GPD 4065 transmitted 10 April 1945 (message 43), TNA, HW 16/43.

66. message CX/MSS/C.487, TNA, HW 5/706

67. CIRO/PEARL/ZIP/GPD 4080 transmitted 11 April 1945 (message 1), TNA, HW 16/43.

68. Kastner-Report, p. 317; Alexandra-Eileen Wenck, *Bergen–Belsen*, p. 891; Eberhard Kolb, *Bergen-Belsen*, p. 160 und 315.

69. First U.S. Army Prisoners of War Interrogation Reports dated 16 April 1945, PWI Report No. 6, 15/16 April 1945, US NARA, RG 498 Box 65.

70. Ueberschär/Müller, *Deutschland am Abgrund*, p. 118; *Kriegsende*, p. 91; John Erickson, *The Road to Berlin*, p. 532.

71. *Kommandant in Auschwitz*, p. 185 (not in the English edition).

72. CIRO/PEARL/ZIP/GPD 4075 transmitted 12 April 1945 (msg 3), TNA, HW 16/43; reported in *Hagener Zeitung* dated 13 April 1945.

73. Kuby, p. 130 f. – These reports published in, e.g., *Hagener Zeitung* dated 13 April 1945 and the Nazi Party newspaper *Völkischen Beobachter*.

74. BAK, Z 42 IV/6871, denazification case of Heinrich Vetter, witness statement by former Gauleiter Albert Hoffmann dated 24 Nov. 1948, p. 292.

75. Ueberschär/Müller: *Deutschland am Abgrund*, p. 126 f.

76. *Hagener Zeitung* dated 13 April 1945.

77. Percy E. Schramm, *Kriegstagebuch des Oberkommandos der Wehrmacht 1944-1945*, Teilband II, p. 1239 f; Schramm, *Die Niederlage 1945*, p. 355.

78. Schellenberg's report, cited in Count Folke Bernadotte, *The Fall of the Curtain*, pp. 78-79.

79. Albert Speer, *The Slave State*, p. 243.

80. Diary of Alisah Sheck, entry for 13 April 1945, in *Theresienstädter Studien und Dokumente 1964*, p. 184.

81. Heinz Höhne, *Order of the Death's Head*, p. 572.

82. Andrew Cunningham papers in King's College London, Liddell Hart Centre for Military Archives; Admiral Sir Andrew B. Cunningham (1883-1963), C-in-C Mediterranean 1939-1942; 1st Sea Lord, August 1943 to 1946.

83. Extract from the order of Reichsführers SS Himmler to the Commandant of Dachau and Flossenbürg, 14 April 1945 in: Summary of Information No. 30, June 1945, U.N.W.C.C. (Research Office), TNA, WO 309/217. This does not have the last sentence of the message, publ. in Reimund Schnabel, *Macht ohne Moral*, D 63, p. 203. The original order has not be located in archives. For the existence of Himmler's orders of 14/18 April 1945, in *Dachauer Hefte* 1 (1985), p. 219 ff.

84. Trial testimony of Rudolf Höss at IMT Nuremberg, 15 April 1946, IMT, Bd. XI, p. 450.

85. Statement of Fritz Suhren, 30 Dec. 1945, TNA, WO 235/310.

86. Statement on oath of Hermann Pister, 2 July 1946 (Nuremberg doc. NO–254); Karin Orth, *System der nationalsozialistischen Konzentrationslager*, p. 312.

87. Deposition on Oath of Max Pauly, 30 March 1946, TNA, WO 309/408.

88. [U.S.] CI Intermediate Interrogation Report (CIIIR) No. 25 of SS-Gruf Jürgen Stroop dated 18 Oct. 1945, TNA, WO 208/4508.

89. Milton Shulman, *Defeat in the West*, pp. 280, 429, quoted in Gerald Reitlinger, *The SS: Alibi of a Nation 1922–1945*, p. 419.

90. Walther Hubatsch (Hg.), *Hitlers Weisungen für die Kriegsführung 1939-1945*, Doc. 74, p. 308-310; Percy E. Schramm, *Kriegstagebuch des Oberkommandos der Wehrmacht 1944-1945*, Teilband II, p. 1587-1589; H. R. Trevor-Roper (ed.), *Hitler's War Directives*, pp. 297-300.

91. Walther Hubatsch (Hg.), *Hitlers Weisungen für die Kriegsführung 1939-1945*, Doc. 75, p. 311; Percy E. Schramm, *Kriegstagebuch des Oberkommandos der Wehrmacht 1944-1945*, Teilband II, p. 1590; H. R. Trevor-Roper (ed.), *Hitler's War Directives*, pp. 300-301.

92. Alexandra–Eileen Wenck, *Bergen-Belsen*, p. 381 f; Karin Orth, *System der nationalsozialistischen Konzentrationslager*, p. 309.

93. SS-Stubaf. Otto Barnewald, Administration Officer at KL Buchenwald, in: Eugen Kogon, *Theory and Practice of Hell*, p. 117.

94. Interrogation of Kurt Becher in the presence of Dr Rezsö Kasztner, 7 July 1947, T/37 (235) = T/689 = PdI 774, MF 12.

95. Kasztner-Report, p. 177, T/37 (237) = T/113 = PdI 900, MF 15.

96. Interrogation of Kurt Becher for the Eichmann–Trial, Israel, 20.06.1961; http://www.kokhavivpublications.com/kuckuck/archiv/karc0005.html

97. *Ich, Adolf Eichmann*, p. 476.

98. *Ibid*, p. 415 f.

99. Jochen von Lang, *Das Eichmann-Protokoll*, p. 233; PdI, Adolf Eichmann, Vol. I, pp. 308–310.

100. Statement on oath by Hermann Pister, 2 July 1945, IfZ-Archiv, Nuremberg doc. NO-254; Karin Orth, *System der nationalsozialistischen Konzentrationslager*, p. 311.

101. Karin Orth, *System der nationalsozialistischen Konzentrationslager*, pp. 310-311.

102. John Erickson, *The Road to Berlin*, pp. 555-558.

103. Glücks to Martin, 16 April 1945, intercept CX/MSS/C.476, TNA, HW 1/3713.

104. Karin Orth, *System der nationalsozialistischen Konzentrationslager*, p. 315.

105. Speer's manuscript dated 16 April 1945, BAB, R 3/1557; cited in Albert Speer, *Inside the Third Reich*, pp. 564-566 footnote 5.

106. H. R. Trevor-Roper, *Last Days of Hitler*, p.113; Anton Joachimsthaler, *Hitlers Ende*, p. 483.

107. David Irving, *The Secret Diaries of Hitler's Doctor*, p. 218.

108. TOP SECRET U, C/9040 (T524/78), TNA, HW 1/3712.

109. U.S. interrogation of Dr Karl Brandt, CCPWE#32/DI-17 dated 30 June 1945 (at Ashcan interrogation centre), TNA, FO 371/46778.

110. Albert Speer, *Inside the Third Reich*, p.465.

111. Jochen von Lang, *Der Adjutant*, p. 280.

112. Translation of a highly confidential letter from F. Bernadotte at Wisborg to G. Storch, Stockholm, 17 April 1945; The Wiener Library, MF Documents 054, roll 2/46 (Fleming Papers).

113. Heinz Höhne, *Order of the Death's Head*, p. 574; Jochen von Lang, *Der Adjutant*, p. 280.

114. David Irving, *Götterdämmerung*, p. 532, footnote 2. – Wolff's appointment with the Führer 'before staff conference' on Apr 18 is noted on Hitler's desk pad, preserved in British Cabinet Office files.

115. Final Interrogation Report (FIR No. 7) dated 11 July 1945, of Arthur Scheidler, TNA, WO 208/4478.

116. Peter Black, *Kaltenbrunner*, p. 271 f; Klaus-Dietmar Henke, *Die amerikanische Besetzung Deuschlands*, p. 896; Karin Orth, *System der nationalsozialistischen Konzentrationslager*, p. 313.

117. Interrogation of SS-Staf. Anton Kaindl during his trial, the Sachsenhausen-Prozesses Berlin 1947; *SS im Einsatz*, p. 201.

118. The journal *Stern* Nr. 2 dated 6 Jan. 1983, p. 65.

119. *Ibid*.

120. Walter Schellenberg, *The Labyrinth*, pp. 390-391.

121. Diary of Lutz von Schwerin–Krosigk, entry for 22 April 1945; William L. Shirer, *End of a Berlin Diary*, pp. 197-199.

122. The journal *Stern* Nr. 2 dated 6 Jan. 1983, p. 65.

123. Final Interrogation Report No. 7 of SS-Ostubaf Arthur Scheidler dated 11 July 1945, TNA, WO 208/4478.

124. Radio message Kaltenbrunner to Fegelein, undated [April 1945], Nuremberg doc. PS-2519, IMT, Bd. 30, p. 587; Miroslav Kárný, "Kaltenbrunners Reise nach Theresienstadt und der Prominententransport im April 1945," in *Theresienstädter Studien und Dokumente 2000*, p. 67.

125. IMT Vol. XI (English language), p.303.

126. Notes of Benjamin Murmelstein about his discussions with Rahm 16-20 April 1945, Nuremberg doc. L 637; Miroslav Kárný, "Kaltenbrunners Reise nach Theresienstadt und der Prominententransport im April 1945," in *Theresienstädter Studien und Dokumente 2000*, p. 74 f.

127. Hermann Kaienburg, *Konzentrationslager Neuengamme 1938–1945*, p. 276.

128. Reinhard R Doerries, *Hitler's Last Chief of Intelligence: Allied Interrogations of Walter Schellenberg*, p.177.

129. Undated "Notes on interrogation of PW CS(AM) 2235 Ogruf BERGER", TNA, KV 2/172.

130. Count Folke Bernadotte, *The Fall of the Curtain*, p.52.

131. Interrogation of Hermann Göring, report SAIC/X/5 dated 24 May 1945, US NARA, RG332,

Entry ETO MIS-Y Sect., Box 73.

132. BAB, R 3/1661, p. 14.
133. Artur Axmann, *Das kann doch nicht das Ende sein*, p. 417 ff.
134. Special Interrogation of Werner Grothmann, 29 Sept. 1945, TNA, KV 4/354.
135. BAB, R 62/13, p. 3; Anton Joachimsthaler, *Hitlers Ende*, p. 141; Marlis G. Steinert, *23 Tage der Regierung Dönitz*, p. 36 f.
136. CIRO/PEARL/ZIP/GPD 4066 transmitted 20 April 1945 (message 5), TNA, HW 16/43.
137. Testimony of Friedrich Karl von Eberstein before IMT Nuremberg, 3 August 1946, IMT, Vol. XX, p. 337.
138. Ruth Bettina Birn, *Die HSSPF*, p. 332, 339.
139. Final Interrogation report No 20, SS-Ogruf Gen d Pol Otto Winkelmann, 17 Aug. 1945, Annex No II: "Winkelmann's Activities 1 Apr-8 May 1945", US NARA, RG 165 Entry 179 Box 737.
140. CIRO/PEARL/ZIP/GPD 4066 transmitted 20 April 1945 (message 64), TNA, HW 16/43.
141. Jean-Claude Favez, *Warum schwieg das Rote Kreuz?* p. 501.
142. Marlis G.Steinert, *23 Tage der Regierung Dönitz*, p. 138.
143. H. R. Trevor-Roper, *Last Days of Hitler*, p. 155.
144. Reinhard R Doerries, *Hitler's Last Chief of Intelligence: Allied Interrogations of Walter Schellenberg*, p.178.
145. Interrogation Report 031/G.0915/I on Heinz Macher, 10 Nov. 1945, TNA, WO 208/4431.
146. Percy E. Schramm, *Kriegstagebuch des Oberkommandos der Wehrmacht 1944-1945*, Teilband II, p. 1453.
147. Interim Report in the case of Werner Grothmann, 13 June 1945, TNA, WO 208/4474.
148. Count Folke Bernadotte, *The Fall of the Curtain*, p. 53.
149. Wiener Library, London, ref. OSP 60.
150. H. G. Adler, *Der Kampf gegen die Endlösung der Judenfrage*, p. 108.
151. Norbert Masur, *En Jood talar med Himmler*, cited in Gerald Reitlinger, *The Final Solution*, p. 521.
152. Norbert Masur, *En Jood talar med Himmler*, p. 45 f; Alexandra-Eileen Wenck, *Bergen–Belsen*, p. 368, footnote 123.
153. Walter Schellenberg, *The Labyrinth*, pp. 392-394.
154. Count Folke Bernadotte, *The Fall of the Curtain*, p. 53; Gerald Fleming, *Hitler and the Final Solution*, pp. 182-183.
155. BAB, R 3/1661, p.14.
156. Walter Schellenberg, *The Labyrinth*, pp. 395-396.
157. Karl Koller, *Der letzte Monat*, p. 48.
158. Undated "Notes on interrogation of PW CS(AM) 2235 Ogruf Berger", TNA, KV 2/172.
159. C.S.D.I.C.(UK), report S.R.G.G. 1315 (C) dated 4 July 1945, TNA, KV 2/172.
160. Robert Kübler (ed.), *Chef KGW. Das Kriegsgefangenenwesen unter Gottlob Berger*, p. 62 f.
161. C.S.D.I.C (U.K.) G.G. Report S.R.G.G. 1322 (C): Conversation SS Gruppenführer Ohlendorf, p. 4, 7 July 1945, TNA, WO 208/4170.
162. Secret monitoring of a conversation between von Herff and von Woyrsch, Report CSDIC (UK), SRGG 1317 (C) dated 4 July 1945, TNA, KV 2/172.
163. Heinz Höhne, *Krieg im Dunkeln*, p. 464; Allen Dulles/Gero v. S. Gaevernitz, *Operation 'Sunrise'*, p. 197; Smith and Agarossi, *Operation Sunrise*, pp. 135-136.
164. TNA, HW 5/700.
165. TNA, HW 5/706, message CX/MSS/C.484.
166. Jean-Claude Favez, *Warum schwieg das Rote Kreuz?* p. 502.
167. Percy E. Schramm, *Kriegstagebuch des Oberkommandos der Wehrmacht 1944-1945*, Teilband II, p. 1453f.
168. Diary of Martin Bormann, p.188.
169. Interrogation of Gen. (der LW) Eghard Christian, Chef Luftwaffen-führungsstab (at Latimer House [Britain]), 15.10.45, TNA, KV 4/354.

170. Walter Schellenberg, *The Labyrinth*, pp. 396-397.

171. C.S.D.I.C.(UK), report S.R.G.G. 1315 (C) dated 4 July 1945, TNA, KV 2/172.

172. CSDIC (UK) S.I.R. 1706 dated 30 Sept. 1945 by Otto Ohlendorf, entitled "Amt III (SD Inland)", TNA, WO 204/11505.

173. Interim Report in the case of Werner Grothmann, 13 June 1945, TNA, WO 208/4474.

174. Walter Schellenberg, *The Labyrinth*, pp. 397-398.

175. TNA, HW 5/706.

176. Karl Koller, *Der letzte Monat*, p. 54 f.; H. R. Trevor-Roper, *Last Days of Hitler*, p. 167.

177. CIRO/PEARL/ZIP/GPD 4078 transmitted 22 April 1945 (message 1), TNA, HW 16/43.

178. TOP SECRET ULTRA, CX/MSS/T531/60, KO 1492, radio message dated 22 April 1945 from Brandt to SS–Ogruf. Rediess, Oslo, TNA, HW 1/3729.

179. TOP SECRET U [ULTRA], CX/MSS/R.533 (A) dated 29 April 1945: Communication of 22/4 [1945] from SS-Staf Brandt marked for forwarding immediately to SS–Ogruf Rediess, Oslo, TNA, HW 5/699. – Negotiations between the German civilian authorities in Oslo and the Swedish General Consulate in Oslo resulted in the release of 54 prisoners from Berg and Grini camps on 2 May 1945 and their transfer to Sweden, in Oskar Mendelsohn, "Norwegen," in Wolfgang Benz (ed.), *Dimension des Völkermords*, p. 197.

180. Special interrogation of Werner Grothmann, 26 Sept. 1945, TNA, KV 4/354.

181. H. R. Trevor–Roper, *Last Days of Hitler*, p. 165; Marlis G. Steinert, *23 Tage der Regierung Dönitz*, p. 145, 375.

182. H. R. Trevor-Roper, *Last Days of Hitler*, p. 165.

183. Erich Kessler, "Theresienstädter Tagebuch," entry for 22 April 1945, in *Theresienstädter Studien und Dokumente 1995*, p. 308.

184. (Unpublished) Diary of Eva Mändl, entry for 22 April 1945, p. 86 f.

185. Jürgen Thorwald, *Die große Flucht*, p. 438.

186. CSDIC (UK) S.I.R. 1706 dated 30 Sept. 1945, report entitled "Amt III (SD Inland) RSHA", TNA, WO 204/11505.

187. C.S.D.I.C.(UK), report S.R.G.G. 1315 (C) dated 4 July 1945, TNA, KV 2/172.

188. Testimony of Gottlob Berger before IMT Nuremberg, 20 Sept. 1945, IMT, Bd. 32, PS–3723, p. 523; Robert Kübler (Hg.), *Chef KGW. Das Kriegsgefangenenwesen unter Gottlob Berger*, p. 78f.

189. CIRO/PEARL/ZIP/GPD 4078 transmitted 22 April 1945 (message 68), TNA, HW 16/43.

190. TNA, HW 5/706.

191. TOP SECRET U, CX/MSS/R.537 (A), radio message dated 23 April 1945 from Himmler via SS-Brig Rode to SS-Ogruf Berger; TNA, HW 5/701.

192. message CX/MSS/C.481, TNA, HW 5/706

193. Count Folke Bernadotte, *The Fall of the Curtain*, p. 55.

194. Walter Schellenberg, *The Labyrinth*, p. 398.

195. Percy E. Schramm, *Kriegstagebuch des Oberkommandos der Wehrmacht 1944-1945*, Teilband II, pp. 1455-1456.

196 Allen Dulles, *Secret Surrender*, p. 183.

197. http://fr.wikipedia.org/wiki/Fichier:Last_trace_of_Hans_Kammler.gif

198. Jean-Claude Favez, *Warum schwieg das Rote Kreuz?* p. 503.

199. Hans-Günter Richardi, *SS-Geiseln in der Alpenfestung*, pp. 167-170.

200. Arno Rose, *Werwolf*, p. 319.

201. Walter Schellenberg, *The Labyrinth*, pp. 399-400; Count Folke Bernadotte, *The Fall of the Curtain*, pp. 56-60.

202. TNA, PREM 3/197/6.

203. *Ibid.*

204. Handwritten letter of Himmler to the Swedish Foreign Minister Günther, 24 April 1945 (copy), BAK, Nachlaß Himmlers, NL 126/19; Gerald Fleming, *Hitler and the Final Solution*, p. 184,

205. Radio message of US–Ambassador in Schweden, Herschel V. Johnson, to the Department of State, 25 April 1945, cited. in: Department of State, For the Press No. 409, p. 1, 2 May 1945, TNA, FO 371/46785.

206. CSDIC (UK) S.I.R. 1706 dated 30 Sept. 1945 by Otto Ohlendorf, entitled "Amt III (SD Inland)", TNA, WO 204/11505.

207. US NARA, RG 319, Entry MLR 134B, Box 85, folder XE 000632.

208. TOP SECRET ULTRA, CX/MSS/T531/39, TNA, HW 1/3729.

209. BAB, R 3/1661, p.15.

210. Albert Speer, *Inside the Third Reich*, pp. 486-487.

211. Gitta Sereny, *Albert Speer: His Battle with Truth*, pp. 534-535.

212. Deposition of Dr Hans Bachmann, Winterthur, 11 April 1946; publ. in IMT, Bd. XL, p. 325.

213. Percy E. Schramm (ed.), *Kriegstagebuch des Oberkommandos der Wehrmacht 1944-1945*, Teilband II, p. 1442.

214. Special interrogation of Werner Grothmann, 26 Sept. 1945, TNA, KV 4/354.

215. H. R. Trevor-Roper, *Last Days of Hitler*, p. 193 footnote 1.

216. James P. O'Donnell, *The Bunker*, p. 187f.

217. TOP SECRET U, CX.MSS/C.498; TNA, HW 5/706.

218. Summary Report No. 1013, 29 April 1945, TNA, HW 13/183.

219. TNA, PREM 3/197/6.

220. *Ibid.*

221. *Ibid.*

222. *Ibid.*

223. Karin Orth, *Das System der nationalsozialistischen Konzentrationslager*, p. 223;

224. TNA, FO 188/526.

225. CIRO/PEARL/ZIP/GPD 4069 transmitted 26 April 1945 (message 12), TNA , HW 16/43.

226. TOP SECRET U, CX/MSS/R.536 (A), TNA, HW 5/700.

227. TOP SECRET ULTRA: CX/MSS/C.509, TNA, HW 5/706; copy shown to Churchill, HW 1/3744.

228. CIRO/PEARL/ZIP/GPD 4069 transmitted 26 April 1945 (message 75), TNA, HW 16/43.

229. TNA, HW 5/706, message CX/MSS/C.503.

230. CIRO/PEARL/ZIP/GPD 4069 transmitted 26 April 1945 (message 4), TNA, HW 16/43.

231. TOP SECRET ULTRA, Report CX/MSS/SC 1 dated 30 April 1945, TNA, HW 5/706; copies shown to Churchill, TNA, HW 1/3739.

232. *Ibid.*

233. CIRO/PEARL/ZIP/GPD 4069 transmitted 26 April 1945 (message 61), TNA, HW 16/43.

234. CIRO/PEARL/ZIP/GPD 4069 transmitted 26 April 1945 (message 51), TNA, HW 16/43.

235. CIRO/PEARL/ZIP/GPD 4069 transmitted 26 April 1945 (message 75), TNA, HW 16/43.

236. Stenographic record of the conference, 27 April 1945, publ. in *Der Spiegel*, Nr. 3, 1966; Albert Speer, *Inside the Third Reich*, pp. 478-482.

237. Percy E. Schramm (ed.), *Kriegstagebuch des Oberkommandos der Wehrmacht 1944–1945*, Teilband II, p. 1445.

238. Joachim Schultz, *Die letzten 30 Tagen aus dem Kriegstagebuch des OKW*, p.39; Gerald Reitlinger, *The SS*, p. 434.

239. Statement on oath of Kurt Becher, Oberursel, 8 March 1946, Nuremberg doc. PS-3762, IMT, Bd. XI, p. 370; and with correction in IMT, Bd. XXXIII, p. 68 f; Peter R. Black, Ernst Kaltenbrunner, p. 251, "a Kaltenbrunner order demanding the *liquidation* of one thousand Mauthausen inmates each day."

240. Jean-Claude Favez, *Warum schwieg das Rote Kreuz?* p. 503f, 586.

241. Special interrogation of Werner Grothmann, dated 26 Sept. 1945, TNA, KV 4/354.

242. *The Memoirs of Field-Marshal Keitel*, p. 214.

243. Karl Koller, *Der letzte Monat*, entry for 27 April 1945, p. 94 ff, 101.

244. Karl Dönitz, Memoirs, *Ten Years and Twenty Days*, p. 211.

245. G.R.G.G. report 341 on Walter Dornberger, CSDIC (UK), 11 August 1945, TNA, WO 208/4178.

246. TOP SECRET U, CX/MSS/T534/43, TNA, HW 5/699.

247. TNA, HW 5/700.

248. Report CX/MSS/500, shown to Churchill, TNA, HW 1/3739.

249. Lew Besymenski, *Die letzten Notizen von Martin Bormann*, facsimile p. 231; Anton Joachimsthaler, *Hitlers Ende*, p. 173; Ian Kershaw, *Hitler 1936–1945*, p. 819.

250. Aktenvermerk Bormann, 27 April 1945, in David Irving, *Göring*, p. 26.

251. Count Folke Bernadotte, *The Fall of the Curtain*, pp. 61-62.

252. Walter Schellenberg, *The Labyrinth*, pp. 401-402.

253. *The Memoirs of Field Marshal The Viscount Montgomery of Alamein*, p.334.

254. Percy E. Schramm, *Kriegstagebuch des Oberkommandos der Wehrmacht 1944-1945*, Teilband II, p. 1461.

255. British Intelligence, MI 14 War Records, "I" Notes, 1/1/45-14/5/45, File No. 5, "I" Notes for 1 May 1945, TNA, WO 208/5489.

256. H. R. Trevor-Roper, *Last Days of Hitler*, p.202; Gerald Reitlinger, *The SS*, p.434; Cornelius Ryan, *The Last Battle*, p. 392; Heinz Höhne, Order of the Death's Head, p. 578.

257. Radio message Bormann to Großadmiral Dönitz, 28 April 1945, 04:05 hours, BAB, R 62/10; Marlis G. Steinert, *23 Tage der Regierung Dönitz*, p. 43.

258. Boris Chavkin/A.M. Kalganov, "Die letzten Tage von Heinrich Himmler. Neue Dokumente aus dem Archiv des Föderalen Sicherheitsdienstes," in *Forum für osteuropäische Ideen- und Zeitgeschichte*, 4. Jg. (2000), Issue 2, Doc. 1, p. 258.

259. TOP SECRET U[LTRA], CX/MSS/T533/59, TNA, HW 5/699.

260. Message CX/MSS/C.498,502, TNA, HW 5/706

261. Percy E. Schramm, *Kriegstagebuch des Oberkommandos der Wehrmacht 1944-1945*, Teilband II, p. 1463; Anton Joachimsthaler, *Hitlers Ende*, p. 182.

262. Interim Report of Werner Grothmann, 13 June 1945, TNA, WO 208/4474.

263. TNA, HW 5/706, report CX/MSS/C.503.

264. TNA, HW 5/701.

265. TOP SECRET U[LTRA], CX/MSS/R.534 (A), TNA, HW 5/699.

266. report CX/MSS/C.504, TNA, HW 5/707

267. report CX/MSS/T534/79, TNA, HW 5/699

268. Lew Besymenski, *Die letzten Notizen von Martin Bormann*, facsimile p. 231; Anton Joachimsthaler, *Hitlers Ende*, p. 174.

269. Jean-Claude Favez, *Warum schwieg das Rote Kreuz?* p. 503, 586.

270. William L. Shirer, *End of a Berlin Diary*, pp. 43-44.

271. Count Folke Bernadotte, *The Fall of the Curtain*, p.62.

272. *Nazi Conspiracy and Aggression*, Supplement B (Red Series), publ. U.S. Government Printing Office, Washington, 1948, p.1632.

273. Walter Schellenberg, *The Labyrinth*, p. 402.

274. H. R. Trevor-Roper, *Last Days of Hitler*, pp. 277-278.

275. Anton Joachimsthaler, *Hitlers Ende*, p. 184.

276. Percy E. Schramm, *Kriegstagebuch des Oberkommandos der Wehrmacht 1944-1945*, Teilband II, p. 1591f.

277. *Ibid*, p.1592; a copy of this radio message was decrypted by Bletchley Park and shown to Prime Minister Churchill, TNA, HW 1/3744.

278. Percy E. Schramm, *Kriegstagebuch des Oberkommandos der Wehrmacht 1944-1945*, Teilband II, p. 1466.

279. Lew Besymenski, *Die letzten Notizen von Martin Bormann*, facsimile p. 232.

280. Adolf Hitler, "Mein politisches Testament", 29 April 1945; facsimile in: Anton Joachimsthaler, *Hitlers Ende*, p. 191 f; photostatic copy of the first part of Hitler's political testament, in Gerald Fleming, *Hitler and the Final Solution*, plate 10 (6 pages) and pp. 186-189; IMT, Bd. XLI, Doc. Streicher-9, p. 549 ff.

281. TOP SECRET ULTRA, message from "C" to Prime Minister Churchill on 30 April 1945. It contains the radio message from Himmler to Kaltenbrunner in Salzburg, sent at 1530 hours on 29 April 1945, TNA, HW 1/3741; separate copy in HW 5/706.

282. Second Preliminary Interrogation Report of G-2, Special Section, S.H.A.E.F. on Otto

Ohlendorf, 10 June 1945, US NARA, RG 319, Box 165A, Ohlendorf folder.
283. TNA, HW 1/3739, information shown to Prime Minister Churchill.
284. *Ibid.*
285. *Ibid.*
286. TOP SECRET U, CX/MSS/R.535, TNA, HW 5/700.
287. TOP SECRET U, CX/MSS/T535/8, TNA, HW 5/700.
288. Count Folke Bernadotte, *The Fall of the Curtain*, pp. 63-64.
289. Marlis Steinert, *23 Tage der Regierung Dönitz*, p. 76.
290. TNA, HW 1/3744.
291. *Memoirs of Field-Marshal Wilhelm Keitel*, pp. 222-223.
292. Percy E. Schramm, *Kriegstagebuch des Oberkommandos der Wehrmacht 1944-1945*, Teilband II, p. 1464f.
293. *Ibid*, p.1449.
294. Interim Report in the case of Werner Grothmann, 13 June 1945, TNA, WO 208/4474.
295. Special interrogation of Werner Grothmann, 26 Sept. 1945, TNA, KV 2/354.
296. TNA, HW 1/3744.
297. Karl Dönitz, *Zehn Jahre und zwanzig Tage*, p. 432 f; zit. nach: Anton Joachimsthaler, *Hitlers Ende*, p. 206f; Marlis Steinert, *23 Tage der Regierung Dönitz*, p. 77f.
298. TOP SECRET U, CX/MSS/T537/6, TNA, HW 5/701.
299. TNA, HW 1/3744.
300. Anton Joachimsthaler, *Hitlers Ende*, p. 282f.
301. Karl Dönitz, *Memoirs*, pp. 212-214.
302. message CX/MSS/C.512, TNA, HW 5/706.

MAY 1945
1. Walter Schellenberg, *The Labyrinth*, p. 404.
2. Deposition on oath of Georg Henning Graf von Bassewitz–Behr, 20 April 1947, TNA, WO 309/408.
3. Percy E. Schramm, *Kriegstagebuch des Oberkommandos der Wehrmacht 1944-1945*, Teilband II, p. 1468; Anton Joachimsthaler, *Hitlers Ende*, p. 277.
4. Gerald Reitlinger, *The SS*, p. 442; León Degrelle, *Die verlorene Legion*, p. 475.
5. Walter Schellenberg, *The Labyrinth*, p.442.
6. Radio message Bormann to Dönitz, 1 May 1945; Percy E. Schramm, *Kriegstagebuch des Oberkommandos der Wehrmacht 1944-1945*, Teilband II, p. 1469; Anton Joachimsthaler, *Hitlers Ende*, p. 281.
7. TOP SECRET ULTRA: CX/MSS/T537/29, TNA, HW 1/3747.
8. TOP SECRET ULTRA: CX/MSS/T537/34, TNA, HW 1/3747.
9. Churchill College, Cambridge, The Churchill Papers, CHAR 20/12/15.
10. Radio message Goebbels und Bormann to Dönitz, 1 May 1945, in Anton Joachimsthaler, *Hitlers Ende*, p. 282; Percy Ernst Schramm (ed.), *Die Niederlage 1945*, p. 420.
11. Diary of Lutz von Schwerin-Krosigk, entry for 1 May 1945, TNA, FO 371/46781, p. 27.
12. BAB, R 3/1661, p. 16.
13. Interrogation report FR 105 Dr Giselher Wirsing, Appendix C (page iii), dated 25 Oct. 1946, TNA, KV 2/140.
14. Interim Report on Interrogation of SS Standfue. Dr Brandt, Rudolf, 10 June 1945, p. 3, US NARA, RG 319, entry MLR 134B, Box 85, folder XE 00 06 32.
   15. Marlis G. Steinert, *23 Tage der Regierung Dönitz*, p. 141.
16. Second Preliminary Interrogation Report, G-2, Special Section, S.H.A.E.F. of Otto Ohlendorf, 10 June 1945, US NARA, RG 319, Box 165A, Ohlendorf folder.
17. CSDIC (UK) S.I.R. 1706, 30.09.1945, by Otto Ohlendorf, entitled "Amt III (SD Inland)", TNA, WO 204/11505.
18. TOP SECRET U, CX/MSS/T536/47, TNA, HW 5/700.

19. TOP SECRET U, CX/MSS/C. 515, TNA, HW 1/3744.

20. British Intelligence, MI 14 War Records, "I" Notes, 1/1/45-14/5/45, File No. 5, "I" Notes for 4 May 1945, TNA, WO 208/5489.

21. Klaus–Dietmar Henke, *Die amerikanische Besetzung Deutschlands*, p. 929.

22. Radio broadcast and daily order of Dönitz, 1 May 1945, Nuremberg doc. D-444, IMT, Vol. XXXV, pp. 116-118.

23. Letter by Hermann Voosen, 30 May 1945, TNA, FO 371/50986, p. 81.

24. Letter by Heinz Samuel, June 1945, TNA, FO 371/50986, p. 87 .

25. TOP SECRET U, CX/MSS/C.524, TNA, HW 5/706.

26. William L. Shirer, *End of a Berlin Diary*, pp. 171-172.

27. Percy Schramm, *Die Niederlage 1945*, pp. 420–423.

28. Albert Speer, *Inside the Third Reich*, p. 494.

29. Percy E. Schramm, *Kriegstagebuch des Oberkommandos der Wehrmacht 1944-1945*, Teilband II, p. 1470.

30. Interrogation of Dr Hans Ehlich by Mr. Wartenberg in Nürnberg, 17 Dec.1946, p. 11f, US NARA, FC 6075 = BAK, 830 K.

31. Rüdiger Kahrs, Die Evakuierung des KZ-Außenlagers Lübberstedt bei Bremen nach Ostholstein 1945; http://www.akens.org/akens/texte/info/36/93.html.

32. Preliminary Interrogation Report 031/Misc 20 of Heinz Macher, 24 May 1945, TNA, WO 208/4431.

33. Interim Report on the Interrogation of SS Standfue. Dr Brandt, Rudolf, 10 June 1945, US NARA, RG 319, Entry MLR 134B, Box 85, folder XE 00 06 32.

34. Interim Report in the case of Werner Grothmann, 13 June 1945, TNA, WO 208/4474.

35. C.S.D.I.C (U.K.) G.G. Report S.R.G.G. 1322 (C): Conversation SS Gruppenführer Ohlendorf, 7 June 1945, TNA, WO 208/4170.

36. Holger Piening, *Westküste 1945*, p. 103.

37. BAOR/JAG 19 Feb. 1946: Activities and personnel of Amtsgruppe "D" of the SS Wirtschafts– und Verwaltungshauptamt, p. 2, TNA, WO 311/435.

38. BAK, NL 1023/7, Nachlass Karl Werner Best.

39. Gerhard Paul, "Rette sich wer kann war die Parole des Tages. Der Norden als Zuflucht von SS und Gestapo," in *Flensburger Tageblatt* dated 7 March 1995; Holger Piening, *Westküste 1945*, p. 103.

40. TNA, HW 12/316, message 144764.

41. William L Shirer, *End of a Berlin Diary*, pp. 51-52.

42. Report by Wilhelm Walter, 30 April 1946, TNA, WO 208/4431.

43. Holger Piening, *Als die Waffen schwiegen*, p. 27.

44. Interim Report on the Interrogation of SS Standfue. Dr Brandt, Rudolf, 10 June 1945, US NARA, RG 319, entry MLR 134B, Box 85, folder XE 00 06 32

45. Preliminary Interrogation Report 031/Misc 19 of Werner Grothmann, 24 May 1945, TNA, WO 208/4431.

46. Preliminary Interrogation Report 031/Misc 20 of Heinz Macher, 24 May 1945, TNA, WO 208/4431.

47. Jürgen Huck, *Ausweichstellen und Aktenschicksal des Hauptamtes Ordnungspolizei im 2. Weltkrieg*, p.141.

48. Percy Schramm, *Die Niederlage 1945*, pp. 423-426.

49. Karl Dönitz, *Memoirs*, p. 229.

50. Count Folke Bernadotte, *The Fall of the Curtain*, pp. 66-67.

51. *Commandant of Auschwitz*, pp. 194-195, 240.

52. BAOR/JAG 19 Feb.1946, Activities and personnel of Amtsgruppe "D" of the SS Wirtschafts – und Verwaltungshauptamt, TNA, WO 311/435.

53. Jan Erik Schulte, *Zwangsarbeit und Vernichtung*, p. 429; interrogation Wilhelm Burger, 26 Jan.1968, ZStL, 413 AR 178/65, Vol. 6, p. 1142.

54. "Zum Kriegsende zog sich die Spitze der deutschen Wehrmacht nach Angeln zurück. Hauptquartier im Bauerndorf", in *Flensburger Tageblatt* dated 4 May 2000;

55. C.S.D.I.C (U.K.) G.G. Report S.R.G.G. 1322 (C): Conversation SS Gruppenführer Ohlendorf, 7 July 1945, TNA, WO 208/4170.

56. Percy Schramm, *Die Niederlage 1945*, p. 426f.

57. Witness statement Oberstleutnant Werner Baumbach, Nuremberg, 27 August 1946, IMT, Vol. XLI, p. 537f.

58. Albert Speer, *Inside the Third Reich*, p. 496.

59. Walter Schellenberg, *The Labyrinth*, pp. 408-409; Reinhard R. Doerries, *Hitler's last Chief of Foreign Intelligence. Allied Interrogations of Walter Schellenberg*, p. 197.

60. Count Folke Bernadotte, *The Fall of the Curtain*, p. 66.

61. Holger Piening, *Westküste 1945*, p. 77; Hillgruber/Hümmelchen, *Chronik des Zweiten Weltkrieges*, p. 283.

62. TNA, HW 5/706, CX/MSS/C.529.

63. Ulrich Herbert, *Best*, p. 400.

64. Marlis G. Steinert, *Die 23 Tage der Regierung Dönitz*, p. 225.

65. *Ibid*, p. 143.

66. Hillgruber/Hümmelchen, *Chronik des Zweiten Weltkrieges*, p. 283.

67. *Ibid.*

68. Walter Schellenberg, *The Labyrinth*, p. 409.

69. Percy Schramm, *Die Niederlage 1945*, p. 429f.

70. TNA, HW 5/706, CX/MSS/C.530.

71. *Ibid.*

72. Secret report GRGG 338 (C) dated 10 August 1945, information provided by von Herff: Himmler's Last Conference with SS-Ogrufs and SS-Grufs, TNA, WO 208/4178.

73. Secret monitoring of a conversation between von Herff and Berger, Report CSDIC (UK), SRGG 1315 (C) dated 4 July 1945, TNA, KV 2/172.

74. Report on the Preliminary Interrogation of Hans Jüttner, 28 May 1945, TNA, WO 208/4474.

75. C.S.D.I.C (U.K.) G.G. Report S.R.G.G. 1322 (C) dated 7 July 1945, TNA, WO 208/4170.

76. Deposition of [Rudolf] Franz Ferdinand Hoess – alias Franz Lang, OC 92 Field Security Section, 14 March 1946, TNA, WO 309/217.

77. Count Folke Bernadotte, *The Fall of the Curtain*, pp. 66-67.

78. CSDIC (UK) S.I.R. 1706, 30 Sept.1945, by Otto Ohlendorf, entitled "Amt III (SD Inland)", TNA, WO 204/11505.

79. Preliminary Interrogation Report 031/Misc 20, 24 May 1945, by Heinz Macher, TNA, WO 208/4431.

80. Preliminary Interrogation Report 031/Misc 19, 24 May 1945, by Werner Grothmann, TNA, WO 208/4431.

81. Holger Piening, *Westküste 1945*, p. 104.

82. TNA, HW 5/706, CX/MSS/C.528; also, HW 1/3756.

83. Percy Schramm, *Die Niederlage 1945*, p. 431f.

84. C.S.D.I.C (U.K.) G.G. Report S.R.G.G. 1322 (C), 7 July 1945, TNA, WO 208/4170.

85. Marlies G. Steinert, *Die 23 Tage der Regierung Dönitz*, p. 198, 244.

86. Interim Report on the Interrogation of SS Standfue. Dr Brandt, Rudolf, 10 June 1945, US NARA, RG 319, Entry MLR 134B, Box 85, folder XE 00 06 32.

87. Interrogation report by Wilhelm Walter, 30 April 1946, TNA, WO 208/4431.

88. Interim Report by Werner Grothmann, 13 June 1945, TNA, WO 208/4474.

89. Hillgruber/Hümmelchen, *Chronik des Zweiten Weltkrieges*, p. 284.

90. *Ibid*, p. 285.

91. Further Interrogation Report by Heinz Macher, 23 Oct.1945, TNA, WO 208/4431.

92. *Ibid.*

93. Hillgruber/Hümmelchen, *Chronik des Zweiten Weltkrieges*, p. 284.

94. Preliminary Interrogation Report 031/Misc 19 by Werner Grothmann, 24 May 1945, TNA, WO 208/4431.

95. Albert Speer, *Inside the Third Reich*, p. 496.

96. Helmut C. Pless, *Lüneburg 1945, Nordostniedersachen zwischen Krieg und Frieden*, Lüneburg 5. Aufl. 1989, p. 137.

97. Interrogation Report 031/G.0915/I by Heinz Macher, 10 Nov.1945, TNA, WO 208/4431.

98. Jan Erik Schulte, *Zwangsarbeit und Vernichtung*, p. 429.

99. Preliminary Interrogation Report 031/Misc 20, 24 May 1945 by Heinz Macher, TNA, WO 208/4431.

100. Preliminary Interrogation Report 031/Misc 19, 24 May 1945, by Werner Grothmann, TNA, WO 208/4431.

101. Preliminary Interrogation Report of G-2, Special Section, S.H.A.E.F. on Otto Ohlendorf, 31 May 1945, US NARA, RG 319, Box 165A, Ohlendorf folder.

102. Second Preliminary Interrogation Report of G-2, Special Section, S.H.A.E.F. on Otto Ohlendorf, 10 June 1945. US NARA, RG 319, Box 165A, Ohlendorf folder.

103. US Military Tribunal, Case 9, trial transcript (English language), pp. 510-511.

104. Fraenkel/Manvell, *Himmler*, p. 244.

105. Death certificate, TNA, WO 309/217.

106. Interim Report on the Interrogation of SS Standfue. Dr Brandt, Rudolf, 10 June 1945, US NARA, RG 319, entry MLR 134B, Box 85, folder XE 00 06 32.

107. Report on Gebhard Himmler, 12 June 1945, US NARA, RG 319, Entry MLR 134B, Box 85, folder XE 00 06 32.

108. Interrogation report by Wilhelm Walter, 30 April 1946, TNA, WO 208/4431.

109. Percy Schramm, *Die Niederlage 1945*, p. 439.

110. *After the Battle*, No. 14 (1976), p. 29.

111. Himmler's strong boxes, report of 15 Sept.1947, TNA, WO 208/4431.

112. Notice, Major Bessler about Ministerial meeting with Reich Foreign Minister, 13 May 1945, BAB, R 3/1625; ADAP, Series E, Vol. VIII, Doc. 349, p. 646.

113. Preliminary Interrogation Report 031/Misc 20, 24 May 1945, on Heinz Macher, TNA, WO 208/4431.

114. Interim Report on the Interrogation of SS Standfue. Dr Brandt, Rudolf, 10 June 1945, US NARA, RG 319, entry MLR 134B, Box 85, folder XE 00 06 32.

115. Major Norman Whittaker established at Ülzenerstr. 31 a, Lüneburg. an interrogation centre for prominent prisoners. The diary of Major Whittaker was consulted at the home of his son, Ian Whittaker. Entry for 15 May 1945. We thank Ian Whittaker for his courtesy.

116. TNA, FO 1093/191.

117. Holger Piening, *Westküste 1945*, p. 105.

118. Preliminary Interrogation Report 031/Misc 20, 24 May 1945, on Heinz Macher, TNA, WO 208/4431.

119. Interim Report on the Interrogation of SS Standfue. Dr Brandt, Rudolf, 10 June 1945, US NARA, RG 319, Entry MLR 134B, Box 85, folder XE 00 06 32.

120. Interim Report of Werner Grothmann, 13 June 1945, TNA, WO 208/4474.

121. TNA, FO 371/46777.

122. TNA, FO 371/46748.

123. Diary of Major Whittaker, entry for 16 May 1945.

124. Report on Gebhard Himmler, 12 June 1945, US NARA, RG 319, Entry MLR 134 B, Box 85, folder XE 00 06 32.

125. Percy Schramm, *Die Niederlage 1945*, p. 448

126. Diary of Major Whittaker, entry for 17 May 1945.

127. Further Interrogation Report on Heinz Macher, 23 Oct.1945, TNA, WO 208/4431.

128. TNA, FO 371/46914; Major General Rooks served with the US Army, and head of the S.H.A.E.F control party at O.K.W. at this time.

129. *After the Battle*, No. 14 (1976), p. 29 with photograph.

130. Diary of Major Whittaker, entry for 18 May 1945.

131. Interim Report on the Interrogation of SS Standfue. Dr Brandt, Rudolf, 10 June 1945, US

NARA, RG 319, Entry MLR 134B, Box 85, folder XE 00 06 32.

132. *Ibid.*

133. Interim Report of Werner Grothmann. 13 June 1945, TNA, WO 208/4474.

134. Preliminary Interrogation Report 031/Misc 20, 24 May 1945, on Heinz Macher, TNA, WO 208/4431; copy of Arrest Report, kindly supplied by the Sayer Archive.

135. Boris Chavkin/A.M. Kalganov, *Die letzten Tage von Heinrich Himmler*, Doc. 2, p. 258 f.

136. *The Memoirs of Field Marshal The Viscount Montgomery of Alamein, K.G.*, p. 372.

137. Interim Report of Werner Grothmann, 13 June 1945, TNA, WO 208/4474.

138. TNA, WO 209/4431.

139. Diary of Major Whittaker, entry for 22 May 1945.

140. TNA, WO 204/12603.

141. Statement by Lt Col B A Stapleton, 22 May 1950. Documents 20152, Imperial War Museum.

142. Interim Report of Werner Grothmann, 13 June 1945, TNA, WO 208/4474.

143. Fraenkel/Manvell, *Himmler*, p. 274, "Additional Note".

144. TNA, WO 208/4431.

145. TNA, WO 32/19603.

146. Manvell/Fraenkel, *Himmler*, pp. 247-248, 273-274.

147. *Ça Ira*, The Journal of the West Yorkshire Regiment (The Prince of Wales's Own), Vol. XII, No. 1, pp. 33-34 (available at the Imperial War Museum).

148. Diary of Major Whittaker, entry for 23 May 1945.

149. TNA, WO 208/4474.

150. Hugh Thomas, *SS-1*, p.165.

151. TNA, WO 204/12603.

152. War Diary – Second Army Defence Company, TNA, WO 208/4474.

153. Diary of Major Whittaker, entry for 24 May 1945.

154. Fraenkel/Manvell, *Himmler*, p.247.

155. Statement of Lt Col. B A Stapleton, 22 May 1950, Documents 20153, Imperial War Museum.

156. Peter-Ferdinand Koch, *Oswald Pohl*, p. 194.

157. William L. Shirer, *End of a Berlin Diary*, p. 77.

158. Copy provided courtesy of the Sayer Archive.

159. TNA, WO 208/4474.

160. TNA, WO 208/4431.

161. *Ibid.*

162. Diary of Major Whittaker, entry for 25 May 1945.

163. War Diary – Second Army Defence Company, TNA, WO 208/4474.

164. Hugh Thomas, *SS-1*, photograph preceding p. 133.

165. Rainer Klöfkorn, Die letzten Tage von Heinrich Himmler, in: *Heimatbeilage der Bremervörder Zeitung*, 18. Jg., Nr. 5, 20 May 1995, p. 4.

166. Ursula von Kardorff, *Berliner Aufzeichnungen*, p. 248.

167. Diary of Major Whittaker, entry for 26 May 1945.

168. War Diary – Second Army Defence Company, TNA, WO 208/4474.

169. *Ibid.*

170. Interim Report of Werner Grothmann, 13 June 1945, TNA, WO 208/4474.

171. *After the Battle*, No. 17 (1977), p.1.

172. War Diary – Second Army Defence Company, TNA, WO 208/4474; also, Diary of Major Whittaker, entry for 27 May 1945.

173. Himmler's strong boxes, 31 Jan.1948, TNA, WO 208/4431.

174. TNA, WO 204/12603.

175. TNA, WO 204/11578.

176. Rainer Klöfkorn, Die letzten Tage von Heinrich Himmler, in: *Heimatbeilage der Bremervörder Zeitung*, 18. Jg., Nr. 5, 20 May 1995, p. 4.

177. *Frankfurter Allgemeine Zeitung*, 28 Sept.1964, following an article in *Freiwilligen* (HIAG).

Abbreviations

AA	Auswärtiges Amt; German Foreign Office
Abt	Abteilung; Department
ADAP	Akten zur deutschen auswärtigen Politik; Documents on German Foreign Policy
A.K.	Armee Korps; Army Corps
AOK	Armeeoberkommando
Art.	Artillerie; Artillery
BA MA	Bundesarchiv Militärarchiv Freiburg im Breisgau
BAB	Bundesarchiv Berlin-Lichterfelde
BAK	Bundesarchiv Koblenz
BAL	Bundesarchiv Ludwigsburg
BArchP	Bundesarchiv Potsdam
BBC	British Broadcasting Corporation
BDC	Berlin Document Center
BdO	Befehlshaber der Ordnungspolizei; Commander of the Order Police
BdS	Befehlshaber der Sicherheitspolizei und des SD; Commander of the Security Police and SD
CdO	Chef der Ordnungspolizei; Chief of Order Police
CdS	Chef der Sicherheitspolizei; Chief of Security Police
C-in-C	Commander-in-Chief; Oberbefehlshaber
CSDIC	Combined Services Detailed Interrogation Centre (British)
Div.	Division
DÖW	Dokumentationsarchiv Widerstands, Vienna
FHQ	Führerhauptquartier; Führer Headquarters
Gen.	General
Gestapo	Geheime Staatspolizei
HGr	Heeresgruppe; Army Group
Hptm	Hauptmann; Captain
HöSSPF	Höchster SS-und Polizeiführer; Supreme SS and Police Commander
HSSPF	Höhere SS-und Polizeiführer; Senior SS and Police Commander
ICRC	International Committee of the Red Cross
IdO	Inspekteur der Ordnungspolizei; Inspector of the Order Police
IdS	Inspekteur der Sicherheitspolizei und des SD; Inspector of the Security Police and Security Service
IfZ	Institut für Zeitgeschichte, Munich
IMT	International Military Tribunal, Nuremberg

Inf.	Infanterie; Infantry
ITS	International Tracing Service, Arolsen
JuNSV	Justiz und NS-Verbrechen
Kdo.Stab	Kommandostab; Command Staff
KdS	Kommandeur der Sicherheitspolizei und des SD; District Commander of the Security Police and SD
KL	Konzentrationslager; Concentration Camp
KTB	Kriegstagebuch; War Diary
KZ	Konzentrationslager; Concentration Camp
LG	Landgericht; County Court
LKW	Lastkraftwagen; lorry, truck
msg	message
Napola	Nationalpolitische Erziehungsanstalten; Political Education Establishment
NSDAP	Nationalsozialistische Deutsche Arbeitspartei; Nazi Party
OB	Oberbefehlshaber; Commander of an Army
OKH	Oberkommando des Heeres; Army General Staff
OKW	Oberkommando des Wehrmacht; Armed Forces General Staff
Pers.Stab	Persönlicher Stab Reichsführer-SS; Personal Staff of the
RFSS	Reichsführer-SS [Himmler]
PKW	Personenkraftwagen; personal automobile
RF, RFSS	Reichsführer-SS
RSHA	Reichssicherheitshauptamt; Reich Security Main Office
SD	Sicherheitsdienst der SS; Security Service of the SS
Sipo	Sicherheitspolizei; Security Police
SS	Schulzstaffel
SS-Ustuf	SS-Untersturmführer; 2nd Lieutenant
SS-Ostuf	SS-Obersturmführer, 1st Lieutenant
SS-Hstuf	SS-Hauptsturmführer; Captain
SS-Stubaf	SS-Sturmbannführer; Major
SS-Ostubaf	SS-Obersturmbannführer; Lieutenant Colonel
SS-Staf	SS-Standartenführer; Colonel
SS-Obf	SS-Oberführer; Brigadier
SS-Brig	SS-Brigadeführer; Major General
SS-Gruf	SS-Gruppenführer; Lieutenant General
SS-Ogruf	SS-Obergruppenführer; General
SS-ObstGruf	SS-Oberstgruppenführer; Colonel General
SSFHA	SS-Führungshauptamt; SS-Leadership Main Office
SSO	SS-Officer file (Berlin Document Center)
SSPF	SS- und Polizeiführer; SS and Police Commander
TNA	The National Archives, Kew, England
US NARA	United States National Archives & Records Administration
WFSt	Wehrmachtsführungsstab; Army Command Staff
WVHA	SS-Wirtschafts- und Verwaltungshauptamt; Economic and Administration Office
ZStL	Zentrale Stelle der Landesjustizverwaltungen, Ludwigsburg

Bibliography

Adler, H. G., *Der Kampf gegen die 'Endlösung der Judenfrage'*, (Bonn, 1958)

Agoston, Tom, *Teufel oder Technocrat? Hitlers graue Eminenz*, (Berlin, 1993)

Aronson, Shlomo, *Theresienstadt im Spiegel amerikanischer Dokumentation*, in: Theresienstädter Studien und Dokumente, (1994)

Bauer, Yehuda, *Jews for Sale. Nazi-Jewish Negotiations 1933–1945*, (Yale, 1964)

Benz, Wolfgang (ed.), *Dimension des Völkermords*, (Munich, 1996)

Bernadotte, Count Folke, *The Fall of the Curtain. Last Days of the Third Reich*, (London, 1945)

Besymenski, Lew, *Die letzten Notizen von Martin Bormann. Ein Dokument und sein Verfasser. Aus dem Russischen übertragen von R. Holler*, (Stuttgart, 1974)

Birn, Ruth Bettina, *Die Höheren SS- und Polizeiführer. Himmlers Vertreter im Reich und in den besetzten Gebieten*, (Düsseldorf, 1986)

Black, Peter R., *Ernst Kaltenbrunner. Ideological Soldier of the Third Reich*, (Princeton, 1984)

Bornemann, Manfred, *Geheimprojekt Mittelbau. Die Geschichte der deutschen V-Waffen-Werke*, (Munich, 1971)

Braham, Randolph, *The Politics of Genocide. The Holocaust in Hungary*, (New York, 1981)

Breitman, Richard, *The Architect of Genocide. Himmler and the Final Solution*, (New York, 1991)

Broszat, Martin, *Nationalsozialistische Konzentrationslager 1933-1945*, in: *Anatomie des SS-Staates*, (Freiburg i. Br., 1965)

Broszat, Martin, *Nach Hitler. Der schwierige Umgang mit unserer Geschichte*, (Munich, 1988)

Buchholz, Marlis, *Die hannoverschen Judenhäuser. Zur Situation der Juden in der Zeit der Ghettoisierung und Verfolgung 1941 bis 1945*, (Hildesheim, 1987)

Chavkin, Boris/A. M. Kalganov, *Die letzten Tage von Heinrich Himmler. Neue Dokumente aus dem Archiv des Föderalen Sicherheitsdienstes*, in: *Forum für osteuropäische Ideen-und Zeitgeschichte*, 4 Jg., (2000, Heft 2)

Czech, Danuta, *Kalendarium der Ereignisse im Konzentrationslager Auschwitz-Birkenau 1939-1945*, (Hamburg, 1989)

Degrelle, León, *Die verlorene Legion*, (Stuttgart, 1955)

Doenitz, Admiral Karl, *Memoirs. Ten Years and Twenty Days*, (New York, 1959)

Doerries, Reinhard R., *Hitler's Last Chief of Intelligence. Allied Interrogations of Walter Schellenberg*, (London, 2003)

Drobisch, Klaus, *Widerstand in Buchenwald, East Berlin*, 1985)

Dulles, Allan W., *The Secret Surrender*, (London, 1967)

Eichholtz, Dieter, *Geschichte der deutschen Kriegswirtschaft, 1943-1945*, Vol. 3, (Munich, 1999)

Erickson, John, *The Road to Berlin. Stalin's War with Germany*, Vol. 2, (London, 1983)

Favez, Jean-Claude, *Warum schweig das Rote Kreuz?*, (Munich 1994)

Fleming, Gerald, *Hitler and the Final Solution*, (London, 1985)

Gorlitz, Walter (ed.), *The Memoirs of Field-Marshal Keitel*, (London, 1965)

Guderian, Heinz, *Panzer Leader*, (London, 1952)

Hackett, David A. (ed.), *Der Buchenwald-Report*, (Munich, 1996)

Heiber, Helmut (ed.), *Reichsführer! Briefe and und von Himmler*, (Stuttgart, 1968)

Henke, Klaus-Dietmar, *Die amerikanische Besetzung Deutschlands*, (Munich, 1995)

Herbert, Ulrich, *Werner Best*, (Bonn, 1996)

Hillgruber, Andreas, Hümmelchen Gerhard, *Chronik des Zweiten Weltkrieges. Kalendarium militärischer und politischer Ereignisse 1939-1945*, (Düsseldorf, 1978)

Hoess, Rudolf, *Commandant of Auschwitz. The Autobiography of Rudolf Hoess*, (London, 1959; German version edited by Martin Broszat, *Kommandant in Auschwitz. Autobiographische Aufzeichnungen des Rudolf Höss*, (Munich, 1963)

Höhne, Heinz, *The Order of the Death's Head. The Story of Hitler's S.S.*, (London, 1969; translation from German: *Der Orden unter dem Totenkopf*, (Hamburg, 1966)

Höhne, Heinz, *Canaris: Patriot im Zweilicht*, (Munich, 1976)

Höhne, Heinz, *Der Krieg im Dunkeln. Macht und Einfluss der deutschen und russischen Geheimdienste*, (Frankfurt/Main, 1988)

Irving, David, *Die Geheimwaffen des Dritten Reiches*, (Gütersloh, 1965)

Irving, David, *Hitlers Krieg. Götterdämerung 1942–1945*, (Munich, 1986)

Joachimsthaler, Anton, *Hitlers Ende. Legenden und Dokumente*, (Munich, 1999)

Janssen, Gregor, *Das Ministerium Speer. Deutschland Rüstung im Krieg*, (Hamburg, 1968)

Kaienburg, Hermann, *Das Konzentrationslager Neuengamme 1938–1945*, (Bonn, 1997)

Kardorff, Ursula von, *Berliner Aufzeichnungen*, (Munich 1962)

Karlsch, Rainer, *Hitlers Bombe*, (Munich, 2005)

Kárný, Miroslav, *Geschichte des Theresienstädter Transports in die Schweiz*, in: *Judaica Bohemiae*, (Vol. XXVII, 1991)

Kershaw, Ian, *Hitler 1936-1945: Nemesis*, (London, 2000)

Kersten, Felix, *Totenkopf und Treue. Heinrich Himmler ohne Uniform*, (Hamburg, 1952)

Klee, Ernst, *Auschwitz, die SS-Medizin und ihre Opfer*, (Frankfurt/Main, 2001)

Koblik, Steven, *The Stones Cry Out*, (New York, 1988)

Koch, Peter-Ferdinand, *Himmlers graue Eminenz. Oswald Pohl und das Wirtschaftsverwaltungshaupt amt der SS*, (Hamburg, 1988)

Kogon, Eugen, *The Theory and Practice of Hell. The German Concentration Camps and the System Behind Them*, (London, 1960; translation from German, *Der SS-Staat*)

Kolb, Eberhard, *Bergen-Belsen*, (Göttingen, 1985)

Koller, Karl, *Der letzte Monat. 14. April bis 27. Mai 1945*, (Frankfurt/Main, 1995)

Krätschmer, Ernst-Günther, *Die Ritterkreuzträger der Waffen-SS*, Preussisch Oldendorf, 1957, 2nd ed.)

Kübler, Robert (ed.), *Chef KGW. Das Kriegsgefangenenwesen unter Gottlob Berger*, (Lindhorst, 1984)

Lang, Jochen von, Der Adjutant. *Karl Wolff: Der Mann zwischen Hitler und Himmler*, (Munich, 1985)

Longerich, Peter, *Heinrich Himmler*, Oxford, 2012; translation of German edition: *Himmler: Bibliographie*, (Munich, 2008)

Lüdde-Neurath, Walter, *Regierung Dönitz. Die letzten Tages des Dritten Reiches*, (Göttingen, 1964)

Manvell, Roger & Heinrich Fraenkel, *Heinrich Himmler*, (London, 1965)

Marsalek, Hans, *Geschichte des Konzentrationslagers Mauthausen*, (Wien, 1995)

Maser, Werner, *Nürnberg. Tribunal der Sieger*, (Düsseldorf, 1977)

Mehner, Kurt (ed.), *Die Waffen-SS und Polizei 1939-1945. Aus den Akten des Bundesarchiv Koblenz*, Bundesarchiv Militärarchiv; Schriftenreihe Führung und Truppe; Band 3, (Norderstedt, 1995)

Messerschmidt, Manfred, *Krieg in der Trümmerlandschaft. 'Pflichterfüllung' wofür?*, in: Ulrich Borsdorf and Mathilde Jamin, Über Leben im *Krieg. Kriegserfahrungen in einer Industrieregion 1939-1945*, (Reinbek, 1989)

Möller, Kurt Detlev, *Das letzte Kapitel. Geschichte der Kapitulation Hamburgs*, (Hamburg, 1947)

The Memoirs of Field Marshal The Viscount Montgomery of Alamein K.G., (London, 1958)

O'Donnell, James, *The Bunker*, (London, 1979)

Orth, Karin, *Das System der nationalsozialistischen Konzentrationslager. Eine politische Organisationsgeschichte*, (Hamburg, 1999)

Padfield, Peter, *Himmler: Reichsführer S.S.*, (London, 1990)

Piening, Holger, *Westküste*, (Heide, 2000)

Reitlinger, Gerald, *The SS: Alibi of a Nation 1922–1945*, (London, 1956)

Reitlinger, Gerald, *The Final Solution. The Attempt to Exterminate the Jews of Europe 1939-1945*, (London, 1968, rev. 2nd ed.)

Rose, Arno, Werwolf 1944–1945, Stuttgart, 1980)

Rückerl, Adalbert (ed.), *NS-Vernichtungslager im Spiegel deutscher Strafprozesse*, (Munich, 1977)

Ryan, Cornelius, *The Last Battle*, (London, 1966)

Schellenberg, Walter, *The Labyrinth*, (New York, 1956); as, *The Schellenberg Memoirs*, (London, 1956)

Schnabel, Reimund, *Macht ohne Moral. Eine Dokumentation über die SS*, (Frankfurt/Main, 1957)

Schramm, Percy E. (ed.), *Kriegstagebuch des Oberkommandos der Wehrmacht 1944-1945*, Teilband II, (Herrsching, 1985)

Schramm Percy E. (ed.), *Die Niederlage 1945. Aus dem Kriegstagebuch des Oberkommandos der Wehrmacht*, (Munich, 1985, 2nd ed.)

Schulte, Jan Erik, *Zwangsarbeit und Vernichtung: Das Wirtschaftsimperium der SS*, (Paderborn, 2001)

Schulte, Jan Erik, Hans Jüttner. *Der Mann im Hintergrund der Waffen-SS*, in: Ronald Smelser/Enrico Syring (eds.), *Die SS: Elite unter dem Totenkopf*, (Paderborn, 2003, rev. ed.)

Seidler, Franz W., *Deutscher Volkssturm. Das letzte Aufgebot 1944/45*, (Munich 1989)

Seidler, Franz W./Dieter Zeigert, *Die Führerhauptquartiere*, (Munich, 2001)

Sereny, Gitta, *Albert Speer. His Battle with Truth*, (London, 1995)

Shirer, William L., *End of a Berlin Diary*, New York, 1947)

Speer, Albert, *Inside the Third Reich*, (London, 1970; translation from German of: *Erinnungen*, Hamburg, 1969)

Speer, Albert, *The Slave State. Heinrich Himmler's masterplan for SS Supremacy*, (London, 1981)

Steinert, Marlis G., *Die 23 Tage der Regierung Dönitz*, (Munich, 1967)

Thomas, Hugh, *SS-1. The Unlikely Death of Heinrich Himmler*, (London, 2001)

Thorwald, Jürgen, *Die grosse Flucht*, (Munich, 1979)

Toland, John, *Adolf Hitler*, (Bergisch Gladbach, 1977)

Trevor-Roper, H. R. (ed.), *The Bormann Letters. The Private Correspondence between Martin Bormann and his wife from January 1943 to April 1945*, (London, 1954)

Trevor-Roper, H. R., *The Last Days of Hitler*, (London, 1962, rev. ed.)

Trevor-Roper, H. R. (ed.), *Hitler's War Directives 1939-1945*, (London, 1964)

Trevor-Roper, H. R. (ed.), *Final Entries 1945. The Diaries of Joseph Goebbels*, (London, 1978; translation from German of: *Die Letzen Aufzeichnungen*, Hamburg, 1977)

Tuchel, Johannes, Reinhold Schattenfroh, *Zentrale des Terrors. Prinz-Albrecht- Strasse 8: Hauptquartier der Gestapo*, (Berlin, 1987)

Tuchel, Johannes, *Die Inspektion der Konzentrationslager. Das System des Terrors 1938-1945*, (Berlin, 1994)

Ueberschär, Gerd R./Rolf Dieter Müller, *Deutschland am Abgrund. Zusammenbruch und Untergang des Dritten Reiches 1945*, (Konstanz, 1986)

Warlimont, Walter, *Im Hauptquartier der deutschen Wehrmacht 1939 bis 1925*, Vol. 2, (Bonn, 1964)

Weck, Alexandra-Eileen, *Zwischen Menschenhandel und 'Endlösung': Das Konzentrationslager Bergen-Belsen*, (Paderborn, 2000)

Witte, Peter, Michael Wildt, Martina Voigt, Dieter Pohl, Peter Klein, Christian Gerlach, Christoph Dieckmann und Andrej Angrick (eds.), *Der Dienstkalender Heinrich Himmlers 1941/42*, (Hamburg, 1999)

Zeigert, Dieter, *Hitlers letztes Refugium*, (Munich, 2003)

Index